This book is due on the last date stamped below.
Failure to return books on the date due may result
in assessment of overdue fees.

DEC 1 6 REC'D

APR 2 3 2007

APR 2 4 REC'D

FINES .50 per day

The Middle East City
Ancient Traditions
Confront a Modern World

Edited by Abdulaziz Y. Saqqaf

A PWPA Book

Paragon House Publishers

New York

Published in the United States by
Paragon House Publishers
2 Hammarskjöld Plaza
New York, New York 10017

A Professors World Peace Academy Book

Library of Congress Cataloging-in-Publication Data

The Middle East City.

"A Professors World Peace Academy book."
Includes Bibliographies and Index.
1. Cities and towns, Islamic—Near East—History—
Congresses.   2. Urbanization—Near East—History—
Congresses.   3. Rural-urban migration—Near East—
History—Congresses.   I. Saqqaf, Abdulaziz Y.,
1951-
HT147.N4M52   1986   307.7'6'0956   86-12385
ISBN 0-943852-32-3
ISBN 0-943852-13-7 (pbk.)

Second Printing

Contents

Part III The Modernization of an Islamic City: The Case of Sana'a

Part IV Jerusalem

Part V Problems of Over-Urbanization: The Case of Cairo

Keynote Address

Crown-Prince Hassan Bin Talal of Jordan

It gives me great pleasure to address this distinguished audience of the Professors World Peace Academy in your conference on the *Middle Eastern City: A Harmonious Environment for the Modern Man.*

The title of the conference, I must say at the outset, implies a future quest rather than a present reality. For, our Middle Eastern city is far from being a harmonious environment and the Middle Eastern Man is too tormented by the ravages of war and conflict all around him to make his transition to modernity smoothly and with a minimum of anguish.

The challenge to you, and indeed to all men and women of good will is to give us a thorough understanding of how the Middle Eastern City has been plunged into its present bleak state of affairs, and more importantly how our cities may be able to transcend this state of affairs in our life time.

In the following remarks, which are personal reflections, I hope to contribute towards enhancing our understanding of the urbanization process in our region.

Contrary to the prevailing stereotype about our region as an arid desert populated by nomads, or a vast empty hinterland sprinkled with oases, the Middle East has been the birthplace of many of the world's first cities.

More than 6000 years ago Mesopotamia and Egypt and then Yemen, witnessed the birth of vibrant cities which were soon to become the seats of empires and the loci of great civilizations. The Middle East has continued ever since to generate varied urban forms as outward signs of complex sociopolitical organization. Baghdad became the first world city to reach one million in population, during the nineth century A.D., at a time when London and Paris were provincial hamlets. Damascus is the oldest continuously populated city in the recorded history of mankind.

Until the 19th century, the Middle Eastern cities reflected the ups and downs of the region's political fortunes. Their growth or decline were functions of whether the region was ruled by a local or an outside power. In all cases, however, the region remained a central link in the highways of world civilization, and its major cities remained important generators of culture or conductors of cross cultural radiation.

Until the 19th century the Middle Eastern city, whether in expansion or contraction, had a physical layout and an inner sociocultural logic based on indigenous values.

The Middle Eastern city managed to evolve its unique symbiosis with the two socioecological forms prevalent in the region; namely, the settled villages and the nomadic tribes. The city dominated the surrounding rural areas from which it obtained its agricultural supplies in return for manufactured goods, urban services, and military protection against tribal raids. The exchange was not always equitable, but it was viable.

The city's relation with nomadic tribes was more complex and subject to greater tension. When powerful, the city either subjugated the tribes or kept them away from rural areas and caravan routes. When it weakened, the city became an easy prey to tribal challenges from the hinterland. A powerful tribal esprit de corps, coupled with religious zeal, often succeeded in dominating the city and establishing its dynastic rule for three or more generations until another tribal challenge from the hinterland repeated the process. Ibn Khaldoun, our brilliant thinker of the 14th century, vividly described this cyclical pattern.

The 19th century was a turning point in the history of the Middle East in general and its cities in particular. It was a century in which the Middle East and the West rediscovered each other. The mutual rediscovery was not a peaceful encounter. At the time when Napoleon's ships anchored at Alexandria, the Middle Eastern cities had long been slumbering. Their last big contact with the West had been their last showdown with the crusaders some six centuries earlier. Napoleon was soon followed by other European encroachments into the Middle East.

The Western penetration and the colonial legacy associated with it triggered far reaching processes for all Middle Eastern societies and in all aspects of life. Of direct bearing on the issue at hand was the demographic transition. Our societies, one after another, began to exert increasing control over the rate of mortality, but little if any over fertility rates. The inevitable result was a steady population growth and rapid urbanization. Thus in the year 1800 the entire population of the Arab World did not exceed 30 million. By the end of the 19th century it reached about 55 million, i.e., nearly doubled in 100 years. But by the early 1980's it topped 177 million. This is nearly a 500% increase in 180 years; and more than 300% increase in the first eight decades of this century. By the year 2000 the total Arab population is projected to reach 270 million. These phenomenal growth rates are unprecedented either in the West or in any other world region. It is true that several developing countries are witnessing similar demographic trends, but none at this magnitude.

The general rapid growth of our population represented a mounting pressure on the cultivable and pastoral land which had sustained the other two human-ecological formations—i.e. village and tribal populations. Population surpluses from the latter began to flow in urban-bound streams of migration. Thus our cities have to contend with their own internal population growth as well as newcomers from the hinterland. Urban population of the Middle East which had not exceeded 5% of total population in 1800, grew to about 15% by 1900 and to 30% in 1960. At present it stands at about 50% of total Arab population. In the last three decades overall population growth rates in the cities averaged about 6%. In some of our countries, the urban growth rates have been much higher, reaching 15% annually. In the Arab Gulf for example, some 80% of the total population lives in urban areas; so much so that some of these countries have become "city-states".

Much of this demographic and urban growth would have been normal and indeed welcomed if it had been an integral part of an indigenous development process. After all, that is what happened in Western societies between the 16th and 19th centuries. But in the West the demographic and urban transformations were congruous with other aspects of change. Urban growth in the West was stimulated by industrialization and general economic growth and the cities attracted, absorbed, and integrated newcomers who were not only incorporated in modern economic sectors, but they acquired an urbanistic outlook and behavioural pattern. They came to the city and became of the city. Urbanization, at first a sheer mechanical and quantitative transformation of residence from village to town, was soon coupled with "urbanism" as a qualitative transformation of values, attitudes, behaviour and lifestyles.

In the Middle East things have not evolved in this fashion. Many of the newcomers to our cities were pushed off the hinterland and were not as easily incorporated in modern sectors of the economy. They came into the city but have not yet become of the city. Urbanization was not coupled with urbanism. Many of the migrants have retained much of their rural and tribal outlook and lifestyles. They added little if any to the modern socioeconomic base of the cities. Yet their very presence in the city has placed mounting burdens on urban services. Municipal services and skills already underdeveloped, have failed to keep pace with the rate of migration. One of the results of all this was the "ruralization" of Middle Eastern cities.

Other complicating factors have been added in recent decades. One such factor is the protracted Arab-Israeli conflict, intra-regional, and civil conflicts. Such conflicts not only divert scarce resources and political energy away from development efforts, but also result in massive displacement of civil population. Many of the latter end up taking "temporary residence" in already strained and overcrowded cities. To cite my own country as a case in point, the capital city of Amman nearly doubled its population during the decade immediately following the 1967 war. Tens of thousands of those uprooted from their homes in Israeli occupied territories have taken what was believed to be temporary residence in Amman and other Jordanian cities. Eighteen years later they are still deprived of their birth rights to return home. A similar story had ensued during the aftermath of the 1948 war. While Jordan in this case has tried everything possible to accommodate the displaced Palestinians, such accommodation is not and will never be an equitable substitute for their right to return to their homeland.

Over-urbanization and under-urbanism in the Middle East have no doubt distorted the sociological and physical landscape of our cities.

Physically our Middle East cities are quickly losing their centuries long architectural character and beauty. The ravages of vulgar development has dwarfed and distorted the architectural treasures of Middle Eastern cities. Again if I may cite the most glaring example of concern to me and millions of other Moslems and Christians around the world that of Jerusalem. The Israeli occupation has mercilessly triggered one of the ugliest urban schemes in and around the historical city of Jerusalem. Massive housing blocks have been constructed in total disregard for the physical, cultural, and human environment of the Holy Places. While in Jerusalem this blight has occurred as a part of a deliberate political strategy, in many of our own Arab cities, lack of planning and control has resulted in much the same ultimate destruction of harmony and architectural integrity.

These remarks have gone longer than I intended. But I must say in conclusion that the present dilemma of Middle Eastern cities reflects the dilemmas of the society at large. If the cities are caught up in the anguish of rapid change, and if they are distorted physically and sociologically by forces from within and without, it is because the whole society suffers from the same processes.

If our cities, and hence our society, are to emerge from these dilemmas, a modicum of peace and stability is a vital pre-requisite. Peace and stability in turn could not be established without equity and justice to all people of the Middle East. Cities represent the most sensitive nerve centers of our society. Therein such pre-requisites must be first felt. It is axiomatic that a harmonious city could not exist in a disharmonious environment. Nothing is more disharmonious than a jungle-like environment in which usurpation is celebrated as pioneerism, and exploitation is hailed as progress.

Even in bleak times such as these, it is comforting to see a group of well-intentioned scholars working towards a better understanding of our problems. I am reminded that in the depth of the great depression, someone thought of constructing the Empire State Building. Others in the midst of mass destruction and killings during both world wars thought of the League of Nations and the United Nations. It is people of vision like those that we need in our troubled Middle East. I hope your meetings and your efforts are targetted in this direction, and I wish you all success in this noble quest.

Conference Chairman's Address

The theme of our conference is the city. The catch title of harmonious environment for modern man is of course very moving. I submit that we do not have in mind a statement of reality but rather a quest for what we hope will happen. Our cities are not at present very harmonious, and I have my doubts that man in the Middle East is all that modern. What exists is probably a mix of modernity and tradition, an outworn polarity of concepts. We all know as social scientists that modernity implies change, and change implies tension, friction, conflict dislocation and so on. So what we're really asking is how to establish modernity with a minimum of disharmony, a minimum of conflict?

The second point I'd like to make, is that the Middle Eastern city is now a very intense place. It has been growing rapidly in recent decades. The average rate of annual urban growth in the region as a whole has been over 6%, that is twice the rate of population growth. That means we are doubling our urban population once every twelve years. So much so that by the year 2000 we'll probably have 80% of our entire population living in urban centers. This is something to think about. Many think of the Middle East as an arid or rural region. Even our policy makers are not really aware of what is happening—that the Middle East is transforming itself very quickly to an urban region. In fact, some states of the region have already become city states, like the Gulf countries.

Our cities are growing rapidly, they are very tense and they are becoming overcrowded not only with people, but with dreams and promises; overcrowded with failures, and frustrations. The Middle East cities magnify the hopes and problems of our societies at large. We now know that our cities are an embodiment of our collective culture and values. They are full of contradictions and glaring contrasts and they are full of our ambitions and hopes. The typical Middle Eastern city (at least the capital cities) are really made up of several worlds living in very close proximity, and often very hostile towards one another. It's true that some of the remnants of Middle Eastern values of compassion and tolerance often dilute the levels of tension that has come to characterize our cities, but even those values are running thin. If we take Jerusalem and Beirut as extreme cases of these hostile worlds living together, living very close to one another with all kinds of potential and actual fear and conflict, then we must say that this is a preview of other big urban centers in the region. We have seen some of these big cities like Cairo, Tehran, Tunis, and Dar Al-Baidha (Casa Blanca) flare up in chaos in response to the slightest provocation. The tension and restlessness is exemplified in the bread uprising in Tunis or the food riots in Cairo. Hostile urban worlds living in close proximity could tear the whole society in flames.

The third point I'd like to make is the heart of the problem in the Middle East—a frantic growth rate. Average annual growth rates have exceeded 6% in all the countries, and in some of them, they reached 15% or 16%. This growth rate is far beyond the imagination and abilities of municipal authorities, and is more than the cities can handle. Therefore disillusion quickly sets in, and the newcomers' brief enchantment with the city quickly gives way to disillusions and discontent. The newcomers are forced into slum areas, and become inflammable materials for any demagogy. This happens especially with the second generation of newcomers—the teenagers and the adolescents of the newcomers who grow up in the city.

The last point I want to make is the fact that there has been at least in the last ten years, two clear methods in dealing with the urban situation by our policy makers. I'm referring to our experience in the Arab world. The first approach notes these potential dangers and uses coersion through a very elaborate security system to keep the city manageable. The other approach has been to emphasize all kinds of programs of social equity, development, services and so on.

The first method unfortunately is more tempting for policymakers. The second method is long range; it taxes the imagination; and it makes our policymakers work much harder. They usually take the easy way; that is, to use covert or overt coersion. In the beginning coersion is used to tame the outskirts of the city, the slums of the city. But soon it becomes a way of life and it carries on to other parts of the city, including the middle and upper-middle classes of the metropolis. However, coersion can only be effective in the short run, in the long run there is no substitute to equitable development programs to deal with the city and the society at large. So with these notes in mind I submit that our work here, our papers, our discussions, can probably help us find other methods or approaches to urban problems. Maybe we will learn more about the dynamics, the inner logic of the city, and hopefully our officials will listen to whatever we can say, if we can say it clearly, loudly and credibly.

Introduction

The world urban population in 1985 is roughly two billion persons, and it grows at roughly double the rate of natural population growth. Urban growth is reflected not only in the size of cities but also in the number of cities. At the turn of the century, there were 11 cities in the world with populations exceeding half a million inhabitants. Today, there are some 200 such cities.

There are three sources of urban population growth. First, there is the natural increase in urban dwellers. According to a United Nations survey of 29 developing countries, it is estimated that at least half of the urban growth rate is due to the natural population increase. Although the general pattern is for urban residents to have a lower fertility rate than their rural compatriates, the urban societies of developing countries still have high rates of fertility. Coupled with a dramatic fall in the mortality rates due to improved health services, hygiene, nutrition, etc., city dwellers end up having high rates of population growth. The second reason is related to the population distribution between cities and the countryside. The rural-to-urban migration is a universal phenomenon which adds considerably to the number of persons in cities. Some 35% of the urban growth rate is due to this migration. Between 1925 and 1950, over 100 million persons in the developing countries drifted from rural areas to towns and cities. Between 1950 and 1975, over 330 million individuals migrated. During the last quarter of this century, some 600 million are expected to move from the countryside and settle in cities. The final source of urban population growth is due to the reclassification of rural areas to urban status. With spatial expansion, villages in the vicinity of cities are swallowed and become part of the urban structure.

Rapid urban growth has been one of the most visible forms of transformation in the Middle East and North Africa (MENA). MENA is the cradle of man's earliest civilizations. The world's first urban forms developed in this region. Although the rate of urbanization in MENA was very low during the last few centuries, it witnessed a dramatic increase during the present century. Table 1.1 provides world comparisons.

TABLE 1.1
URBAN POPULATION GROWTH: 1950-2000

REGION	PERCENT OF URBAN POPULATION			ANNUAL GROWTH RATE	
	1950	1980	2000	1950-1980	1980-2000
Developing Nations	18.9	28.7	40.2	3.4	3.1
Industrial Nations	61.3	77.0	83.7	1.8	1.0
MENA	27.7	46.8	59.9	4.4	4.3
Subsaharan Africa	33.7	49.4	55.2	3.1	2.9
Southern Europe	24.7	47.1	62.3	3.8	2.9
Latin America	41.4	65.3	75.4	4.1	2.9
East Asia/Pacific	19.6	31.9	41.9	4.1	3.1
China	11.2	13.2	20.1	2.5	2.1
India	16.8	23.3	35.5	3.2	4.2

Source: The World Bank, World Development Report: 1984, page 67, Table 4.3.

We can see from the above table that the MENA region has had the highest average annual urbanization rate during the period 1950-1980, and will continue to claim the highest rate for the remainder of this century. As a result, the demographic distribution has gone through a rapid transformation. In 1960, there were only 11 cities in MENA with populations exceeding one million inhabitants; today, there are 38 such cities. In addition, there are some 250 cities with populations between 100,000 and 500,000. One of the main reasons for this strong urbanization trend in the MENA countries is the sedentarization policies pursued in the region. The development programs have entailed policies to settle the bedouins and nomads. Table 1.2 gives the individual urban characteristics of the MENA region and the countries around it.

The growth of cities is not an historical accident, but a conscious human decision regarding the preferred form of human habitat. The benefits derived from urban living are many. Urban centers give industrial, service, administrative, and other activities the benefits associated with economies of scale. The positive externalities derived from living together and in close proximity are immense, especially due to the concentration of suppliers and consumers. Cities also

TABLE 1.2
PERCENT OF URBAN POPULATIONS IN
MENA COUNTRIES: 1960-1985

Country	1960	1970	1980	1985*
Afghanistan	8.0	11.0	15.4	17.9
Algeria	30.4	34.0	43.5	47.6
Bahrain	78.6	78.3	78.1	79.7
Chad	7.0	11.4	17.8	20.3
Cyprus	35.6	40.8	46.3	47.8
Egypt	37.9	42.3	46.8	49.3
Ethiopia	6.4	9.7	13.6	15.9
Iran	33.6	40.9	49.9	52.7
Iraq	42.9	58.4	71.6	74.6
Israel	77.0	84.2	89.1	91.3
Jordan	42.7	49.6	56.3	61.3
Kuwait	72.3	76.5	88.4	91.2
Lebanon	44.4	61.8	75.9	78.8
Libya	22.7	34.3	52.4	59.7
Mauritania	3.4	12.8	23.0	25.9
Morocco	29.3	34.6	40.6	44.2
Oman	3.5	5.1	13.5	18.2
Pakistan	22.1	24.9	28.2	31.1
Qatar	72.4	80.3	86.1	87.5
Somalia	17.3	23.1	30.2	32.8
Sudan	10.3	16.4	24.8	26.3
Syria	36.8	43.3	47.9	50.6
Tunisia	36.0	43.5	52.2	54.8
Turkey	29.7	38.4	46.0	46.7
United Arab Emirates	40.0	57.1	71.9	80.3
Yemen Arab Republic	3.4	8.1	13.7	16.2
Yemen (PDRY/South)	28.0	32.1	36.9	39.2
Saudi Arabia	29.7	48.7	66.9	73.4

Source: The World Bank, World Tables (Volume II: Social Data), Third Edition,
      country pages.
*1985 data are estimates.

provide a forum for an in-depth synthesis of ideas and interdisciplinary research. Thus, most innovations and formulations are generated
in cities and by city dwellers. In terms of socio-cultural contribution,
cities give the identities of their inhabitants a more tolerant and
universal outlook, thus diluting the vernacular and regionalistic
perspectives.

Yet, the analysis of positive externalities associated with urban growth indicates a diminishing return pattern as urbanization proceeds. In fact, as a city attains a certain size (there is no agreement regarding the optimal city size), negative externalities begin to creep in. In addition, the available resources may not be enough to meet the rising needs of the city residents. Thus, large cities are plagued with bottlenecks and difficulties, administrative inefficiencies and corruption, housing shortages, severe unemployment leading to high rates of crime and lawlessness, traffic jams and other forms of congestion, noise/air/water and other pollution, etc. High densities lead to smaller and smaller private space as well as less and less public space and fewer open parks. Traditional values in terms of socio-cultural beliefs as well as in terms of architectural patterns give way to more universal and less durable concepts. Rectifying these developments is a very costly process.

Cities seem to require larger and larger portions of the budget. To alleviate some of the socio-economic problems, governments throughout the world introduced a vast array of subsidies—housing subsidies, food subsidies, public transportation subsidies, medical subsidies, educational subsidies, etc. Urban growth has placed a tremendous burden on government budgets, to the extent that a vastly disproportionate share of public expenditures is earmarked to satisfy urban needs. Yet, this is not enough, and more money is required. This again leads to the issue of optimal urban or city size.

The book at hand attempts to discuss these and other issues with reference to the Middle East. How far has the Middle East come in its urbanization process? What are the urban versus rural expenditure distributions and investment priorities of the Middle Eastern governments? Is there already a serious problem of over-urbanization in the Middle East? What happens to ancient city cores that provide living testimony to Islamic architectural splendor and grandeur? How could these be saved from the aimlessly sprawling new urban phenomenon? What are the socio-cultural and religious implications of the present urban trend? What will the Middle Eastern city look like by the turn of the century, and what should it look like?

Middle Eastern scholars as well as European scholars interested in Middle Eastern urban development attempt to answer those and other questions in this volume. Administrators, anthropologists, architects, bureaucrats, economists, planners, political scientists, sociologists, and other specialists have written research papers on the Middle Eastern city and have discussed the issue at length. Their papers and discussions are given in the following chapters.

Acknowledgments

I am grateful for the assistance of numerous friends, colleagues and organizations in the production of this book. First, I wish to acknowledge the cooperation and understanding of the contributors, especially those who met the original deadline for turning in their manuscripts. I would also like to thank the commentators, discussants and reviewers.

This volume comprises the proceedings of the Second Annual Conference sponsored by the Middle East Chapter of the Professors World Peace Academy. The PWPA International has been instrumental in bringing scholars and practitioners together in a wide range of international and interdisciplinary gatherings focused on topics related to world peace.

Finally, I would like to thank certain individuals without whose support this book would not exist. Many thanks go to Mr. Thomas Cromwell, the able Secretary-General of PWPA-Middle East, who was responsible for organizing the conference. The proceedings required editing, retyping and other services. Toni Muller did most of the typing and Louise Zontek the transcription. Nancy Farlow, the Publications Director for PWPA, coordinated preparation of the manuscript for publication.

Abdulaziz Y. Saqqaf
Sana'a,
Yemen Arab Republic

Part I

The Islamic City

The concept of an Islamic city has not been sufficiently studied, therefore, it is rather difficult to understand let alone explain. At the micro-level, one would be describing the architecture; at the macro-level, the analysis goes into the domain of socio-political organization. So what is an Islamic city, and how is it different from "other" cities? Professor Carl Brown summarizes this problem in the following extract from *From Medina to Metropolis* (The Darwin Press, Inc., Princeton, New Jersey, 1973), pages 19–20.

> *Cities are, in one sense, becoming increasingly alike or at least faced with similar problems and prospects. Yet, anyone who has had the opportunity to experience, say, Fez, Istanbul, or Isfahan would argue that such cities possess a cultural core, however elusive to describe, that is and will ever be distinctive. And even if experts and laymen might dispute what generic label to apply—whether Islamic, Near Eastern, Western Asian, or some hyphenated sub-category such as Arabo-Islamic or Turko-Islamic—there could be a consensus that these cities are properly distinguishable from New York, Paris, Calcutta, Nairobi, or Shanghai.*

Yet, there are those who would argue differently. Ira Lapidus *(The Middle Eastern Cities,* University of California Press, 1969, page 73) goes far enough to deny the existence of any uniqueness in Islamic cities. He asserts:

> *. . . we can no longer think of Muslim cities as unique. . . . None of the characteristic social bodies of Muslim society—the quarter, the fraternity, the religious community, and the state —were specifically urban forms of organization—Cities were physical entities but not unified social bodies defined by characteristically Muslim qualities.*

Of course, most scholars take issue with Professor Lapidus since Muslim cities do have certain distinctive features. They have a unique layout and physical design the central focus point of which is always a maidan (open square) around a castle or palace on the one hand, and al-masjid al-jami' (central mosque specially for Friday prayers) on the other hand. The specialized markets are the most accessible part of the city, while the residential areas have narrow and meandering streets that aim to limit non-local traffic. There is a definite zoning pattern of the three major activities of the city (residential, business/ trade/crafts, and guidance either of religious and/or political nature). In addition, the Islamic city has its social, administrative, religious, political, and economic institutions. *The Islamic City* edited by R.B. Serjeant (UNESCO publication, 1980) gives detailed descriptions of the different unique aspects of the Islamic city.

Yet, our interest is not in the Islamic city as an historical phenomenon, but as a contemporary entity that provides a harmonious environment for its inhabitants. Could or rather should these unique aspects of traditional city cores be preserved? And at what cost? Could these be part of an overall urbanization plan for modern Middle Eastern cities? Socio-economic changes have been so dramatic and profound that the old Islamic "medina" structure is neither suitable nor desirable; yet aspects of the old structure could be integrated in our modern efforts. Professors Ervin Galantay and Cyrus Mechkat, both architects with immense experience in Islamic architecture, tackle this issue in the following papers.

Chapter 1

Islamic Identity and the Metropolis: Continuity and Conflict

Ervin Y. Galantay

_____**TRADITIONS**

The built environment of the modern world has been shaped by four great urban traditions: the Far-Eastern (Chinese); the Indian; the Islamic and the Western, or European.

The Eastern traditions produced urban paradigms which expressed the high value accorded to spiritual factors and the search for harmony based on *permanent* values.

By contrast, the Western mode which has been embraced by both capitalist and socialist countries places a premium on efficiency in spatial organization in order to optimize production and consumption, and expresses a lifestyle in which constant *change* has become a goal in itself.

_____**MODERNIZATION**

During the last 50 years—in the guise of modernization—the Western mode started its encroachment on the territory of the great Eastern traditions. As a result, the cities of Africa and Asia have lost much of their historic tissue, and the impact of modernization has led to a rupture of continuity between the inherited morphology and more recent urban structure.

BUILT FORM AS "MEMORY"

A living culture needs constant reference to the "collective memory" which is largely embodied in the built form of cities. The erosion of this substance results in a loss of identity and leads to cultural dependence. Due to the forced pace of modernization, the conflict between traditional values and imported ideas has been the sharpest in some of the Islamic countries, and recently, the resulting resentment gave rise to fundamentalist movements not only in Iran or Libya but even in such secularized nations as Turkey.

SINGLE-LINE EVOLUTION?

Some will argue that modern technology is not a monopoly of the Western civilization but the consequence of universal progress in scientific thought. Hence, modernization is an inevitable result of global interconnectedness, and since spatial organization is no longer culture-specific, the conflicts arise simply from the difficulties of transition from pre-industrial to industrialized societies. In this view the world has become too small to permit cultural diversity in its urban areas; the evolution or "progress" of global society is unilineal. The modernization of Islamic cities is only a matter of time lag and of "catching-up." After all, haven't the European cities also undergone a painful metamorphosis and much loss of historical substance until a new equilibrium with modernity has been reached?

PARALLEL-LINE EVOLUTION

On the other hand, if we value cultural diversity we should not accept the theory of single-line cultural evolution as *destiny* and examine the possibility of the continuation of parallel-line development, each line keeping its distinct identity. As far as the morphology of cities in Islamic countries is concerned, the question is twofold:

- Can we assure the survival of the special character of the historic "medina"?
- Is it possible to infuse Islamic identity in the spatial organization of New Towns and modern town extensions?

Let us first attempt to define the essence of the Islamic tradition.

ISLAMIC TRADITION

Most of the great cities of the Islamic world were built in a hot, arid zone which stretches from the Maghreb to Afghanistan between the 10th and 35th parallels north of the Equator.

Within this vast area there developed a common[1] "pattern language" which still impresses by its unity more than its diversity.

URBANIZATION

The heartlands of Islam cover regions which once gave rise to the most ancient urban civilizations. Today most Islamic nations are highly urbanized while others are urbanizing with astonishing rapidity, e.g., the population of Libya is now 81% urban, more urban than Italy.

METROPOLI

Very large agglomerations have emerged due to rampant primacy: Cairo with its 10 million inhabitants may reach a population of 16–20 million by the year 2000.[2] Teheran may be close to the size of Cairo at present,[3] and Istanbul, now having about six million inhabitants, will reach 10 million within 15 years.[4] But apart from these metropoli of international importance, even smaller national and regional centers show astonishing growth: i.e., Ankara which in 1923 had only 23,000 inhabitants now has over three million and is likely to reach a population of six million people by year 2000.[5]

THE MEDINA

All these fast-growing cities include as a core a relatively small historic medina as well as some other islands of traditional urban tissue surrounded by a vast and amorphous agglomeration in which formally planned projects in the Western mode are juxtaposed with illegal and informal development. While the historic substance of the medinas is eroding, one looks in vain for signs of Islamic identity in the New Town extensions.

INFLUENCE OF CLIMATE

In asking the questions about continuity and identity we have to define, first of all, what exactly is *specifically Islamic* in the inherited environment? Three factors have shaped the built form of Islamic cities and, of these, two are *not* culture-specific. The first is the climate: characteristic responses, such as the intraverted courthouse, the use of roof-terraces, windcatchers, and the close packing of cubic volumes to maximize shading, all go back to *pre-Islamic* civilizations.

MATERIAL CONSTRAINTS

The second factor is the preference for certain building techniques and materials: it has been determined by resource constraints such as the scarcity of timber or stone, which made the use of brick and of vaulting a rational choice. The recent availability of steel and particularly of cement has rapidly transformed the townscapes once dominated by brick into ones of reinforced concrete. In fact, the cement consumption of Arabic countries is staggering.[6] In the Gulf States cement used per capita is far in excess of the per capita consumption in Europe, the U.S. or the USSR.

CULTURAL FACTORS

Putting aside the parameters of climate and traditional building techniques, we can now identify the culture-specific determinants which are the religious practices and legal traditions of Islam and a lifestyle based on separate roles of men and women in Islamic society.

UMMA

Fundamental to the understanding of Islamic tradition is the concept of the community UMMA which is based on faith rather than on kinship. Thus Islamic ideology is democratic although—descending from the authority of the Khalifs—there has always been an elite which collected and managed the "zakat" and provided leadership in need.

TAKAFUL

Basic also is the concept of social solidarity TAKAFUL and the distinction between needs (hajiyat) and absolute necessities (daruriyat) which must be met by alms if necessary. There is also provision for public consultation by open meetings (shūrā).[7]

SHARI'AH

The legal system is value-loaded and oriented toward the ultimate objectives of Islam: MAQASID AL-SHARI'AH.[8]

IJMAH

Although the legal system SUNNA admits at least four different systems of interpretation, there emerged an agreement about the proper use of land and of behavior in space based on customary law (AL MASALIH, AL MUSALAH) derived from the IJMAH—a principle attributed to the Prophet's—saying "my community will never agree in error."

LAND OWNERSHIP

Customary law establishes that all land belongs to Allah, then to the Muslim community, i.e., to the state, and while the individual has beneficial rights of title "this amounts to trusteeship or *stewardship* rather than to outright freehold" in the Western sense. It appears that Islamic law does not condone the degree of collectivization and regulation by the state as found in socialist "regimes"[9] but it does include the right of *expropriation* for public needs after payment of just compensation. Rights of title may not be abused to deny access to land owned by others or to visually invade the privacy of other families, i.e., by opening a window into their court. While Western law distinguishes only between freehold and leasehold, Islamic law permits more intricate systems of interlocking ownership and servitudes.

PRIVACY

Customary law also caters to a refined sense for multiple layers of privacy which led to the recognition of special rights and responsibilities of neighbors living like an extended family in a cluster of buildings sharing access from the same cul-de-sac alley. In fact, until quite recently in cities such as Fez[10] the alley had a gate which was closed at night.

HORMA OR FEMININE SPACE

Islamic tradition assigns separate roles to men and women and goes to great length to safeguard privacy and female modesty. In principle, public space is considered unsafe and "to be eschewed by women" and even within the home private space is layered to permit further reclusion for individual privacy. An arrangement of a string of interconnected bedrooms "en suite"—crossed by streams of servants and visitors as in Versailles—would be quite inconceivable in Islamic society. The concern with female modesty dictated such solutions as separate entrances for men and women, separate waiting rooms, hidden or indirect entranceways (called "chicane" by the French) and the ingenious "Mashrabiyya" of Cairo, the "Kafess" of Medina or "Rawshin" in Jeddah—variations of balconies screened by wooden grill-work.

SHARAF

The strong sense of SHARAF or family honor which includes the extended family along male bloodlines resulted in the need for controlled semi-public space serving a cluster of buildings inhabited by members of the same clan. These clan members have special rights and responsibilities which later have been transferred to the proximate neighbors living around the same DERB and often sharing communal equipment such as wells and baking ovens.[11]

MAHALLE

On a somewhat larger scale of social organization we find the neighborhood completing the hierarchy of intraverted cells from the room, to the courthouse, the cluster with its semi-private alley and to the MAHALLE[12] with its mosque, school, hammam, etc. separated from other neighborhoods by streets carrying through traffic.

CELLULAR ORGANIZATION

This concept of spatial organization is based on distinct "territories" with the movement system and public open space confined to the residual, interstitial areas between cells. This is in total contrast with the spirit of Western townplanning which assigns priority to the movement system by first reserving space for the street grid and public places and then proceeding to the subdivision of the grid squares or islands for lots and different land uses.

CHARITY

A basic requirement of Islam is charity. In cities the collection of the alms was based on the neighborhood units which conferred to the MAHALLE the status of a legal entity.

THE WAQF

The economic institutionalization of charity gave rise to the numerous pious foundations of public fountains, schools and hospitals and the creation of the WAQF for their administration and management. Since the WAQF property was inalienable, a very sizable percentage of the real estate in Islamic cities eventually passed into public hands.

CONNECTIVITY

In contrast to European cities where public buildings often focus on market squares or are free-standing like sculptural objects, the major communal buildings of the Islamic city (mosques, medreses, hammams, hans, etc.) are tightly woven into the urban fabric and interlink linearly along the bazaars which run gate-to-gate as continuations of the main regional roads. At the same time, they provide the essential interface and exchange among inhabitants of adjacent Mahalles.

INTROVERSION

Apart from the bazaars the other through-streets separate, more than link, the neighborhood territories. Unlike the extraverted European buildings where the ostentatious facade serves to advertise the social standing of the owner, the Islamic house only reveals its richness in the interior. This made possible the juxtaposition of houses of the rich and the poor and permitted the co-existence of families of different income levels within the same Mahalle.

FUNCTIONS OF THE MODERN CITY

Let us now examine the impact of "modernization" on the structure of the archetypical medina. In a thoughtful article presented at a recent conference on the Unity of Sciences, Dr. Abdulaziz Saqqaf[13] defined the roles to be played by the modern metropolis:

- A generative role: diffusing knowledge by education and telecommunications;
- A transforming role: molding the inhabitants to become members of programmed consumer society;
- A mobilizing role: supportive of production goals and based on efficiency principles, norms and standards;
- A decision-making role: implying integration with the international system, high "connectivity" and "coupling" with multinational technocracy.

It is obvious that every one of these roles is disruptive of the medina and incompatible with its traditional functions. Thus, policies are required to prevent the new "metropolitan" functions from establishing themselves within the limits of the historic medina since this would result in its destruction.

CENTER-PERIPHERY RELATIONS

As Professor Cyrus Mechkat[14] explained in another paper read at the same conference, each urban spatial system establishes its own mode of regulation. Within the framework of the international division of labor and the "Center-Periphery Model" there is a need for the rise of a modern "central" enclave fully coupled with other international decision-making centers by high "connectivity" in terms of telecommunications.

CBD-FORMATION

This implies a high-technology "enclave" providing the location for headquarters of local businesses of international stature, branch offices of international organizations and multinational conglomerates. Such a modern Central Business District (CBD) will provide for interface of local decision-makers with members of the technocracy which is replacing the old patriarchal order. Unfortunately, the linkage needs of a modern CBD are incompatible with the structure of the medina.

Apart from offices, the "enclave" requires access to a modern airport and very special amenities such as luxury hotels and restaurants, entertainment areas, golf courses, and, above all, street space for cars and for parking.

IMPACT OF CARS

Needless to say, the spatial requirements of the automobile —whether in movement or stationery—cannot be met within the narrow streets of the medina in which beasts of burden used to be the predominant mode of transportation unlike the wheeled vehicles favoured in the pre-industrial cities of Europe.

ROAD CLEARANCE

Unfortunately, the voracious spatial needs of the automobile often resulted in clearing 100 foot- and even 165 to 175 foot-wide access roads through dense tissue of mahalles and bazaars, causing irreparable damage. One of the worst offenders was Reza Shah of Iran who started by cutting two intersecting orthogonally main axes through Tehran. Similar measures of "traffic improvement" followed in Ispahan, Mashad and Yazd accompanied by attempts to "free" for the view and thus physically isolate mosques and shrines. A frightening example of such an approach was Darius Borbor's project to clear a wide field by razing dense urban tissue around the Imam Reza shrine of Mashad and then encircling it with eight-story office buildings sitting on a three-story parking and commercial platform. Similarly disruptive projects have been carried out in Iraq, for example, the 100 foot-wide cut of Al-Keefah street leading to the Al-Gaylani shrine in Baghdad.[15]

IMPACT OF HIGH-RISE BUILDINGS

Such cuts not only result in the insensitive severing of bazaars and mahalles but have, as a consequence, the erection of high-rise buildings along their right of way. But high-rise buildings reduce the attractiveness of the adjacent courthouses by destroying their visual privacy, casting permanent shadows on their gardens, and preventing the flow of cooling winds. By generating excessive traffic, they also contribute to noise and air pollution.

DECLINE OF THE MEDINA

If the new Central Business District is established outside of the original medina, the threat of wholesale demolition of historic buildings is diminished. However, the shifting away of the center of economic activity often results in a decline of the bazaar as the prestigious businesses move out, followed by the transfer of the homes of the rich and the middle class to more fashionable areas; the slum formation by the splitting up of large houses in small rental units; neglect of maintenance; decay of the physical structure; overcrowding and the breakdown of social coherence.

SPECULATION

At the same time, the slow process of incremental renewal of the urban fabric is profoundly upset by land speculation triggered off by the search of space for the new CBD and the rapid rise of land values in zones upgraded by infrastructure improvement. The impact is often exacerbated by the insensitivity of foreign planners, architects and contractors to whom large-scale projects are assigned.

IMPACT ON LIFESTYLES

Although the outward signs of "modernization" are the most evident, the indirect impact of the imported value system on traditional lifestyles is even more destructive.

The competitive, dynamic and aggressive nature of Western capitalism and the high value given to "progress" contrasts with the importance accorded to continuity and incremental change in the patriarchal order.

DEMAND FOR FEMALE LABOR

The demand for ever faster production of ever larger quantities of goods and services creates a voracious appetite for the mobilization of manpower and a stimulus for bringing women out of the shelter of the home and into the active labor force.

The education of women, coupled with the impact of telecommunications (films, radio, TV, travel) is a secularizing force reducing the persuasion of the Islamic rules on privacy and female modesty. This influences authority relations within the family when it comes to mate selection, career choice, or cohabitation, for example, young wives refusing to subordinate themselves to the authority of their mothers-in-law (as poignantly described in "A wife for my son" by the Algerian author Ali Ghalem).

OVERCROWDING

Indirectly, the very increase of the extension and densities of the modern city are also working toward the breakdown of the extended family. The size of the nuclear family is not yet decreasing—in fact, in Libya, average family size increased from 4.6 persons to six within the last 25 years. High natural increase coupled with accelerated rates of migration to the cities result in overcrowding in the medinas and even in the informal housing areas rising illegally on the periphery. In conditions of extreme crowding the traditional separation of the home in spheres of privacy can no longer be maintained. Standards vary: while in Istanbul[16] the average house still provides a comfortable 12 square yards per inhabitant, in the Jebel Lamar[17] "gourbi" or spontaneous settlement of Tunis, average floor space is only about six square yards. Similarly, in Cairo[18] no less than 26% of all dwelling units (some 380,000 D.U.S.) consist of only one room, and since the average family size is five persons, privacy is non-existent.

HETEROGENEITY

Another "modernizing" factor is the increasing heterogeneity of urban populations resulting in a loss of social cohesion and solidarity. Doing research in Istanbul's Küçük Ayasofia Mahalle,[19] we found considerable friction among migrants from different Anatolian regions—each mutually hostile group frequenting its own kahveh-outlet and disinclined to cooperate with any "outsiders." Such recent migrants tend to use the traditional inner-city neighborhood as a staging point for urban acculturation before moving out to settle permanently in the peripheral areas and thus have no stake in the improvement of the physical or social environment. Even more disruptive is the influx of foreigners even if they are temporary workers or refugees from other Islamic countries.

The lifestyle of foreign consultants and businessmen is emulated by the rapidly secularizing Islamic middle class. The presence of large numbers of Asiatic contract laborers, i.e., the 250,000 Philippinos and Koreans in the Gulf States, is yet difficult to fathom.

THE FAST RATE OF CHANGE

Even more upsetting than the discontinuity in lifestyles is the extremely fast rate of change of the built environment. In the pre-industrial city, change used to be slow and incremental, mostly resulting from marital and inheritance arrangements. Now most urban interventions are "megaprojects." Clusters of houses used to be settled by cohesive and compatible family groups, but now the state often builds tens of thousands of dwelling units and then assigns them at random.

SOCIAL INSTABILITY

As proof that the rate of change of the urban spatial environment can be a powerful irritant leading to social instability, no better example could be cited than the Iranian revolution. The pace of modernization led to land speculation, corruption, and the collusion of decision-makers with local elites syphoning off excessive and indecent profits to foreign banks.

THE CASE OF SHAHASTAN PAHLEVI

Apart from the fact that the accumulation of excessive profit is contrary to the egalitarian and charitable principles of Islam, no doubt the ultimate irritant to trigger off the riots in Tehran was the Shah's ambitious project to create a new business and administrative center. This vast project called SHAHASTAN PAHLEVI[20] was to be located in the hills on the northern periphery of the capital, on land mostly owned by the Shah's own family. The building of modern infrastructure and of a subway system using public funds would have yielded enormous windfall profits for the owners of real estate in this area. At the same time, the success of the project—planned for a daytime working population of 330,000 people—would have depressed land values in the traditional center and ruined the bazaar merchants who had to face the alternative of moving to the new high-rent area in Shahastan Pahlevi or face declining sales in the neglected bazaar, already poorly served by congested narrow streets. The anger of the bazaar merchants combined with the distaste of the mullahs for the rampant secularization of life which threatened their power base, and both fanned the fires of revolution and prepared the ground for the advent of the fundamentalist Khomeini regime.

FUNDAMENTALIST POLICY

It is too early to tell whether the new regime can successfully block Westernization in other than purely superficial aspects. The growth of Tehran has not been checked: on the contrary, due to the influx of refugees from the war zone and in response to unfulfillable promises to provide housing for the needy, the population has been growing even faster than in the last years of the Shah's rule. Now the Shariah has been invoked, the size of urban plots limited to 1200 square yards and the resale of property made difficult. Yet there has been little change in the typology of buildings or the layout of neighborhoods. The building of extraverted Western-style free-standing blocks of flats continues. The only positive element is that the building of imported "megaprojects" by expatriate contractors has stopped, interventions are more incremental and also much reduced in volume.[21]

RECOMMENDATIONS

What policy recommendations can we distill from this brief critical analysis of "modernization" and the current practice of planning and building in Islamic countries?

MEDINA CONSERVATION

As far as the medina is concerned, it is important to realize that, in leading cities, the historic core only occupies a tiny fraction of the area of the metropolitan agglomeration—.4 to 1.6 square miles. (The area of Greater Cairo is 1160 square miles; of this the densely built-up area covers 104 square miles. The Fatimid old town is only 1.5 square miles—one–sixtieth of the built-up area. The medina of Tunis only occupies 1.1 square miles, the medina of Aleppo .8 square miles, the walled city of Lahore .9 square miles, etc.)[22]

The optimal strategy would be the conservation of the entire medina area by declaring it a "tradition island" to be saved from further erosion by specific legislation. If this is not politically or financially feasible, a "low-investment strategy" could still aim at the conservation of entire neighborhoods embracing a wide range of activities and a maximum diversity of elements in a compact assemblage.

Within the conservation area the reduction of densities and overcrowding is indispensable. But this should certainly not be done by clearance operations or street widening, but by relocating the numerous temporary dwellers who give the medina a transitory character and—having no stake in its improvement—are one of the chief agents of its decay. This implies that the perpetuation of the present composition of inhabitants is incompatible with the conservation goal. But what then should be the new function of the medina?

MEDINA-CBD COMPLEMENTARITY

As explained previously, it cannot accommodate the CBD functions, but it could profit from the proximity of a new CBD. In this case the medina could play a complementary "tandem" role, providing a congenial setting for certain types of business and artisanal activities.

ACTIVITY MIX

Polluting, noisy and traffic-generating industries as well as wholesaling and warehousing must be removed and relocated. On the other hand, since it is desirable to maintain an optimal mix of activities, cultural and educational facilities should be attracted. The medina must remain a predominantly pedestrian precinct.

PEDESTRIAN ZONE

The penetration of the automobile, or at least of heavy traffic, must be reduced. Truck access can be limited to certain hours of the day or night. However, it is well known that car owners want to keep an eye on their cars by parking them preferably in direct proximity of their houses. This results in congestion due to off-street parking. Also, unsightly activities such as washing and repairing of cars on the curb reduce the recreational use of the street space. For this reason it seems to be desirable to concentrate on the medina residents who do not require or cannot afford automobiles, i.e., students (who primarily use motorcycles), retired educators, public servants and officers, and institutions such as old-age homes, orphanages, maternity homes and hospitals.

GENTRIFICATION

In any case, the upgrading of infrastructure will raise the value of real estate and rents, forcing out the lowest income residents and leading to what in the U.S. is called "gentrification."

Hotels, guest houses, hans and certain types of entertainment activities may also be compatible with this commercial-institutional mix although not the international style nightclubs catering to foreign tourists.

The medina might be developed to attract internal—i.e., Islamic —tourism, the potential of which should not be underestimated. Traveling has a venerable tradition in Islam due to the obligation of the Hadj. With the rise of an educated and prosperous middle class and greater pride taken in Islamic identity, a visit to the splendid relics in Istanbul's Topkapi Place, the great mosque of Kairouan, and the remnants of Fatimide Kairo may prove as attractive as a trip to Europe or the United States.

ISLAMIC IDENTITY IN NEW DEVELOPMENT

While the revitalization of the medina seems to be within easy reach, our second goal of infusing some Islamic identity in modern developments seems much more difficult to achieve.

INFORMAL SETTLEMENTS

In many countries of the Maghreb, in Egypt as well as in Turkey, much of the growth occurs in illegal settlements, in "gourbis" and "geçekondus." While these squatter settlements lack adequate infrastructure, their morphology is much more in harmony with the traditional use of space than that of planned developments. If possible, they should be upgraded rather than razed as in Libya where nearly all gourbis have been replaced by non-descript, free-standing, pre-fabricated units totally at variance with Islamic lifestyle. In such "modern" housing projects the provision of street space and so-called "green areas" is far in excess of European standards. At the same time, the size of the unit has been squeezed down to a minimum and there is no place for private courts or gardens where receptions involving the larger family and friends could take place, although there is still a demand for such gatherings in Arab households. If possible, larger lots should be provided since the minimum standard may provide adequate shelter but may not suffice for the survival of the Islamic lifestyle. In the Maghreb, spontaneous housing offers the best guarantee for a continuity of Islamic traditions. In

Turkey and in Iran the builders of informal housing units seem to have taken as role models the secularized middle class with their preference for Western-style isolated buildings. Maybe it is not too late to change this by enforcing appropriate guidelines.

SHORTCOMINGS OF HIGH-RISE BUILDINGS

In the formal provision of mass housing, high-rise construction should be avoided. Most of the high-rise projects of the last decades have been provided by foreign contractors who have probably never given a thought to Islamic customs.[23] Negative examples abound. Nasr City in Cairo, designed in 1956 by Soviet consultants, packed 60,000 people in 3- to 14-story blocks on 600 acres. The Jeddah Rush Housing Project built by American contractors can claim the dubious record of concentrating 10,000 inhabitants on only 35 acres (in densely packed 15-story towers on 3-story platforms for parking and commerce) at a net density of some 3,000 persons per acre.[24]

HIGH-DENSITY LOW-RISE

It can be demonstrated that reasonably high densities can be achieved in low-rise developments by grouping 1- to 3-story units and reducing public circulation space to a minimum.

In line with Hassan Fathy's[25] experiments in GOURNA-el GEDIDA and elsewhere, 20 to 25 units should be grouped into clusters and assigned to a compatible group of inhabitants selected on the basis of common regional background, kinship, or some other social bonding force. Reasonable plot sizes should permit core houses to expand incrementally to allow at least 12 square yards' floor space per habitant which is sufficient to safeguard the requirements of privacy and female modesty.

Self-help construction may offer a wide field for the application of traditional materials and building methods as pioneered by Hassan Fathy.

PREFABRICATION

However, these materials (such as mud-brick) and methods (such as vaulting) have never been conceived for the rapid satisfaction of mass housing needs. Therefore there is undoubtedly some merit in attempting to use modern technology consisting of the assemblage of prefabricated units.

MEGAPROJECTS

The monotony of a prefabricated environment could be reduced by using an incremental approach, building on scattered sites rather than "megaprojects."[26] A decentralization of construction sites and reduced-scale operations would permit the maximal mobilization of local enterprises. Also, less use should be made of "package deals" assigned to foreign designers and contractors. It seems that, due to the vast scale of projects preferred by the decision-makers in the Arab world, no more than 25% of all building contracts has been carried out by local Arab companies in the last 20 years.[27]

DESIGN MEASURES

Another attempt to break monotony would be to avoid rigid orthogonality and wide right of ways.[28] Hassan Fathy points out that in historic medinas even the longest straight stretch of street never exceeded 1000 ft. To provide more perceptual variety, various configurations of prefabricated houses should be tried. Inspiration should be sought in Arabic music which is not the endless repetition of the same tune but infinitely rich variations on a single theme—as in the stories of the "Arabian Nights" which keep returning unfailingly to the basic yarn of the narrator.

HUMAN SCALE

Keeping in line with the traditional size of the mahalle of 6 acres, clusters should be formed with 250 to 600 dwelling units per acre and not exceed a density of more than 2500 persons per acre. Having promoted greater social homogeneity on the mahalle level, it is desirable to restore to it some local autonomy. The institution of the waqf could be revived to take on the management of communal socio-cultural equipment on the neighborhood level, to promote activities, and to provide maintenance of public grounds and buildings.

MOTORIZATION

Mahalles could be juxtaposed on one side on linear bazaars and on the other side on service streets with strips for car parking. Continued motorization could perhaps be slowed down by a deliberate policy of making the purchase and operation of private automobiles difficult. On this issue, of course, opinions are widely divided. Colonel Khadafi, on the occasion of an official visit to Antanarivo (Madagascar), startled his hosts by stating that the Bedouin tradition of unrestricted mobility should be met by providing each Arab with a car instead of a camel!

In large cities, however, existing street space is already often congested to saturation levels. In 1973 in Istanbul there were only 70,000 registered cars, and in Cairo no more than 220,000.[29] If these numbers are going to increase tenfold until the year 2000 as predicted, there will be a dire need for more street surface and parking areas. More emphasis on public rapid transit is called for.

Major efforts are needed to control speculation. These could include the measures already introduced in Iran of limiting the maximum size of plots, making property transfer difficult and all development subject to severe control for conformity with guidelines.

Among non-physical measures it might be useful to tie property taxes to the declared value of real estate and simultaneously make it known that property can be expropriated any moment at the tax value. This would generate adequate income for municipal purposes by ensuring taxation based on a fair assessment of real estate. Positive measures of enticement, tax rebates, etc. should also be employed to assure the optimum use of land in harmony with the Islamic concept of the trusteeship of real estate—of which the ultimate owner is Allah.

It seems to me that the implementation of these simple recommendations could provide the preconditions for the rise of settlements more in harmony with Islamic principles. It is important to emphasize that these principles define an appropriate use of *space* and of *behavior* in space. By contrast, the cosmetic use of traditional decorative elements, applied skin-deep to the exterior of Western-style buildings, is dishonest trickery and should be avoided.

CONCLUSIONS

Leaders of the modern states in the countries of Islamic tradition often seem exasperated with the conditions of the inherited environment[30] which seems antiquated, unsanitary, overcrowded, decaying, and plagued by traffic congestion, air and noise pollution. Yet there is nothing outdated in the Islamic *principles* or the spatial organization derived from it. The task is to reduce the conflict of tradition and modernization to be able to enjoy some of the benefits of continuity.

Speaking as a "Western" planner and addicted to rationality and quantitative methods, I nevertheless hope that the Islamic traditions will show a way for a new paradigm of urban spatial organization based on more spiritual values.

Is it too much to hope that an Islamic urbanism will emerge that will elevate the art of city planning through levels of sublimation as asked by the Sufi philosophers from the mere "world of forms" to the "world of spiritual perception," "the world of imagination" and "the world beyond form"?[31]

NOTES

1. Janet Abu-Lughod, "Contemporary relevance of Islamic urban principles" in *Ekistics* 280. Jan/Feb. 1980.

2. B. Jensen, K. Kunzmann, and S. Saad-el-Din, "Taming the Growth of Cairo" in *Third World Planning Review*. May 1981, pp.201–233.

3. Cyrus Mechat, "The Metropolis in Islamic Countries," Proceedings of the 13th ICUS, Sept. 2–5, 1984, Washington D.C., ICF, New York.

4. Istanbul Master Plan Bureau and Colin Buchanan and Partners, "Istanbul Urban Development Project," 1977.

5. G.K. Payne, "Ankara" in *Cities*. Feb. 1984, pp.210–214.

6. The European Cement Association in Paris estimates that while world-wide average cement consumption was 415 lbs. per capita in 1982, it amounted to 1584 lbs. per capita in Bahrain and no less than 7700 lbs. per capita in the United Arab Emirates!

7. Nur-al-Islam: al-Azhar, Matba'ah al-Ma'ahid al Diniyah; Cairo 1351 h./1933, vol.3, English Supplement pp.24–25.

8. Othman, B. Llewellyn, "The Objectives of Islamic Law" in *Ekistics* 280. Jan/Feb. 1980, pp.11–13.

9. *Ibid.*

10. Min. de l'Habitat et de l'Aménagement du Territoire, Royaume du Maroc "Schéma Directeur de l'urbanisme de la ville de Fez", PNUD et UNESCO, Paris 1980.

11. Janet Abu-Lughod, "Urbanization and Social Change in the Arab World" in *Ekistics* 300, pp.223–231.

12. HĀRA in Cairo and in Damascus, HAWMA in Algiers, and HĀĀRAT in Yemen.

13. Abdulaziz Y. Saqqaf, "The Islamic Metropolis: A Commentary," Proceedings of the 13th ICUS, September 2–5, 1984, Washington, D.C., ICF, New York.

14. Mechkat, *op. cit.*

15. J. Warren, "Baghdad, Two Case Studies of Conservation" in *The Arab City*. pp.242–250.

16. Istanbul Master Plan Bureau, *op. cit.*

17. Distric de Tunis "Réhabilitation du *Jebel Lamar."* 1974.

18. *Cahiers IAURIF* no. 74, Dec. 1984 *La Region du Grand Caire* and text. In this document "Greater Cairo" includes the three Governorates of Cairo, Gizeh and Kaliubah with a present population of 11 million, about 22% of the population of Egypt. This metropolitan area covers 1160 square miles; however, the built-up area is less than one-tenth, about 108 square miles.

19. Swiss Federal Institute of Technology, Zurich, INDEL-Program "Küçük Ayasofia Mahalle Conservation and Renewal Study, Istanbul", report of graduate field-study group under the direction of Prof. E. Galantay, ETH-Zurich, 1977. See also: P. Schubeler, "Localization of small-scale enterprise in Istanbul." ETH-INDEL 1977, Zurich.

20. J. Robertson, "Shahastan Pahlevi," Proceedings of the 1st Congress of the International New Towns Association, Teheran 1975.

21. Sadat, student report submitted to the author, Nov. 1984.

22. Compare these areas to the size of historic Venice: 1.8 square miles or that of the city of London: 1 square mile. See also: Samuel Noe, "Old Lahore and Delhi" in *Ekistics* 295. July/Aug. 1982, pp.306.

23. Youssef Belkacem, in *The Arab City. op. cit.* p. 11. "In Algeria people continue to sacrifice sheep on *Aid* even on the 15th floor balcony. In Algeria where the sacrifice of *Aid* is observed even by the urban population, some people in modern housing projects are obliged to kill sheep on 15th floor balconies."

24. A. Farahat and M.N. Cebeci, "A Housing Project: Intentions and Realities" in *The Arab City*. pp.302–311.

25. Hassan Fathy, "Interviewed by Jorick Blumenfeld" in *Architectural Association Quarterly,* Vol.6, 1974, no.3/4.

26. Entirely alien in conception are the vast projects carried out by the U.S. Army Corps of Engineers, such as the King Khaled Military City in Saudi Arabia which will accommodate 70,000 people, or the Suwaihan military city in Abu Dhabi planned by the Bechtel Corp. However, equally insensitive is the concept of the new industrial town of Ariashahr in Iran, provided by the Soviet State Planning Institute GIPROGOR of Moscow and built with Russian help in 1968–76. For a discussion of Ariashahr see: Ervin Y. Galantay, *New Towns.* New York: G. Braziller, 1975.

27. A. Zahlan, (an Arab labor consultant) quoted in the *International Herald Tribune*. Nov. 16, 1984.

28. It is useful to recall that Rasullah's recommendation for an appropriate street width in reconstructing Medina and Mecca is "at least seven zirah's," i.e., 9.2 yards. Somewhat later Sydgna Omar planned the main roads of Basra 15.4 yards wide (20 zirah's) while side streets were kept at 6.9 yards (9 zirah's). In fact, in traditional Islamic medinas primary streets vary by 4.4 to 13.2 yards and the main thoroughfares rarely exceed 13 to 22 yards. By contrast modern roads built in Kuwait and Libya have R.O.W. widths of 77 yards and even 110 yards. See also: Ali Afak, "Urbanism and Family Residence in Islamic Law" in *Ekistics* 280. Jan/Feb. 1980. p.23.

29. Istanbul Master Plan Bureau, *op. cit.* and *La Région du Grand Caire, op. cit.*

30. "The traditional Middle Eastern city is no 'paradise lost.' But even if it were, it would be futile to lament its loss . . ." Prince Hassan Ibn Talal of Jordan in his message at the PWPA Symposium on the Middle East City, Paris, 1985.

31. N. Ardelan and L. Bakhtiar, *The Sense of Unity*. Chicago: University of Chicago Press, 1973.

    The "seven levels of realization" are in ascending order:

    1. ālam i tabiat (the world of man)
    2. ālam it sūrat (the world of forms)
    3. ālam i ma'nā (the world of spiritual perception)
    4. ālam i malakūt (the world of imagination)
    5. ālam i jabarūt (the world beyond form)
    6. ālam i lāhūt (the world beyond Nature)
    7. ālam i hāhūt (the world of divine essence)

REFERENCES

The Arab City. Proceedings of a symposium held in Medina, Kingdom of Saudi Arabia 1401 AH/1981. Ismael Serageldin, Editor.

International Conference on "Urbanization and Social Change in the Arab World." Bellaggio, Italy. 1982 and special issue of *Ekistics* 300. May/June 1983.

International Symposium on Islamic Architecture and Urbanism 1930. King Faisal University, Dammam S.A.

Chapter 2

The Islamic City and the Western City: A Comparative Analysis*

Cyrus Mechkat

THE ARABO-IRANIAN AREAS AS DIRECT PROTAGONISTS IN THEIR HISTORY

Since the early seventies, because of the so-called Third World's outburst and the rise in the prices of raw materials, the Arabo-Iranian areas have become direct protagonists of new periods in their own history. This phenomenon is particularly noticed in countries newly engaged in an industrialization program. Each reorganization plan has in consequence given rise to an important territorial remodelation as well as to the growth in building activities. In that manner, and for the past 10 years, the North African, Red Sea and Gulf areas have had the most intensive construction activity ever known.

This rate of construction growth has been abated with the coming of the world economic crisis. There remains some superficiality in the modernity attempt, mixed with a tendency to react against such deceptive modernity, seeking its legitimization in an out-dated past. With respect to urban landscape, it remains the superposed images of subsisting traditional elements and unfinished parts of New Towns. The prevailing image is of an interrupted development process which hereafter becomes impossible to realize conformably to schemes based on the standards and concepts of Western advanced societies. To modernize, as if the East's history was since ever blended with the West's history, can only lead to a dead end. Five centuries of

*Translated from the original French

relationships and confrontations with a triumphant Western world have furthermore altered the economic, political and socio-cultural background of the Arabo-Iranian world.

The traditional East has lived out its life and the modern Orient remains a new-born project, but one that cannot ignore its past. A comparison between the history and formation theory of Arabo-Iranian cities and the rise and development of Western towns will reveal the considerable differences between those two urban forms.

THE EASTERN TRADITIONAL CITY HAS NOTHING IN COMMON WITH THE WESTERN TOWN

The territory conquered by the Muslims had been inhabited by Greeks, Carthagians, Romans, and Persians. These territories had been conquered by different civilizations before the advent of Islam which remodeled them from the seventh century, from which time they were controlled quasi-uninterrupted for more than 10 centuries. Before this, the same regions, extending from the Tigris and the Euphrates to the Nile, had already experienced the first stages of urban phenomenon and had evolved writing. The question of the Babylonian city's influence on the Arabo-Iranian pattern keeps its pertinence. If it appears that most of the constitutive elements of the habitat and city exist before Islam, it is however true that the socio-cultural formation settled in the Islamized regions knew how to assimilate these same elements; to transfer and reproduce them in their newly conquered regions.

The West's influence, i.e., the laic and industrialized centers, was felt in the Arabo-Iranian periphery at the middle of the nineteenth century only. It was the first time in history that expansionist Europe found itself confronted with a strongly structured society and had to compound with territories endowed with a network of cities, routes and equipment services. However, we should not, according to common implicit practice, qualify as towns the urban entities of Eastern or Islamic origins. The forming of towns is peculiar to the industrialized world. An understanding of this fundamental difference is imperative in order to avoid confusion at a later stage.

The Iranian shahr as well as the Arabian medina are born and nurtured in socio-cultural, economic and political contexts which have nothing in common with the advent of Western industrial town. In this paper, the purpose of the use of endogenous words is to avoid the implicit philological transfer of modern Western concepts on pre-modern investigated items.

So far as the urban level is concerned, the first European realizations in the Arabo-Iranian area were erected within the framework of colonial relationships and were based on a destruction/substitution process as can be seen in lower Algiers. At a later stage came the creation of European-type towns. In this case, the town was built outside the boundaries of the medina, sheltering—as seen in the Maghreb—European inhabitants. The decolonization process of the fifties led to a rapid expansion of the urban framework and further destructions, even destruction of cities and ancient living quarters. This very process had already started in the twenties and thirties in non-colonized independent countries such as Turkey or Iran.[1]

However, the conditions of passage from a traditional, oriental, social formation to a modern social formation have nothing in common with the passage from a medieval society to a mercantile, and then industrial, society. Likewise, the conditions of passage from an oriental city of the Islamic period to a modern town are not a mere repetition—with a five-century delay—of the transition from a medieval city to a mercantile, then industrial town, ending up as a contemporary metropolis.

The city invested by Islam reflects the religious purpose to permanently maintain and safeguard its values. The industrial town is the product of an enterprising society, welcoming inventivity, innovation and renewal. Within the two urban entities, human relationships differ fundamentally. Wage reproduction has nothing to do with man's domestic reproduction. Mass production and mass consumption create human relationships as well as goods production and distribution relationships that are totally foreign to the handicraft mode of production and the total economic dependence on the traditional sector. These differences can be seen in the very design of the distribution networks' territory, production and usage sites—the factory or the stall, the habitat, equipment.

The Western industrial society's world-wide economic influence and the cultural side effects on the corpus of habits, on the "habitus,"[2] forbid the reproduction of totally outdated conditions of the past. However, the problem would not be solved should the peripheral countries merely adopt the center's conditions. By ignoring the fundamental differences between modern and traditional societies and the primary context of those urban entities, there has been a thoughtless transfer of the pattern of the center's towns towards the periphery right when, considering the economic crisis, this pattern is evolving in a yet-hard-to-define direction. Confronted with the failure of such a transfer, there is a strong temptation to return and to take refuge in past norms, most attractive "traditional values": this is yet a less viable solution than the preceding one.

The constitutive elements of the peripheral Arabo-Iranian town must be reappraised. Such analysis requires a thorough knowledge of the traditional city, and must be formulated with the precision applied to the knowledge of the industrial city. Terms of a new urban project will arise from the combination of the attainments of both urban forms along with the autonomous creation project of a new life framework.

This paper sketches out some elements related to traditional urban form and the history of cities in the Arabo-Iranian area, re-examined with the new urban and architectural design in prospect.

WHAT PRODUCES THE UNITY AND THE UNIQUITY OF THE ARABO-IRANIAN CITY

It is dangerous to attempt to generalize on an area so vast and over a period of 10 to 12 centuries during which the cities had different destinies and were subject to several important or reversible internal changes.

Various geophysical factors, the extreme rapidity of the jihad and the economic and socio-cultural structures do permit elements in common which impact the unity of the Arabo-Iranian area.

The common denominator of the geographical entity is essentially the existence of a huge plain which facilitates access and communication, and extends from the east Afghano-Iranian plains to the western extremity of North Africa. Most of the area is arid, with a few fertile regions. It is bordered by the Atlantic coast, by the high mountain range situated on the northern limit and the Sahara on the southern limit.

The rapidity of the conquest and of the Islamization marks through its contemporaneity the profile of the settlements and intensifies the resemblance as well as the recurrence of the re-managed urban landscapes.

The repartition of the population in highly cultivated nuclei is directly linked to the availability of water. Such population centers in pre-Islamic and later in Islamic periods are where the princes reside, the imperial city of the Asiatic despot: the focus of religious practice, administrative control, military base, and later, the principal trading activity center throughout the long road from the Maghreb to distant China.

The birth of Islam as a religion takes place in such "foyers de sédentarisation"[3]—foci of sedentarization—and in such a commercial environment. The practice of Islam is easier in such an environment. The medina, the city pattern adopted by Islam, manifests certain characteristics in as much as it had existed prior to the Islamic conquest or had taken place in the framework of conquest. Its situation in the Western Islamized world with a Greek, Roman or Byzantine past, or in the Eastern Islamized world which has a Persian cultural past, constitutes new elements of particularity.

The mentioned rapidity of Islamic expansion necessitates the assimilation of the cultures of conquested regions. The early Islam, engaged in its jihad, had no need for creating new large cities since it was spreading over the most urbanized regions of the Mediterranean basin: Damascus, Antioch, Jerusalem, Alexandria. However, in later years, Islamic conquerors founded, resettled or remodeled cities such as Basra, Fustat (Cairo), and Baghdâd. They established new capitals in al Maghreb, such as Qayrawan, Fes, Marrakesh, in al Andalus, Spain, such as Ishbiliya (Sevilla) and Qurtuba (Cordoba), while in the Eastern regions other cities appear or begin to grow, such as Kashân, Isfahân, Nishâpur, Bukhara, Tashkend and Samarkand. All these cities conform to the new urban configuration, which was precisely shaped between the ninth and the thirteenth centuries—a period of political expansion and cultural radiance.

The inhabitants of the medina and shahr, including the largest among them—Istanbul, Damascus, Cairo, Baghdad, and Kashân, do not live from spices or artisanry, but principally from agricultural products of their outlying areas, the income from which form their real wealth.

The territory is structured in fiscal units. These are delimitated by established ruling entities which control and manage the urban and rural settlements, the equipment of water supplying, the production and trading activities, the caravaning and caravanserais network.

Islamic ideology is egalitarian: every man is· equal in the sight of God. Nevertheless, the society is ruled by a small elite. This group concerns itself with the maintenance of law and order (sharia), the collection of taxes (zakat) and the provision of some elementary public services. It is necessary to make a distinction between egalitarianism and the Western concept of democracy. The Eastern traditional authority has a despotic nature. This tradition tends to continue and constitutes a major obstacle to real modernization of the civilian society. Without such evolution, progress will be held back. It is the politico-military group, often of foreign origin, that has the de facto control over the different aspects of the life in the medina in collaboration with the Ulama, the religious elite.

The advent of a new dynasty can change the status of a city towards an essor or a decline. In his discourse on the universal history, Al Mugaddima, Ibn Khaldûn writes: "If the dynasty is short, the existence of city will not survive . . . on the contrary, a prolonged dynasty gives rise to new buildings, to the growth of palaces, to the extension of fortifications."

THE INVOLUTIVE DEVELOPMENT
PROCESS OF THE MEDINA

The classic Hellenistic polis and the Roman civitas are cities characterized by the urban disposition of their public spaces. The medieval European cities are conditioned by the rural and domestic dominances of their socio-economic formation. The Western town is regulated by the prefigurated disposition of the urban design and the premeditated arrangement of public spaces and streets, the layout of façades and the articulation with internal rooms. The city, in the Islamic agreement, is ruled by the predominating role of privacy and by the strict distinction from public activities. The respective spaces of internal life (batîn) and external or visible life (zâhir) are precisely separated according to the dominating conditions of life. The physical organization of the city is controlled by a process of development from the private domestic space to the public urban space, by the separation of residential neighborhoods from the commercial main quarter.

The sense of collectivity does not prevail. Except religious spaces, peculiarly inside the mosques, there is no imperative necessity for important collective and civil open spaces. Existing examples are initiated by more or less generous individual purposes. However, excluding some well-known realizations—among them the Meidan-é Shah of Safavid Isfahan, originally reserved for equestrian plays—the open spaces, when they exist inside the city's circumvolution as they do in the Southern Arabic peninsula, are not conceived as elements of meeting for the city communities but rather as no man's land and separate elements between the ethnic groups. Public meeting areas are sometimes managed outside the medina, near cities' fortified gateways or between outer and inner gateways.

Numerous elements, such as ramparts, gates, markets, khans, and public baths (hamam) are service elements inherited from preceding urban forms. The central power takes place in a commandment space (qasr), palace or castle lying in kasbah or ark respectively in Arabic or Farsi. The citadel is generally built at the edge of the medina or shahr, easy to defend and far from the people's curiosity.

Inside the ramparts, the main built entity is composed of the masjid al-jami, the Friday mosque, associated with a complex of institutions forming the medina's pole of attraction. This complex may include the major madrasa (the theological university), a library, and some other annex services. Its role is to put the population in conformity with the Islamic way of life which determines all aspects of the city, conceived as a confraternity of believers.

The suk, or bazâr, with its qaysariya-funduk, khan, etc. forms a complex of shops, workshops and warehouses composing the commercial urban entity. This offers a grand variety of goods according to the importance of the medina which it serves. It constitutes a continuous space linked with the network of other medinas and their rural set.

The subsistance economy is based on a system of land tenure where agricultural land is owned by the state, the direct cultivators and the notables having the right of enjoying the use of property. Crops are cultivated for local urban and rural consumption. The community is generally self–sufficient. Most of the grain is destined for the medina as tax and removed from rural areas. The shaykh of the village administers the land and collects the taxes.

All professional activities, except some very messy or polluting jobs, are sited around the main suk or along the ways leading to it. The more precious activities such as jewelery or perfume making are the closest to the masjid al-jami.[4] According to the regions and periods, the urban craft guilds acquire more or less importance, enjoying protection of the state, gradually becoming instruments of control on the economic activities of populations. With the Ottomans and Persians, they grew in importance, acquiring political authority and considerable religious significance. Their responsibility was to check the quality and quantity of manufactured goods. These are produced to satisfy the prince and all his suite, to be sold in the suk of the medina, or to be exported. The responsibility of the guilds also expands on the determination of the number of shops per profession, on the verification of the production and performances of each good and on the approval of every change. The guilds form a rigid hierarchy of masters, journeymen, and master or ordinary apprentices in which the master plays the part of an ethic and religious example while the apprentice has to follow this example.

The residential quarters, hawma, harah mahala, form the basic society unit and the relational space of social solidarities. They swerve from the main public and commercial area of the city, essentially frequented by the male adult population. They shelter a succession of progressively more secluded and private space until the houses, which are haram (that is, sacred) become non-transgressible. This is the lieu of the woman's daily existence. The medina is built up through the most fundamental ties—kinship, common origin and ethnic identity, clientage, religious or sectarian appartenance. The quarters are the social areas in which these established ties appear and work. The quarters are also administrative units, headed by shayks or aqil appointed by the governor to assist him in tax collection, order maintenance and ceremonial occurrences. Thus, the formal institutions are reduced to their simplest form, when not completely non-existent. In the hawma, social control is tightened to the extent that the norms of interiorized behavior and self-discipline are strong enough to solve any difference which might arise between people and to pass by the administrative institutions.[5]

The configuration of public traffic equipment is the residual result of the piled buildings. It is directly negotiated among the concerned neighbors. There are chief arteries receiving the main buildings of the medina. They go through the city and give way to fortified gates managed in the ramparts and beyond them to the caravan routes and their caravanserais. Secondary arteries lead to the quarters; along them are sited the usual equipment of the quarter, such as masjid, madrasa, suk or bazârtcheh, and hamam. Branching cul-de-sacs constitute new limits to more privacy; they give access to the housing units, with these turning their back on the external space.

The system of circulation in the medina is conceived in tree pattern, imposing exclusive coming and going peddler movements through an apparatus of successive thresholds. The access to a derb and then to a cul-de-sac is reserved to ever more selected groups of inhabitants, who in turn are more secure as well as more socially controlled. This tree pattern is completely different from the circulation system of the Western towns, even the medieval cities, which corresponds to a network or an open grid pattern.

The Islamic law recognizes the enlarged family, the parental group, (táefah), as the entity between the individual level and the level of the whole community of believers. These live in introverted residential units which are the expression of a way of life, of a kind of social organization, of habits and practices. The elementary arrangement of the house is uniform; it is generally shaped by four covered rooms, delimiting a central open space, the inner courtyard. The house configuration springs from the complex combination of the patriarchal system, the Islamic ideology about privacy and the seclusion of women, as well as physical conditions such as topography, climatic data, and finally subsistance of pre-Islamic habitat patterns, adopted as well as adapted to the new ruling context. This introverted house works in complete privacy within the medina, even insulated from its neighbors.

THE MEDINA AS THE EXPRESSION
OF A TACIT AGREEMENT

The medina, conceived to correspond to the Islamic way of life, presents repetitive plans with a certain margin for local interpretation according to specific conditions such as cultural heritage, relations with the hinterland and with physical imperatives. Nevertheless, it corresponds to a generalized way of life through the whole area. Even if there are no rigorous and explicit rules on housing and city planning, the Islamic religion exercises an indirect but real influence through the control upon land and building appropriation rules, upon production and professional guilds, upon diffused administration of each quarter, upon housing, upon communication systems, upon education, etc. The medina is the expression of a certain tacit agreement of a community's way of life through the appropriation of areas and relations. It offers an effective balance between the economic system by which it is ruled and the necessary mode of regulation for the functioning of this specific system. Like this, it would not be able to satisfy any other system. It must be considered apart from the city of the Middle Ages, from the mercantile European town, from the town of industrial capital, from the modern metropolis. This difference lies in history, namely, the rigidity of politico-economic institutional structure, the cultural conception, the administrative functions, the property laws, the weak degree of autonomy permitted by the princely power to each social category, particularly that of merchants and entrepreneurs. These are limited in their initiative in order to hinder all eventual rise of an accumulate productive capital which can compete with the established political authority. The difference is apparent in all institutions as well as being mirrored in the habitus furthered by the medina.

THE TRADITIONAL CITY SUPPLANTED
BY THE COLONIAL TOWN

But what is the Islamic conception of the Western world, successively known as conquested, as rival, then as dominator before the decolonization? There is a tendency to forget that in a world organized into closed social entities, the Arabo-Iranian world was for centuries the "center of the world"; and it is the only civilization simultaneously in contact with Africa, the Far East, Northern Asia and Europe. Custodian throughout the centuries of Greek and Roman cultural heritages, it is the essential historical link between the ancient world and the Western renaissance. It is only towards the end of the Middle Ages that Europe began to discover other worlds. In a few decisive decades, Europeo-centralism supplanted "Islamo-centralism."

There is a plethora of informative literature on these discoveries, especially on the "discovery" of Islam by the Europeans, but there is a dearth of knowledge on the discovery of Europe by the Arabo-Iranian world and the successive phases of the formation of this knowledge.

The first Europeans to venture into the Islamized world were the crusaders of the eleventh century. They stayed until the thirteenth century, founding numerous, small fortified principalities isolated from the rest of the region. The "jihad" of the crusaders can be compared to the Muslim "reconquista," pealing to the Islamization of Eastern Europe. The crusaders were vanquished, but the European merchants who had come with them were encouraged to remain in the Levantine ports. They lived in small communities doomed to failure, victims of the aftereffect of the crusades. Nevertheless, their written testimony, after that of the crusaders, is a new source of information on the Islamic world which will be enriched by the description of travelers.

The Arabo-Iranian world of the thirteenth and fourteenth centuries is aware of its unchallenged superiority, and therefore makes no attempt to develop relations with Europe apart from trade relations established with the merchants who had remained in the Levantine area. But internal rivalries contradict the concept of a great, universal destiny of Islam. Every new ruler makes changes within the boundaries of his territory. In the sixteenth century the Middle East could boast of only three great established states: Turkey, Egypt and Persia. But the rulers of these states considered themselves each to be the supreme ruler over all the followers of Islam.

If the Orient was uninterested in the Occident, the reverse is not the case. The crusades were a resounding failure, religiously speaking, but they resulted in a new awareness on the part of the European merchants who were quick to perceive the existence of a great wealth to be snatched, if one only had the means. This was the European perspective of the ensuing centuries, and Venice and Genoa were particularly active in opening up this new trade possibility. However, it is between sovereign European and Arab or Iranian partners that commercial exchanges were developed right up to the middle of the nineteenth century, with a few notable exceptions, namely Algeria, which had fallen under French domination in the 1830s. European products became increasingly interesting for oriental leaders, such as manufactured goods, transportation equipment, arms, civil-engineering, luxury articles, etc.

It is remarkable indeed to note to what degree the Islamic thought isolates itself from current developments, introverted as it is in its superiority complex. It remains in quasi ignorance of profound changes and revolutions which affected the West and the world map. It was only towards the end of the nineteenth century when colonization was widespread that the Islamic leaders realized the profundity of the differences between the two societies. The reaction was defensive in the extreme, and the first primitive impression of the West, forged in the Islamic imagination, was intensified.

The regions of the Middle East, on the way to British India, and of North Africa are not sheltered by colonization and its consequences. The Ottoman Empire lost its Mediterranean territories. The Maghreb fell under French domination; Libya under the Italian sphere of influence; Egypt under British control as well as the coast of the Arabian peninsula and the Indian sub-continent. World War I marked the end of the Ottoman Empire.

The establishment of massive metropolitan populations modified the social and physical character of colonized regions. This phenomenon led to new types of settlements: the Dutch towns of Southeast Asia, the English settlements in India and the destructive French interference in Algiers. The initial phases of British settlement in India were not carried out according to any particular urban plan, except for certain large official buildings. Experience was gradually acquired. One can attempt a definition of new colonial construction, intended for military, administrative, economic, and housing uses, including the famous colonial bungalows.[6]

The French intervention in Algeria started along the same lines. Colonists were installed in houses abandoned by their original inhabitants who were chased out of Algiers. The first urban operations took place within the limits of the old city. But opening new places with the purpose of military parades, new avenues and building new street fronts in a traditional urban web was not an easy task. An extension of the Kasbah began on adjoining land which culminated in a new fortified enclosure around the Kasbah. Most of the old port area was pulled down, for "sanitary reasons." A new waterfront was built along with the new port in neo-classic style. Such massive destruction was met with hostility by the local people. This groping context led to building new European towns, outside the indigenous cities. Reorganization projects were set into motion throughout the territory. The traditional cities of the interior, turned towards the countryside, were abandoned in favor of coastal development. After the waterfront of Algiers, the plans for the new European towns of Casablanca, Meknès, Fes, Marrakesh and especially Rabat, designed on Lyautey's order,[7] became the classical examples of colonialist urban development at the beginning of the century. This created the instruments, techniques, rules and regulations necessary for the realization of the designs and made the master plan mandatory for each town.[8]

The importance of these projects extends beyond the colonial empire. It is indeed the first experience of intervention on such a massive scale at the time. These plans serve as points of reference for the establishment of plans and ideas for numerous French towns. It is interesting to note that these experiences can only be accumulated under special circumstances—mixing the most advanced directives with the traditional royal dahir (order). The colonial town is and remains a domination act—for those who engineer such domination as well as those forced to submit to it. Installed side by side, directly alongside the traditional city, it becomes a direct instrument of its disintegration.

Towards the end of the nineteenth century the economy of several areas of the whole region was progressively transformed from a self-sufficient, domestic economy into a new export-oriented economy adapted to the international economies of Europe and North America. At the end of the nineteenth century, various parts of the region were more or less drawn into the international network of trade and finance.

The process of transfer of the urban poles towards the coast was the general trend throughout the area: Casablanca, Oran, Bône, Bizerte, Port-Saïd, Alexandria, Suez, Haïfa, Beirut, Jeddah, Aden, Abadan, Khorramshahr. The populations followed the movement of the town to the coasts. Modern hygienic measures[9] resulted in a sharp increase in the population. The capital and technology export and the increase of European business and businessmen also increased. England, France, Germany and North America were the main driving forces behind such transfers of capital. The most prosperous of the receiving countries were able to use these funds for building expensive infrastructures such as railways and civil engineering projects. But in less structured societies, such injections of foreign capital served less to develop than to colonize and to put the power in the hands of a few local bosses. Foreign competition resulted in the breakdown of indigenous handicrafts and production.

THE IMPOSSIBLE RESISTANCE

The relative speed at which these changes reached the Arabo-Iranian area poses problems which need a thorough investigation from the very beginning of the phenomenon. The decline had started in the sixteenth century, even though certain elements fed the illusion that this was not the case. Does not history accumulate examples of apparently vigorous civilizations that were in reality on the edge of decline? Successive invasions had shaken the Arabo-Iranian world, introverted as it was into itself and hindered by a stagnant superiority complex. The introversion precluded an objective view of the historical changes irrevocably in progress. From the sixteenth century, the world politico-economy tendency within the Oriental city networks had begun to disintegrate with the advent of European maritime expansion and the first bastions of capitalism.

Because of the rapid growth of the colonial powers, only at the end of the nineteenth century did the Eastern world become aware of the gap, without having the means to answer the challenge. The development imposed upon ancient cities of these areas[10] has nothing to do with an indigenous development. It proceeds, in fact, from that taking place in European towns caught up in the industrial revolution. From the very beginning of this process, the ancient urban structure gave way. The supreme politico-religious magistracy of the caliphate declined. The traditional system of control fulfilled by the shayks on the life in the city fell into disuse and was progressively replaced by the newly established municipal administration.

The former dominant social orders, the zamindâran (members of the aristocracy, tribal leaders, merchants motivated by social prestige) and the peasants fell into decay. Their eventual reconversion into import-export business with the Western industrial center did not promote any pro domo productive infrastructure. The ulama, custodians of the waqf (lands granted to religious institutions, the revenue of which is used for investments in schools, hospitals and charitable organizations) saw their operational field vanish for the benefit of the state controlled apparatus.

Members of the other social groups of population played a subordinate role. They were for the most part merchants in the bazâr, engaged in the commercialization of traditional products; the artisans as well as the other groups submitted to them. The changes in production relations spelled the diminution of the power of the guilds, nay even their disappearance or prohibition. They became of evident secondary importance and had to content themselves with a sterile and defensive policy in an attempt to retain the last vestiges of their obsolete authority. This latter was founded on the preservation of political context rather than on economic developmental purpose. Contrary to Western corporations, the Eastern guilds placed themselves under direct domination of the politico-religious authority.

Because of that, they structurally, culturally and even professionally were incapable of engendering an autonomous development initiative.

All these population groups historically belonged to the dominant order and were unable to transform themselves into real entrepreneurs able to initiate the development of capitalistic relations of production, to exploit the urban areas with the goal of rent formation and capital accumulation, and lastly to remodel the traditional city into a modern town.

REVISED AND NEW KNOWLEDGE ABOUT CONTEMPORARY URBAN AND HOUSING DESIGN

In what sense can this kind of knowledge serve contemporary urban planning and architectural design? The urban and architectural question in the Arabo-Iranian area proceeds from two fields of distinct and divergent concerns, that is to say, the archeological investigation and the professional practice. The archeological investigation is conceived according to the specific scientific, dynamic, historical researches. The urban and architectural design springs from professional rationality as working in Western socio-cultural and economic urban environment. The connection between these two isolated concerns is of prime importance. This will show how much the Eastern traditional city and the Western industrial town are two alien urban forms. The medina has nothing to do with the modern town, nor with the society which gave rise to it. The medina has a completely separate history. It is born in a time, in places, under social conditions and relations appropriate to those of a despotic authority, of pre-capitalism and of an Islamic religion's environment. It corresponds to a body of institutions and habitus totally foreign to those which characterize the Western town. The idea of a soft transition between the medina and the Western town must be abandoned. Its result is nothing more than a pale patina of modernity. The various development plans propose solutions to as yet non-existent problems in the area which stem directly from the experience of the industrialized Western city transplanted to a different setting. The proposed plans will become inoperable. The success of such plans requires some preconditions, such as the historical maturity of the ruling classes to engage in an appropriate modernization strategy, an adequate cultural environment, the rise of a workforce with the industrial and technical know-how, the self-effacement of the patriarchal family structures, a democratic political system with different levels of consensus, guaranteeing salarization, and a rational administrative state apparatus. Similar arguments can be mentioned about urban housing in the Arabo-Iranian area.[11] This may be put into four categories as outlined below:

- Traditional housing situated in the ancient cities, in the medina
- Colonial (or semi-colonial) period housing, that is, of nineteenth and early (first half) twentieth century construction, situated in the new European cities
- Post-war modern housing, planned on the Western economic growth model, situated in the suburbs
- More or less precarious housing, incorrectly called "spontaneous" housing, built without any license by people of limited means.

Shanty towns and slum areas are to be added to this list, these being the most precarious form of housing.

The respective importance of each of these urban sectors and the proportion of each type of housing mentioned are determined by differences in each regional situation being examined.

However, the new housing programs generally conform to the Western models, with similar performances, surfaces, materials, and equipment. The plan of dwellings composed by specialized cells is alien to the social norms and lifestyle of people who live in such housing, and the rent is too high for their purchasing power. In other words, housing is produced according to the practices and consumption norms of Western salaried employees and workers even before the corresponding economic situation has been achieved, and comes in anticipation of supposed productivity earnings, in anticipation of supposed wage earnings, on the coming mass consumption, and on the future economic growth. In the meantime, large parts of the state revenue are allocated to housing and this enormous investment greatly swells the external debts.[12]

On the other hand, the difficulties in modernization cannot be substituted by a mechanical return to the past. Too many things have changed, in internal as well as in external terms. The traditional context is irrevocably past and not recusitable, while the self-centered conditions of a new situation are not yet brought together. What still remains in this "in between"[13] context? On one side, atrophied or disused traditional elements—on the other side, parts of towns being shaped in urban sprawl. The prevailing image is of an interrupted development which becomes impossible to realize because the economic conditions for such a realization no longer exist. Everything remains suspended.

The accomplishment of schemes based on the standards and concepts of an advanced Western society, however attractive they seem to be, are in reality merely cultural and economic anticipation and are therefore out of reach. Inversely, the same can be said of reliance on traditional and appropriate local concepts and techniques. However ingenious and admirable they might appear to be, they have not been designed to meet contemporary needs of a remodeled urban context and of mass-housing.

THE TOOLS OF THIS POLITIC

The question is how to break out of the present deadlock, how to introduce different social and technical relations, and how to promote production processes better adapted to indigenous cultures and conditions. A resolved choice of such autonomous and self–centered economic development and of such protection of cultural identities marks the beginning of efforts to take in hand our own way of life.

Such projects can only be realized if the concerned societies find the strength and imagination necessary to carry out reforms which first of all have to be identified and set into motion. The pursuit of such an original way goes through the combination of three factors springing from inventivity, indigenous cultures and industrial civilization.

Inventivity, creativity and imagination start with the search for new processes and solutions or with the reformulation of old ones. The purpose is to set up an environment corresponding to the situation of transition ("in between") but also able to go beyond this—a propitious environment for change and progress.

Indigenous cultures do not have to be considered a last refuge, as a defensive item on which to fall back, nor as a final goal, but as a point of departure. Chosen aspects of cultural inheritance must be reconsidered and updated to new identified needs. But the development of the aptitude to invent is not an ex nihilo creation. It supports itself on the traditions of indigenous cultures and on the modernity of industrial civilization.

Modernity and industrial civilization must not be considered as the finality, but reexamined through their achievements which can be mastered and locally exploited.

The combination of these three items has to make itself known at three levels of production of the built environment: firstly, conceptualization; secondly, realization; and thirdly, socialization. Conceptualization is the phase involving the formulation of ideas, of the elaboration of the plans, projects and designs. These may be the tagleed (the imitation of ancestral city and housing patterns) or, on the contrary, the product of the intellectual work of contemporary urbanists, architects and engineers. Realization is the phase involving the construction of the designed cities and houses. This can be achieved by traditional craftsmen and guilds or, on the contrary, by modern local or international entrepreneurs. The socialization phase is the utilization of urban elements and built houses. This can be ruled by two different categories of inhabitants, living in patriarchal or conjugal family units, according to auto-consumption and domestic reproduction or to salarized way of life.

The concept, springs, manifestations, and effects of modernity on urban planning and architecture have been and remain the subject of reflections and scientific studies in the Western context; that is to say, in this very context where modernity has appeared and developed. But modernity has different effects in different contexts especially in the ones to which it has violently been transferred. Very often, the analytical proceeding has also been transferred and mechanically applied to a body of objects for which it had not been intended.

The results are truncated if the knowledge of the historical background—on which the modernity is grafted—is weak, or founded on alien schemes.

The differences existing between two urban forms, the medina or the oriental city and the Western town, make necessary the constitution of a corpus of theoretical and specific knowledge to be verified through practical experimentation and the insistance of a rational understanding of the past and of the benefits of the present civilization in designing our habitat.

NOTES

1. Cyrus Mechkat, "Teheran, de la ville islamique à la métropole contemporaine," *La ville arabe dans l'Islam.* Tunis-Paris: Centre d'etudes et de recherches économiques et sociales—Centre national de recherches scientifiques, 1982, pp. 475–537.

2. According to Pierre Bourdieu's definition.

3. Dominque Sourdel, *L'Islam medieval.* Paris: Presses Universitaires de France, 1979, p. 51.

4. Eugen Wirth, "Zum Problem des Bazars (suq, çarşi)," *Der Islam —Zeitschrift für Geschichte und Kultur des Islamischen Orients.* n. 52, 1, Berlin, February 1975, p. 246.

5. Mohamed Naciri, "La medina de Fes: trame urbaine en impasses et impasse," *Présent et avenir des medinas.* Tours: Equipe de

recherches associée au Centre national de recherches scientifiques, 1982, p. 242.

6. Anthony O. King, *Colonial Urban Development.* London, Henley, Boston: Routledge & Kegan Paul, 1976, pp. 146–155.

7. Jean Royer, "Henri Prost" urbaniste," *Urbanisme.* n. 88, 1965, pp. 11–16.

8. Brian Brace Taylor, "Planned Continuity—Modern Colonial Cities in Marocco," *Lotus International.* n. 26, 1980, pp. 53–66.

9. Michèle Jole, "L'hygiène public et l'espace urbain," *Bulletin économique et social du Maroc.* n. 147–148, non-dated, pp. 101–116.

10. Jallal Abdelkafi, "La medina de Tunis, l'espace historique face au processus d'urbanisation de la capitale," *Présent et avenir des medinas.* n. 5, pp. 201–218.

11. Cyrus Mechkat, "Production d'architecture, Concentration du capital et migration du travail dans le golfe Arabo-Persique," *The Production of the Built Environment.* Proceedings of the 1982 Bartlett International Summer School, University College, London, 1983, pp. 4.8–4.46, (text also available in English: "Production of Architecture, Concentration of Capital and Labor Migration in the Persian Gulf").

12. Cyrus Mechkat, "Periphérie et métropolisation: le cas des pays arabes et de l'Iran." Proceedings of the School of Architecture of the University of Geneva, March 1985.

13. Daryush Shayegan, *Qu'est-ce qu'une révolution religieuse?,* Paris: Les Presses d'Aujourd'hui, 1982, pp. 124–178: "Entre l'agonie des dieux et leur mort imminente ou la destinée historique des civilisations traditionnelles."

DISCUSSION

Saqqaf

What is the Islamic concept of a city? How different is this from the contemporary Western model? Can Islamic cities escape the Western onslaught and can they survive in today's world? All these are questions which trouble the minds of many of us, including the author of the paper on which I am commenting, Professor Ervin Galantay. In a well-thought-out paper, "Islamic Identity and the

Metropolis: Conflict and Continuity," Professor Galantay thinks aloud about a number of issues. I shall not address the same issues, but I shall follow up by comparing a few characteristics of the Islamic city with its modern counterpart.

The rise of Islam brought into sharp focus the Ummah's habitat —the city—by settling the nomadic Arabs. From the very beginning when the Prophet Muhammad started the Islamic community, he gave them a model. Old Yathrib was renamed as Al-Madinatul Munawwarah (the enlightened city). Many new cities were then created on the basis of the model; these include Baghdad, Cairo, Kufah, Samarra, Tunis, etc. In addition, there were ancient cities which, having fallen into decadence, found renewed vigor and prosperity with their entry into the "Paz Islamica" such as Balkh, Bukhara, Cordova, Damascus, Halab (Aleppo), Istanbul, Samarqand, Sana'a, Seville, etc. There is no doubt, therefore, that the Islamic civilization was an urban one, and that the urban structure expressed in concrete material terms the abstract and spiritual conviction which is embodied in the social, political, cultural, and economic system of the Islamic religion.

The present urban structure creates many socio-cultural complications to Muslim urban dwellers. The Islamic city requires social cohesion and compulsory cooperation among its inhabitants. Residents have an obligation, in concrete economic and social terms, towards their neighbors in a radius encompassing as a minimum, 40 houses. Therefore, neighborly cooperation, and full knowledge of the members of the neighborhood is necessary. This contrasts visibly with the alienation of today's city dwellers who do not know (and may not want to know) who lives next door. The togetherness of Islamic city inhabitants compares markedly with the loneliness of modern city people. Given that one's neighbors are determined by chance, one is neither really at home nor together.

Another aspect of the social cohesion required by the Islamic city is the collective responsibility of all inhabitants in the well-being of their city. This draws from the principle of "al-amr bil maroof wal nahyi anil munkar" which demanded every citizen to intercept any wrong deed, and to promote useful and beneficial activities. This attitude helped control the rates of crime, pollution, and other urban malaise. Today, however, the citizens have lost much of their collective responsibility, thus leading to an urban life characterized by fear, anxiety, and restlessness. Modern cities, especially in the West, are making a comeback to the Islamic concept of collective responsibility through such efforts as "citizens' arrests," voluntary organizations to control crimes, pollution, etc.

A third aspect of social life in cities has been the emphatic demand for a minimum of privacy. The Islamic city, through its layout and through design of houses, provides this privacy. Every family lives in a house surrounded by a compound which provides a transition zone between family privacy and the public space. Within the house, different rooms and corridors carry different levels of intimacy and privacy. In today's cities which are troubled by exploding populations, officials import mass-housing models and put hundreds of families into gigantic dormitory towns such as Nasser City in Cairo, Madinat Al-Thawra in Baghdad, the massive dormitory complex near Jeddah Airport, or al-Madinah Assakaniyyah Musaik in Sana'a. The uniform and banal structure and space have erased the threshhold of transition, thereby leading to a total confusion as to what is private and intimate space and what is public. This kind of "new" alienation that takes away one's privacy leads to strong tendencies to protect oneself. Thus, Muslim women who have never before worn the veil in their own villages take to wearing it in the city, in a forlorn attempt to shield themselves. But if the tall dormitories are not the answer, neither are the spacious pavilions. It is true that most Islamic dwellings were low-rise houses that resemble the pavilion in their structure, but these used to house more than just one family, given the extended family system. With the breakdown of the extended family system, more space and more houses are needed, and a different architectural design is needed.

The layout of Islamic cities was very distinct. The city was divided into quarters (hayy, singular; ahya', plural), which in turn were divided into sub-quarters or haraat. The focal point for a hara was the mosque around which everything else revolves. Connecting one hara to another were two things: a) the roads; and b) the suq which was the lifeline of the haraat. At the hayy level, in addition to the mosque there are public buildings representing the authorities. Depending on the importance of the hara, this could be a citadel, or the residence of a sheikh of sahib al-shurta, al-muhtasib, etc. At the city level, the dar al-imarah is the most important government building and in it lives the amir, or al-wali. Dar al-imarah also houses the treasury, and with it, of course, the army.

Islamic cities, therefore, had their own zoning system. Within the suqs, every profession and line of business had its own alley. The residential ahya' and haraat are separated from each other by the maidans (city squares). There were certainly large areas of open space in the pattern of Islamic urbanization, but the greenery that is envisaged in many of the modern Muslim cities, whether it be Teheran or Karachi, Riyadh, or Algiers, have become no more than dust collectors. In the Islamic pattern, the residents of the quarter were responsible for "their" gardens and open spaces; in today's structure, ineffective municipal authorities are supposed to take care of them.

Geographers and travelers have described Islamic cities as very clean. The linkage process which helped recycle products had created a very efficient system of sanitation. Human residue and solid garbage were used as fuel in the furnaces of the hammams (public baths). The ashes were then used as fertilizers in the city gardens, whereas the hammam water goes to the farms outside the city. Even within the house, precious resources such as water are recycled from one use to another in a hierarchy established by history. Today, the affluent Middle Eastern cities produce more garbage than anything else—heaps of plastics, papers, metal cans, bottles, abandoned cars, furniture, and all kinds of products. Per capita water use has tripled over the last 15 years, thereby threatening the exhaustion of the underground water supply, and also threatening the foundations of old quarters and houses.

Islamic architecture reflects a strong aesthetic value. This is manifested in the façades and gateways of buildings, street decorations, the colorful designs and writings, the different arches and geometric shapes, the extroverted gigantic public buildings (mosques, palaces, citadels, etc.), and the introverted residences and private buildings, the beautifully carved stones and pillars, the meandering streets and the covered alleys, etc. Today's cities, however, have lost much of that aesthetic value. Cost-conscious inhabitants build rush houses that are neither as durable nor as beautiful. The tendency has been that once a building is constructed, a few decorative additions at the surface level are supposed to give it an Islamic touch, and this is happening, for example, in many cities of the Arab Gulf. In part, Islamic cities draw some of their beauty and durability from the local building materials, such as burned bricks, hard stone, clay with straw, lime, and so on. The pattern of dwellings in today's cities is to use cement blocks with reinforced concrete beams, glass windows, metal doors, etc. These are not only less durable and less beautiful, but they also interrupt the ventilation and lighting systems, thereby requiring heating in the winter and cooling in the summer. The large glass windows, which could have provided a good lighting effect, are rendered useless by heavy curtains and drapes which are put there to limit pedestrians' ability to see inside the house.

There are many distinct features that characterize Islamic cities and urban settlement patterns, some of which continue to exist. Will these continue for long given the internationalization of Western values and culture? The present upsurge of Islamic values may help recreate the Islamic city.

Of course, the drive towards revival of the Islamic city should not neglect the necessities of modern life. The different modes of transportation, the consumption pattern, the production structure, the living conditions, etc., require a totally different pattern of urbanization. Preservation of the old Islamic city with the simultaneous growth of Western urban centers alongside will not work. The experience of North Africa and other regions indicates this. If societies pursue the dual effort of "preserving the old" while planning new cities alongside them, the affluent members of the old city tend to move out to the more convenient "new parts of the cities." The areas which they evacuate in the old towns are filled by an influx of poor elements in the community. Therefore, the biggest challenge is not preservation, but creating livelihood by generating income and work opportunities in the old towns.

The issue at hand, therefore, is to plan our cities by incorporating something of the old and the new, that is, making the old liveable and making the new meaningful.

Munro

What I have to say is more in the nature of an observation. I was interested to find that one of our speakers said that we must go back to the past for traditional models on which to develop our future cities, and another speaks of the past as gone forever. Oddly enough, I think both are right, and I think this is true, generally speaking, of the Middle East today. The modern Arab man is schizophrenic and the cities are schizophrenic, and I don't think there is a model for a modern Middle Eastern city. I think we're just going to live in a makeshift environment for the foreseeable future.

If you ask someone what kind of house he would like to live in he will say that he would like to live in a modern Western-style house. However, what is interesting, and we see this in Beirut at the moment with the breakdown of law and order, is that people move into these Western-style houses, but they very quickly establish their oriental ways inside those houses. So, on the one hand, you have a desire to engage in a Westernized consumerist activity, and, at the same time, you have the traditional way of life established inside the home. Therefore, we just have to live with schizophrenia for the foreseeable future.

Khayutman

I want to refer to the particular part about the future of the medina in the Arab city. I haven't visited many cities but of course there is Jerusalem, which I've seen. So I want to say that much of what

Professor Galantay has proposed should be done in the future there. It has already been done in Jerusalem with a combination of factors which may not be typical. These are topography, which puts around the medina from three quarters a physical separation which has simply become a garden, a park connecting the two parts of the city—Arab and Jewish. Then there is a very strong planning control, the Jerusalem committee, 60 of the world's most famous architects. Then comes a resurgence of economic activity inside the old city.

What is happening there is that much of this vision, (its being a center) is due to the new consciousness in the traditional society. There is resurgence of interest which is centered somehow in the old city, which hasn't been there before. If this is a precedent for what may happen in other cities, I want to emphasize the role of education in facing this issue.

Maybe future tourists will go to the old city, to the medina, and find enough reasons for pride in the tradition. The medina should be some kind of a living museum which, again, the old city of Jerusalem is managing to become, and people will make their own hejra. This has already happened in Jerusalem, and it may be an interesting example.

Schleifer

To reinforce the comment that was made by the first speaker about the relationship between social stability and unthinking modernization, I would have two comments to make. A professor of mine once engaged in a dialogue with an old colleague of his, was making a point which was challenged by this colleague. The point was that there were great dangers ahead for the region if modernization continued to push forward without any sensitivity at all to tradition, to culture, to the questions of authenticity. Now the man he was debating with said, "Well look, this is simply a lot of nonsense because the needs for development are so great that we must push ahead at whatever cost," I'm quoting exactly, "at whatever cost"! Now that gentleman who said that at the time was the director of planning of Iran.

Secondly, almost as a sort of parallel to that, I'd like to comment on the remark made by the second speaker that the past is unrecoverable. One of the proofs he gives to that is from his recent visit to the Islamic Republic of Iran where he noticed that the housing developed under the republic follows the same extroverted model. Well I don't think that in any way reflects on the issue. All that illustrates is that simply what we are defining as Islam is fundamentalism as observed in Iran or elsewhere.

The Islamic fundamentalist, in his own peculiar way, is often as indifferent to tradition as the secularizing modernist. It's just that he sort of tragically combines the virtue of piety with a lack of discernment. That is tragic because, in traditional piety, discernment is part of piety. What we have here is a case of reaction. Falling back on Islamic fundamentalism is not the tradition, but the reaction.

Ragette

The problems we are discussing here today have been discussed on many other occasions before, and I think you will agree that the Middle Eastern city has been disturbed by the adoption of Western ideas. It may have started with the car, new mobility, and then the demand for the private, independent, individual, detached house and all that. The West has faced and experienced all these problems through many generations, whereas they are experienced in the Middle East by a single generation. Combined with all the money available through the oil boom, the experience has reached explosive dimensions.

I am impressed with the similarity to the problems which are now being tackled in Europe. What we are lamenting here about the Middle East has also been felt very much in the West, especially in Europe with its old historic centers and its historic ways of life. We can learn a great deal from what happened in Europe. There and in the United States actions are taken which address problems similar to the ones faced in the Middle East, for instance, harnessing the car. This can only be done by promoting public transportation.

Khuri

We have been using the word "medina" frequently. Medina simply refers to the place where sanctions are made. Therefore, its definition relates to and symbolizes authority rather than anything else. This is why, for example, in the Quran, Egypt is called El Medina, and when the Prophet migrated from Mecca to Yathrib, Yathrib changed its name to El Medina, the place where the first Islamic community was established. So El Medina actually means the place where law and order prevails in peoples' activities. Thus, the term medina does not refer to the traditional Islamic core of our cities.

Saqqaf

Although Dr. Khuri's explanation is correct, I believe that the word "medina" now refers to the old core of cities when urban experts use it.

Part II

The Middle Eastern City

All cities of the Middle East are engulfed with problems associated with rapid urbanization, especially over the last three decades. Rapid urbanization is the result of persistent high birth rates coupled with a dramatic fall in the death rates; rural-to-urban migration; and the unprecedented spatial expansions of urban centers which swallow the surrounding villages.

It is evident that a spectacular phenomenon associated with those factors has been the level of mobility. Within the city itself, people drive/walk/ride from one part to another constantly. In addition, massive waves of people move from one country to another. Laborers from Yemen, Egypt, and Somalia travel to the oil-exporting countries in the Gulf and Libya; teachers from Syria, Egypt, Jordan, and the Sudan work in Yemen, Algeria, Saudia Arabia, the United Arab Emirates, etc.; and students from Kuwait, Bahrain, Yemen, etc., study in Egypt, Syria, and Iraq. Traders and businessmen from Lebanon, Tunisia, Morocco, etc., criss-cross to sell their products in the different market countries of the region. In a sense, this mobility has made the different Arab groups aware of one another and has broken the isolation among them. Of course, population mobility has been a major factor contributing to urbanization. Dr. Osman discusses the waves of inter-Arab migration.

The urbanization issue also involves major socio-cultural changes. Dr. Khuri discusses these values in the cities and compares them to values in the countryside. Since most urban dwellers are first-generation immigrants from the countryside, he finds that the cities have been ruralized because of the prevalence of rural values in them. But the urbanization evolution will re-structure the rural value systems and "rationalize" them to urban needs. Although this process has started, Dr. Khuri says it has a long way to go.

Chapter 3

Population Movement and Urbanization in the Arab World

Osman M. Osman

It has been permanently argued that in the Middle East the dominant threads of urbanization are geographic continuity and Islam.[1] This is especially true since the mid-1970s. It seems that the geographic factor is of a static and—perhaps—a passive character. Thus, the low level of urbanization in countries such as Libya, Saudi Arabia, and the two Yemens up to the late 1960s is explained by the influence of geography[2] which serves as a deterrent to urbanization. Surprisingly enough, this same geography embodied the wealth which has been destined to change the character of many states in the region.

The upsurge of oil revenues since 1973 quickly transformed these economies from traditional to modern. Even the landscapes of these desert states changed as expenditures rose in keeping with oil incomes.[3] Oil wealth has increased the capacity of the oil-endowed states to invest, and thereby enlarged their scale of development and their industrial ambitions.

This drive for faster economic change and expansion of services was reflected in a growing demand for labor. Because of the small size of the population and working force of the oil-rich countries, increasing demand for labor has been met by the international migration of workers from over-populated and less fortunate countries in the region.

The purpose of this paper is to examine the impact of the sudden growth of labor and population movements on changing levels and patterns of urbanization in the Arab Middle East.

The paper first discusses the magnitude and characteristics of recent population growth. Then it addresses the questions of urbanization: its level, tempo and components. A crude measure of migration's contribution to the growth of the urban sector has been calculated. The paper finally throws light on some prospects and problems of population movements and urbanization in the region.

SCALE AND PATTERN OF POPULATION MOVEMENTS

The phenomenon of population mobility within the Arab world is an old bedouin nomad tradition. However, labor migration for work has grown in the last decade to be of a regional importance. In 1975 more than 1.6 million migrant workers were employed outside their home countries.[4] Gross population that has been affected by the phenomenon is estimated at 3.1 million in the same year. By 1985 the figure for migrant workers is projected to rise to 3.4 million. Total migrant population is expected to reach a figure around 10 million.[5] This population movement has had a profound impact on the pace of development and social changes in the region. To examine some of the influence this phenomenon has had on the level and growth of urbanization, five main factors of relevance are discussed below.

Immigration of Large Proportions of Workers

The recent large population movement has been a function of economic forces, namely, huge investment projects in oil-endowed states. Until 1972 the pace of economic development of these countries remained moderate. In 1972, before oil prices increased, there were probably about 800,000 migrant laborers working in the various countries of the Middle East. This number doubled by 1975.[6] In 1980 the figure of Arab migrant workers alone was 2,283,000.[7] The scale of this phenomenon has exceeded all expectations. Birks and Sinclair had estimated the Arab migrant workers in 1980 at 1,754,000, a figure which exceeds the World Bank projections for 1985.[8] The actual figure may even be higher. The Arab migrant workers in the Middle East in 1983 was estimated in the Unified Arab Economic Report at four million.[9]

The large-scale Arab workers' movement is not the most expressive feature. Compared to the European 6.4 million migrant workers outside their home countries, the absolute number of migrants in the Middle East may be seen as moderate. However, the relative importance of migrants in the region is much greater. Migrant workers represented 17 percent of total employment in the oil-rich states in

1975. In some states the non-national share of the labor market is considerably higher. Kuwait, Libya, Oman, Qatar, Saudi Arabia and the UAE have work forces of which 44 percent are non-citizens.[10]

By 1985 the overall share of migrant workers in total employment in the labor-importing states is expected to exceed one-third. The smaller countries of the Arabian Gulf show an even greater dependence on expatriates: the non-citizens' share of the total work force in the UAE will be over 90 percent in 1985 and in Qatar 86 percent. In Kuwait the work force will retain 66 percent non-citizens[11] if the present trend persists.

Gross Numbers Moving

The settling of workers' dependents and their tendency to increase have a deep impact on urbanization and its future growth in both labor-importing and labor-exporting groups of countries. Population migration has been mainly concentrated in urban sectors of the labor-importing states. On the other hand, it highly mobilized the rural-to-urban flow within the labor-exporting countries. Simultaneously, this emmigration of workers and dependents may have reduced urban density in the large cities of their home countries. Moreover, there is ample evidence that labor movements affect fertility rates and the overall demographic structures.[12]

In 1975 there were 1.6 million migrant workers along with 1.5 million dependents. Some studies have projected that the total non-citizen communities in the major importing countries will increase from 3.1 million to 9.5 to 11 million, depending on the performed rates of economic growth.[13] Based on changes in crude activity rates, we have estimated the total number of non-citizen population in 1980 at 6.8 million (Refer to Table 3.1.)

Thus, the migrant population has increased its share in the total population of the major labor-importing countries from 24 percent in 1975 to 42 percent in 1980. Though the absolute number in 1980 is less than the projected level for 1985, its share became rather close to the projected level for that year. Moreover, this overall percentage share makes considerable difference among individual countries, which range from one-fifth of the Omani population to a majority of the population in the U.A.E., Qatar and Kuwait.

In contrast, the migrant population from Egypt, the major exporting country, accounted for only five percent of its total population. This percentage, however, is higher in the case of the two Yemens. (Refer to Table 3.2.)

TABLE 3.1
PERCENTAGE OF NON-CITIZEN POPULATION (IN THOUSANDS)

Country	1975			1980			1985		
	Total pop.	*Non-cit.*	%	*Total pop.*	*Non-cit.*	%	*Total pop.*	*Non-cit.*	%
Bahrain	267	58	22	400	142	36	758	284	49
Kuwait	1,027	555	54	1,400	836	60	1,817	1,154	64
Libya	2,680	501	19	3,000	1,287	43	5,404	2,186	41
Oman	686	136	20	900	187	21	1,283	272	21
Qatar	180	127	71	280	158	79	474	395	84
Saudi Arabia	5,990	1,398	23	9,000	3,211	36	13,711	4,594	36
U.A.E.	551	351	64	1,000	785	79	1,961	1,666	85
Total	11,381	3,126	27	15,900	6,605	42	25,275	10,911	43

Sources: 1975 and 1985 data from Surageldin, *op. cit.,* table 6.3. Projections for 1985 are based on the high economic growth scenario. For 1980 total population data is from U.B., *World Development Report 1981.* Non-citizen population is estimated using work force numbers from Ibrahim Saadeldin, *Movement of Arab Labor, op. cit.,* table 1.27, and adjusted rates of crude activity from Serageldin, *op. cit.,* table 6.1.

TABLE 3.2
PERCENTAGE OF OUT-MIGRATING POPULATION
IN TOTAL POPULATION OF LABOR EXPORTING
COUNTRIES IN 1980 (IN THOUSANDS)

Country	Total pop.	Migrant pop.	%
Misr (Egypt)	39,800	2,139	5.4
Yemen A.R.	7,000	981	14.0
Jordan & Palestine	3,900	1,075	33.6
Yemen PDR	1,900	267	14.1
Syria	9,000	361	4.0
Lebanon	2,700	206	7.6
Sudan	18,700	264	1.4
TOTAL	82,300	5,293	6.4

Sources: *World Development Report,* 1981.
Highest population: as in Table 3.1.

Concentration of Migrant Workers in Modern Sectors

Labor migration in the Middle East has intensified urbanization. A wide body of evidence suggests that the rapid growth of the oil exporting countries has stimulated mobility between economic sectors. Basically, transfer of workers implied a shift of workers from agriculture to modern sectors. According to the World Bank study, the largest proportion of non-citizen workers in 1975 were employed in construction (35 percent of the total stock of migrants). The next largest proportion was in services, which absorbed 29 percent of non-citizen workers. Trade and finance employed 14 percent. All in all, the non-agriculture (urban) activities have absorbed almost 94 percent of migrant workers.[14] (Refer to Table 3.3.)

TABLE 3.3
MIGRANT WORKERS BY ECONOMIC SECTOR IN LABOR-EXPORTING COUNTRIES

Sector	1975		1985	
	Number (in thousands)	%	Number (in thousands)	%
Agriculture	94.8	5.9	514.6	14.5
Mining & Quarrying	24.2	1.5	55.5	1.6
Manufacturing	97.8	6.1	223.2	8.3
Utilities	24.6	1.5	62.8	1.8
Construction	563.9	35.3	881.2	24.8
Trade & Finance	221.6	13.8	436.4	12.3
Transport & Comm.	116.8	7.3	261.4	7.4
Services	457.1	28.6	1,113.3	31.3
TOTAL	1,600.8	100.0	3,548.4	100.0

Source: Serageldin, *op. cit.,* table 4.4.

It is true that in many of the Gulf desert- or city-states agriculture and pastoral employment was never great. However, the urgency attached to "modernity" and development of industry has largely absorbed the traditional sector or decimated it. Many studies have predicted increasing dependency on foreign labor in all sectors with the exception of construction. Even in agriculture where the presence of non-nationals was very low in 1975 migrants may account for 39%

of total manpower requirements in 1985.[15] Nevertheless, actual data indicates that the share of construction sector in employment continues to grow.[16]

Replacement Labor and Rural-Urban Migration

The impact of labor migration on the process of urbanization is not limited to the major labor-importing states. In fact the system of migration becomes more complex, since it is no longer a one-track movement from one group of countries to another. The expanding replacement migration has a considerable multi-dimensional impact on rural-urban relations in both sending and receiving countries. (A replacement migrant is an immigrant who comes into the country to fill a vacancy created by the departure of a national for employment abroad. See Birks and Sinclair, *op. cit.,* p. 87.)

This impact depends crucially on government policies. In some cases, while international labor migration has been a main cause of accelerated rural-urban movement of workers, replacement migration contributes towards reducing labor shortfalls. In Jordan, for example, the net result of upward occupational mobility in response to out-migration of workers is the shortage of rural and unskilled labor. This cannot be met by domestic supplies of manpower, and it is at this skill level that most replacement immigration takes place. In 1980, there were 75,000 replacements.[17] This process is illustrated schematically in Figure 3.1.

Similarly, peripheral areas in Saudi Arabia are starved of workers because of rural-urban drift and the periodic migration of menfolk from the villages. Yemeni and some Omani replacement migrants work in rural areas.[18] If this is perceived as a positive factor in its effect on urbanization, replacement migration has a deleterious impact on the rural sector and indirectly on urban centers, too.

Distortions in agricultural labor and products' markets induce more rural-to-urban migration, but because in many of the labor-sending countries the modern sector is small, it fails to create large numbers of new jobs. Replacement migration makes things even worse. Due to labor market inflexibility, replacement migration of labor came to Egypt, a country with over one million unemployed.

Semi-skilled and even unskilled expatriate labor from the Far East is being used in certain construction work. In Yemen, because Asians are employed in urban centers and in the modern sectors of the economy, their continued presence limits the participation of nations in those parts of the economy. Some authors believe that expatriate laborers fill jobs which Yemenis are capable of undertaking themselves, and even if employing Asians makes good economic sense

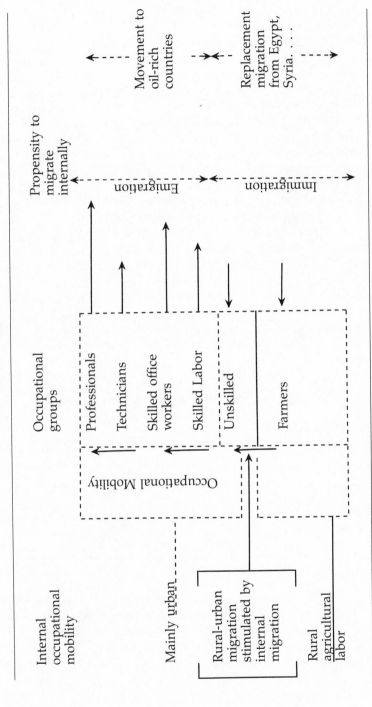

FIGURE 3.1
DIAGRAMMATIC REPRESENTATION OF REGIONAL AND INTERNAL
LABOR MOBILITY

Source: Based on a diagram designed by Birks and Sinclair, *op cit.*, p 93

from the employers' point of view, it does not assist in the development of the YAR in the long run.[19]

Increasing Migration from Outside the Region

The early waves of migration into the oil rich countries were almost wholly from the region. This was due to linguistic and religious unity, geographic proximity, cultural similarity and ethnic affinity. Today, there is a rising proportion of labor from outside the region.

With the growth of non-citizen communities in labor-importing countries, attitudes towards labor composition have changed. These communities affect their host countries in several ways.[20] First, they pose the threat of outnumbering their hosts. Second, they present the country of employment with a growing responsibility to provide infrastructure, utilities, education and health services. Third, these communities' requirements are increasing with rise in numbers of those acquiring citizenship. (The number of migrant workers who acquired Kuwaiti citizenship in 1970-75 amounted to more than 50,000. This represents 40 percent of net migration into Kuwait. See Fargues, *op. cit.,* p. 77.)

These factors, together with the nature of the recent economic development slow-down in oil-rich countries, explain the shift in priorities in ethnic composition of migrant workers. In 1975 some 65 percent of them were Arab, with 35 percent non-Arab. (Refer to Table 3.4.)

TABLE 3.4
MIGRANT WORKERS BY NATIONALITY

Nationality	1975		1985	
	Number (in thousands)	*%*	*Number (in thousands)*	*%*
Non-citizen Arabs	1,041	65	1,843	52
Indians & Pakistans	348	22	902	25
East Asians	21	1	371	11
Other	192	12	433	12
TOTAL	1,601	100	3,548	100

Most of the best studies on the subject have predicted that the regional pattern of employment is clearly swinging away from the use of Arab labor. These predictions depended on the decline of the Arab share from 70 percent in 1975 to 63 percent in 1980. Consequently, the percentage share of non-Arab workers increased from 26 percent in

1975 to 34 percent in 1980 (to almost one million workers).[21]

The increased participation of workers from outside the region has been associated with the location policy of new industries in the oil-rich countries, thus bringing different modes to the urbanization. Planners have chosen to separate physically new industrial areas from existing urban areas. In order to limit the cost of providing infrastructure and social services at these industrial sites they are operated on a work camp basis.[22] The work force on large projects stay within the limits of the site area. They are kept in isolation from the local population and from the immigrant communities in the urban centers already established in these capital-rich states.[23]

URBANIZATION: NEW TRENDS AND A DIFFERENT PATTERN

I have presented some of the factors which influence labor and population movements and their impact on the process of urbanization in the Middle East. On the basis of this, it is now possible to examine the level of urbanization, its growth rates, and the components of this growth.

Level of Urbanization

The level of urbanization of a country is measured by the percentage of population living in urban areas. The definition of the urban population of a country is to some degree arbitrary, and definitions change from country to country. In general however, an urban center is one which has at least 25,000 inhabitants, according to United Nations classification.

There are several reasons for paying attention to the level of urbanization. First, at low levels of urbanization, economic policies should be dominated by a concern for the rural sector. Second, there is a close association between the level of urbanization and the level of economic growth as measured by the per capita GNP. Figure 3.2 demonstrates this correlation.

As it was shown earlier, oil-rich countries could, and will, sustain fast growth rates in GNP by mainly industrializing their economics. This effort has been facilitated by overall population growth. Third, at low levels of urbanization, migration becomes the main source of growth of the urban sector; at high levels, the main source of total urban growth is the natural increase of the resident population.

Table 3.5 presents the basic urbanization indicators in the Middle East for 1980 and 1982. The divergence among the countries of the region is extremely pronounced. In 1960 the level of urbanization was very low in North Yemen, Oman and Sudan. With the exception of Kuwait, no country reached the 50 percent mark. In 1982 all countries of the region had higher levels of urbanization than before, but country differentiation persisted. At one end of the spectrum are Kuwait, the U.A.E. and Saudi Arabia (Lebanon too had a high level, 77 percent). At the other end of the spectrum are the same group of countries with low levels of urbanization.

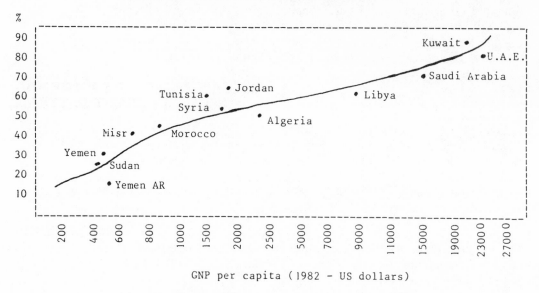

Figure 3.2 *Degree of urbanization compared with per capita*

In the middle is a group of countries which are close to the 50 percent mark of urbanization, with intermediate levels of income. With their emphasis on infrastructure and the emergence of a large-scale public sector, major urban functions have tended to gravitate toward a few metropolitan regions. While many of these countries attempt to face urban housing shortages, overcrowding and the lack of public services by control of rural-urban migration, rich countries with high levels of urbanization tend to be more worried about non-citizen migration.

Tempo of Urbanization

The speed at which a country is urbanizing reflects the pressures on the urban sector and conditions in the policy environment. The United States calculates the tempo of urbanization for each country as

TABLE 3.5
URBAN INDICATORS IN THE MIDDLE EAST

Country	Urban population				Urban pop. % in largest cities		Number of cities over 500,000 pop.	
	% total pop.		average growth					
	1960	1982	1960–70	1970–82	1960	1980	1960	1980
Algeria	30	45	3.5	5.4	27	12	1	1
Tunisia	36	54	3.8	4.0	40	30	1	1
Morocco	29	42	4.2	4.1	16	26	1	4
Sudan	10	28	6.8	5.8	20	31	–	1
Misr (Egypt)	38	45	3.5	2.9	28	39	2	2
Yemen AR	3	14	10.2	8.3	—	25	–	–
Yemen PD	28	28	3.5	2.7	61	49	–	–
Jordan	43	60	4.7	4.0	31	37	–	–
Syria	37	49	4.8	4.6	35	33	1	2
Lebanon	40	77	6.9	2.8	64	79	1	1
Iraq	43	70	5.8	5.3	33	55	1	3
Oman	4	20	6.3	15.6	—	—	–	–
Libya	23	58	8.4	8.0	57	64	–	1
Saudi Arabia	30	69	8.4	7.6	15	18	–	2
Kuwait	72	91	10.1	7.4	75	30	–	–
U.A.E.	40	79	14.9	14.4	—	—	–	–

Source: *World Development Reports,* different issues.

the difference between the rate of growth of the urban population and that of its rural population.[24] In fact, the observed differences between the rate of urban and rural population growths is a good indicator of the speed at which urbanization is taking place.

There are different ways a country can have a high value of the urban-rural growth differential.[25]

a) A country at a low level of urbanization can have a high rate of urban growth because the absolute base is very small.

b) A country may have a high rate of urban growth because of "international" migration combined with a declining rural population.

c) A country may have a high total population growth rate and a high rate of farm-out-migration with its rural population still growing.

Available data provides no indication that any of the countries in the region has been so far experiencing an absolute decline in its

TABLE 3.6
RURAL AND URBAN POPULATION GROWTH (1950–2000)

Group of countries	% Urban pop.			Average growth rates			
	1950	1980	2000	1950–80		1980–2000	
				R	U	R	U
All developing countries	18.9	28.7	—	3.4	1.7	—	—
without China	22.2	35.4	43.3	3.8	1.7	3.5	1.1
Low-income countries:							
Asia	10.7	19.5	31.3	4.4	2	4.2	0.9
China	11.2	13.2	—	2.5	1.8	—	—
India	16.8	23.3	35.5	3.2	1.8	4.2	1.1
Africa	5.7	19.2	34.9	7.0	2.5	5.8	1.5
Middle-income countries:							
East Asia	19.6	31.9	41.9	4.1	1.8	3.1	0.9
M.E. & N. Africa	27.7	46.8	59.9	4.4	1.6	4.3	1.6
Africa (sub-Sahara)	33.7	49.4	55.2	3.1	1.0	2.9	1.7
Latin America	41.4	65.3	75.4	4.1	0.9	2.9	0.4
South Europe	24.7	47.1	62.3	3.8	0.5	2.9	−0.2
Industrial countries	61.3	77.0	83.7	1.8	−0.7	1.0	−1.1

Source: *World Development Report,* 1984, Table 4.3.

"rural" population. Table 3.5 presents the average growth rates of urban population for the 1960s and 1970-82. It is interesting to note that, with the exception of the Maghreb countries and Oman, growth rates of urbanization for all countries were higher in the first period than in the latter. As it is expected, oil-rich, labor importing countries had higher rates of urbanization than other countries in the region.

Generally, urbanization in most of the Middle East countries has been growing at higher rates than that of the advanced industrial countries. For one thing, the Middle East started from a low level of urbanization (Table 3.6). On the other hand, countries with the highest rates of urbanization growth had the largest shares in non-national migrant population.

The rural-urban growth differential for 1950-70 is presented in Table 3.7.

Components of Urban Growth

The relative importance of the two major components of urban growth—natural increase of the urban population and migration—is of major significance to urbanization policy. To be accurate, an analysis of the components of urban growth requires the use of separate information on fertility and mortality in cities, on the age structure of the population, and on urban annexation.

According to the World Bank's comprehensive report on "World Development—1984," the impact of internal and international migration on the rate of urbanization has been generally limited worldwide. From a United Nations sample of 29 developing countries, it is estimated that 60 percent of the urbanization growth is explained by the natural increase of population. Another 8 to 15 percent is due to redefinition of urban population and annexation.[26] The report shows that neither permanent nor temporary migration provides a real addition to the urban population.

TABLE 3.7
URBAN-RURAL GROWTH DIFFERENTIAL

(1950–1970)

COUNTRY	DIFFERENTIAL	COUNTRY	DIFFERENTIAL
Kuwait	7.53	Mexico	3.29
Yemen AR	6.92	Yemen PD	2.89
Lebanon	5.85	Egypt (Misr)	2.66
Algeria	5.35	Libya	2.58
Saudi Arabia	4.43	Sudan	2.55
Iraq	4.18	Tunisia	2.50
Jordan	3.45	Syria	1.72

Source: B. Renaud, National Urbanization Policy, *op. cit.,* App. D Table D.1.

As we have already seen, the case of population movements in the Middle East provides a different pattern from the world-wide experience. Although it is difficult to separate the impact of rural-urban migration on urbanization from the similar impact of international migration, we find such a distinction unnecessary for the purpose of this paper.

Reference has been made to the influence of labor migration for work in oil-rich countries and to rural-urban migration in both labor sending and labor-receiving countries. Suffice it to estimate the percentage of net migration in the growth of the urban sector. This has been obtained by taking the difference between the urban growth rate and the total population growth rate and dividing it by the urban growth rate. Orders of magnitude for the percentage of urban growth from net migration are presented in Table 3.8.

Contrary to the World Bank conclusion, the results show that the

TABLE 3.8
PERCENTAGE SHARE OF NET MIGRATION IN URBAN GROWTH

COUNTRY	URBAN GROWTH	POP. GROWTH	MIGRATION SHARE	
	1970–82	1970–82	1970–75	1970–82
Yemen AR	8.3	3.0	76.3	63.9
Saudi Arabia	7.6	4.8	61.9	36.8
Sudan	5.8	3.2	61.8	44.7
Morocco	4.1	2.6	52.9	36.6
Yemen PD	2.7	2.2	50.0	18.5
Tunisia	4.0	2.3	45.2	42.5
Lebanon	2.8	0.5	44.4	82.1
Algeria	5.4	3.1	43.9	42.6
Misr (Egypt)	2.9	2.5	43.6	13.8
Jordan	4.0	2.5	34.7	37.5
Iraq	5.3	3.5	34.0	34.0
Kuwait	7.4	6.3	24.4	14.9
Syria	4.6	3.5	21.4	23.9
Libya	8.0	4.1	16.0	48.8
Oman	15.6	4.3	—	72.4
U.A.E.	14.4	15.5	—	−7.6

Source: Based on data from "the World Development-1984."
Percentage share of migration in urban growth =

$$\frac{\text{urban growth rate} - \text{total population growth rate}}{\text{urban growth rate}} \times 100$$

contribution of migration to urban growth is generally significant. It is particularly high at low levels of urbanization as well as at very high levels, but for different reasons. Population migration has operated in two ways.

First, some countries have experienced higher rates of urbanization because of international migration. They are small and among the fastest urbanizing countries: Kuwait, and Saudi Arabia. Second, a few countries have benefited from international migration that has shown the growth of their rural population.

The share of migration in urban growth ranges from 60–70% for Yemen and Saudi Arabia, and -7 percent for the U.A.E. The rank of individual countries according to the percentage share of migration in urbanization growth has differed dramatically from 1970–75 to the latest period. In the period of 1970–75 migration explained more than 40 percent of urban growth in most of the countries. The reason is the high growth rates of urbanism during the period. For a longer period

(1970–82) the higher shares of net migration in the urban growth of Yemen and Lebanon are a result of relatively high rates of growth of urban population as compared to modest total population growth. Oman is the opposite case.

CONCLUSION

The level of urbanization in the Middle East was still below the 50 percent mark in 1980. It is, however, higher than the level of urbanization in many parts of the developing world. Urbanization in the Middle East has been growing at relatively high rates over the last two decades. Divergence among the countries of the region is considerable. Saudi Arabia, Lebanon, Iraq, U.A.E. and Kuwait are the highly urban states. The two Yemens, Sudan and Oman are the least.

One major reason behind such growth of urban population is the increasing mobility of population seeking work in oil-endowed countries, or replacing migrants in urban centers. Although labor requirements of oil-rich countries are expected to continue to rise over the remaining years of the century, the impact of population movement on urbanization seems to relax. Urban areas will no longer play an increasing role in absorbing large shares of the population. For one thing, some of the oil-rich states are becoming highly urban. Other countries became very sensitive to non-national communities, and they discourage permanent stays (or acquiring nationality) of non-citizen workers. In most of the Middle East countries the major concern of the policy should be directed towards solving problems of urban centers—and rural development—than speeding urbanism.

NOTES

1. J. Abu-Lughod, "Problems and Policy Implications of Middle Eastern Urbanization," *Studies on Development Problems in Selected Countries in the Middle East.* New York, 1973.

2. Bernand Renaud, *National Urbanization Policy in Developing Countries.* Renaud, New York: Oxford University Press, 1981, p.48.

3. I. Serageldin, *Manpower and International Labor Migration in the MENA.* by Serageldin New York: Oxford University Press, 1983, p.26.

4. Ibid. p.29.

5. Ibid. p.60.

6. J.S. Birks and J. Sinclair, "International Migration and Development in the Arab Region." ILO, Geneva, 1980, p.26.

7. I. Saadeldin and M. Abdel-Fadil, *Movements of Arab Labor.* (in Arabic), CAUS, Beirut, 1983, p.70.

8. Saadeldin and Abdel-Fadil, *op cit.,* p.18.

9. *Asharq Al-Awsat,* Dec. 23, 1984.

10. Serageldin, *op. cit.*

11. *Ibid.*

12. Fargues, *Manpower Reserves and Oil Revenues.* (in Arabic) CCES, Beirut.

13. Serageldin, *op. cit.,* pp.58–59.

14. *Ibid.* p.28.

15. *Ibid.* p.30.

16. Saadeldin and Abdel-Fadil, *op. cit.,* p.66.

17. Serageldin, *op. cit.,* p.83.

18. Birks and Sinclair, *op. cit.,* p.89.

19. Serageldin, *op. cit.,* p.84.

20. *Ibid.*

21. Saadeldin and Abdel-Fadil, *op. cit.,* p.62.

22. Birks and Sinclair, *op. cit.,* pp.110–111.

23. Serageldin, *op. cit.,* p.50.

24. Renaud, *op. cit.*

25. *Ibid.,* and Johannes F. Linn, *Cities in the Developing World.* New York: Oxford University Press, 1983.

26. World Bank: "World Development Report," 1984, p.88.

Chapter 4

Ideological Constants and Urban Living

Fuad I. Khuri

In his article "Village and City: Cultural Continuities in Twentieth Century Middle Eastern Cultures," John Gulick makes the point that "many details of life are essentially the same for villagers and urbanites," and that "although there are some very striking differences between them, the village and city subcultures have many traits in common" (Gulick 1969:122). Among those traits he discusses "patrilineal segmentary kinship structure," "factionalism," "sexual alienation," "household size and domestic family structure," and "personalized environments" (Gulick 1969:124–140). The problem with Gulick's paper is not the idea but the argument, in the sense that many of the above-mentioned traits he discusses are not essentially peculiar to Middle Eastern cultures; they are common to many other cultures as well, in Africa, Asia, and Latin America. Segmentary kinship structures, factionalism, sexual alienation, and/or personalized environments are cultural traits spread in varying degrees in different societies in the world. However, aside from these ethnographic details with which one may not agree, Gulick's idea that village and city are alike at one point or another, never caught interest, not because it lacks evidence, but because it stands in contraposition to many socially and mentally accepted stereotypes that take the distinction between village and city for granted.

Not only do these standardized stereotypes draw sharp distinctions between village and city, but they hold the city ways to be of a higher moral order than village ways. Even a careful scholar, like Janet Abu-Lughod, could be trapped by such stereotyped distinctions. For example, her description of the "modern-urban" style of life in Cairo as opposed to the "rural" (1971:185–86) corresponds to distinctions between the rich and the poor, regardless of whether they are rural or urban in origin. "A fairly adequate income, European styled furniture, high enrollment of children in schools, low ratio of person-to-room in dwelling units," all of which she attributes to the "modern-urban" type, are clearly indexes of middle- or upper-class characteristics. By contrast, "minimal furnishings, a few mattresses and quilts, some cooking pots, several glasses for tea, perhaps a trunk or two, one or two rooms accommodating a family of 10 or more, marginal subsistence, unfashionable clothes," all of which she considers to be rural in origin (Abu-Lughod 1971:186), are indexes of lower-class characteristics. Thus, when villagers migrate and settle in the city, they "ruralize" the city, a term used to indicate a series of unfavorable behaviors often attributed to slums in Western cities: crowded streets, lack of spatial specialization, high-density population, low standard of living, non-Western costumes, staple food consumption patterns, clustering of family or village groups in individual neighborhoods. To "ruralize" the city is to make it slummy. By the same token, a Lebanese expresses dissatisfaction with another by saying: "you are a villageman," indicating the display of rough and unrefined manners. The reverse is also true; when villagers catch up with city standards of living, they are "urbanized."

Concerning the distinction between city and village, it must also be noted, furthermore, that the native category of *badu,* and *ḥadar* lumps villages and cities together as *ḥadar,* whereas Ibn-Khaldun's model of *'aṣabiyya* and *mulk* take into account tribal-nomadic organization and urban structures and ignores altogether "villages" which constituted no less than 70% to 80% of the total Middle Eastern population in Ibn-Khaldun's days. Neither the native category of *badu* and *ḥadar,* which is essentially based on ecological conditions, nor the analytic model of Ibn-Khaldun's *aṣabiyya* and *mulk,* which is based on power-authority differentiations, captures the value orientations that bring both village and city together as manifestations of a single ideological formulation. Even the cultural traits which Gulick holds to be common to village and city structures are nothing but simple manifestations of this ideological formulation, namely, the syndrome of endogamy that characterizes the processes of group formation in Arab culture; this is so irrespective of whether the setting is urban or rural. Before discussing the details of this "syndrome of endogamous formulations," otherwise called "ideological constants" in this paper, and showing how they relate to urban living, I would like, first, to present some ethnographic observations on the city of Beirut before and during the Lebanese war.

In my work on Beirut just before the war (Khuri, 1975), I was so misguided by the literature on urban social ecology as to believe that cities have inner parts ringed by stratified residential belts (the workingmen's houses, the homes of the middle classes, and the commuter's zone) and surrounded by suburbs, and that all of these zones, rings and belts make up the totality of the city. This is what is referred to in the literature as "the Chicago School" following Wirth, Park, McKenzie and Burgess who worked in and on Chicago. Burgess, for example, divided Chicago into five "concentric circles" (Burgess 1938:218) encompassing the whole city limits. My data on the suburbs of Beirut then did not quite conform to this model of analysis as evidenced by the generality and independence of the socio-economic organization of individual suburbs. Unlike Western suburbia, suburbs in Beirut lack specialization and tend to develop multifunctional services in the sense that jobs, services, recreational centers, schools, clubs, welfare societies, places of worship, cultural activities, banks, hospitals, you name it are all centered in individual suburbs. So much is the case that within a radius of about 200 yards one may get all the necessary services he needs daily. Because of this generality and independence, about 91 percent of the labor force in my work were found residing within the suburb's limits; the rest (9%) commute to different parts of the neighboring areas for work (1975:214). What is called city-center, al-Burj in Beirut, does not serve, strictly speaking, the urban communities in the city. The city-center is simply an extension of the port and it operates as a terminus for traffic coming from the countryside. Were it not for the heavily centralized bureaucracy in the country which led to the concentration of all kinds of services and facilities in the capital (Beirut), the Burj area would have been far less active than it actually was. In other words, the city-center is a *suq* (market place) that serves the whole nation and not simply an organic part of the city structure *par excellence;* it happened to be in Beirut, close to the port. As a matter of fact, many cities in the Middle East like Fez, Aleppo, Sana'a, Damascus, etc., used to, and many still, have weekly *suqs* located outside the city limits; literally speaking, they have no "downtowns."

The image of Beirut as a single organism, where parts constitute an integrated whole, does not reflect socio-economic realities. It is better seen as series of individual "tents" bounded together in a constellation—like form rather than a single, monolithic unit. This same image or model is observed in Abu-Lughod's work on Cairo where she refers to the "tents" as "sub-cities" that emerged at different times in the history of Cairo. With some alterations here and there, the same thing can be said about other cities as well. For example, the city of Al-Ain in Abu-Dhabi today is inhabited by various tribal factions, each clustering in a specific section of town; so was Basra at the onset of the Arab-Muslim conquest.

Perhaps nowhere did this image of the city, as made up of series of "tents" or semi-independent urban nuclei, come up as vividly as it did during the Lebanese war. Conflict situations, at times, illustrate the pattern or norm better than non-conflict conditions. In a survey carried out in 1980 with the help of many graduate students at the SBS department of the American University of Beirut, I counted 42 para-political, para-military "associations," local militias, that spread in different sections of the city of Beirut. Built upon a series of social solidarities, these associations had divided the city, perhaps consciously and more likely unconsciously, into mutually exclusive spheres or zones of influence, or what they call "operation grounds"; the presence of one excludes the others. It may happen that the same street is divided in half, each under the control of a given "association." This is precisely where straight streets laid down according to a geometric design may be an embarassment, difficult to divide socially and then politically and militarily. The twisted streets of Beirut, like other Middle Eastern cities, are a mirror of social agglomerations interwoven by kinship and traditional ties of neighborliness. In a micro-research I carried out on a small neighborhood in Ras Beirut, it was found that buildings are erected on plots subdivided according to inheritance patterns. It is the social assemblage that matters more than the physical design; the urban society is fitted into a social map, not a spatial one. This may explain the virtual absence of public gardens and the disrespect for anything "public." Whenever I mention the word public ('umūmi) two things come to my mind: shared taxi which is called in Arabic "'umūmi car," and a brothel, which is called "'umūmi sūq."

True, these para-political, para-military associations are grafted onto wider political organizations—in 1980 many of them adopted PLO slogans—but this sort of grafting did not eliminate the measure of independence they exercised in dealing with local affairs within individual neighborhoods. Indeed, in 1978 when the PLO tried to incorporate these local "militias" into its military body, it was met with stiff resistance and consequently the attempt was withdrawn. It looks as if these local micro-militias rush to adopt macro-political ideologies just to safeguard their local autonomy and enclose upon themselves as unpenetratable solidarities. Through this process of enclosure they ward off the possibility of being assimilated into impersonalized national structures. I fear it is precisely this double process of "grafting" and "enclosure" that works against the rise of free and open political party systems as well as free and open urban neighborhoods and, therefore, macro "horizontal" structures of any kind. As soon as these free and open macro-movements begin to develop, built-in endogamous solidarities creep in, encapsulate the inner moral authority of the movement, and redirect its orientation inwardly again in order to reinforce the very endogamous character of the solidarity itself. Consider, for example, how Wahhabism reinforced the endogamous character of Al-Saud and how the Ba'th party reinforced the endogamous character of a religious community in Syria and a "village" community in Iraq.

The theme is that city social ecology, like many other macro structures such as political parties, national liberation mass movements or religious movements, is built around a series of endogamous solidarities that graft themselves onto the general body without being assimilated into it. This is why it looks at times that what matters in a conflict situation is not the resolution of the conflict as much as the attainment of the group's social solidarity. If so, then why? I maintain that this theme can be explained by the ideological insistence on endogamy as a desired way of life, a model of social mobility in Arab culture. I use the word "endogamy" here in a generalized sense to refer to a wide variety of actions, behaviors, beliefs, customs and practices which include, among other things, marriage, visitations, class distinctions, group formation, ethnicity, or what have you. It is indeed a syndrome of preferences. By understanding the endogamous character of Arab culture, it is then possible to appreciate the different aspects of its political and organizational characteristics including the organization of urban life.

It is important to realize, at the onset, that there are no secondary associations, "lodges" or "rites of passage" in Arab culture that interfere in the process of socialization other than the family, nuclear or extended. Given the practice of first-cousin marriage, it is possible for two married brothers or sisters, or brother and sister, to constitute a total society. Within this small kinship unit a person is able to fulfill all the necessary cultural requirements of life focusing on birth, puberty, or death.

Life is a process that continues uninterrupted by the stages of biological growth; the category of *al-shabāb* (youth) lumps together anybody between six and sixty. Just as this lumping explains why many militia organizations train children between six and ten, it also explains the absence of public playgrounds for children, or, for that matter, why we tend to be more intelligent than innovative. The fitting of children into adult models restricts fancy and curbs inventiveness.

Believers see life continuing after death, and religion (ad-dīn) organizing man's life here and in the hereafter. Religion in Islam does not oppose the "world" (al-dunya); the world opposes the other world *(al-'akhirah),* and religion organizes both. In this continuing and uninterrupted process, a person is seen as a link in a chain *(silsilah),* and the chain as a single solidarity. It is interesting to note that the concept of solidarity and internal cohesion is often symbolically expressed in words signifying seriation of individuals: *silsilah* (chain), *tasalsul* (descent), *sulalah* (genealogy), *habl* (rope or cable, as revealed in the Qur'an, sura 3, no. 103: "And hold fast, all of you together, to the cable of Allah, and do not separate"), *nasab* (patrilineality, also means alliance *"tahaluf), hasab* (mother's patrilineality, also means high social reputation), *takatuf* (shoulder to shoulder), or *tacadud* (pillar to pillar). No wonder why beads have a wide popular appeal in Arab culture; we call them "praise" *(sabbaha)* beads, not "worry" beads, as is oftenly falsely translated into English. In other words, we praise through beads; we do not worry.

Obviously, the person, as "link", is believed to be bound to a group, as "chain," formulated on the basis of genealogy, descent, or lineality; he is therefore distinguished by the solidarity thus formulated. People of high status are known as *'usul* or *'ansab,* which means a kinship category that has long and traceable genealogy. Indeed *'asīl* horses are those whose parents are known, and the *ta'sīl* means in-breeding. Arabs in-breed *(yu'assil)* horses, camels, hawks (for hunting), and dogs, and all of these are prestige investments often possessed by people of high status and social notability.

Because of these ideological formulations, endogamy and social enclosure become desirable models of action and behavior. Endogamous behavior is an instrument to attain "enclosure" and, therefore, internal solidarity. The ethnographic record on Arab society strongly supports this conclusion as evidenced by the high ratio of intermarriage among the *'usūl;* the one-way visitation traffic between notables and commoners where the latter visit the former but are not visited by them; the tendency for high-status families to cluster in space; the expression of high status by long genealogical records—i.e., as soon as a person achieves notability through wealth, power, or professional practice, he adopts, along with it, a long genealogy of origin. In brief, as people move up the social ladder, they turn inwardly rather than outwardly, thus becoming *khassa* (the private) rather than *camma* (commoners). While social celebrities in the West focus on the "private" life of the elites, such as marriages, divorces, travels, hobbies, etc., celebrities in the Middle East focus on the elites' formal and public engagements: visits, projects, meetings, meals.

This is perhaps the reason why we tend to have many Thatcher-like and Healey-like elites, but very few Dianes or Charleses. In Arabia, when a commoner meets a notable he salutes with "peace," the notable responds by asking about wives, homes, children, jobs, work, earnings; these are private matters the notable never divulges in public. The notables are the *khassa,* the private enclosed solidarity.

Many other customs, concepts, and practices in Arab culture including honor and shame, face *(wajh),* revenge and vengeance, kinship systems and organizations can be dealt with as instruments of endogamy that turn relations inward rather than outward. However, what concerns us in this paper is the way or ways endogamy as an ideological system, a desirable model of action, bears upon urban living. And in this connection, two related fields of action and behavior must be stressed: first, the image of the city as composed of series of semi-independent solidarities that are distinguished socially and ethnically, and sometimes politically and economically; second, the sharp division between private and public domains with obvious moral preference given to the private. In other words, there is a clear relationship between endogamous forms of action and behavior, as desirable models, and the constitution of cities as a series of "tents" or urban nuclei each corresponding to a social solidarity of a kind and enjoying the very facilities and services enjoyed by the others. Social solidarity may express itself sometimes in ethnic terms, sometimes in religious and sectarian idiom, and sometimes in kinship, community-based ties, or in the three arenas of action woven together into a single solidarity, each reinforcing the others.

The stress on endogamous behavior as a desirable model of action also makes "the public," however defined, take on a secondary moral value. What matters is "the private" domain, especially women and family; everything else—space, streets, traffic, parking, garbage, gardens, schools, states, laws, parliaments—is of subsidiary importance. The readiness and ease by which public property is confiscated in Beirut to the objection of none strongly supports the point. Private shops fencing a segment of the street to designate it as theirs, flower shops and peddlers occupying the pavement, parking or double parking in any open space, confiscating part of the highway in order to expand the limits of a building lot, stealing electricity from municipal cables—these scenes occur so frequently in Beirut today, as well as in many other Arab cities, that they can easily go unnoticed. Not only do people ignore these misdeeds, but to the actors, they are a source of pride.

In these basic ideological commitments, we, villagers or urbanites, are alike. In Beirut where I live, the urban native population blames these mishaps upon the recently settled rural migrants; the migrants, in turn, blame it all upon the urban natives. None is to be blamed; it is simply an expression of ideology.

REFERENCES

Abu-Lughod, Janet, *Cairo.* Princeton: Princeton University Press, 1971.

Burgess, Ernest W., "Residential Segregation," in *Social Ecology,* by Miller Alihan. New York: Columbia University Press, 1938.

Gulick, John, "Village and City: Cultural Continuities in Twentieth Century Middle Eastern Cultures," in *Middle Eastern Cities,* by Ira M. Lapidus. Berkeley: University of California Press, 1969.

Khuri, Fuad I., *From Village to Suburb.* Chicago: University of Chicago Press, 1975.

DISCUSSION

Ibrahim

I have some soul-searching questions about the propositions Dr. Khuri laid before us. The first proposition actually ties the content of this paper with some of the papers presented in the first session about authenticity and modernity. Dr. Mechkat and Dr. Galantay talked about whether it is really possible to reconcile the old and the new, and the Crown Prince in his opening remarks talked about the traditional Islamic city as a paradise lost, and hard to recover. Dr. Khuri's paper seemed to be saying that, whether we try or not, the traditional ideological metaphor persists and will probably continue to persist for some time.

The question here is, what is the basis of solidarity in the modern or contemporary Arab city? Is it the old bonds of solidarity of cohesion, such as kinship, ethnicity, guilds and so on, as Dr. Khuri seemed to imply, or do we have a new basis for solidarity and cohesion —occupation, class, etc.?

We have both models in the Arab world today. The description of Beirut is interesting. However, I find that it does not really hold for Cairo, for example, in which kinship, ethnicity, and tribe do not seem to constitute the basis of social cohesion in the contemporary city, except for newly migrant groups who cluster in the outskirts of Cairo, and who probably make up no more than 15–20% of the total population of the city. But the rest of the city is based on new bases of solidarity, or new models of cohesion, and that is something to take note of because we have more than one model to explain the present scene in the Middle East.

Even in Beirut, we find an area, the Alhamra area, which probably represents a preview of things that could have come, had the evolution of Lebanon, both in social and political terms, proceeded without a civil war. Here the basis of solidarity is different—it is not kinship, it is not tribe, it is not ethnicity. You have a pocket in Beirut with a high degree of mix, but it is a mix determined by modern determinants, such as occupation or class.

So what I'm really arguing here is when does a linear model help us explain a contemporary city, and whether that linearity is reversible. I cannot help think that linearity from the traditional bonds of cohesion to modern bonds of cohesion is reversible, as illustrated by the case of Beirut. When under stress, when under conditions of civil war, people seem to retreat back to the primordial bonds of religion, of sect, or tribe, of family, and so on. But to say that this is an eternal feature of an Arab city may be overexaggerating the case.

Cromwell

Alhamra is rather a curious case. It is perhaps collectively the most economically advantaged part of all Lebanon, and I don't think you can take Alhamra as a kind of bellwether for the rest of the country at all. In fact, I think it's significant that most of the people who did live in harmony with one another in that part of Beirut have, in fact, emigrated. In other words, they were the ones with the professional skills and they were the ones with capital. So I don't think that we really can take Alhamra as a representative case which might be a harbinger of better things.

Khuri

It's probably because of lack of social solidarity in Alhamra that it had suffered most.

Schleifer

What is striking about Alhamra was precisely the absence of solidarity. It was convenient, extremely convenient, which is why most people lived there. It had access to international standards, international communications, and international values (Western values). It did not have social solidarity; it is the area that is most crimeridden; it was the area that was least capable of defending itself. The only way that people in Alhamra have defended themselves was by making deals with outside militias. In fact, Alhamra became for me the symbol of everything wrong with New York, especially the breakdown of cohesion.

The great tragedy is that those institutions which opened up endogamous solidarity to a cosmopolitan view unfortunately have disappeared in the last 100 years. These institutions such as the tareeqa, or the madresa or the awqaf systems didn't confront endogamous solidarity head on, but were openers for cosmopolitanism.

Finally I would suggest that one look at Cairo. One would note that the most successful sector would be the family business. A typical case, which I'd offer you, is of two brothers who were working in the Gulf. They saved their money and sent it back where it was managed in a joint venture by a third brother or an uncle. When we look at the proliferation of economic activity in Cairo, be it a small business, a manufacturing firm, or a retail operation, invariably it is a family firm. The same can be said of all the successful trading companies that have come out of the Gulf and Saudi Arabia as for the most successful banking and industrial companies in Pakistan.

Galantay

The additional metaphor which you mentioned applies in Arabic countries mostly to the very rich and the very poor. The very poor carry only the traditional metaphor and the very rich are rich enough to be able to afford the refinements of multiple layers of privacy and so forth. But it no longer seems to apply to the middle class, which is very rapidly secularizing and Westernizing. This is actually a question I wanted to ask because I think that you can either say the traditional metaphor applies or, if it no longer applies, then the question is "to whom does it apply"? One has to somehow distinguish between these categories.

Khayutman

In Egypt we find just these two giant cities and none in between, and this has to do with the political tradition of a country united and centralized for thousands of years. Whereas in Lebanon, the divisions in Beirut reflect the situation of the whole country. The internal struggles over Beirut interest me because I do propose for Palestine/Israel some sort of a tribal arrangement in order to ease the alienation. It seems that it's so difficult to modernize with this heterogeniety. Yet there are a lot of positive things and points about these mosaic neighborhoods and communities, but we do see the weakness in maintaining law and order, and maintaining urban economics. I wish to stress those principles that transcend and build metropolitan organization out of this high degree of autonomy which the different groups of families and tribes enjoy.

Schleifer

Dr. Khuri did then say we could separate Arab characteristics from Islamic. I think one of the problems intellectually with just coming to grips with these problems for the past 50 years is the tendency that we as Moslems, when we find something in the Islamic tradition that we have difficulty with, rule it out and say it is not part of Islam. I think that if we're going to come to grips with the authentic tradition and deal with it, then we have to sort it out. For instance, now egalitarianism has been very much a fashion in the West for the last 200 years. Therefore, there is great pressure on Moslem intellectuals to rule out anything that appears to be an impediment to the equivalent of Western egalitarianism. Certainly Islam, as an Eastern civilization is egalitarian within Eastern terms; it doesn't have a caste system. The egalitarianism of Islam, the egalitarianism of the mosque, of priorities to piety, is not the same as the egalitarianism of the French Revolution, or the egalitarianism of twentieth century bourgeois society.

Islam does contain hierarchy, and I think that any of these characteristics that Mr. Khuri has identified are recognized as realities without it not being egalitarian. I mean, the old do take priority over the young, which is a hierarchy; the pious take priority over the laymen; the learned take priority over the unlearned, etc. These do not negate egalitarianism in Islam, yet tribal and family affiliations have always been one of the structural foundations of Muslim societies. The Moslem armies have marched out of Medina under tribal banners yet their tribal solidarity is not greater than the solidarity with the Ummah.

Even in the distribution of charity, family takes priority over strangers. That's very important. Maybe that's why we don't have a welfare problem in the Moslem world, because the family structure remains. So I think what we can try to do is to stay on these factors and try to see what forces will enable them to perform constructively to the degree that we can rehabilitate our tradition—what forces will enable them to perform constructively and positively rather than constrictively and narrowly.

Part III

The Modernization of an Islamic City: The Case of Sana'a

INTRODUCTION

The case of Sana'a was chosen to represent Middle Eastern cities that still have an intact original urban core that is vibrant and economically active. Yet, this original core—Old Sana'a—faces the challenge of a sprawling and expanding "modern" urban phenomenon. The urbanization of Sana'a is studied from three different angles.

Engineer Ali Oshaish is an official responsible for Old Sana'a at the Ministry of Municipalities and Housing in Yemen. His paper indicates that Old Sana'a is a model of the Islamic City. "Old Sana'a is a typical medieval city organized similarly to sister Islamic cities' and this model is "the [only] Islamic city that remained untouched and intact." The approach reflects the author's profession—architecture and engineering. Thus, the paper stresses the physical layout and urban plan of the city.

Fritz Piepenberg is a journalist who has lived in Sana'a for a long time. During this time, he has been fascinated by the beauty of the city. Thus, the thrust of his paper is towards the preservation of Old Sana'a. He insists that "safeguarding Sana'a Al-Qadimah (Old Sana'a) is a matter of urgency and does not permit any further delay." He provides a summarized narration of what has been done and what could be done in this direction.

The third paper deals with Old and New Sana'a together as one urban entity. Professor Abdulaziz Saqqaf, an economist at Sana'a University, stresses the need to study the urbanization process of the whole city rather than any part of it. In addition, the interaction between Old Sana'a and the city as a whole is analyzed.

The papers are followed by many comments—notably the comments of Dr. Ahmed H. Rasool of Baghdad University and Dr. Osman M. Osman of the National Planning Institute of Cairo.

Chapter 5

Old Sana'a: An Existing Model for the Islamic City

Ali Oshaish

Sana'a is considered by many as one of the oldest cities of the world. An exact date for its establishment is unknown, but if we rely on the existing sources of Yemeni tradition, Sana'a dates way back in history to the time of "Shem," son of Noah. The inscriptions provide an explanation for the origins of the name Sana'a, which means "The Fortified Place." These inscriptions date back to the Himyaritic era about 2000 years ago.[1]

In the "Description of the Arabian Peninsula," Al-Hassan Bin Ahmed Al-Hamdany (4th A.H./10th A.D.), Yemeni geographer and historian describes Sana'a as the oldest city on earth and "Shem" as the founder of the city. A great landmark of the city of Sana'a is the "Ghamdan" Palace, which is confirmed by Al-Hamdany and Himyaritic inscriptions dating back to around 200 B.C. This famous monument is believed to have been built by "Sharah Yahdub the First,"[2] one of the early kings of the Himyaritic dynasty. However, historical accounts have to be substantiated through excavation of sites.

Sana'a is located right in the center of the Yemen Arab Republic. It lies in a rich valley that runs from south to north and is surrounded by the mountains of "Nagum" on the east and "Aiban" on the west. It is cold in the winter and warm in the summer, but relatively dry most of the year. It has two limited rainy seasons—the first during March/April and the second from July to September.

The old city of Sana'a has all the elements that make a city, even in the pre-Islamic period. Sana'a was fortified by a circumference wall about 200 B.C.; it had a market inhabited by "kings" and "governors," and it contained different forms of associations—all being the characteristics of a city[3]. In addition, Sana'a has always been well populated. "Al-Razy" mentions that Sana'a embodied about 6,500 houses, thus giving it a population of about 65,000 people.

Sana'a had a good legal system to which its suburbs were effectively linked. This provided an economic and political system for traders and merchants, craftsmen, civil workers, etc., who lived in the city, and it regulated the relations with the farmers and peasants outside the city walls. The coming of Islam gave the city a new socio-political structure and strengthened its legal system.[4]

THE ISLAMIC URBAN AND ARCHITECTURAL HERITAGE

The old city of Sana'a is known to be one of the few Islamic cities that remained untouched and intact from the urban and architectural standpoints. The physical layout of Sana'a revolves around an original core. As Nikita Elisseff states, "the form of a city depends upon its origin."[5] Elisseff also categorizes the Islamic city as being "the symbol of the religious, political and social system."[6]

The urban layout of Sana'a and the unique architecture that it ensembles were the product of the continuous interaction between the ancient Yemeni building techniques and the Islamic influence through the centuries.

Describing Sana'a, Paolo M. Costa wrote, "Sana'a is a unique city of magnificent houses, mosques so different from the rest of the Islamic world, and markets in which survives a perfectly efficient medieval organization. But the exceptional quality of Sana'a lies not only in these things; it comes also from all the other survivals, however humble and poor they may be, which compose a picture still exceptionally intact despite all the damage and mutilation to which it has been subjected."[7]

Old Sana'a encloses 6,500 houses of rare beauty, nearly 100 mosques, 14 "Hammams" or baths, several public open green spaces, many private gardens, and a traditional market located in its center. Above all, enclosed by its wall, is the citadel.

Old Sana'a is characterized by its groups of houses around the open spaces in the various neighborhoods of the city. Those spaces serve as collection points for the houses and the neighborhood drainage. At the same time, the green spaces provide natural scenes of beauty. This is the kind of layout that made Costa speak of Sana'a, explaining "the built-up area of Islamic Sana'a takes on a characterization layout with the various quarters and groups of houses mainly disposed around open spaces which are lower in level and cultivated as vegetable gardens,"[8] and which are "ideally suited for cultivation since they formed the collecting points for all the drainage waters in the area."[9] Other than green spaces, the city has several spaces spread in its various neighborhoods which are used as playgrounds, public gathering and market places. Further, Costa indicates that "other open spaces were allocated to marketplaces, and particularly large areas were left for cattle and forage suqs."[10]

The 23 mosque minarets of Old Sana'a interact harmoniously with the multi-storied houses and form a unique skyline. Old Sana'a embodies a sense of magic to its visitors. Again, Costa summarized this in a few words: "Sana'a enjoyed a surprisingly harmonious development practically uncontaminated by foreign intrusion."[11] It can be added that Old Sana'a is the only city in the Islamic world that was built during the early Islamic period with a medieval urban layout, and it continues to exist as it did. We will examine Old Sana'a's historical, structural and architectural evolution.

The present citadel was built by Yemenis in respect to the ancient and great "Ghamdan" Palace. It was built on the eastern hills of Sana'a, but its exact date is historically undefined. Some believe that it was built during the Himyaritic era, others believe it was founded by "Ibn Yafur" in the ninth century,[12] who also constructed one of the city walls as well. The present citadel was known by the name of "Ghamdan" and the "Sana'a" Palace, but since the revolution it is known as the "Weapons Palace." It consists of storages of weapons, grains, a furnace, grinding mill, hammam or bath, two mosques (the second was built by the Turkish "Murad Pasha" in the sixteenth century), two prisons, and two palaces used as detention quarters for rivals from the noble families. It is believed that the "Citadel" was built in different periods.[13]

The history of the wall encircling Old Sana'a could be traced to the early Islamic period, but it is believed that the ancient city of Sana'a had a similar wall built by "Sharem Awtar," one of the Himyaritic kings. However, the city wall was destroyed and rebuilt several times and there are no reliable details to be examined. Most of the present wall is made of mud, and it was built by the Ayyubides (twelfth century). The towers, water gates, and city gates were built of stones. The wall is about 12 feet thick and has bastions roughly at 44-yard intervals, with two flood gates located on the southern (entry) and northern (exit) parts of the city wall.[14]

Old Sana'a is known to have six gates, some of which still exist to this day. Those gates were either part of the ancient walls and/or rebuilt or added at later historical periods. The gates include the southern gates of Bab-Sitran, Bab-Al Yaman and Bab-Khuzaimah, the northern gates of Bab-Shaub and Bab-Al Sebah, and Bab-al-Salam in the east.[15]

The city's residential areas or quarters, appear clearly as the product of continuous urban development of the old city through the ages. Each group of houses and facilities is organized in units reflecting the date of its development. The oldest quarters are believed to be Al-Sirar and Al-Quatiee[16] located on the east of the Great Mosque, forming a north-south urban axis. These quarters contain the ancient "Ghamdan" Palace and "Al-Qalis"—the Christian cathedral built on Abraha's orders during the year 525.[17] Those two quarters date back to pre-Islamic times. They are the most congested quarters of the old city.

The other quarters, along with the rebuilt and redeveloped parts of the old quarters, clearly carry an Islamic imprint of a continuous development and organization throughout the different Islamic periods.[18] Thus, the various neighborhoods are named by their mosque names (mosques often named after the Prophet's companions, or builders' names). Also, larger green spaces were introduced. Houses were better organized and more air circulation, lighting, and Islamic decorations were used.

Old Sana'a is famous for its typical Islamic and medieval markets. The market space is occupied by several specialized markets and located at the center of the city. The market's original buildings are believed to be the "Samaser" (warehouses). Those "Samaser" were used as trade exchange spots, storages and as hotels for visitors. Some of those "Samaser" were found to be of exceptional architectural value, with the use of repetitive arcaded loggias and "facades of over a thousand motifs of rare finesse."[19] Similar to "khans" of sister cities of Damascus, Aleppo and Cairo, the "Samaser" in Sana'a were poorly maintained and, in the case of Sana'a, still await costly maintenance.

The specialized markets were organized and named according to the crafts, occupations and/or materials traded. For example, there are the grain, cattle, silver, grape, salt, cloth, and coffee markets. Some of these markets have disappeared (e.g., the sewing and thread markets) and other new markets are lately developed and expanded, such as the "Jambiah" (the traditional Yemeni dagger) market.

The city's greatest Islamic imprint lies in that for a city of such size, it contains nearly 100 mosques, including the city's "Great Mosque" which is "the greatest Islamic monument in existence from the early Islamic period."[20] The Great Mosque was originally built in the year 6 A.H. on the orders of the Prophet himself. Then it was expanded during the "Ummayad" and the "Abbasid" periods. Further significant expansions were made by the "Yafurids" in the ninth century and major maintenance carried out by the "Sulaihis" in the twelfth century. Thus the Great Mosque was completed in its present form in the ninth century.[21] Twenty-one of the old city mosques have tall minarets and five have multi-tombs. Together with towering houses, they form a rare and beautiful skyline.

The old city still has about 14 hammams spread out in its various neighborhoods. It was mentioned by Ismael Al-Akwa, that "Sabaa and Shoukr baths are the oldest two,"[22] and date back to the pre-Islamic period. The baths are well situated and designed within the city residential neighborhoods. They provide proper and continuous (from 4:00 a.m. to 6:00 p.m. daily) services. They use human and animal excrement or bones as fuel.

Old Sana'a is a typical medieval city. Its layout and topographical map show the narrow and meandering pathways, cul-de-sacs, public gathering courts and playgrounds. It was also mentioned by Ismael Al-Akwa that Ibn Rusta and Ibn Batuta (the two famous fourteenth century travelers) acknowledged that "Sana'a's roads were covered by stones and when it rains, they are well cleaned and washed."[23]

The building technique of Old Sana'a is simple and complex at the same time. It can be defined as a single-column structural system. All of its structural elements are attached and connected to the staircase, the "gutb," which is the major carrying structural element. It is usually located in the center of the building and measures about 4.8 square yards, built of stones with hard mortar of lime and earth from ground to the top floor. The other elements are the foundation, walls and close interval wooden beams used to carry slabs and tied to the staircase directly wherever used.

The foundation is stepped-type, built of black basalt stones or wadi bed stones using hard mortar of earth and lime. It extends about 20 inches below ground level and about five feet above ground level, including the ground floor.

The walls have two sides: the facing (exterior) and the interior with varying thickness. The upper floors are clean, dried red bricks (yajoor), using lime or gypsum mortar as well. The slabs and the wooden carrying beams are connected to the bearing walls and/or directly to the major structural element in the house, the staircase.

All of the internal elements such as walls and ceilings are plastered with gypsum. As such, the treated gypsum material is used in all stages of construction as well as for internal decoration.

The living space of an Old Sana'a house varies from house to house and the height usually ranges from four to eight floors, with each floor about 10 feet high. The ground floor is used for storage and similar uses. The first floor is either used for official meetings between the owner and visitors or as living space for the owner's farm workers. The second floor usually consists of several large rooms called "Dawaween," some extending from one side to the other side of the house without any partitions, and are usually used during family occasions and events for large gatherings. The third floor is used by the women in the family. The uppermost floors are usually kept for men's affairs. Normally, each floor has its own restrooms, bath and kitchen and can be used as a separate family unit.

Most of Old Sana'a's houses have a room located on the top floor, exactly above the "Gutb" called "Al-Mafraj." It is of a rectangular shape and has large windows made of beautiful gypsum and colored glass arcs with extensive decorations. This room overlooks the surrounding scenes of the city and its activities and is used for afternoon entertainment.

Thus, the organization and uses of each floor, the various air and light openings, the application of decorated wooden "Mashrabiah," the use of arcs and facades, the contrast between the bricks (brownish-red) and the gypsum (white) colors are certainly some of Old Sana'a major building architectural elements. These elements are a further evidence of Sana'a's originality, uniqueness and exceptionality.

CONCLUSION

The growth of Western influence, particularly during the past few decades, has been the product of the opening up of the Islamic world and its cities to Western civilization. The process started during the colonial period and continued through the oil-boom and since. At the same time, the opening up of Islamic countries and its peoples to education in the Western world has left a marked effect on the planning and architectural policies of Middle Eastern cities which created problems with the geographic and cultural environment.

Local tradition and culture is at variance with certain Western attitudes, therefore, city planning and architecture as now practiced create many difficulties.

It is necessary that researchers, whether from the East or West, should aim at avoiding blind imitation of any given style of planning and architecture without precise studies and an understanding of all aspects of a given culture and/or country. A precise study of the cultural, religious, social and political background of a society should be the base for modernization, especially in city planning and architecture.

The Islamic urban pattern is part of the heritage of man, therefore it should be protected. At the same time modernization should take place in a manner beneficial to tradition.

GLOSSARY

Ahmed Al Razy——An historian from the 5th/11th century and the author of a descriptive book called *Tarikh Madinat Sana'a.*

Al Gutb——A thick column of wall connecting different parts of the house.

Al Mafraj——The highest and most beautiful room in Yemeni houses.

Al Mashrabiah——The decorated wooden cases attached to the upper floors of the house which facilitate looking outside the house.

Dawaween——Plural of "Diwan," the long rectangular rooms of any house, serving as living/reception rooms.

Ghamdan Palace——An ancient palace that was built during the Himyaritic era by Sharah Yahdoob. Al-Hamdany mentioned that it contained 20 floors, each floor being about 10 feet high.

Jambiah——The Yemeni dagger which consists of an upper handle made of animal horn and a lower knife made of quality steel.

Jum'a Mosque——Friday prayer mosque, with a quorum of a minimum of 40 people for Friday noon prayer.

Samaser——The plural of "Samsarah," which is a caravanaserai that consists of storages, animal stables, and lodging rooms for merchants.

Sana'a——A fortified palace, as was found on Himaritic inscriptions.

NOTES

1. Ismael Al-Akwa, "Lamha Tarikhiah An Sana'a," *Al-Ikleel* Magazine. September 1981, p. 9.
2. *Ibid.*
3. Abdo Al-Jabar Naji, "The United Understanding of the Islamic City," *The Arab Town Organization* Magazine. November 1984, pp. 47–56.

4. "The Arab Understanding of the Islamic City," pp. 46–57.

5. R.B. Serjeant, *The Islamic City.* Cambridge, U.K.: UNESCO, 1980, p. 90.

6. *Ibid.*

7. *Ibid.,* pp. 164–165.

8. *Ibid.,* p. 156.

9. *Ibid.*

10. *Ibid.*

11. *Ibid.,* p. 160.

12. "Lamha Tarikhia An Sana'a," p. 10.

13. *Ibid.,* pp. 9–13.

14. *Ibid.* and *Sana'a: An Arabian Islamic City,* p. 129.

15. "Lamha Tarikhia An Sana'a," p. 12.

16. *Ibid.,* p. 9.

17. *Sana'a: An Arabian City,* p. 51.

18. *Ibid.,* p. 132.

19. Abdel Aziz Al Doulati, "The Restoration, Rehabilitation and Enhancement of the Old City of Sana'a." Consultant Report. Paris: UNESCO, 1982, p. 5.

20. *The Islamic City,* p. 155.

21. "Lamha Tarikhia an Sana'a, pp. 9–13.

22. *Ibid.,* p. 12.

23. *Ibid.,* p. 11.

Chapter 6

Sana'a Al-Qadeema: The Challenges of Modernization

Fritz Piepenberg

It was never easy to reach Sana'a, located as it is in the very heart of mountainous Yemen on the southwestern corner of the Arabian peninsula. Yet those who did take upon themselves the tiresome journey on donkey or camel-back felt both awed and inspired by the tall rising houses of the age-old capital. Aràbs and foreigners alike have expressed their impressions in numerous pieces of literature. Just a few excerpts are given below.

_____Some Early Comments by Arab Writers

"La budda min Sana'a—Sana'a must be seen . . ." are famous words first attributed to Imam Muhammed Ibn Idris Al Shafi'i (768–820) who visited the ancient capital several times. Even though his true motivation for taking up the long journey south might have been his ceaseless striving for more religious knowledge (and Sana'a was famous for her Ulama), he hardly could have failed to appreciate the city's unique architecture and heritage. Many who followed the example of Al Shafi'i have been deeply impressed by the striking beauty of the tall stone and brick houses.

Ibn Rustah, the geographer of the early tenth century, is one of the early Arab travelers to describe the city. In his "Book of Precious Records" he gives the following description: "It is the city of Yemen—there not being found in the highland or the Tihama or the Hijaz a city greater, more populous or more prosperous, of nobler origin or more delicious food than it . . . Sana'a is a populous city with fine dwellings, some above others, but most of them are decorated with plaster, burned bricks and dressed stones. . . ."[1]

A contemporary of Ibn Rustah, the well known Yemeni geographer and historian Al Hamdani, marveled at the cleanliness of the city: "The least dwelling there has a well or two, a garden and long cesspits separate from each other, empty of ordure, without smell or evil odours, because of the hard concrete and fine pasture land and clean places to walk."[2]

A century later, Al Razi, another Yemeni scholar, described the tall houses of the northern part of the town in his "History of the City of Sana'a": "(they) stretch up to the sky, with dwelling places and high rooms of the most splendid construction and most beautiful workmanship. They were the most imposing of the dwellings of Sana'a —they were the dwelling places of such governors as came from Iraq (the Abassid governors)."[3]

The famous Arab traveler Ibn Batutah visited Sana'a probably in 1331. In his notes he commented on the city as being large and well constructed, built with bricks and plaster. He stated that the rain waters were drained by flowing into Wadi Sa'ilah: "The city is wholly paved, and when it rains the water washes and cleans all the streets."[4]

Sana'a as Viewed by Early European Visitors

When the first visitors from Europe arrived at Sana'a, they were not less impressed than their Arab colleagues. The Englishman John Jourdain, arriving in Sana'a from Aden in 1609 to visit the Turkish Pasha, remarked: "This city of Sana'a is not a great city, but well seated in a valley and walled about with earth in the manner of a great stone square . . . having every forty paces distance a watch house or a little tower with battlements."[5]

The Dutchman, Pieter van der Broecke, followed the footsteps of Jourdain only seven years later. Impressed by the antiquity of the city, van der Broecke retells many of the ancient legends about Sana'a. His accounts of a mosque with more than 100 columns, each made from a single stone and containing pre-Christian engravings, probably referred to the Great Mosque.[6]

Carsten Niebuhr, arriving in Sana'a in 1763, describes the city as lying at the foot of Mount Nuqum, with ancient ruins on top, which the Arabs suppose to have been built by Shem. He said that the city appeared to be more populous than it was in reality, because of large and beautiful gardens within the walls. According to his description, there were many noble palaces, built by the imams.

Niebuhr was one of the first Europeans to visit the Jewish quarter Qa'Al Yahud. He commented on the Yemeni Jews as being the best artisans in Arabia, mostly potters and goldsmiths.[7]

Charles Cruttendon of the Indian Navy remarked on Sana'a, during his visit in 1836: "The first thing that struck us on entering the city was the width of their streets and their cleanliness. . . . The houses are large and the windows of those of higher classes are of beautiful stained glass. A handsome stone bridge is thrown across the principal street, as in wet weather a stream of water runs down it."[8]

Another detailed description of Sana'a in the late nineteenth century comes from Walter Harris following his visit in 1892. He gave a well-presented account of the suqs, of the capital and their caravan-serais. On the style of architecture he remarked: "a style impossible to describe, for it is a style that exists nowhere else. It is purely and essentially Yemenite, though in some cases, gateways and windows are found of Byzantine and Gothic forms."[9]

For renewed negotiations on the Anglo-Yemeni Treaty, Harold Ingrams arrived in Sana'a in 1934 with other British officers. In his words, the town was "the greatest Arab city I had seen—unspoiled by European influence."[10]

Even today, Imam Al-Shafi'i's words still hold true. Entering Bab Al-Yaman, the southern gate of the old city has never failed to fill the casual tourist, the historian or the architect with awe and inspiration. Passing by the Great Mosque and penetrating into the very heart of the old city, the twentieth century visitor will feel the same dignity and nobility emanating from the old houses as described by earlier travelers.

And if he is lucky enough to climb to the top of one of the tall houses, he will find himself surrounded by a marvelous skyline of higher and lower top floors whose rich brickwork decorations are highlighted by a whitewash of gypsum. Wherever he looks, he will be captivated by the geometrically patterned window arches filled with multi-colored pieces of glass, the whitewashed pinnacles of the roof gardens and the tall minarets rising steeply into the blue sky. It is still the same city as described by Ibn Rustah, "unrivaled in her greatness, population, prosperity and nobility of origin."

In fact, the people of Sana'a are known to be rather conservative, stubbornly clinging to traditional ways. The Sana'a that Al-Shafi'i knew 1200 years ago and the Sana'a of the twentieth century, after all, may not be too different!

ISLAMIC SANA'A: AN UNCHANGED PATTERN OF LIFE

The Three Centers of Islamic Sana'a

a) The Great Mosque, the spiritual center

It was the arrival of Islam, traditionally dated from the year 6 of the Hijrah (628), that gave Sana'a her three new centers of religion, politics and commerce. The splendid cathedral, the ruins are now known as Ghurqat Al-Qalis, built by the Axumite Christian ruler Abraha, had been deserted ever since the Persians, in cooperation with the Himyarite nobility expelled the Ethiopians from the peninsula. The new spiritual center of the city was to become the Great Mosque, built according to the detailed instructions of the Prophet himself "between the ruins of Ghamdan and the Mulamlim stone in the royal gardens." Early Muslim missionaries were sent by the prophet to help in the construction of the new "house of Allah."

The Great Mosque gives a curious reflection of Yemen's history. Among the 183 pillars, the Sabean period is represented by those columns taken from Sabean temples and public buildings. The construction of the exterior walls, with each level slightly recessed from the one beneath but still keeping the wall exactly vertical, is another characteristic of Sabean architecture.

Other columns richly decorated with accanthu leaves or stylized patterns of vine leaves, come from the Himyarite kingdom (115 B.C.-525A.D.). Panels with South Arabian inscriptions near the eastern door and the engraved metal sheet covering the Mihrab door are believed to originate from the Ghamdan Palace of the Himyarite kings.

Capitals, with clearly visible Greek crosses at their center, are a reminder of the brief Christian rule (525-575). Those capitals, together with the wooden lintel of the main door in the center of the southern facade showing vine tendrils, leaves and rosettes typical of the Byzantine art of the sixth century, may have been taken from the Al-Qalis cathedral.

Persian influence on the architecture is also visible. The ceiling in front of the Mihrab, culminating in small domes or lanterns with alabaster skylights for illumination, is most probably a Persian innovation. It is quite striking how the architectural contributions of bitterly opposed military and religious factions exist side by side under the roof of the Great Mosque!

b) Qasr Al-Silah, the political center

The famed Ghamdan Palace, rising up to 20 floors with a translucent roof of alabaster, has served as a royal palace for the Sabean and Himarite kings of Yemen. It was finally destroyed as a symbol of paganism when the Islamic rulers and governors moved their seat to the far east of the city, reconstructing (probably on the foundation of a pre-Islamic fortification) what is now known as Qasr Al-Silah. The fort sits on a natural elevation overlooking the entire city. Some historians maintain that this early Sabean fortification was the center from which all subsequent urbanization began.

c) Suq Al-Milh, the commercial center

Probably at the time of the arrival of Islam, the seasonal and weekly market at Sana'a that was still held outside the city walls up to that time became a permanent part of the city. The market soon moved into the very heart of the expanding city and became the center of trade and craftmanship for the Sana'a province. Much of the centuries-old market order (Qanun Sana'a) remains intact, regulating the daily life of the suq today.

The Traditional Urban Texture

a) Infrastructure and Gardens

What makes Sana'a so delightful to visitors is the perfect individuality yet seamless harmony with which the tall houses cluster inside the city walls. The narrow lanes running in an amazing labyrinth between the quarters are kept in cool shade for most of the day protected by the steeply rising walls of the houses. At certain points, the small lanes suddenly open up into squares bordered by the decorated fronts of the lofty facades.

Sana'a also has a number of large gardens, carefully hidden behind walls of clay and stone. Since ancient times, these gardens were used to grow fruit and vegetables. The upper rooms of the houses, with a view over the gardens, give an especially pleasant view.

b) Local Architecture

All houses are built on a solid foundation of hewn basalt blocks, one and a half feet below and one and a half feet above ground. The outer walls of the next two floors are formed by a beautiful combination of tufa and limestone. The dark tufa has its place on the corners and follows the window arches in one or two layers. The limestone in between can be of various colors: white, yellow, green or red. Only one face of the stone is dressed smoothly by the masons. Yet from the outside, all stones fit together perfectly, leaving no gaps.

The upper three to six levels are built with burnt clay bricks. Protruding bricks form a variety of geometric patterns, running in ornamental patterns along the roofs and windows. The highest room, the mafraj, has windows on two or three sides that give magnificent views of the city. Windows are of particular interest given their highly decorated arches. The double arches are laid out from the inside with colored glass, allowing the evening sun to draw beautiful patterns on the opposite wall of the room. Traditional alabaster windows that can still be seen in many houses.

The ground level serves as accommodation for sheep, goats and chickens, while the floor above that serves for storage of flour, cereals and dried vegetables. A steep staircase of high steps winds around the "Umm Al-bayt, "(staircase) to the very top floor. The Umm Al-bayt is a massive pillar of heavy stones, built up through the middle of the house like a spinal cord. Local architects say that any damage to the house can be repaired, as long as the Umm Al-bayt remains strong.

The Diwan, a large room for family celebrations on the third floor, always has a south facing position, allowing the sun to warm it up after the cool winter nights. The kitchen lies north, allowing the smoke to drift away from the house. Each floor has its own toilet, with the liquid waste running down a specially constructed runway on the outer wall of the house, to be dried up by the sun. The solid human waste is collected and dried in a small excrement chamber that is emptied from time to time. The other side of the house usually has a well, providing fresh water that can be drawn up to the highest floors.

The Social Fabric

Old Sana'a is divided into four quadrants, excluding the market area. Each quadrant has a number of city quarters called Harat. The quarters are of very ancient origin and mostly center around a small mosque, often taking its name. The residents choose the "Akil Al-harah" (quarter's headman) who is then confirmed in his post by the authorities, and he keeps the job for the rest of his life. His duties include solving the disputes among his people, keeping a watchful eye on foreigners entering the quarter, providing security at night by organizing a watchman system, and collecting the religious taxes.

Life in old Sana'a is organized well and efficiently. Its proud and hardy inhabitants developed a high degree of individuality creating even their own peculiar dialect. They have never abandoned their city even during hard times when the city was sacked by power-hungry conquerors time and again. Thanks to the unyielding traditional views of the citizens, the capital so far has bravely endured all attacks threatening her sovereignty. The biggest challenge, however, has not been met yet. It is the challenge of modernization that gnaws at the foundations of the old city, threatening her very life.

MODERNIZATION AND ITS THREATS TO THE OLD CITY

It was with the country's political change from the Imamate to the Republic that Yemen finally opened its gates to the rest of the world. The whole country was awakened to the fact that it was living in the twentieth century, and found out it was far behind developments in other countries of the Middle East. A desperate struggle followed in an attempt to catch up with the rest of the world as quickly as possible, and values and attitudes began to change. Old and traditional is being identified with backwardness and underdevelopment, while things alien and imported are regarded as signs of progress. Usually such a nation takes a while to appreciate its own heritage once more to the point of being proud of it. This period of rapid transformation, from the beginning of large-scale modernization until the reconsideration of the nation's own roots and traditional values, can be most fruitful for technical development, but also most destructive to its historical identity.

PIERCING THE OLD CITY'S NATURAL BOUNDARIES

In the early years of the revolution (1962-1967) large segments of the city wall were knocked down. The areas of Abdul Mughni Street and around Bab Al-Yaman were the first victims of those unhappy events. The stone mantle of the remaining city was used in the new buildings thus leaving the naked clay cores of the once famous and strong walls. Most of the gates were too narrow for the rapidly increasing traffic and were knocked down.[11] The same destiny befell the Sailah, where the entire wall stretching in arches over the waterway was removed to make way for traffic. The natural boundary of the old city was thus pierced on all sides, as if in an attempt to weaken the old city's natural defenses against modernization.

The Ever-Increasing Traffic

In addition, the deafening noise of blowing horns and roaring engines disturb the peace of the old city. The narrow lanes are simply not designed to take wide vehicles, still less two-way traffic. The clay roads are damaged by the heavy traffic which causes clouds of dust to envelop pedestrians. The corners of houses have been damaged by careless drivers, prompting the placement of heavy rocks at those centers for protection. The eroded lanes are no longer able to discharge the rain water in the Sa'ilah, and now turn into pools of mud during the rainy season, thus making the houses very vulnerable.

The Water and Sewage Problems

Water and electricity moved in shortly after the traffic, and again, with a total lack of planning. Electricity and telephone cables form a dense net of wires stretching wildly from house to house and across the streets.

Given the dramatic rise in water consumption,[12] the traditional water supply from wells within the houses or from the Ghayls of Sana'a (the old underground water channel leading the water from southern wells to the city) were suddenly no longer sufficient. An emergency network of water supply was constructed, with pipes connecting as many houses as possible. Again, this was done in a rather confused manner, with the pipes appearing on the surface of the roads and running curiously up the house facades. An additional complication, leaking joints, pose a serious threat to the foundations of the multi-story houses.[13]

The traditional sewage system could not cope with the volume of waste water. The excess sewage water was discharged in the streets where it formed stinking rivulets. Householders reacted by digging underground Balu'ah (cesspits), again threatening the foundation of the houses, carrying immense pressure from the upper floors. The moist and eroding clay undergrounds of houses have given way to high pressure,[14] leading to ugly cracks in the outer facade, or even causing the collapse of houses.

The Solid Waste Problem

The ever-increasing solid waste, the packaging from all kinds of imported goods, has become too much for the city's traditional cleaning system. The times when the old city was spotlessly clean have long gone. Most regrettably, the Sa'ilah, for example, has become a public dumping place for all sorts of waste materials. The consumers who are flooded with neatly wrapped Western goods have not yet learned how to dispose of all the plastic covers, tins and glasses after consuming their contents. The easiest solution is to throw the refuse on the streets, where the passing traffic would either crush it to pieces or at least evenly distribute it along the lane.

Attacks on the Social Fabric

Another serious threat is the disintegration of the city's social fabric. The influence and authority of the Aqil Al-harah is severely curtailed as individual families begin to withdraw and to care for their own immediate concerns only.

The useful role of the Shayk Al-ruba', the headman of the city quadrant, disappeared completely. Sana'a's inhabitants, overburdened by the challenges of modernization, no longer have the strength to clean up the lanes in front of their houses or cope with the increasing water consumption and sewage. People retreated into their houses, neglecting even the green gardens and, in certain cases, the external appearance of the house. Others have attempted to repair breaking walls with cement that looks ugly and doesn't fit well with traditional building materials such as clay and brick.

To escape all these troubles, young families in increasing numbers choose to move out from the old city into newly built houses outside the city walls. Rents have dropped sharply in old Sana'a, with many houses being occupied below capacity. Poorer classes are moving into the old city, but they have neither the motivation nor the financial means to maintain the buildings.[15]

Challenges to the Suq

The central market area, never belonging to any of the four quadrants, suffers from all the problems brought to the old city by modernization. There is the uncontrolled traffic, the flood of Western goods with its problems of solid waste disposal, the neglect of important buildings, such as the caravanserais (samsarah) and even most mosques. Most unfortunate is the rapid disappearance of local handicrafts, giving way to cheap imported goods. One example is the silver market, where genuine Yemeni silvercrafts are sold to tourists without manufacturing new ones (Yemeni women are now interested in only golden ornaments). It is a matter of time before all the silver bracelets and necklaces will have disappeared completely. Again the fatal consequence is the moving out of business people to larger shops in the new city, abandoning the traditional suq altogether.

HOPEFUL MOVES TOWARDS THE SAFEGUARDING OF THE OLD CITY

Steps towards the safeguarding of the old city have been taken. It was the foreign visitors who first expressed admiration for the old city and demanded her preservation and protection from the adverse effects of modernization. Qadhi Isma'il Al-Akwa, president of the Organization for Antiquities and Libraries, said, "Until recently, we Yemenis did not have much appreciation for our architectural heritage. The people of Sana'a and indeed the people in many Islamic countries were not sufficiently aware of the treasures contained in their cities that were worth preserving. . . . Foreign architects and experts registered their concern over our heritage. They praised the beauty of our architecture, the types of buildings and the traditional buildings of Sana'a!"[16]

However, the Yemeni government, represented by Qadhi Isma'il's organization, did issue a number of significant decrees protecting Yemen's architecture and cultural heritage as early as 1972. Among the population of Sana'a Al-Qadimah, it seems to be the upper class that is especially aware of the disintegration of the city.

International Concern for Old Sana'a

a) **An early example by a Frenchman**
The French architect Alain C. Bertaud, a United Nations town planner, was the first to be given a chance to demonstrate his proposals for the upgrading of the lanes and squares of the old city. In the early seventies, he paved the roads leading to and from the Abhar square with cobbles. The square was newly divided with stone benches and trees at its center. Streets of the square were lit by beautifully designed street lights. It was a laudable experiment that gives a feeling, albeit limited, of how the entire city could be.

b) **Efforts by UNESCO**
Sana'a was classified as one of the three most endangered cities in the world by UNESCO in the mid-1970s. During its 21st general conference in November 1980, UNESCO decided to authorize the financing of necessary technical studies for developing a draft plan of action.

A number of missions were sent to Sana'a. In September 1982, Professor Ronald Lewcock, a well-known specialist on Yemeni architecture from Cambridge University, completed his important research entitled: "The Campaign to Preserve the Old City of

Sana'a."[17] The report proposed to launch an international campaign by UNESCO for the rescue of the Yemeni capital. Site visits by important officials, TV and radio interviews, video films and a whole range of articles in UNESCO and other publications aimed to create a general awareness of the problem.

The most recent step by UNESCO came when Mr. Mbou, Secretary-General, officially announced Sana'a a world heritage city. This was done during the Islamic Foreign Ministers' Conference in Sana'a in December 1984. Thus UNESCO has given the green light for an international campaign to raise funds for the old city.

c) The Aga Khan Seminar

Sana'a featured and continues to feature prominently in many seminars on urbanization in the Middle East. The Aga Khan Award for Architecture held one of its regular seminars in Sana'a at the end of May 1983, focusing on a single Muslim country, Yemen, and in particular her ancient capital. Among the participants were eminent scholars from other Arab countries and Europe as well as Yemeni public figures holding positions of key responsibility.

In the seminar's concluding remarks, the establishment of a "National Institute of Construction Arts and Sciences" in Sana'a was suggested. This is to include distinguished members of society including people from both the public and private sectors. Other suggestions include undertaking research on the promulgation and the creation of a program of public professional information on Yemeni construction. Former Prime Minister Abdulkarim Al-Iryani told the audience at that time: "We, in the Yemen Arab Republic, extend our hands to all organizations and individuals concerned with the architectural heritage of Yemen and wish to cooperate with them in protecting and preserving this heritage. We believe that this heritage is not the property of the Yemenis alone; it is a heritage of all mankind."[18]

d) Contributions by the German Voluntary Service

Smaller, yet valuable, studies have been compiled by two volunteers of the German Voluntary Service. Tomas Winzer, a civil engineer, has been proposing a solution to the traffic problem of the old city in the form of cul-de-sacs.[19] Architect Werner Lingenau, assisting in the research of Ronald Lewcock, proposed his own "Draftplan of Action" for safeguarding the old city. His primary concern was the exodus of richer families, replaced by economically weaker groups who eventually are unable to provide for the expensive maintenance of the tall houses. He therefore does not merely suggest a campaign of conservation, but rather the redevelopment of the city's social life, going beyond a merely architectural approach.[20]

e) Research by the Italian organization "Studio Quaroni"

The most recent study, which also is the most comprehensive and detailed, was completed as recently as June 1984 by the Italian organization Studio Quaroni. Quaroni presents, in its own words: "a study, which, if it had taken twice as long, would have run the risk of finding the decay so far advanced . . . as to prejudice seriously any recovery of the old city."[21]

The first part of the study, the reconnaissance phase, stipulates that Sana'a Al-Qadimah should be dealt with as a separate entity, contrasting with Sana'a Al-Jadidah, the new city. Principles and strategies useful and true for Sana'a Al-Jadidah cannot be simply transfered for tackling the problems of Sana'a Al-Qadimah. To keep the old city alive, a separate organizing body is needed to take full consideration of the traditional social structures and modes of architecture.

The establishment of a masonry school becomes inevitable, where the traditional "Usta," the building master, can document and formulate his ancient building knowledge, passing it on to young students.

Studio Quaroni is not only concerned with the "safeguarding" of the old city, but sees it as becoming self supportive and an economically viable part of the future capital.

The study calls for the dynamic and harmonious interchange between Sana'a Al-Qadimah and Sana'a Al-Jadidah. The interchange is seen as one between the old center as a cultural focus, nurturing culture, arts and religious studies, albeit with basic facilities, and the new center, symbolizing a dynamic and modern Sana'a. While the modern city will fully live up to the requirements of a modern capital, the old city will be a haven for scholars, students of arts and culture, religious "Ulama"—thus providing the city with a sense of tradition and history.

The second part of the study, the proposal phase, makes detailed suggestions on four major features of the old city: 1) the traffic and its regulations through one-way streets and pedestrian zones; 2) the preservation of the borders of the old city, namely the Sa'ilah and the remaining city walls; 3) the preservation of the urban texture; and 4) the reorganization of the suq.

The study provides for an orderly parking space within the old city for 1400 cars that belong to the residents, merchants, and relevant parties. Space will partly be provided by already existing squares, and partly by the large gardens that presently are hidden behind high clay walls. Vehicular traffic in and out of the suq is to be strictly limited to specified hours. The entire Bab Al-Yaman area is to be kept as a pedestrian zone. Concerning the Wadi Al-Sa'ilah, Studio Quaroni seems to propose a compromise between the idea of leading the waters through two box-shaped channels with a broad street leading on top of the channels along the course of the Sa'ilah, or alternatively simply paving the bottom of the Wadi and fortifying its banks with local stone masonry. The box channels would be constructed underground, thus keeping the street on the present level of the Wadi bed. Both banks are to be kept free from traffic and turned into pedestrian promenades and walkways.

Concerning the urban texture, Studio Quaroni, in common with previous studies, envisions paved roads, either asphalted, or better, cobbled. Benches, small fountains, trees, playgrounds and parks will be a regular feature of old Sana'a, as will be smaller health clinics, elementary schools, restaurants, and meeting places for each quarter. However, as the study poignantly states: "before starting to implement those plans, a new and revived land and property registration has to be drawn up, strictly dividing public and private property." Detailed case proposals are offered for restoring and strengthening the foundations and the walls of the old houses.

The largest part of the study is dedicated to the suq. In many ways the suq can be considered an encapsulation of the old city with all its problems. The proposal reads: "It cannot be denied that the hypothesis of designing the whole area of the Central Suq afresh appears to be the most appropriate (solution) and perhaps the only one . . . in view of the theme assigned to our organization."[22] The small shops, being of rather poor architectural quality and almost beyond repair, should be completely replaced by an adequately designed new shop system, including a second and even third level. Studio Quaroni puts forward a detailed proposal for rebuilding the suq, and for restoring and refurbishing the old caravanserais as centers for handicrafts, urban services, exhibition halls or small scale hotels. Studio Quaroni does not discuss how much such a large scale undertaking would probably cost. Also before breaking down the shops and constructing a new suq, the complicated and sensitive question of ownership has to be resolved first. In any case, such large-scale interventions into the life

of the suq are only possible with the full agreement and cooperation of those working in it.

Efforts by the Yemeni Government

Yemeni projects to improve life in the old city are of a more practical
nature and usually in response to the most urgent needs voiced by
large sectors of the population. Valuable assistance to foreign reconnaissance missions was extended by the Organization of Antiquities
and Libraries.

a) Service-related ministries

To satisfy the rising demand for fresh water, the National Water
and Sewage Authority (NWASA), subordinate to the Ministry of
Electricity and Water, launched the "Sana'a City Water Supply
Project," completed in 1982. The main pipeline was connected to
an earlier "emergency system" provided by the U.S. Agency for
International Development.[23] The water supply project connects
most of the houses in the old city.

The same authority has finally begun to tackle the sewage
question by contracting the Korean Sam Whan Construction
Company for laying some 90 miles of sewage pipes in old and new
Sana'a. The 45-million-U.S.-dollar project is expected to be completed by April 1986.[24]

The Yemen Electricity Corporation, again subordinate to the
Ministry of Electricity and Water, has just completed a project to
improve the electric supply and wiring of the old city. Six and a
half miles underground and 80 miles overhead cables have been
installed, supplying the houses and some 2000 newly installed
street lamps in the old city alone.[25]

b) Efforts by the mayor's secretariat

Another remarkable step has recently been taken by Ahmed
Muhammad Al-Akwa, the mayor of Sana'a. According to a
republican decree of 1983, the duties of the mayor's secretariat
include such important tasks as "the preservation of the historic
character of the city, the preservation of dying handicrafts and the
supervision of the cleanliness of the capital." Mayor Al-Akwa
plans to organize the headmen of the city quarters into larger
units, supervised by government-appointed district leaders. The
district leader is a municipal employee and thus provides the
important link between the quarter's headman and the mayor.

According to the plan, the 'Aqil, who is expected to know the
residents of his quarter personally, will supervise his people's
performance on a whole set of new duties.

The secretariat offers awards to exemplary citizens and punishes offenders of the new regulations. The good citizens will receive a letter of thanks from the secretariat after a period of three months of cooperation. Three months later their names are favorably mentioned on the billboard of the local mosques. And another three months of exemplary behavior earn them medals to be affixed on the front doors of their houses as examples to others. The lists of punishments for repeated noncompliance ranges from temporary imprisonment to expulsion from the quarter.[26]

c) **Establishment of the "Council of Trustees for the Preservation and Upgrading of Old Sana'a"**

Yet the most recent and decisive undertaking on the part of the Yemeni government has been the establishment of the "Council of Trustees for the Preservation and Upgrading of Old Sana'a." In May 1984, representatives from the Ministry of Municipalities, the Organization of Antiquities and Libraries and the mayor's secretariat met with people of Studio Quaroni to discuss possible future steps. It was agreed that a project of such magnitude as the safeguarding of Old Sana'a can only be successful if supervised by a council headed by no less a person than the prime minister himself.

In December of the same year, a republican decree issued by the president and the prime minister established the "Council of Trustees for the Preservation and Upgrading of Old Sana'a." The same decree announced the beginning of a "national and international campaign for safeguarding Old Sana'a." The council, which is headed by the prime minister, includes among its members the ministers of awqaf, interior, municipalities and housing, education, the president of the Sana'a municipal council, the president of the Sana'a local development association, the mayor, the vice president of the general tourism corporation and five additionally named persons, well known for their personal and academic commitment to the city.[27]

WHAT REMAINS TO BE DONE

The list of requirements for safeguarding the old city is both long and urgent. Many of the ideas and proposals mentioned in the previous sections have not yet passed the level of studies. In order to preserve the unique character of Sana'a for future generations, a comprehensive approach to the problem has to be taken with short–and long–term strategies.

Urgent Administrative Improvements

a) For organizing a sound plan of action, a complete and updated housing and property ownership registration becomes inevitable. The exact borderlines of the quarters and the quadrants need to be defined. Together with a clear definition of rights and duties of the headmen, an administrative base will be established for rapid implementation of any decisions or measures.

b) The naming of streets and numbering of houses go hand in hand with the property registration. A "project for numbering the houses" was announced by the Ministry of Municipalities in July 1984. But so far, nothing has been implemented.[28]

c) There is an urgent need for upgrading municipal services,[29] such as exact metering for electricity and water consumption, a fast connection of the houses to the sewage system upon completion, and an effective way of solid waste collection with the active participation of the residents. A small tax for the solid waste collection and vigorous campaigns to "make the city beautiful" will create an awareness for cleanliness and hygiene. Connecting the houses by underground cables to a common TV antenna would solve the aerial forest on the roofs.

The Establishment of New Organizations

a) The recently established Council of Trustees for the Preservation and Upgrading of Old Sana'a needs to become an effective and fast working body to help and support the people of old Sana'a. It is not sufficient, however, to merely establish the institution. The question is how to make it function effectively, so as to win the trust and confidence of the concerned inhabitants.

b) An advisory center, as part of the council, should be created, answering inquiries from residents and coordinating the cooperation between the council and the inhabitants. A substantial part of the advisory center's efforts should be focused on educating the people about the value and historical importance of the old city and the need to take good care of this treasure. This can be achieved primarily through the mass media, but also through special programs in schools and city centers.

c) An Institute for Building Arts and Sciences could document and develop unique aspects of Sana'a, especially in the field of architecture.

d) Connected with the institute, a masonry school teaching traditional building style would enable the experienced Usta to pass on his knowledge and experience to the younger generation.

Immediate Action for Safeguarding the Architecture

a) A thoroughly planned and firmly enforced traffic regulation is urgently needed, especially for the suq area. Regulations must be supplemented with designated parking space and pedestrian zones.

b) The preservation of the remaining city walls calls for immediate action, because the clay stumps, stripped of their protective stone mantles, are rapidly disintegrating with each rain that descends upon them. If something is not done soon, the few remaining walls will disappear in a few years.

c) A good solution for the Sa'ilah has to be agreed upon, since it is an historic part of Sana'a, just as are the city walls and gates.

d) The inhabitants need counseling and incentives for choosing the right methods of house repairing. This will be one of the main tasks of the advisory center. The center should also advise on how to modernize bathrooms and kitchens.

e) The traditional gardens should serve as recreation areas, playgrounds, small tea houses, and so on.

Long-Term Strategies

a) All roads should be paved with cobblestones, combined with an effective system of water drainage.

b) A comprehensive new design for the suq (as the one proposed by Studio Quadroni) becomes necessary for upgrading and developing the commercial center of the old city. However, the full understanding and cooperation of the shop owners, tradesmen and craftsmen of the suq has to be secured.

c) Sana'a, and indeed Yemen as a nation, needs a new national museum with ample space and archeological laboratories. The existing national museum, the former imam's palace Dar Al Shukr, is part of the Mutawakkilite complex including Dar Al-Sa'adah, another large palace, the Al-Mutawakkil Mosque and the royal gardens. The entire complex could become a cultural center, fulfilling this purpose much the same way it did in pre-republican days and could be the principal joint between Sana'a Al-Qadimah and Sana'a Al-Jadidah.[30]

d) Other historic monuments worthy to be preserved include the Qasr Al-Silah, the ruined Ghurqat Al-Qalis, the former Jewish quarter (Qa'Al-Yahud) and the historic baths. A section of the Great Mosque could be opened for non-Muslim visitors.

CONCLUSION

Safeguarding Sana'a Al-Qadimah is a matter of great urgency and does not permit any further delay. Dr. Paolo Costa, a former archeological advisor to Yemen, demanded at a meeting held at the Middle East Center of Cambridge University in mid-1976: the protection of the Jabbanah near Bab Sha'ub from fast encroaching buildings; the preservation of the Khanadiq, the city wall leading across the Sa'ilah; and the restoration of the remaining stretches of the Bir Al-'Azab walls. Only a few years later, Dr. Costa's appeals were completely overtaken by events: the age-old Jabbanah (built during the lifetime of the Prophet) gave way to a modern mosque built entirely of cement and concrete; the Khanadiq has been knocked down to make way for the traffic; and the remaining stretches of the Bir Al-'Azab wall have disappeared altogether.

Sana'a Al-Qadimah is a wounded city, badly hurt by the attacks of modernization. If anybody wants to know what might happen if worse were to come, let him go east and visit the old city of Marib. Old Marib has become a ghost town. The few families that have remained so far no longer take the trouble of clearing the lanes from the rubble of the broken houses, but simply walk over the piles of stones and clay bricks.

However, if the responsible departments and organizations can only agree on a common strategy to save the city and combine their efforts, Sana'a Al-Qadimah will regain her attractions and mysteries that impressed countless Arab and non-Arab visitors during past centuries. Only then will the words of Imam Al-Shafi'i hold true for all future generations "la budda min Sana'a . . . "—"Sana'a must be seen, however long the journey. . . ."

NOTES

1. *Kitab Al A'laq Al Nafisha*. Liber viarum et regnorum ed. M.J. deGoege, Leiden 1892, VII 109.

2. Abi Muhammad Al Hassan Al-Hamdani, *Al-Iklil*. Ar Al-'Awdah,

Beirut, Dar Al-Kalimah, Sana'a.

3. *Tarakh Madinat Sana'a.* Ed. Husayn b. 'Abdullah Al-'Amri and Abdullah Al-Jabbar Zakkar, Damascus 1394/1974.

4. *The Travels of Ibn Batutah,* Trans. H.A.R. Gibb, Hakiyt Series, Cambridge 1956-1971.

5. John Jourdain, *Journal of John Jourdain.* Hakluyt Series, London, 1905, p. 93.

6. Pieter van den Broecke, *Dutch Travelers in Arabia.* Trans. C.F. Beckingham, IRAS London, 1951, pp. 170-181.

7. Carstein Niebuhr, *Travels through Arabia.* Edinburgh, 1792, p. 373.

8. Charles Cruttendon, *Narrative of a Journey From Mokha to Sana'a in July and August 1836.* IRGS London, 1838, pp. 267-289.

9. Walter Burton Harris, *A Journey Through the Yemen.* Edinburgh, 1893, p. 19.

10. Harold Ingrams, *A Journey in the Yemen.* IRCAS London, 1946, pp. 58-69.

11. From the ten city gates, indicated by Rathjens and Wisemann in their city map of Sana'a from 1934. Only Bab Al-Yaman and two gates leading to Qasr Al-Silah have remained.

12. In his report to UNESCO, Ronald Lewcock claims that leaking water pipes are the primary cause for cracking house walls, eventually leading to their collapse. "The Campaign to Preserve the Old City of Sana'a" Consultant Report by Ronald Lewcock, UNESCO, September 1982.

13. According to Studio Quaroni, water consumption amounting to 5,535 inches per day will have increased to 10,055 inches per day by 1985 and rise to 25,397 inches per day by the year 2000. Reconnaissance Phase, Table V/2.

14. The pressure on external walls amounts to 31.71 tons per yard. Pressure on the cross walls is even higher with 38.84 tons per yard. Studio Quaroni Reconnaissance Phase III Data Sheet No. 2.

15. A recent World Bank study claims that the solid waste collection in Sana'a has come close to a complete breakdown. The report states: "The situation in Sana'a is critical. All system segments are rapidly approaching the end of their life, and if not replaced, the system will break down shortly." "Yemen Arab Republic–Urban Sector Memorandum" World Bank, August 1984. p. 22.

16. In his report to UNESCO, Ronald Lewcock estimated the average

costs for maintaining a medium-sized house at 900 U.S. dollars per year. Putting a house back into condition that had been neglected for a few years would cost between 18,000 and 27,000 U.S. dollars. These figures are likely to have increased over the last two years.

17. "Development and Urban Metamorphosis: Yemen at the Cross-roads." Vol. I, the Aga Khan Award for Architecture, Proc. of Seminar VIII in Sana'a YAR, May 25-30, 1983, p. 14.

18. "The Campaign to Preserve the Old City of Sana'a." Consultant Report by Ronald Lewcock, September 1983, p. 14.

19. Thomas Winzer, "Improvement of the traffic system in the old town of Sana'a." GVS report for the Ministry of Municipalities and Housing, Sana'a, November 1983.

20. Werner Lingenau, "Draft Plan of Action: 1. Restoration and Presentation of the historic city of Sana'a. 2. Draft Proposal for the conservation of the old city of Sana'a." GVS report for the Organization of Antiquities and Libraries, February 1982.

21. *Ibid.,* p. 6.

22. *Ibid.,* p. 4.

23. Sana'a is threatened by an increasing water supply shortage. According to the 1984 World Bank study, wells designed for a total production of 14,400 inches produce less than half (p. 20). Agricultural demands still account for 70-80% of the water use in the Sana'a basin. The NWSA is already unable to connect new households. During the hot months, water supply is temporarily being cut to lower situated city quarters to have the water level reach the higher ones. A "Supreme Council for Water" was established in 1981 to tackle the problem of fresh water supply.

24. Even though the works of the sewage network are progressing at great speed, the placing of the treatment plant seems to pose a problem. Studio Quaroni reports that the original place chosen by the British consultant was earmarked by the government for another purpose.

25. An important task that remains to be done by the Yemen Electricity Corporation is the removal of the useless and dead wires that wildly run from house to house and across the lanes.

26. The appeal of the mayor was published in the official newspaper *Al-Thawrah,* August 12, 1984.

27. From a conversation with employees of the Ministry of Munici-pality and Housing.

28. From an article published in *Al-Thawrah* on July 21, 1984.

29. See summary of the World Bank Report 1984, p. V and p. VI.

30. This remarkable proposal was first given by Dr. Paolo Costa, a former Italian government archeological advisor to Yemen, in "The Islamic City." Selected papers from the meeting held at the Middle East Center, Faculty of Oriental Studies, Cambridge, U.K., July 1976. Ed. by R.B. Serjeant, UNESCO 1980.

Chapter 7

Sana'a: A Profile of a Changing City

Abdulaziz Y. Saqqaf

_____**HISTORICAL EVOLUTION**

"Then Sam Ibn Nooh (Shem son of Noah), discomforted by life in the "north," headed south in search of a better living environment. He reached the land of Yemen, and there he chose to build his home on top of Mount Ghamdan in the fields of Sana'a."[1] So goes the legend of the founding of Sana'a, proclaimed to be the oldest living city on earth. It is this legend that gives Sana'a its popular name of Madinat Sam (Shem's city).[2] Ancient references call Sana'a by still another name, Azal or Uzal, (referred to in Genesis 10, verse 27) which is the name of one of the sons of Yaqtun, son of A'ber, son of Shalekh, son of Arfkhshed, son of Sam, Son of Nooh.[3]

Regardless of the founding person and date, Sana'a did not attain much significance before the time of Christ. One century after Christ, the Himyarite king Sha'ram Auter built the first wall around the city.[4] During the second century after Christ, the Himyarite king Ely Sharh Yahdhub[5] rebuilt the great Ghamdan Palace which ever since has been the symbol of power in the city. Although growing in importance, Sana'a never became Yemen's capital city until the coming of the last Himyarite king, Yusuf Asar Yath-ar, commonly known as Dhu Nuwas, at the end of the fifth century. Since the time of this Jewish Yemeni king, Sana'a has remained the capital city except for short intervals in sporadic times of history.[6]

With the fall of the "Eastern" Yemeni civilizations (Ma'een, Saba, Himyar, etc.), the desert caravan trade route passing through Hadhramaut, Shabwa, Marib and northwards towards Mecca was replaced by the trade routes of the coastal plains (the Tihama), and the mountain routes passing through Zhafar, Sana'a, Sa'adah, and northwards towards Mecca. As a result, a major market developed in Sana'a within the chain of Arab annual markets. Thus, the first market of the year starts in Dowmat al-Jandal in what is today Jordan, then moves southeast to Hajer (today's Al-Hafoof in Saudi Arabia), then moves south to Suhar wa Duba', and further south to Shire Muhra in Hadhramaut, turns east to Souq Aden, and north to Souq Sana'a, and further north to Souq O'kaz. The duration of each market season varies from one region to another but extends between two weeks to six weeks. Sana'a's market and storage facilities[7] soon eclipsed most of the others to the extent that it became the destination of all astute merchants and serious scholars. Thus, the famous phrase repeated by Arab travelers states: "One must arrive in Sana'a, however long the journey, though the hardy camel droop, leg-worn on the way."[8]

With the coming of Islam, Sana'a attained full bloom. In addition to its political and commercial importance, Sana'a also became the center for theology, and scientific research. Among the disciples of the prophet Muhammad who taught in Sana'a were Muadh Ibn Jabal, Wabre Ibn Yahnus Al-Khuza'i, Farwat Ibn Musaik Al-Muradi, and of course Ali Ibn Abi Taleb. Yemen also produced its share of ulama, scholars and poets like Wabh Ibn Munabbih, Abdul-Razzaq Al-Sana'ani, Al-Hasan Ibn Ahmed Al-Hamdani, A'lqamat Dhi Jidan, Waddah Al-Yaman, Abdul-Khaliq Ibn Abi Attalh Ashihabi, Bishr Bin Abi Kibar Al-Blawi, and many others.

During the Sulaihi rule of Yemen in the eleventh century, King Ali bin Muhammad Assulaihi reconstructed the circumference wall of Sana'a and established its six gates, some of which can be recognized today.[9] The city expanded steadily thereafter, especially during the Ayyubide rule of Yemen during the twelfth century when, to the west of the city, a new quarter called Hayye Annahrain (the Two Rivers' Quarter) was established. Attached to the southern periphery of this quarter was the residence of the governor at a place called Bustan Assultan (the Sultan's Garden). During the sixteenth century, with the first Ottomon rule of Yemen, another quarter further to the west was added and its name still is Beer Al-A'zab.[10] There was another addition during the seventeenth century when Qa'al-Yahood (the Jewish quarter) was established. A century later, numerous palaces, mosques, and public baths were constructed by Imam Al–Mutawakkil Al-Qasim. This was followed by a number of military garrisons to the south of Bab-el-Yemen built during the second Ottomon rule (nineteenth century). By the twentieth century, the butterfly shape of the walled city had been completed as the map (Figure 7.1) on the following page indicates.

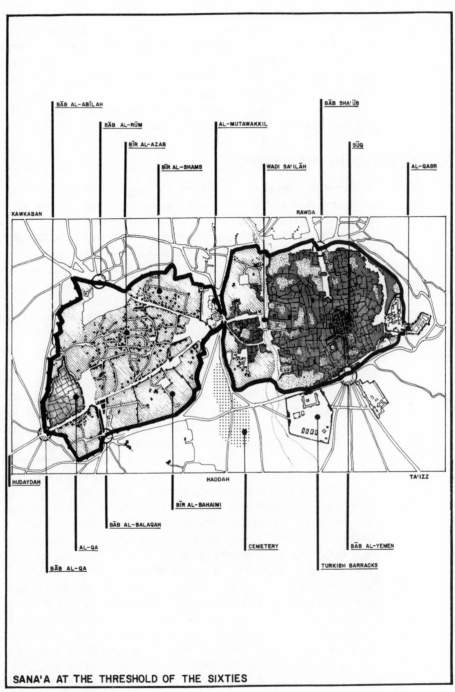

BĀB AL-ABĪL AH

BĀB AL-RŪM

BĪR AL-AZAB

BĪR AL-SHAMS

BĀB SHA'ŪB

AL-MUTAWAKKIL

SŪQ

WADI SA'ILĀH

AL-QASR

KAWKABAN

RAWDA

HUDAYDAH

HADDAH

TA'IZZ

BĪR AL-BAHAIMI

BĀB AL-BALAQAH

AL-QA

CEMETERY

BĀB AL-YEMEN

BĀB AL-QA

TURKISH BARRACKS

SANA'A AT THE THRESHOLD OF THE SIXTIES

Fig. 7.1: *Sana'a in the 1950s.*

The oldest map of Sana'a available to us today was done in 1763 by C. Niebuhr, reprinted in "Terrae Yemen" in *Voyage to Arabia,* Amsterdam, 1974. Over a century later, R. Manzoni did another map in 1879 in his work "Pianta della citta di Sana'a" in *El Yemen, tre anni nell'Arabia Felice,* Rome, 1884. Researched during 1929, H. von Wissman's work "Plan of Sana'a" was printed in *Landskundliche Ergebnisse,* Hamburg, 1934. Today, many detailed plans of the old and new quarters are available for researchers and scholars.

THE OLD CITY: THE BUTTERFLY

At the beginning of the 1960s, Sana'a covered slightly less than 750 acres and had the form of a butterfly extending its wings in an east-west direction at the foot of Jabal Nuqum, as the map indicates. The beauty of the urbanistic system and the harmony of the physical setting were reflected in the smooth social and economic organization of the city. In 1962, an estimated 35,000 inhabitants lived within the walls of Sana'a.[11] Yet, Sana'a included the belt of villages beyond its walls which were the home of an additional 15,000 persons. The city produced and exported goods and services to its tributary territory from which it obtained its daily food and other supplies. "The countryside was the natural and logical extension of the city because they were mutually reflected in each other."[12]

The intricate and coherent organization of the city encompassed all aspects of life. Social relationships—at the family, neighborhood, and city levels—were clear-cut and well-defined. The city was subdivided into haraat (singular harah meaning quarter or district), each headed by an "aqil" (the headman or wise man). Each individual was fully aware of his sense of "belonging" to his family, extension to his neighborhood (to whom he has blood ties, in any case), and recognition of the obligation to provide mutual assistance.

The two focal points of socio-economic activities are the mosque and the suq.[13] The role of the mosque, especially the Friday noon prayer, is undeniably the most important social event that repeats itself every week. The 100 or so large and small mosques[14] have played, and continue to play, a prominent role in the lives of the Sana'anis. The markets are just as important. W. Dostal enumerated 40 markets that make up the suq of Sana'a which is the center of the economic activities of the people.[15] Of these the prominent are Suq Al-Milh (The Salt Market), Suq Al-Bazz (The Cloth Market), Suq Al-Habb (The Grain Market), Suq Al-Baqar (The Cattle Market), Suq Al-Hareer (The Silk Market), Suq Al-Fiddha (The Silver Market), Suq Al-A'laf (The Animal Feed Market), Suq Al-Fitlah (The Yarn

Market), Suq Al-Buharat (The Spice Market), Suq Annuhas (The Copper Market), Suq Azzabeeb (The Raisin Market), etc. The market was thus divided in terms of specialized commodities with their storage and distribution systems. In addition, the market included shops of artisans (carpenters, colored glass and tool makers, locksmiths, utensilmakers) categorized according to lines of production. There are also sections for pottery, dying, sweets, sesame oil mills, etc.

With the coming of Imam Ahmed Bin Yahia Hameed Eddeen to power in 1948, Sana'a lost its capital city status to Taiz, and as a result the seat of government and the connected institutions moved out. Thus, the growth of the city was slow and gradual, the transformations were absorbed into the urban organism, and the final evolution led to the confirmation of Sana'a as mainly the home of private persons (notably merchants and artisans) rather than the site of monumental public places. This has given Sana'a a unique image among Islamic cities. Sana'a never evolved in the Islamic urban "skyline and profile" that is so well propagated by the European perception of the "panorama" of the Islamic City in the Middle East, Indo-Pakistan, or central Asia. This European perception of the Islamic City projects the image of "high profile" dominated by public buildings—tall minarets, impressive domes, monumental castles and palaces, etc—with the residential quarters forming a fabric of low-profile houses serving as a connecting structure. Sana'a's profile does not fit this pattern. Here the image consists of elegant and sumptuous residential buildings rising up to eight stories high.

THE TRANSFORMATION: SINCE 1962

Of the butterfly-shaped Sana'a, the western wing has already been incorporated into the modern Sana'a. What is left of Old Sana'a is merely a circular-shaped enclave slightly more than half a mile in diameter. This has come to be known as "Sana'a al-Qadeemah." Sana'a al-Qadeemah today is less than 10% of the whole city in terms of population, area, and socio-economic activities. The rapid transformation that has taken place will be outlined in the following pages:

a) **Population Growth**

In the beginning of the 1960s, the population of Sana'a was roughly 35,000; by the end of 1984, it is estimated at close to 300,000 persons. Table 7.1 gives the evolution of the number of inhabitants.

TABLE 7.1
POPULATION GROWTH
IN SANA'A

Year	Population
1962 (*1)	35,000
1968 (*2)	59,766
1972 (*3)	77,922
1975 (*4)	135,600
1981 (*5)	217,600
1984 (*6)	300,000
2000 (*7)	972,800

Sources:
(*1): Consensus estimate.
(*2): Alain C. Bertaud—"Updating of Demographic Data for Sana'a" (UN/OTC Town and Country Planner Report, Sana'a, 1972), Appendix III, page 2.
(*3): ITALCONSULT Survey, June 1972.
(*4): The CPO: Population Census results, 1975.
(*5): CYDA: Population Census results, 1981.
(*6): Author's estimates on the basis of a 7.1% per annum growth rate, plus the incorporation of villages at the periphery of the city like Rowdha (population 4,139), Hadda (1,312), Al-Wadi (3,852) and other villages varying in population from 1,000 to 2,000.
(*7): World Bank—*Urban Sector Memorandum*, Report No. 5196-YAR, August 3, 1984, page 2.

The influx of rural populations on Sana'a has led to a compounded annual growth rate of roughly 10% during 1962-84, from a population of 35,000 to 284,910. Although the low starting base explains the high rate of growth, it still reflects a phenomenal explosion in the number of people living in Sana'a. By the year 2000, the population according to the World Bank estimate will reach nearly one million persons. These calculations are based on an 8.2% annual growth rate: but even if the rate is reduced to 6.5%, Sana'a's population will still climb to 800,000 by the year 2000.[16]

The government has started many programs recently to curb the population growth in Sana'a. One major attempt has been the hinterland-oriented new investment plan. The Second Five-Year Development Plan (1982-86) has been aptly called the "rural plan" because of its strong drive towards creating sources of income in the countryside, thereby aborting population movements from the hinterland to the cities. Another attempt is the city-based tax collections. This means that earnings in the city will be more heavily taxed. Finally, the government pays more for its employees who work in the rural areas. Thus, teachers, doctors, administrative staff, etc. receive a rural allowance over and above their city salary. All these efforts, however, may end up reducing the rate of rural influx, but they will definitely not be able to stop it.

b) Land Use

The dramatic expansion of Sana'a has eaten away almost all the fields and gardens that once claimed 90% of the plateau on which the city is built. In 1962, urban Sana'a covered a land area of 740 acres; today it covers over 7500 acres. The rising cost of real estate has motivated farmers and owners of gardens and open fields to sell plots of land for house construction purposes.

Land ownership in Sana'a is of three kinds: privately-owned, government-owned, and waqf land (either designated for special purposes or left open for any use). The government has been using most of its real estate to build government institutions, schools, hospitals, police stations, roads, parks, etc. The army has reserved large plots of land as barracks in different parts of the city which were originally at the periphery. Waqf land has been used to build mosques and religious centers, in addition to waqf-sponsored investments in real estate like shopping centers and general markets. Considerable volumes of waqf land have been leased to the private sectors, and these have been used in an identical way as privately-owned land. As a result, the distribution of government-financed services is directly dependent on the distribution of land ownership in the different quarters of the city, thereby leading to an uneven distribution of those services. In many instances, the government was forced to expropriate land on which schools, hospitals, police stations, roads, etc, are built. The inability of the government to pay speedy and adequate compensation is a major hindrance in the continuation of this practice.

The phenomenal rise in the cost of land in the city has led people to settle further and further away from the center where the cost of land is still reasonable. This phenomenon has expanded the city in all directions at a very fast rate, yielding a low density urban area. The direct results have been a shapeless city where services such as water supply, electricity, sewerage, telephone, garbage collection, and public transportation have cost the government extraordinary amounts because of the nature of the settlements and the long distances involved.

To control land speculation and the aimlessly sprawling urban expansion, the government started zoning procedures. The zoning law depends for its enforcement on the building permit requirement. But a person may obtain a building permit and may change the use of the building. For example, a residential building may be transformed into an office, a restaurant, a shop, etc. In collaboration with the ministries of public works, electricity, water, and communications, the Ministry of Municipalities intends to enforce a new set of regulations. According to these regulations, any violators of the zoning laws will be unable to obtain telephone, water, sewer, and electric services. To tap into the system, people must adhere to the new urban development laws, especially the zoning laws.

c) **The Social Fabric**

The traditional social hierarchy is gradually giving way to a more secular authority based on the civil code. The role of the traditional centers of authority—the mosque, the family, tribal ties and kinships, the neighborhood—are no longer as strong as they were. "Today, individuals are much more independent."[17] Yet, the change is not complete, and the society lives today in a dual socio-cultural system. The rising costs of land, and the inability of individuals to support "relatives" or to provide them with lodgings in their houses or adjacent to them have had two major effects:

1) The extended family system is, by and large, broken. The new generation prefers to start up new homes away from the guidance (interference) of the parents and grandparents. The fact that relatives cannot cluster together in one house or group of houses because of pressures in cities has led to breaking the extended family system.

2) The mono-culture homogenous society is gradually replaced by a multi-culture heterogenous group. As a result, different value systems live side by side, and are tolerated (accepted). Not only are the different "subcultures and values" able to live side by side, but they influence one another, and a certain amalgam is taking place. This trend is intensified because of the influx of foreigners and Yemenis who had lived abroad.

The co-educational system has led to work conditions in which males and females work together. The fact that females can now increasingly support families and mix with men has tormented the older generation, and is creating many problems within the family. The visibly surbordinate role of women has given way to a more assertive female role. At another level, the near-total authority and dictatorial attitude of parents towards their children is increasingly being replaced by a more "understanding" attitude on the part of parents. The attitudinal gap that has resulted from a sudden exposure to foreign ways of life has placed a strain on the social fabric.

The traditional foota, thowb, zanna have been replaced by foreign clothes—shirts, trousers, skirts, etc. Although traditional clothes continue to be in use, especially inside the houses and during leisure time, people in general wear Western clothes to go to work, school, and other public places.

Eating habits of the residents of Sana'a are beginning to change although traditional meals continue to dominate Yemeni life. Nonetheless, many foreign dishes, including a few of the fast foods, have already found their way into the Yemeni diet. The ingredients in the diet now include quite a few imported items. Qat (a mild stimulant that is grown by farmers) continues to grow in importance and has become a focal point for meeting friends. Additional occasions for meetings in restaurants, coffee shops, cinema halls, etc, are becoming prevalent. Friendship ties, based on school/work/neighborhood relationships steadily replace blood ties.

In short, the social transformation of urban Sana'a is still in its early stages, and it has already created too many problems. The future socio-cultural values are directly dependent on the urbanization process on the one hand, and the educational system on the other.

d) The Economic Activities

Traditionally, the residents of Sana'a worked in one of four jobs. They were either merchants, craftsmen, (artisans), government-employed, or agriculturalists. Today, the work options are much larger, and more rewarding. The rapid industrialization and the rise of formidable administrative, commercial, and service institutions in both the private and public sectors have changed the old pattern of employment in the city. Today, clerical activities constitute the largest single source of employment as Table 7.2 indicates.

The relatively low labor participation ratio is a visible characteristic of the whole country because of the low female participation rate. Women are, by and large, housewives. The participation ratio of Sana'a is lower than the national average (38.6% as compared to 47%) because of the larger proportion of the student body on the one hand, and the resultant higher dependency ratio (4.3 for Sana'a, and 3.1 for the nation), on the other hand. If the students

TABLE 7.2
LABOR FORCE CHARACTERISTICS &
EMPLOYMENT, 1984

Working age (15–55 years) group	59.8%
Labor force participation ratio	38.6%
Total employable as % of population	23.1%
Unemployment rate in Sana'a	4.5%
Employment rate as % of population	18.6%
Sectoral Distribution of Employment:	
Daily wage workers and laborers	23.5%
Business, commerce, sales workers	20.4%
Military, police, etc. personnel	15.9%
Office clerks, bureaucrats	12.4%
Technicians, professional workers	11.1%
Service workers	8.7%
Managerial & administrative personnel	6.1%
Agricultural workers	1.9%

Source: Author's estimates based on the 1981 Pilot Demographic Survey.

(15 years and above) are added to the labor force, over 90% of the
male residents of Sana'a either work or study.[18]

The median household income in 1984 is estimated at 1800 U.S.
dollars per inhabitant in Sana'a. Although this figure is higher
than the official per capital income, it is corroborated by results
from partial surveys. For example, the television tax indicates that
there are 47,500 subscribers, which means that roughly every
family has a television set. Of the 145,000 cars registered in Sana'a
Province, 36,000 cars are private vehicles. Of these, roughly 25,000
are owned by Sana'a city residents, which means that one of every
two families has a car. Other evidence regarding per capita
consumption further confirms this estimate.

e) The Architecture
Old Sana'a has its own distinguished architecture in terms of
layout, structure, and building materials. The overall layout or
plan of the urban structure of Sana'a is different from those in
many Islamic cities. In the other Islamic cities the public buildings
(impressive castles and palaces, mosques with their imposing
domes and tall minarets) shape the skyline; whether it is Istanbul
with its great palaces and mosques lined with lead, or the gigantic
citadels and beautiful mosques of Iran with the yellow, green and
blue floral backgrounds; or the impressively huge castles and large
mosques of Cairo; or the historic monuments and pink sandstone

mosques of India. Examples of this skyline are many including the great Islamic cities of central Asia. However, the skyline of Sana'a is dominated by private houses—houses that belong to ordinary merchants and craftsmen. This phenomenon immediately reflects the mercantile origins of the city, and therefore, its extroverted residential buildings, as in so many mercantile cities in Europe —Venice, Florence, Genoa, Flanders.

The tall buildings usually have four to eight stories, and every story has a different layout with the necessary facilities. Domestic intimacy and family privacy increase in the upper floors, except for the uppermost floor. The middle floors (usually two of them) are left for the exclusive use of the women. The double windows, which may be opened in the lower part to allow air circulation, and the thin slits and the vertical shutters all add to the level of privacy. The general layout for the building is based on the extended family structure, so that different generations occupy different floors.

The foundations and the first floor are often built with granite rocks, whereas the upper floors are built with cubic bricks made of burnt clay. The width of the rooms (varying between 6 and 10 feet) is determined by the length of the wooden beams obtained from local trees that support the ceilings. Other building materials include the sawed bands of teak combined with the long carved stones for the lintels, the closely bundled twigs to weave the ceilings, the clods of lightly damped soil to cover the vegetal texture of the floors, the chalky mix for the roofs or for the vertical flow of the storm water along the facades, the colorful window glasses, the beautiful mashrabiyyas made of aromatic wood that combine the functions of windows and balconies, and the prevalent whitewash.

The buildings in the modern sector are totally different. Cost-conscious, the inhabitants of new Sana'a are happy with a one-story (maximum two-story) residence made of cement blocks. The ceilings are made of reinforced concrete supported by vertical and horizontal beams. Metal doors and windows have replaced the traditional wooden ones. The cost of land and other overheads have made the construction of independent residence units limited to only the rich. Thus, a further transformation of the architecture has led to the coming of new high–rises—the apartment buildings. Towards the northeast, the Yemen Bank built 500 apartments, and has plans to build 1500 more in the future. In the northwest, Sana'a University's prefab buildings house more than 150 families of the faculty staffmembers, and roughly 1000 students. Numerous other residential complexes are made up of tall apartment buildings.

The modern construction industry is directly dependent on imported cement (partially), iron bars, aluminum, glass, wood, etc. It is sadly discovered day after day that neither the imported designs (in terms of privacy, ventilation, natural lighting) nor the imported building materials are satisfactory. Yet, the alien architectural pattern is increasingly gaining ground in Sana'a.[19]

f) Finances

Funds for infrastructural development and municipal services in Sana'a come from government allocations, and bear little relationship with the revenues collected. As a result, it is very difficult to determine the urban households' willingness to pay for the services they receive and their consumption priorities. Given the rising level of urban expenditures, there is now increasing interest in indexing future government expenditures to the revenues collected. That may mean imposing specific taxes on city dwellers.

The YAR Government has been investing nearly 400 million Rials annually in Sana'a or an average of YR.1,334 per resident per annum. If we add recurrent government expenditures, the share of the Sana'a resident per annum jumps to YR.3,000/=against a national average of YR.1,285/=per person per annum. Total revenues collected from Sana'a residents (taxes, customs duty, fees on buildings permits, business licenses, user charges on municipal and infrastructural services, etc.) cover roughly 45% of total costs. Total revenues cover a higher percentage, if the analysis is limited to recurrent expenditures. During 1982, for example, total revenues of the municipal office of Sana'a represented 77.2% of the recurrent expenditures.[20]

A few years back, total expenditures by the government were negligible in Sana'a, or in any other city for that matter. Today, however, given the need for putting in place a modern infrastructure (roads, electricity, water supply, sewer systems, telephone lines, lighting, waste disposal, parks, schools, hospitals, police stations, administrative units, etc.), total government expenditures in Sana'a have been rising year after year. This has led to initiating serious efforts to mobilize financial resources by asking Sana'a dwellers to pay for at least the recurrent expenditures of those services.

SANA'A TODAY: CONCLUDING REMARKS

Sana'a today is made up of two distinct cities: Sana'a Al-Qadeemah

(Old Sana'a) and modern Sana'a, the capital city of the Yemen Arab Republic. The evolution of the urban image and profile has resulted in a dual nature. The unrelenting vigor of the "modern" Sana'a that sprawls in all directions threatening whatever "has been left behind from the past" is matched only by the obstinate persistence of the old to remain intact. This situation has created two urban realities that interact and co-exist. Any meaningful urban planning in Sana'a must pay sufficient attention to the relationship between the old and the modern based on a city-city dialectic rather than on a city-district basis. The truth is that old Sana'a, even though reduced to a mere 10% of the total Sana'a population and area, has managed to preserve itself as a "city." Because, unlike what has occurred in so many urban centers in Europe, Asia, or even other Arab countries where time has had the opportunity to eat away and erode the old tissue and where technology has worked in favor of the progressive adaptation of the historic elements to the new realities of the urban structure, the old core in Sana'a is able to hold out. Thus, while old Sana'a continues to be a defiant living expression—in full vigor—of the archetypal city, the modern Sana'a is a young and growing city that is planning its own future with the aim of providing its citizens with the facilities, services, entertainments, and organization in keeping with the requirements of today.

Yet, the city requires new urban policies. The most pressing issue revolves around the uneasy interaction between the two segments of Sana'a, and whether an eventual "osmosis" is likely or even desirable. The old, an embodiment of a long and precious human heritage, has a message to offer—a message of a harmonious way of life—the very essence of our discussions in this conference. Yet, the old city is in harmony with itself only because it is oblivious to the outside world. In a sense, it is the bliss of ignorance. Therefore, to pass on its important message to the new city, the old must, in some way, accept certain rules of the modern. And the modern urban system, sprawling impetuously outside the ancient walls and absorbing by force everything that has been "left behind by history" must, in order to give itself "a minimum level of harmony, an identity, and a quality of life," take as its own some of the extraordinary lessons of coherence and harmony offered by the organism of the past.

The dilemma faced by urban planners in Sana'a also challenges planners in other cities with an ancient core, especially if that core does not "want to die," and should not die. Urban policies for Sana'a should aim at the preservation of the old core by giving it new roles and functions in its relations with the modern Sana'a. The process should not be set in finalistic terms of conservation; it should be viewed as a means, not an end, in itself. The end should be to enable the old core to continue to be viable in socio-economic terms for its inhabitants. Therefore, conservation should be taken to mean a "re-alignment" of the functions and uses of the old in light of its organizational and physical capabilities, so it can make economic sense in its relations with the modern. The conservation policies must not lead to the banishment of the old to the category of things that are kept at a respectful, or even reverent, distance. It must be viable in economic terms, otherwise it may degenerate to "functional obsolescence" and become a large museum.

Modern Sana'a also has its problems. These are mainly of an identity crisis because of the internationalization of the architecture, social relations, and the way of life. The special things that used to distinguish Sana'a and its residents are being lost because of "progress." Sana'a is becoming just another city on the map.

Through the first and second Urban Development Projects, Yemeni officials are trying to take into consideration the economic, social, cultural, and political factors that shape Sana'a, and to formulate policies that will create the aspired urban pattern for Sana'a as one whole unit. The actions and decisions taken in this regard, over the next few years, will determine the destiny of this special city.

NOTES

1. Ahmed Al-Hasan Al-Hamdani, *Al-Ikleel.* Volume 8, pp. 36–37, (Arabic).

2. Ahmed Bin Abdullah Ar-Razi, *The History of Sana'a City.* p. 170, (Arabic).

3. The lineage as listed in Genesis, Chapter 10, verse 27.

4. Scripts on Stone 12, Sana'a Museum (Naqsh Nami 12).

5. R.B. Serjeant and R. Lewcock, *Sana'a—An Arabian Islamic City.* London: 1983.

6. Yusuf M. Abdullah, "Sana'a—An Arabian Islamic City," in *Majallat Al-Ikleel.* Special volume on Sana'a, 1982, p. 285, (Arabic).

7. For a detailed study of the suq of Sana'a, read Walter Dostal, *Suq Sana'a,* 1979.

8. These lines of poetry are attributed to Al-Imam Muhammad Ashafii (768–820 A.D.) before journeys to Sana'a.

9. Bab-al-Yemen, Bab-Sha'oub, Bab-As-Sabha, Bab-Sitram, Bab-al-Balaga, Bab-al-Qa'.

10. Qadhi Ismail Al-Akwa', "Sana'a," in *Majallat Al-Ikleel.* Scecoa, volume on Sana'a.

11. *Safeguarding of Sana'a Historical Center,* Reconnaissance Phase, Section I: Urban Planning Approach, Studio Quaroni, Rome, December 1983, p. I.5.

12. *Ibid.,* p. I.4.

13. T. Gerholm, *Market, Mosque, and Mafraj—Social Inequality in a Yemeni Town.* Univ. of Stockholm, 1977.

14. There are roughly 20 major mosques and some 60 small and medium mosques in old Sana'a.

15. Dostal, *op. cit.*

16. The World Bank: *YAR—Urban Sector Memorandum.* Report 5196–YAR, August 3, 1984, p. 6, Table I.3.

17. *Safeguarding of Sana'a Historical Center.* Section II, p. II.7.

18. The World Bank, *op. cit.,* p. 9.

19. *Development and Urban Metamorphosis: Yemen.* Proceedings of the Eighth Aga Khan Architectural Seminars, May 25–30, 1983. pp. 47–55.

20. The World Bank, *op. cit.,* p. 58, Table 6.6.

DISCUSSION I

Rasool

I have been asked to comment on Dr. Abdulaziz Saqqaf's paper entitled "The Urban Profile of Sana'a." The paper addresses mainly the issue of the transformation of the city, especially during the last quarter of a century. Dr. Saqqaf has tackled the evolution of the city in terms of area size, social values, economic activities, architectural changes, urban finances, population growth, and so on. There is, in fact, very little to add in discussing these trends. Therefore, I have seen it is best to supplement the paper with a few remarks of my own. These remarks will attempt to shed light on the key location factor of the city, and how this factor, in addition to other factors, was responsible for the transformations that Dr. Saqqaf describes in his paper. The reasons and motivations behind these transformation trends are many, yet the socio-economic ones are the most crucial. Likewise, the socio-economic consequences of these transformations are the most visible and most pressing.

Sana'a is located in the central highlands of the Yemen Arab

Republic, at 15 degrees 22'N latitude and 44 degrees 11'E longitude in a basin surrounded by mountain ranges, Jabal Nuqum (9343 ft.) in the east, Jabal Ayban (10,540 ft.) in the west and Jabal Nahdayn (8292 ft.) to the south.

The major subcenters of Yemen are almost equidistant from Sana'a, Marib being at the distance of 117 miles to the east, Hodeidah at the distance of 144 miles to the west, Saadah at the distance of 138 miles to the north and Taiz at the distance of 159 miles to the south.

The central location of Sana'a was always an advantage in economic, social and political contexts. After 1969 the importance of Sana'a as the capital of the Y.A.R. increased due to the fact that many foreign diplomatic missions, representatives of international organizations, and multinational companies settled in the city. After 1969 it also started to play a leading role in internal and external commercial activities, a position which was held before by the cities of Taiz and Hodeidah.

In the industrial context Sana'a became the booming nucleus, not only of the Yemeni highland region, but for the whole country. According to the preliminary results of the 1980 Industrial Survey[1] 37 percent of the total number of all factories with more than 10 employees were located in Sana'a.

As Sana'a plays a leading role in the commercial, industrial and political contexts, it also occupies the first position culturally among all Yemeni cities. The only university of the country, which was founded in 1970, is located in this city. In addition, most technical, industrial and commercial institutions and administrative training institutions necessary for qualifying the national cadres are located in Sana'a.

The development of Sana'a in all functional and administrative aspects encouraged part of the rural population to migrate to Sana'a. When questioned, the migrants mentioned the possibilities for employment, extended social activities and better standards of living in the capital as dominant pull-factors. As a result of the internal migration the population of Sana'a increased nine times between 1982 and 1984 as shown in Table D-1.

TABLE D-1
SANA'A POPULATION
INCREASE 1962–1984

Year	Population
1962[a]	35,000
1975[b]	135,625
1984[c]	300,000

Sources: (a) Consensus estimate
(b) CPO, Statistical Yearbook 1983, Sana'a, p. 27
(c) Estimate

The increase in population resulted in an increase in the built-up area from 1.2 square miles in 1962 to 12 square miles in 1984. Previously, the land in the vicinity of Sana'a was used mainly for agriculture but nowadays large parts of the area are used as building sites for industrial estates, building of houses for tertiary sector functions, and especially private houses. This is documented by the increase of licenses for private house construction which were issued between 1973 and 1983 and the consequent increase in the built area as shown in Table D–2.

TABLE D-2
NUMBER OF LICENSES ISSUED FOR HOUSE CONSTRUCTION AND THE AREA IN THE FOUR MAIN CITIES, AND SANA'A, IN Y.A.R.

| Year | FOUR MAIN CITIES* | | SANA'A | |
	Licenses	Area (sq. yards)	Licenses	Area (sq. yards)
1973	2201	730,039	987	301,401
1974	1653	570,532	818	326,376
1975	1793	524,109	820	334,880
1976	3744	1,404,177	1598	661,814
1977	4157	1,257,009	2423	941,992
1978	5185	1,918,176	2862	1,192,764
1979	4450	1,785,604	2172	995,283
1980	4355	1,700,073	1674	684,276
1981	4418	1,437,753	2362	903,369
1982	5147	1,400,876	3478	1,093,693
1983	4901	1,441,509	3124	1,034,913

Source: Statistical Yearbook 1983, Sana'a p. 118
*The four main cities are: Taiz, Hodeidah, Ibb and Dhamar.

The number of licenses issued during these years added up to 53.2 percent of the total number of licenses, and the area permitted for use for the construction of houses added up to 60 percent of the total area permitted for this purpose by the Ministry of Municipalities in the Y.A.R.

The urban sprawl of Sana'a between 1962 and 1984 led to a tremendous increase of activities in the building sector as a consequence. Between 1980 and 1982 approximately 500 workshops in the building sector were established in the city of Sana'a and its surroundings.

The main functions of these workshops are:

a) the production of building materials, such as cement blocks, bricks and tiles; and

b) the production and assembling of wooden doors and windows, iron gates and water tanks, and aluminium doors and windows.[2]

The urban sprawl between 1962 and 1984 had, as a consequence, a close relationship between Sana'a and its hinterland due to the improved road and public transport connections.

The change in consumer taste concerning agricultural products resulted in a change of producer activities of the farmers in the vicinity of Sana'a. It was observed that the agrarian structure changed completely from a home consumption-oriented system to a market production-oriented system.

The price of agricultural land around Sana'a rose sharply during the past two decades, and high investments are needed to ensure a reliable high production level due to the low rainfall, e.g., YR 500,000 are necessary for the drilling of a well and the installation of a pump for irrigation purposes. The consequences of this development had to be that only high-value cash crops could be grown, such as vegetables, qat and grapes.

With these remarks I end my commentary, knowing full well that the floor discussion will enrich the subject at hand by raising additional commentaries.

NOTES

1. CPO, Preliminary Results of the 1980 Industrial Survey. November 1980, p. 5.

2. Gunter Meyer, "Arbeitsmigration und Wirtschaftsenwicklung in der Arabischen Republik Jemen, untersucht am Beispiel der Beschaftigten im Bausektor von Sana'a," in Jemen-Studien Band I by Horst Kopp and Gunther Schweizer, Wiesbaden 1984, p. 145.

REFERENCES

Al-Ikleel, Majallat, special volume on Sana'a, no. 2 and 3, second year 1983 (Arabic), Sana'a.

CPI, Statistical Yearbook. 1983, Sana'a.

CPO, Preliminary Results of the 1980 Industrial Survey. November 1980.

Kopp, Horst and Schweizer, Gunther, "Entwicklungsprozesse in der

Arabischen Republik Jemen." Jemen-Studien Band I, Wiesbaden, 1984.

Rasoul, A. Habib, "Some Economic Aspects of Y.A.R.," in *Iraqi Geographical Society Magazine.* no. 11/1980, Baghdad, pp. 75–130.

Rasoul, A. Habib, "Cement Industry in Y.A.R.," in *Center of Yemenian Studies Magazine,* no. 15/1984, Sana'a, pp. 1–77.

Serjeant, R.R. and Lewcock, R., *Sana'a: An Arabian Islamic City.* London, 1983.

Shahir, Jamal Agha, *The Physical Geography of North Yemen.* (Arabic), Damascus, 1983.

The World Bank, "Yemen Arab Republic, Manufacturing Industry: Performance, Policies and Prospects." Report no. 3651. YAR, November 12, 1982.

DISCUSSION II

Sobhi

European cities have conserved their historical identity in the form of a very well preserved part of the downtown area. These parts are pedestrian areas and in many cases most of the very important historical monuments are located here. They are preserved, renewed, and very well maintained, and complimentary touristic services are· provided. They are very pleasant, middle-aged quarters which exist quite harmoniously in the heart of very modern and advanced big cities.

Actually, this is a kind of living museum. People live and work in these quarters. It is not that they are depopulated to be preserved or kept a historical area.

In the same way we can keep our past alive in selected old parts of our cities by carefully and quickly preserving in a methodological way without conflicting with modern ways of life which dominate many of our big cities. This would apply very precisely to Cairo, a city very much modernized and Westernized, and a city with more than one type of ancient history. It should not be very difficult to achieve this since the total area of such old parts is not very big compared to the total area of Greater Cairo.

Of course, this is not exactly the case with Old Sana'a which is rather small compared to Cairo, and does not suffer from the same kind of problems, and therefore it stands a better chance of succeeding in terms of preserving its old and historical Islamic heritage.

Osman

I believe that Sana'a is a very lucky city, not because it's free of problems to be solved, but because intellectuals have spent a good time and indeed a lot of work on the problems of Sana'a, and officials recognize its problems. There is now a council headed by the Prime Minister of Yemen, and recently international circles represented by UNESCO called for raising three billion dollars for the safeguarding of Old Sana'a. So it's really a good example of how intellectuals have a good deal of influence on the officials and on international opinion.

However, it's very dangerous to concentrate on one aspect of the city of Sana'a, especially Old Sana'a, its history and development through its architecture. The impact of Islam on Sana'a is evident and clear. There are about 100 mosques in Old Sana'a alone and because of Islamic theology Sana'a became famous for its Ulema. The mosques in an Islamic city are not just places of prayer. The Quran Sunna urge moslems to build mosques for several functions. It is not by chance that Old Sana'a and Islamic Cairo are quite similar in the pattern of building residential quarters (harat) around a mosque. The quarter would usually take its name from the mosque at its center.

Both cities, Islamic Cairo and Old Sana'a, are quite different from Alexandria, for example, in this respect. The three pillars of Islamic Sana'a are its commercial, political and religious functions. It is historically known that cities were first established to foster trade, this being the earliest urban function. In this regard, the transformation of the Sana'a market into a permanent one influenced the expansion of the city significantly. Then, around the time of Christ, Sana'a became the political capital of the country. Finally the coming of Islam added to Sana'a's third function—the religious role which added to its importance significantly.

Yet, we have to examine the challenges that Old Sana'a is destined to face. The biggest challenge is the arrival of modernization, we are told by Mr. Piepenberg. I beg to differ with this view. One may have one of a number of notions as to what modernization is. But this is beside the point. However, the way he sees the threat of modernization reflects, in my opinion, an over-riding concern with the old and traditional.

Galantay

Sana'a cannot be preserved as a historical Disneyland for tourists. I think that it is not enough in a conservation area to conserve the architectural elements, the cosmetic part. But one has to think about the new functions to be given to the historic area, and who is supposed to live there. It's not to say 15% of the population, but *which* 15%, and to work out a strategy of systematically attracting the various fields of enticements to people of whom you want to compose the new population—preferably, that section of the population that is willing to preserve some of these traditional values which are built into the physical urban structure.

Dr. Galantay suggested maintaining the past, maintaining traditions, or hopefully preserving stability. I wonder whether this is, in fact, possible.

    It is a wonderful idea to put retired people, institutions, schools, and various other things into Old Sana'a. Although I'm not an expert on Sana'a, I think it's highly unlikely that people would actually move there, given the fact that the Yemeni people appear to be extremely individualistic. I don't think that they would take kindly to the fact that they were being obliged to move in. My question is, therefore, is it feasible to try and preserve the past, feasible to try and preserve tradition? Can it, in fact, be done given the realities of our present situations?

Munro

One of the major problems faced by Sana'a's buildings today, especially in terms of maintenance costs, is that the same building is owned by so many members of the same family. The inheritance system is such that you don't own the house yourself; you and your 12 brothers and sisters own the house together, and therefore it's not worth entertaining the costs on your own; and, it's very difficult for all these people to agree to enter into a major maintenance investment.

Saqqaf

I feel that when we are talking about the old and new, and question whether we could maintain or hold on to the old in the face of the new, it is very useful to remember that the city is part of the peoples' culture. It's like their language, their dress, their music. The question is really whether we ought really to allow for a cultural invasion to overrun one's culture, or whether one ought really to stand up and try to restore one's own culture in the face of new ideas. When we look at some of our Arab cities we find that there is the new and there is the old, and all are co-existing. I feel that we must hold on as much as possible to our cultural identity, and to try to restore and vitalize it wherever possible. I believe this is most important when we talk about Sana'a, the old city of it, and we must make every effort indeed to make our city a place where we could redefine our identity.

Nasser

I think the question has been asked—who is going to pay for this and what is the price? I would also like to stress another point. The valuable architectural heritage of this city is a non-renewable re-

Galantay

source. It's as important as any other resource, but it's not non-renewable. Once destroyed you can't rebuild it.

Oshaish

Hoda Sobhi mentioned that Sana'a is very small compared to Cairo, I think I agree to this. However, the proportion of Old Sana'a to the city of Sana'a will be the same or even more than what Old Cairo means in proportion to the new or Greater Cairo. It has been mentioned also that the old city of Sana'a is not depopulated; it still lives but the functions are a little bit changed.

I think we need to focus on public relations. We need public participation in the preservation programs because we have to get the people first to understand what we have, what we are losing, and how much it will cost. We are in the beginning of these programs.

Piepenberg

How did Islam change the old city? The city, of course, is older than Islam. We had harat, we had city callers, we had the market, and we had the gardens before Islam. So, how did Islam change and influence Sana'a? One of the obvious changes, of course, is the mosque. Then there is the social life and the subsequent changes in urban forms. Islam re-shaped the structure of the city, and re-defined the relationships among its inhabitants. I think that has been the most persuasive and lasting impact of Islam in Sana'a.

Fig. 1: Minaret and roofs of Old Sana'a with Mount Nugum in the background.

Fig. 2: The tall houses of Old Sana'a built exclusively from hewn natural stones and burned clay bricks.

Fig. 3: The Great Mosque of Sana'a, which was built during the lifetime of the Prophet Mohammed, has become the spiritual center of Sana'a.

Fig. 4: An interior view of the Great Mosque of Sana'a.

Fig. 5: Bab-Al-Yaman is the only existing gate into the old city of Sana'a. This is also the entrance to the Sana'a Market which is the economic center of the city.

Fig. 6: (Above) A shop in the silver market; part of the Sana'a Market, it is now a tourist attraction.

Fig. 7: A view of "Liberation Square." This is a modern extension of Sana'a which was built after the republican revolution.

Fig. 8: Zubayri Street at the foot of Mount Nugum, leading into modern Sana'a. All of the photos in this section by Fritz Piepenburg.

Part IV

Jerusalem

INTRODUCTION

Jerusalem/Al-Quds is probably the world's most troubled city. It is supposed to enjoy the greatest peace. It is also the city that underwent the greatest transformation over the last few decades. In 1948, the city was divided into Eastern Jerusalem, known as Al-Quds, which was under Jordanian rule and Western Jerusalem which was under Israeli rule. In 1967 the two parts were united under Israeli rule. Immediately, Israel embarked on a major town-planning scheme for the Old City and the immediate environs such as the Valley of Hinnom, the Valley of Kidron, and Mounts Scopus, Olives, Offence, etc.

The master plan was completed in 1970, and it classified the different sites in the Old City into religious, historical, and architectural. The plan indicated the inadequacy of existing infrastructure and services, and the serious over-crowding, especially in the Muslim Quarter. Poor maintenance has rendered much of the Old City in ruins, and physical hostilities have damaged many parts of it. Extensive and immediate repairs were needed.

The Israeli government took effective steps to halt the decline of the Old City and several projects were implemented within the overall master plan, especially in the Jewish Quarter covering an area of 35 acres or roughly 16% of the Old City's total area. Buildings were renovated, the bazaar (commercial) center was rebuilt, transportation lines were demarcated, open squares were constructed, utilities and services were introduced. All in all, an impressive achievement.

Yet, the efforts had a political and economic twist. At the political level, Israel's renovation efforts also aimed at changing the demographic structure of the town. The plan called for a ceiling of 20,000 residents in the Old City, so the Arab population was perceived as over-crowding the city. Therefore, many Arab families were evacuated, some of whom were, in some cases, relocated elsewhere. Yet, in the hope of transforming Jerusalem into a uniformly Jewish city, Jewish residents were moved in. The progressive evacuation of Christian and Muslim residents of the Old City and its repopulation by Jews has become an explicit policy of the Israeli government. At the same time, expansions in the Jewish Quarter have steadily encroached on the Christian Armenian Quarter to the west, and the Muslim Quarter to the north. Also, the restructuring of the bazaar ate away at the Christian Quarter in the northwest and the Muslim Quarter in the north. At the economic level, the Israeli efforts transformed, in part, the sacred sites and shrines from places of pilgrimage for the devout to points of attraction for the tourists. To cash in on the tourist-generated profits, several major hotels, businesses, and other services quickly sprang up in the city.

We have three papers on Jerusalem, and each author represents one of the three religions of the Middle East. Henry Cattan is a Christian Palestinian Arab; Abdullah Shleiffer is an American Muslim; and Yitzhak Khayutman is an Israeli Jew. These papers complement and complete each other.

Chapter 8

The Repercussions of Israel's Occupation of Jerusalem

Henry Cattan

INTRODUCTION

The problem of Jerusalem is one of the most emotional and explosive issues in the world. Unlike other issues of the Arab-Israeli conflict, its importance and dimensions transcend the Middle East and its peoples.

Jerusalem is unique among all the cities of the world because of its association with three great religions. It is the spiritual and religious heritage to one half of humanity and is holy for 1,000 million Christians, a similar number of Muslims and 14 million Jews.

Jerusalem is the birthplace of Christianity. Almost all the holy places, sacred shrines and sanctuaries connected with the birth, life and death of Christ are found in Jerusalem and in nearby Bethlehem: the Holy Sepulchre, the Via Dolorosa, the Church of the Nativity, the Cenacle, the Garden of Gethsemane, the Mount of Olives and 38 churches.

Jerusalem is also holy for Islam: "All Islamic traditions and sacred writings point to the unmistakable fact that Jerusalem is holy for all Moslems, second only in holiness to Mecca and Medina. It is the *gibla* (direction of prayer) and the third of the sacred cities."[1] The name of Jerusalem in Arabic is *Al-Qods,* which means "The Holy".

On the site of the Haram Al-Sharif in the Old City of Jerusalem stand two famous Islamic sanctuaries: the Mosque of the Dome of the Rock which was built in the seventh century, and the Mosque of Al-Aqsa, meaning "the farthest," which was built in the eighth century on the place associated by Islamic tradition with "the farthest mosque" mentioned in the Koran (*surah* xvii:1)[2] In addition to these two historic mosques, there exist 34 other mosques in Jerusalem, 27 of which are located in the Old City and the others outside the walls.

To Judaism, Jerusalem has been a holy city since the building of the Temple of Solomon. This temple, completed in 962 B.C., was destroyed by the Babylonians in 587 B.C. A second temple was built around 515 B.C. after the return of the Jews from captivity, but was again destroyed by the Macedonians in 170 B.C. It was reconstructed in Herod's time only to be destroyed for a third time by the Romans following the Jewish insurrection in 70 C.E. Today the most important Jewish sanctuary in Jerusalem is the Wailing Wall which the Jews consider to be the remnant of the Western Wall of Herod's Temple.

The significance of Jerusalem, however, does not lie merely in the holy places and sanctuaries of the three great religions. In addition, all three have a vital interest in preserving the living presence of the adherents to their faith in the Holy City.

Jerusalem has been the scene of many dramatic events and the cause of many wars during the 38 centuries of its known existence. It has suffered more than 20 sieges, changed hands more than 25 times, was destroyed 17 times, and its inhabitants were massacred on several occasions. The last act in the drama of Jerusalem occurred in our lifetime. Zionist Jews, who had come to Palestine as immigrants during the British mandate, established the State of Israel in 1948, seized Jerusalem and displaced and dispossessed most of its original inhabitants.

THE FOUNDING OF JERUSALEM

Jerusalem is one of the oldest cities in the world. According to Josephus, who wrote in the first century of our era, it was founded by the Canaanites, Josephus wrote:

> But he who first built it (Jerusalem) was a potent man among the Canaanites, and is in our tongue called Melchisedek, The Righteous King, for such he really was; on which account he was (there) the first priest of God, and first built a temple (there), and called the city Jerusalem, which was formerly called Salem.[3]

As Melchisedek was a contemporary of Abraham (*Genesis* 14:18), this would date the founding of Jerusalem in the 18th century B.C. Hence, the city was in existence several centuries before the arrival of the Israelites to the land of Canaan. In fact, the Jewish Encyclopedia mentions that in Hebrew annals "Jerusalem is expressly called a 'foreign city' not belonging to the Isrealites (**Judges** 19:21), and the Jebusites are said to have lived there for very many years together with the Benjamites."[4]

After taking Jerusalem around 1000 B.C., "David dwelt in the fort and called it the city of David" (2 *Samuel* 5:9). According to the classical custom of the time, a captured town was given the name of its conqueror.[5] The Bible, however, contains a reminder to the city's new occupiers of its non-Jewish origin:

> And say, thus saith the Lord God unto Jerusalem: Thy birth and Thy nativity is of the Land of Canaan; Thy father was an Amorite, and Thy mother an Hittite. (Ezekiel 16:3)

Without ascribing any particular date to the founding of Jerusalem, Father R. de Vaux, an eminent archaeologist, states that about 1800 to 1550 B.C., Jerusalem was one of several cities protected by ramparts which sprang up in Palestine.[6]

It seems necessary to stress the fact that Jerusalem was founded by the Canaanites long before its capture by David because some present-day Israeli politicians falsely claim that it was founded by the Jews. Thus, at the time of the capture of the Old City of Jerusalem in June 1967, Ygal Allon, then Israel's Deputy Prime Minister, was reported by the press to have said: "The world must reconcile itself to the fact that the city has at last returned to the nation that founded it and turned it into a Holy City" when, in fact, Jerusalem existed as a Canaanite sacred city for several hundred years before the Isrealites set foot in Palestine.

The fact that Jerusalem existed long before the arrival of the Israelites is further borne out by its vassalage at a period of its history to the pharoahs of Egypt. The Tell El–Amarna Tablets, which were discovered in 1887 but date back to the 14th century B.C., embody appeals made to the pharoah of Egypt by the king of the city—then called *Urusalim*—for assistance against invaders. In fact, Jerusalem was under the overlordship of the pharoahs between the 12th and the 15th centuries B.C.

Jerusalem was inhabited by the Jebusites, a Canaanite subgroup. It was one of the oldest and most illustrious royal cities in the country[7] and for some 800 years it remained a purely Canaanite city.

The influx of Jews to Palestine in general, and Jerusalem in particular, was partly a function of their persecution in Europe. In consequence of the persecution of the Jews in Western Europe and their expulsion from Spain (1492) and Portugal (1496), some of them sought refuge in Palestine and in other Mediterranean countries. As a result, some Jews came to live in Jerusalem. According to Rappoport, there were 70 Jewish families in Jerusalem in 1488, 200 families in 1495 and 1,500 families in 1521.[8]

In the nineteenth century, the Jewish population of Jerusalem began to increase. According to the Reverend Edward Robinson, professor of Biblical literature at Union Theological Seminary in New York, who visited Jerusalem in 1838, the population of the city was 11,000, made up of the following:

Muslims	4,500
Christians	3,500
Jews	3,000
TOTAL	11,000

Following the Russian pogroms of 1881 and 1882, a number of Jews emigrated to Palestine and settled in Tiberias, Safed and Jerusalem. In 1917 the Jewish population of Jerusalem numbered 30,000.[9] The Jewish immigration permitted by the British government during the mandate materially affected the demographic situation in Jerusalem. In 1922, according to the census of the government of Palestine, the Jewish population of Jerusalem reached 33,971 out of a total population of 62,578 in the urban area of Jerusalem. The 1931 census shows an increase of the Jewish population to 51,222 out of a total population of 90,503 within the municipal limits of the city. At the end of 1946 the Jewish population of the City of Jerusalem, envisaged by the U.N. as *corpus separatum,* had risen to 99,690 compared with 105,540 non–Jews.

Throughout history there has always been one city of Jerusalem, but as a result of demographic and political developments new appellations were coined to describe three different urban areas of the city. These new appellations were: the Old City, Modern Jerusalem and *corpus separtum* of the City of Jerusalem. An explanation of these new appellations is necessary for a proper understanding of the troubles of Jerusalem.

Jerusalem has at all times been a walled city. The present massive walls of the Old City were built in 1542 by Suleiman the Magnificent, the Ottoman Sultan. In the Old City are found the Holy Sepulchre and other holy places of Christianity. Within the Old City are also found the two famous mosques in an area called Haram Al–Sharif by the Muslims and Temple Mount by the Jews who consider it the site of the Temple of Solomon.

Until the 19th century the inhabitants of Jerusalem lived in the Old City and no buildings or habitations existed outside its ramparts. The gates of the city were locked every day in the evening not to be opened until the following morning. As the population of the city increased in the latter half of the 19th century, new residential quarters were built outside its walls by Arabs and Jews. Two appellations then came into use: the "Old City" to describe the walled city, and "Modern Jerusalem" or the "New City" to describe the new residential quarters which grew up outside the walls. Following the war of 1948, during which the Jews occupied most of the area of Modern Jerusalem and Jordan occupied the Old City, including a small section of Modern Jerusalem lying to the east and to the north, new appellations were created, such as "Jewish Jerusalem" and "Arab Jerusalem" to indicate the sectors occupied respectively by the Jews and the Arabs.

It seems necessary to emphasize that while the Old City, with the exception of its old Jewish quarter, is entirely Arab and is inhabited by both Christians and Muslims, Modern Jerusalem was, until its seizure by Jewish forces in May 1848, a mixed urban area comprising several residential quarters, inhabited by Christians, Muslims and Jews. In fact, Modern Jerusalem comprises fifteen Arab residential quarters in which lived the majority of the Christian and Muslim inhabitants of Jerusalem. Twelve out of these fifteen residential quarters, namely, Katamon, Talbieh, Ratisbonne, Greek and German colonies, Musrarah, Nebi Daoud, Mamillah, Deir Abu Tor, Upper and Lower Bakaa and Sheikh Jarrah were seized by Israel in 1948 and were emptied of their Arab inhabitants.

Regarding land ownership in the urban area of Jerusalem in 1948, Sami Hadawi, a former government officer of the Department of Land Settlements, calculated on the basis of survey maps and taxation records the following information:[10] In the Old City the Jews own five dunoms out of 800.

In Modern Jerusalem, or the New City, land ownership is as follows:

Arab-owned	40.00 percent
Jewish-owned	26.12
Others (Christian communities)	13.86
Government and municipal	2.90
Roads and railways	17.12

Jewish land ownership outside the urban area was also insignificant. The official statistics of the government of Palestine indicate that in 1946 the percentage of Jewish land ownership in the sub-district of Jerusalem did not exceed two percent (UN Doc, A/AC. 14/32, p. 293.)[11]

To the preceding appellations, one must add a third one: the *corpus separatum* of the city of Jerusalem. This new appellation is derived from Resolution 181 of the General Assembly of November 29, 1947 which called for the partition of Palestine into Arab and Jewish States and for the creation of a *corpus separatum* for the City of Jerusalem to be subject to a special international regime administered by the UN. The resolution also provided that the City should be demilitarized, its neutrality should be declared, and no paramilitary formations or activities should be permitted within its borders.

The city of Jerusalem was delineated by the resolution to include the municipal boundaries of Jerusalem as they existed at the time plus the surrounding villages and towns, the most eastern of which was Abu Dis, the most southern, Bethlehem, the most western, Ein Karem, and the most northern Shu'fat. By extending the area of the internationalized zone beyond municipal limits, the General Assembly sought to include certain holy places and sites, namely Bethlehem, Bethany, and Ein Karem, birthplace of John the Baptist.

The population of the *corpus separatum* of the city of Jerusalem as it stood in 1946 is shown in the following table which was then prepared for the United Nations:

Muslims	60,560
Christians	44,850
Others	130
Total of Arabs and Others	105,540
Jews	99,690
TOTAL	205,230[12]

This was the position with regard to population and land ownership in Jerusalem in May 1948 when the British mandate came to an end and the war erupted between the new State of Israel and the neighbouring Arab states.

CHANGING THE CITY'S REALITIES

Israel's occupation of Jerusalem has changed the realities as they existed before 1948. Violations of human rights were committed, as well as breaches of the Geneva Convention relative to the Protection of Civilian Persons in Time of War of August 12, 1949.

In 1948, as we have seen, Israel seized Modern Jerusalem, including 12 of its 15 wholly Arab residential quarters. The plan to seize Jerusalem was put into effect before the withdrawal of the Mandatory. In fact, all the Western part of the *corpus separatum* and some parts of the modern section of Jerusalem were seized by Jewish forces while British forces and the British High Commissioner were still present in Jerusalem. The Arab residential quarters of Modern Jerusalem, namely Katamon and Sheikh Jarrah, were seized and occupied by Jewish forces on April 25 and 30 respectively. Other Arab quarters of Modern Jerusalem were overrun by Jewish forces on May 14 and 15. Thus, the Jews had completed the occupation of most of Modern Jerusalem before the day on which war broke out between Israel and the Arab states.

Pablo de Azcarate, Secretary of the United Nations Consular Truce Commission, has described events in Jerusalem on May 14. The British High Commissioner left Jerusalem on the morning of that day by air for Haifa at which time he sailed home. He was followed by British troops so that at about two o'clock in the afternoon not a single British soldier remained in Jerusalem. Here is the story as told by Pablo de Azcarate:

> Hardly had the last English soldier disappeared than the Jews launched their offensive, consolidating their possession of Katamon which they occupied two weeks before and seizing the German Colony and the other southern districts of Jerusalem. The last remaining Arabs were liquidated, and from henceforth, the Jews were absolute masters of the southern part of the city.[13]

The Arab quarters of Modern Jerusalem were completely undefended and their inhabitants had either fled or were killed. In those quarters where the Jews encountered resistance, such as in Musrarah, the Arab residents were terrorized by the Haganah which had been proclaimed the official army of the new State of Israel.

Undeterred by the United Nations internationalization of the city of Jerusalem which was rejected both by Israel which occupied Modern Jerusalem and by Jordan which occupied its Old City, Israel proceeded to annex Modern Jerusalem. On August 12, 1948 it proclaimed that the area it had occupied in Jerusalem was "Israeli–occupied territory" subject to military occupation. Then in February 1949 military rule was abolished and the government declared that such areas should no longer be considered as occupied territory. Thereupon several ministries were moved from Tel Aviv to Jerusalem and in December 1949 the government itself moved to Jerusalem, leaving in Tel Aviv three ministries, including the Ministry of Foreign Affairs. Immediately after, pressure developed to declare Jerusalem the capital of the State of Israel but the Knesset preferred to adopt a resolution on January 23, 1950 which proclaimed that Jerusalem has always been the capital of Israel. Since then Isreal has treated Modern Jerusalem as an integral part of its territory.

Israel seized and confiscated all property—lands, homes, businesses—that belonged to the Palestinians who fled. The seizure was carried out under the Absentee Property Regulations (1948) and the confiscation was consummated by the Absentee Property Law (1950). This last enactment purported to authorize the so-called Custodian of Absentee Property to sell "absentee" property—as Arab refugee property was described—at its "official value." This formula was nothing but a thin disguise for its confiscation at a nominal consideration. All the Arab residential quarters of Modern Jerusalem were thus "sold" to the new Jewish settlers. The magnitude of this plunder of Arab refugee property can be appreciated when it is realized that the Arabs had owned the greater part of the properties in Modern Jerusalem.

The United Nations Conciliation Commission/Palestine asked Israel to abrogate the Absentee Property legislation and to suspend all measures of requisition and occupation of Arab homes and lands. But Israel refused. In 1950, the General Assembly by its Resolution 394 (V) directed the Conciliation Commission "to continue negotiations with the parties concerned regarding measures for the protection of the rights, property and interests of the refugees."

The second chain of changes regarding the city came less than two decades later. On June 5, 1967 Israel went to war against Egypt, Syria and Jordan. In a lightning surprise attack, Israeli annexed the Gaza Strip, the Sinai Desert, the Golan region, the Old City of Jerusalem and the West Bank. Despite the issue of several cease–fire orders by the Security Council, Israel pursued its attacks until it achieved its territorial objectives. On the evening of June 7 the Old City of Jerusalem, as well as all the rest of Palestine, was in Israeli hands.

Although on the first day of the war, Israel's prime minister, Levi Eshkol, proclaimed that Israel had no territorial claims and Israel's defence minister, Moshe Dayan, declared that "we have no aim of territorial conquest," Israel proceeded with the annexation of the Old City soon after its capture. On June 27, 1967, it enacted the *Law and Administration Ordinance* (Amendment No. 11) which provided that the law, jurisdiction and administration of the state should apply in any area designated by the government by order. On the following day the Israeli Government issued an order which declared that an area comprising the Old City of Jerusalem and some adjacent territory shall be subject to the law, jurisdiction and administration of Israel. On the same day the area of the Municipal Corporation of Jerusalem was enlarged to include the annexed area. This meant an expansion of the municipal area of Jerusalem from 40 to 100 square kilometers.

Compared with the *corpus separatum* of Jerusalem as delineated by the United Nations in 1947, the expanded municipal area remained approximately the same at the east and west, but was extended to the north to include Kalandia airport, and was cut back in the south to exclude the three Arab towns of Bethlehem, Beit Jala and Beit Sahur. In effect, Israel annexed the entirety of the *corpus separatum* of Jerusalem as defined by the United Nations in 1947 to the exclusion of the three above-mentioned towns.

Since then Jerusalem and its surrounding area have been severed politically, administratively and economically from the other territories occupied in June 1967. This has since been treated as Israeli territory, except with regard to the national status of the inhabitants who have remained Jordanian citizens. The action of Israel, described as "integration," was officially declared to be "irrevocable" and "not negotiable."

On March 22, 1979 the Security Council adopted Resolution 446 which, *inter alia,* called upon Israel to rescind its actions and not to transfer its civilian population into the occupied territories. The resolution also charged the president of the Security Council to appoint a commission to examine the situation with regard to settlements in the Arab territories occupied since 1967, including Jerusalem. In its report dated July 12, 1979 (S/13450), the commission mentions that 17 settlements were established in and around Jerusalem. In the Old City, 320 housing units were established for Jews, 160 Arab houses destroyed, 600 homes expropriated and 6,500 Arab residents evicted.

It appears from the commission's report that Jewish settlement in and around Jerusalem was more intensive than in other occupied areas. The commission states that the number of settlers in Jerusalem and the West Bank had reached 90,000. The commission gives no breakdown of this figure, but it seems that the largest number of those 90,000 settlers are found in the Jerusalem area.

The commission observed in paragraph 231 of its report that the Arab inhabitants still living in those territories, particularly in Jerusalem and the West Bank, are subjected to continuous pressure to emigrate in order to make room for new Jewish settlers who, by contrast, are encouraged to come to the area.

Israel has followed a process of the judaization of Jerusalem which has resulted in the tripling of the Jewish population there, which has risen from 100,000 in 1948 to 300,000 in 1985, compared with 100,000 Arabs presently living in the city. It may be noted that most of the city's original Christian and Muslim inhabitants have been permanently displaced and were not allowed to return and that the number of Christian inhabitants has dwindled from 25 percent to 4 percent of the total population of the city.

It is obvious that Israel's actions in Jerusalem since 1948 have sought and succeeded in the alteration of dominion, demography and land ownership with the object of obliterating the Muslim and Christian character of the Holy City and exhuming the Jewish state which disappeared more than 25 centuries ago into the dust of history. The drawing of a curtain by Israel over the history of Palestine is noted by Father Joseph L. Ryan, who observes: "As a result of Zionist presentations, the impression is given that history of any consequence stopped in Palestine in the year 70 A.D. and only began again with the Zionist movement under Herzl.[14] This is confirmed by the "basic law" enacted by Israel in July 30, 1980, which proclaimed Jerusalem its eternal capital.

Israel's action in adopting the law proclaiming Jerusalem its eternal capital was censured in the strongest terms by the Security Council on August 20, 1980 in Resolution 478 which was adopted by 14 votes to zero with the United States abstaining. The Council declared that the enactment of the basic law on Jerusalem was a violation of international law and that all legislative and administrative measures and actions taken by Israel which have altered or purport to alter the character and status of the Holy City of Jerusalem and in particular, the basic law are null and void and must be rescinded forthwith. This resolution of the Security Council was one of a score of decisions adopted by the Security Council and the General Assembly since 1967 condemning Israel's actions on Jerusalem and declaring their nullity.

However, the repeated condemnations by the United Nations of Israel's actions in Jerusalem bore no fruit, and the process of judaization of the city has continued.

The reason for Israel's flaunting of the will and decisions of the international community is that it exploits the religious significance of Jerusalem to Judaism in order to achieve its political objectives. Although Jerusalem possesses an equally great religious significance to Islam and Christendom. Moreover, unlike the Christians and the Muslims, the Jews do not possess any actual holy places in Jerusalem. This was made quite clear by Chaim Weizmann, the author of the Balfour Declaration and the first president of Israel in his autobiography in which he asked himself the reason for opposition to Zionism by the Italians and the Vatican and why the issue of the Holy Places should arouse so much interest. To soothe fears, he wrote:

> *There were no Holy Places in Palestine to which the Jews laid actual physical claims—except perhaps, Rachel's tomb,[15] which was at no time a matter of controversy. The Wailing Wall we did not own, and never had owned since the destruction of the Temple. . . .[16]*

In 1931 an international commission appointed by the Mandatory, with the approval of the League of Nations, found that "the ownership of the Wall accures to the Muslims. . . . and that the pavement in front of the Wall, where the Jews perform their devotions, is also Muslim property."[17]

However, despite the admitted absence of any Jewish holy places in Jerusalem, Israel has not abandoned the ambition to recover what it considers to be the Temple Mount in the city.

Such a policy has encouraged collective as well as individual actions against Christian and Muslim holy places. It suffices to mention the holding of a prayer ceremony by the Chief Rabbi of the Israeli army in 1967 in the area of the Haram Al-Sharif; the arson committed on August 21, 1969 at the Mosque of Al–Aqsa; the arrest of two soldiers (in possession of explosives in 1980 in the Old City) who were charged by the authorities with the intention of blowing up churches and mosques in Jerusalem; the shooting by an Israeli soldier on April 11, 1982 of worshippers at the Mosque of the Dome of the Rock; the attempt made on March 10 to blow up with explosives the Mosque of the Dome of the Rock which was foiled by the Muslim guards of the Mosque; and the arrest in May 1984 of 25 Jews for terrorist attempts, including an attempt to blow up the Mosque of the Dome of the Rock.

The persons arrested are still awaiting trial, but some sections of the population support what they have done. The police investigation yielded the fact that the terrorists arrested had also planned to bomb the mosques from a helicopter, but abandoned the idea for fear that they might damage the Wailing Wall.

The dangerous and explosive situation created in Jerusalem as a result of Israel's occupation of the city which has encouraged the deeds of Israeli extremists calls for effective local and international action so that Jerusalem lives up to its name of the City of Peace.

TABLE 8.1
CHRONOLOGY OF JERUSALEM

		YEARS OF OCCUPATION
Canaanites	From around 1800 B.C. or earlier until the capture of the city by David in about 1000 B.C.	800
Israelites (with intermittent occupations of the city by the Egyptians, the Philistines, the Syrians and the Assyrians)	From 1000 B.C. to capture of the city by the Babylonians in 587 B.C. (destruction of Jerusalem and the Kingdom of Judah)	413
Babylonians	From 587 to 538 B.C.	50
Persians	From capture of the city by Cyrus to Greek conquest: 538 to 332 B.C.	206
Greeks	Alexander's conquest of the city to its emancipation by the Maccabees: 332 to 141 B.C.	191
Jews	Maccabean rule: 141 to 63 B.C.	78
Pagan Romans	Roman conquest of the city to fall of paganism: 63 B.C. to 323	386
Christians	From Constantine to Persian conquest: 323 to 614	291
Persians	Persian rule: 614 to 628	14
Christians	Reconquest of the city by Byzantines: 628 to 638	10
Arabs	Conquest by the Moslem Arabs: 638 to 1072	434
Turks	Seizure of the city by the Turks: 1072 to 1092	20
Arabs	Reconquest of the city by the Arabs: 1092 to 1099	7
Christians	Latin Kingdom of Jerusalem: 1099 to 1187	88

TABLE 8.1 (cont'd)
CHRONOLOGY OF JERUSALEM

		YEARS OF OCCUPATION
Arabs	Reconquest of the city by the Arabs: 1187 to 1229	42
Christians	City ceded by treaty for 10 years to Frederick II: 1229 to 1239	10
Arabs	Revived Arab rule: 1239 to 1517	278
Turks	Occupation by the Ottoman Turks: 1517 to 1831	314
Arabs	Occupation of Jerusalem by Mohammed Ali and Egyptian rule from 1831 to 1841	10
Turks	Restoration of Turkish rule: 1841 to 1917	76
Christians	British occupation and mandate: 1917 to 1948	31
Israelis and Arabs	Modern Jerusalem occupied by Israel and Old City occupied by Jordan: 1948 to 1967	19
Israelis	Capture of Old City by Israel in 1967	

NOTES

1. H.S. Karmi, "How Holy is Palestine to the Muslims?", in *Islamic Quarterly*. Vol. 14, no. 2, 1970, p. 69.

2. Surah xvii:1 states: "Glory to (God) Who did take His Servant for a Journey by night from the Sacred Mosque to the Farthest Mosque, whose precincts We did bless, in order that We might show him some of Our Signs: for He is the One who heareth and seeth (all things)."

3. Josephus Favius, *The Great Jewish-Roman War 66–70 A.D.* (vi. 10). Gloucester, MA: 1970, p. 250.

4. *Jewish Encyclopedia*, Vol. VII, p. 120.

5. Michel Join-Lambert, *Jerusalem*. London: Elek Books, 1958, p. 55.

6. R.G.Vaux, *Histoire Ancienne d'Israel*. Paris: Gabalda, 1971, p. 72.

7. A. Lods (trans.), *Israel*. Paris: Albin Michel, 1930, p. 419.

8. A.S. Rappoport. *Histoire de la Palestine*. Paris: Payot, 1932, p. 210.

9. Ronald Storrs, *Orientations*. London: Nicholson and Watson, 1945, p. 280.

10. Sami Hadawi, *Palestine, Loss of a Heritage*. San Antonio, TX: Naylor, 1963, p. 141.

11. United Nations Document A/AC, 14/32, p. 293.

12. Official records of the second session of the General Assembly, Ad Hoc Committee on the Palestine Question, p. 304.

13. Pablo de Azcarate, *Mission in Palestine 1948–1952*. Washington, DC: Middle East Institute, 1966, p. 43.

14. O. Kelly Ingram, ed., *Jerusalem*. Triangle Friends of the Middle East, Durham, North Carolina, 1978, p. 26.

15. Rachel's tomb is located outside Jerusalem on the road to Bethlehem.

16. Chaim Weizmann, *Autobiography*. London: Hamish Hamilton, 1949, p. 355.

17. See quotations from the Commission's report by Muhammad H. El-Farra, "The UN and Palestine Question," The Arab-Israeli Conflict, Vol. II, Princeton University, 1974, p. 515.

Chapter 9

Islamic Jerusalem as Archetype of a Harmonious Urban Environment

Abdullah Schleifer

When we speak of Islamic Jerusalem, of *Al-Quds* (The Holy) as it is most commonly known today in Arabic, we allude to a spiritual as well as a physical geography that has been visibly recognizable as such for more than 1000 years. We speak now of the Old City or the Walled City which Creswell (who devoted a lifetime to the study of Muslim architecture) described as the most perfectly preserved example of a medieval Islamic city, and not, in general, of the largely Arab-owned but semi-colonial-in-spirit New City which spread along the Western rim of the city in the late nineteenth century and fell to the Israelis in the 1948 War.

But Islamic Jerusalem in the old Arab chronicles and geographical dictionaries also incorporates all of those sites of profound sacred import to the Islamic tradition which range from just beyond the shadows of the city's walls—such as the tomb of Nebi Daoud (the Prophet-King David) or the Mount of Olives where Nebi Isa (Jesus) ascended directly to Heaven—or that rest in distant sight of the Holy City's dominating skyline such as the tomb of Nebi Samwel (the Prophet Samuel.)[1]

Jerusalem is the holiest of the holy in what God describes, in the Quran, as the Holy Land. *(Quran 5:21—surah al-Ma'ida,* the surah which means "The Table Spread" and which seems to allude to the Last Supper.)

This spiritual conception of space is reflected in one of the oldest terms the Muslims use for Jerusalem—*al-Bait al-Maqdis*. Derived from Quranic usage for purity and for the glorification of Allah's name, it is used interchangeably to mean the Holy House or Temple (better known now as *Haram ash Sherif*—the Noble Sanctuary), the Holy City and even the Holy Land in a similar manner to the use of *Bait al Haram* to describe, according to context, the Kaaba in Mekka, the sanctuary (haram) that encloses the Kabba, Mekka itself and its outlying districts.

It is my intention to briefly consider five factors that suggest Islamic Jerusalem as the archetypal Middle Eastern city of a harmonious environment.

The first is the centrality of Islamic Jerusalem as a model for the overwhelmingly Muslim Middle East. The reverence with which this city is held in the religious consciousness of the Muslims is a reflection of the same spiritual centrality that prompted the Prophet Muhammad in a well known hadith (canonic tradition) to designate Jerusalem along with Mecca and Medina as the three centers of equal merit to which the faithful could "journey" for prayer and pilgrimage.[2] It is of such centrality as to have been the first direction *(qibla)* of Muslim prayer and to be revered as such in the religious consciousness of the Muslim. Al-Yaqut devotes as many pages of his remarkable thirteenth century geographical dictionary to Jerusalem as he does to Mecca and Medina and an entire sub-division of Arabic literature—the *fada'il* books, devoted to extoling the spiritual virtues of Jerusalem—flourished from at least the ninth century to the eighteenth, inspiring as well as guiding the millions of Muslims who have made *zi'yar'ah* (formal visits) to the Holy City.[3]

As for the viability of that claim, whoever has observed the proliferation of Islamic calendars and other popular artifacts that feature pictures of the Dome of the Rock from one end of the Muslim world to the other, or whoever recalls that President Sadat justified his peace initiative as a bold attempt to rescue Islamic Jerusalem and lost his life partly because he had clearly failed to do so, or whoever remembers that Iranian military morale has been largely sustained despite truly punishing losses by the image of Iraq as an alleged barrier on the road to Jerusalem, cannot doubt that the Holy City retains its centrality in Muslim religious consciousness.

Yet in the particularities of its claim to archetype, Islamic Jerusalem in contrast to Mecca and Medina—cities of the homogeneric Arabian homeland—stands as a model for much of the Middle East that traditionally contains a mosaic of religious, ethnic and linguistic communities within the unifying field of a broadly defined Islamic civilization: a civilization that drew its characteristic qualities as a social order from the overwhelmingly Muslim character of the population without restricting participation in that civilization to Muslims.

Secondly, Jerusalem is central to the Muslim consciousness of Islam as both heir and seal of Semitic monotheism—of an Islam perceived of simultaneously as the primordial religion that incorporates all the prophetic figures of the Bible as primordial Muslims, as well as an Islam perceived of as a community of believers specific in time and bound by its acknowledgment of Muhammad as the final Prophet.

Adam and Lot, Abraham, Isaac and Jacob, David and Solomon, Jesus, Mary, John and Zakariya—all are associated in one manner or another by Quran and hadith with Jerusalem. "All the prophets have prayed in Jerusalem" is a saying attributed to Muhammad, and the additional popular traditional accounts collected in the "Virtues of Jerusalem" literature elaborate upon and extend the associations which are further reinforced in the prayers of the Muslim pilgrim in Jerusalem as he or she visits the many sites identified with the earlier prophets.

The most direct link between this primordial Islam and the Islam that emerged in seventh century Arabia is effected by the Prophet Muhammad's miraculous journey by night to Jerusalem and his ascension there to Heaven.

The Quranic text, according to its meaning in English, reads: "Glory to God Who carried His servant for a journey by night, from the Sacred Mosque (Masjid al Haram) to the Farthest Mosque (Masjid al Aqsa) whose precients We did bless—in order that We might show him some of Our signs." (*Quran* XVII:1)

The interpretation of this verse and the explanation of this miraculous experience are to be found in the classical commentaries on the Quran, in the canonic collections of hadith and in the nearly contemporary biographies of the Prophet. Escorted by the Angel Gabriel and mounted on a mysterious winged animal called al-Buraq, the Prophet was carried by night from Mecca to Jerusalem. There on the site of the Temple—the farthest mosque—Muhammad is met by the prophets who preceded him (most notably by Abraham, Moses and Jesus); there he leads the preceding prophets in prayer and there he receives additional Revelation. Then, from the same sacred rock prefigured in centuries of Jerusalem's sacred history, the Prophet ascended to Heaven by a ladder of light and was led by stages to the seventh heaven to experience the Beatific Vision. The descent and return to Mecca were accomplished during the same night, before dawn, but the entire experience took but a few minutes of prosaic or worldly time.

It is instructive that the Quranic allusion to this miraculous link between primordial Islam and the Islam of seventh century Arabia is the first *ayat* (verse) of the 17th *sura* that has been titled either *al-Isra*—"the journey" or *"Bani Isra'il*—the tribe of Israel.

For the Arabian army advancing upon Jerusalem only a few years after the death of the Prophet, as well as for the many thousands of Palestinian Jews and Judeo-Christians in the neighboring countryside who rallied to their banner, the coming of Islam was the fulfillment of biblical prophecy.[4] From that perspective, the clearing of the desolate temple site by the Khalifa Omar, the re-institution of regular prayer in this *Haram el Sherif* and its ongoing beautification and visible sanctity in the years that follow under the Ommayid dynasty are all signs of the Temple Rebuilt, and interpreted as such in the earliest chronicle, that of the eighth century Byzantine historian Theophanes.[5]

The earliest known Jewish apocalyptic texts that relate the coming of Islam indicate that even those Palestinian Jews who did not embrace Islam appear to have welcomed it as the vehicle of their redemption prophesized in *Isaiah* XXI:13, and the texts acknowledge in the literary form of apocalyptic prophecy that "some of Israel" will embrace "the religion of Ishmael."[6] More than two centuries later, the Rabbi Saadia Ha'Goan rails against the "Jewish Ishmaelites" among the Muslims of Jerusalem, in his *Responsa*.[7]

The third factor is the centrality of Jerusalem for Muslim spirituality or mysticism. Salman al Farsi, one of the Prophet's companions most closely associated with the transmission of the spiritual path *(tariqa)*, is buried in Jerusalem as is our Lady Rabia al Adawiya al Basra, one of the great saints *(awliya)* of the earliest generations. Sufyan al-Thawri, Ibrahim Adham, Bayazid Bistami, and Abu'l Najib al-Suhrawardi are among the many Sufis drawn to Jerusalem in earliest centuries of Islam and their regard is echoed in the spiritual fever that informs the developing "Virtues of Jerusalem" literature—a literature largely developed by Sufis including such prominent figures as the sixteenth century Egyptian, Sha'rani and the eighteenth century Syrian, Abdul Ghani al Nabulsi. Ghazali journeyed to Jerusalem when he abandoned his public life as a reknowned scholar for the spiritual path, and it was in Jerusalem that he began his opus, the *Ihya ulum al-Din* which inspired an ethical renewal of medieval Islam.

To understand this we must consider that there are two types of relationships between God and man in Islam. The first (the affirmation of which is the basis of salvation for the Muslim) involves the descent from a transcendent God to man via the Prophet as passive vehicle of the final Revelation. This relationship which is profoundly transcendental is acknowledged in obligatory worship, structured around the ritual recitation of the Quran. The symbol of this relationship is the Kabba, or Mecca—where Revelation begins and which serves as the qibla or direction of worship.

The other relationship is ascendant, the spiritual aspiration of the pietist to journey in this life towards an Omnipresent God—to a God Who says He is closer to us than our own jugular vein. The inescapable metaphor for that journeying on a spiritual path is the Prophet's *isra wa'l miraj*— the miraculous journey to Jerusalem, the ascension to Heaven and the Beatific Vision.

Thus, Mecca and Jerusalem are the two poles. Mediating them is the Prophet and his adopted city Medina. I speak here of the Prophet in the present tense, in order to express the vivid way his light still illuminates the consciousness of millions of practicing Muslims. In Medina he implements a divinely ordained social order on the basis of the sacred law *(shari'a)* contained within Revelation. And there he also serves as source and instructor for the superagatory spiritual practices also contained within Revelation which will be elaborated upon as the methodology of *tasawwuf,* Islamic mysticism.

Ibn Arabi, the thirteenth century master, suggests a similar but far more profound polarity in his poem and commentary *Tarjuman al-Ashwaq*—Jerusalem as the station of Holiness and Purity in a spiritual geography wherein Mecca is the perfect heart which contains the Truth and Medina is the place where the spiritual adept seeks the ability to see God in everything.[8]

It is in the unitary nature of Islam that these poles mediated by the Prophet are inseparable. The spiritual malaise reflected in the moral as well as physical weakness of the secularized Muslim world on the one hand, or the lack of moral equilibrium, the lack of generosity and the extremism manifest in much of the contemporary Islamic Revival on the other hand, reflects a contemporary breakdown of that unitary nature.

In the first case, secularized elites of Muslim societies tolerate personal spiritual aspiration within their societies but deny themselves and their societies the moral support that would be available by legitimatizing their political authority by acknowledging the higher authority of sacred law. In the second case, a militant social-religious solidarity denies priority to the traditional practice of a personal spiritual purification which must always play a moderating role, if only by virtue—to mix metaphors—that the man who is aware that all men live in glass houses will hesitate to throw the first stone.

To celebrate the Prophet's birthday or the birthday of any of his family or his saintly followers is to celebrate the Prophet's journey to Jerusalem and his ascension to Heaven and to meditate upon this. There is a wonderful Palestinian custom, still preserved in Jerusalem and the West Bank, that whenever there is some special goodness in our life—the birth of a child, his memorization of the first subdivision of the Quran, his graduation, an important promotion—it is at precisely that moment that is the Prophet's birthday *(mulid al Nebi)*, and the recitation in his honor vividly recalls his miraculous journey to Jerusalem.

Jerusalem, the object of Islamic militance by its very existence as the shadow of a celestial city and the citadel of Islamic spirituality, must be a reminder to the militant of traditional Islamic priorities.

Jerusalem, as indicated in the introduction, is also a symbol of the Islamic city as a "pluralist" civilization. Twice conquered in the historically significant sense by Muslim armies, its non-Muslim native inhabitants were in both cases allowed to remain and guaranteed their lives, property and religious practices. The terms of the second conquest by Sultan Salah-ad-Din so epitomized chivalry that he was immortalized in European literature.

Certainly the contemporary Muslim world, particularly where Muslim values are theoretically again in ascendency, would benefit much from this historic sense of Islamic Jerusalem as the political stage where was made manifest such Islamic virtues as generosity, magnanimity and nobility. But the existence of "pluralism" in Islamic civilization has to do with more than the magnanimity of individual rulers. All that the khalifa Omar conceded to the Byzantine Patriarch at the gate into Jerusalem was guaranteed by sacred law, except, interestingly, the one provision the Muslims ultimately did not abide by, in fact, thoroughly violated. That was the Patriarch's insistence that the Byzantine ban on Jews living in Jerusalem be maintained by the Muslims.

And while the Jewish population never numbered more than a few thousand and often far less, up until the early nineteenth century Jerusalem was to share with Safed the reputation as the great center of Sephardic mystical thought, particularly in the first century of Ottoman rule.

Since Muslim cities could not develop their own autonomous law by virtue of sacred quality and the cosmopolitan way in which jurisprudence developed (which somehow disturbed several London SOAS scholars meeting to discuss the Islamic City a number of years ago), those same legal rights were acknowledged to a greater or lesser degree throughout the Muslim world, and in the Jerusalem region as in Syria, it is only in the mid-nineteenth century after several decades of subversion of the primacy of Islamic law and the local Muslim economy under the guise of modernization as well as economic and legal capitulations to the West that we read of significant communal attacks against non-Muslim minorities, tragically self-identified as the beneficiaries of the semi-colonial forces dismantling the Islamic political economy.

When one reads the accounts of travelers to the Holy City one realizes that most of the sectarian quarrels that the travelers complain about occured within the broadly defined religious communities and not between one community and another. This also suggests that, given the sensitivity inescapably associated with holy sites, there was a certain providential factor at work in the particular harmony that Islamic Jerusalem experienced—a harmony based upon the providentially complementary quality of the traditional, orthodox sensibilities that prevailed until fairly recently in all three religious communities.

The Christian communities have no shrines from which they are excluded on the Haram el-Sherif, nor do they acknowledge the Haram but as that site of desolation prophecized by Jesus; the very desolation in which the Muslims found it. And at least as late as the summer of 1968 when I left Jerusalem the Chief Rabbis of Israel were still insisting that observant Jews not enter the Haram area.

It is providential that all three orthodox religious communities, one in possession of the Haram, one indifferent to its contemporary status and one in a profoundly self-perceived exile have awaited in their respective places the coming of the Messiah, or, in the case of the Muslims and the Christians, for his second coming.

The veneration with which orthodox Muslims again providentially view the prophets of both Old and New Testament assured in principle that no shrines would be desecrated and frequently Muslim notables were called upon to mediate inter-Christian disputes over access and control of Christian shrines.

To avoid the possibility of encroachment, a status quo convention evolved during Mamluk and Ottoman Islamic rule and was more or less honored by the British Mandate authorities—a convention based upon extended and recognized ownership and usages of the shrines. Since, at the time of the Mamluks and the first centuries of Ottoman rule, there were no secular, much less religious, Jewish nationalist parties to advance ownership claims even on the Wailing Wall, the status quo was primarily a way to protect Christian sects from encroaching upon each other or to protect them from Muslim encroachment.

Here too is both a model and a challenge to Middle Eastern harmony. Either all parties respect that status quo or risk perpetual religious war. The status quo was first torn to shreds in 1948. Since then, thousands, perhaps hundreds of thousands, of visitors to Israel have toured the memorial to the victims of the Holocaust without any sense that they were desecrating the site of a Sufi prayer hall and monastery, or have visited the synagogue of King David's tomb without quite grasping that they were desecrating, with their shoes, the mosque of Nebi Daoud.

Since 1967 the situation has still worsened. The shrine of the Moroccan Saint, Shu'aib Abu Madyan (whose grandfather Sidi Abu Madyan was one of the great *muhaditheen* and Sufi guides of the twelfth century) along with an entire quarter surrounding the shrine, the Magharaba quarter, was demolished by Israeli bulldozers a few days after the fall of the city. Within a year the prayer hall of the Abu Saud family adjacent to the quarter was also demolished. There have been repeated and increasingly aggressive intrusions onto the Haram ash Sherif by Israeli Temple Revivalists, and at the Haram Ibrahim (the tomb of the prophet Abraham) a sister sanctuary in the West Bank city of Hebron to the *Haram ash Sherif,* Jewish worshippers and tourists now wear their shoes into the mosque. The choice between restoration of the status quo convention or a permanent invitation to *jihad* is a central issue that must be explored if the Middle East is ever to be a harmonious environment.

Finally I would suggest Jerusalem as an urbanist model of the Islamic city. All the hallmarks of the traditional Islamic city are present:

- The compressed, spinal-cord quality of the main suq.

- The centrality of the *Jumma'* mosque and the educational institutions and hospices clustered about it.

- A very refined sense of public, semi-public and private space in transition from suq to quarter to neighborhood, to compound to house to home.

- The outward homogenerity and modesty of residential architectual form that resulted naturally from local material use and conservatism reflecting the Islamic spirit of public conformity.

- Control of vehicular traffic—cars were barred from nearly all of the Old City, and in the most intimate residential areas even animal drawn carts were barred by street barriers to preserve the privacy and tranquility of the neighborhood.

- The City Wall defines limits. Limits are profoundly important to Muslim sensibility, which is also manifest in the twisting street patterns. The effect is aesthetically pleasing. Everyone can appreciate the new vistas of the twisting city street, but the cause I would suggest is in part metaphysical. Only Allah is Infinite and man in his creations does not imitate the Nature of the Creator. And within these finite limits the uses of space become more ingenious and more organically (rather than abstractly) creative—on site design by rule of eye rather than off-site scale.

- The homogenerity and inwardness of quarters. Before 1967 quarter life lost some of its brilliance for several reasons: first was the voluntary migration of Arab elites from the Old City to the New before 1948 or to the new Arab suburbs east of the Old City after 1948. This reduced the natural leadership role of old family elites within the quarters, and weakened the mutual patronage system or mutual aid exchanges of rich and poor members of extended families and client families which, along with other traditional factors such as *sharif* (honor) and the nobility of piety, did much to offset the differences in wealth. Secondly, the flight or expulsion of the old Jewish Quarter inhabitants in 1948—a tragedy, for if we exclude the 1000 or so fighting men who infiltrated there to the dismay of most of its apolitical elders, there were few Jewish communities in Palestine of longer standing and of more compatability within an Islamic urban civilization than the original and ultra-orthodox inhabitants of the pre-1948 Jewish Quarter. Indeed one of the many tragedies involved in the triumph of political Zionism is that it has so often been the peaceful, non-Zionist Jewish communities who paid the price of Zionist provacateurism. But that harmony did exist is reflected by the extraordinary number of Arab Jerusalemites over the age of 45 who had Jewish Jerusalemite milk-brothers. The relatively deserted Jewish Quarter quickly filled up with Palestinian refugees from the New City who were to be denied, like all 1948 Palestinian refugees, an opportunity to return to their homes. These refugees were made homeless for a second time in 1967 when they were expelled from the quarter as squatters.

- The Control of tourism. The Jordanian prohibition of nightclubs anywhere in the Arab city and the prohibition on the sale of alcohol at least within the Muslim quarter of the walled city did much to set a certain moral tone to tourism, far more than has been done in most other Muslim countries. But the city rather uniquely did its own psychic policing—the sacred quality of so much of Old City public life prior to 1967 so intimidated most visitors that even those without a religious sensibility found themselves adopting the demeanor of pilgrims.

There is a message here for any effort throughout the region at "medina" restoration. If we are concerned with preservation in its fullest sense, and authenticity, then the spiritual ambiance of the old cities must be as much our concern as their physical rescue and restoration. That means encouraging religious tourism and mini-malizing gratuitous tourism.

One of the virtues of a traditional quarter and the even smaller units of residence in a Muslim city (and one still encounters this in old Cairo *harats*) is a healthy suspicion of strangers, coupled with the redeeming ritual politeness and hospitality offered those with a legitimate reason to visit the quarter.

The very biblical exoticness of Islamic Jerusalem also provided a sufficient culture shock to discourage Western tour groups from wandering off a few main thoroughfares.

To more easily perceive the moral implications of a mindless, gratuitous tourism—a tourism of idle curiosity—I think of what would have been the implication of busloads of rich, oddly dressed Arabs driving through the residential neighborhood in a New York City suburb where I grew up, and their periodically piling out of their buses to just look around at the way we natives of Forest Hills lived.

I must confess that I now fear for Islamic Jerusalem what has happened to the traditional quarter of Jaffa—a brilliant restoration job and technically worthy of study—the physical frame of Jaffa's Islamic core brilliantly preserved, the inner structure rewired, reinforced and replastered. But the moral implications are, to say the least, deeply disturbing—the transfer of a once vital but morally conservative Arab quarter into a Muslim-*frie* bohemian artistic quarter and red light district. May God spare Jerusalem such a restoration.

But consider the implications of the changing nature of tourism to the Islamic city. Before 1967 the dominant motif for non-Muslim visitors was pilgrimage. After 1967 the dominant motif for thousands of Israeli visitors who poured in late Friday afternoon and evening and all day Saturday was to find a convenient place to violate the Jewish Sabbath. Is the destiny of Islamic Jerusalem to become the sin city of an intrinsically secular Israel?

- Preservation. In the total architectural integrity of the Old City up until 1967 and in what still remains should be inspiration for the old cities of the Middle East. Even the Arab suburbs to the East maintained a certain linkage to the Old City by building on a low-rise scale and using locally quarried stone at the very least for facing material. This sort of linkage must be stimulated and increased—the Old City preserved not only for its own sake but as a model of authentic values for the larger and newer quarters.

The major reason why Islamic Jerusalem in all of its quarters was so perfectly preserved prior to 1967 was because Jordanian law respected the principle of *waqf,* most adequately translated as "pious foundation."[10] There are two types of *waqf*—what we might classify as regular and family. Both share the following characteristics: that a property is endowed and made inalienable in the lifetime of its owner and its ownership returns to God, to be administered inevitably by religious scholars (and thus once a source of support and independence for this critically important mediating group—a position undermined by the nationalization of waqf administration in most of the Muslim world).

In the regular waqf, the proceeds of the revenues of the waqf (rents, proceeds of agricultural sales, etc.) are designated in perpetuity for purposes pleasing to God—for the benefit of mosques, schools, hospitals, hospices, the maintenance of scholars and assistance to the poor. Family waqf designates ones heirs as immediate beneficiaries but the proceeds are to revert to communal purpose upon extinction of the family line. In either case every document of foundation dedicating property as waqf lays down provisions that it is inalienable, and the document of foundation is irrevocable.

In Jerusalem, where almost all of the Old City was *waqf* and much of that private *waqf,* this had two effects. The first constituted a form of extended family social security. When rents of a family waqf are subdivided by 20 or 30 owners the returns are so minimal that the wealthier members of the family customarily leave their shares in for redivision among the poorer members.

But most important, the inalienability of the waqf property, family or regular, drastically reduces land speculation and the inevitable destruction of neighborhoods that result when restoration improves the land values of a community—as in the gentrification process in American and West European cities.

Jordan's respect for the family waqf, perhaps more than any other factor, enabled the city's architectural fabric to survive for, if the profit at stake is sufficient, private interest usually overwhelms zoning when no other restraints are at work.

That landscape has suffered drastic blows since 1967. Large areas of waqf, both regular and family, have been appropriated by the Israeli authorities and, as in the case of the Quarter, the properties have been demolished. At the same time, extensive archaeological excavation on waqf-administered land has been carried out along the southwestern and western wall of the Haram ash Sherif despite protests by the Awqaf authorities—excavations that the Muslim Council of Jerusalem fears threaten the safety of al-Aqsa Mosque which does not rest on a firm foundation like the Dome of the Rock and has been brought down before by earthquakes.

In 1968 I interviewed Rabbi Levenger shortly after he moved into Hebron at the head of what has become a significant force for the settlement of the occupied Arab territories. At that time Rabbi Levenger acknowledged that an earthquake leveling al Aqsa Mosque might be a divine sign for the recovery of the Haram and the rebuilding of the Temple.

Now it is true that Rabbi Levenger represents a relatively small sector within Israeli politics, but nearly 40 years ago former Prime Minister Begin and the present deputy Prime Minister represented relatively small sectors of political influence, sectors that were denounced at the time by the Israeli establishment as "fascist" and "terrorist."

To the Muslim world the success, until 1967 in Islamic Jerusalem of the waqf, both private and regular, in stabilizing urban land values merits serious study, re-evaluation and, I hope, revival. Since so much of the problem is a complex psychological one, I am tempted to suggest that, if and when the *waqf* is revived or rather de-nationalized, it be passed off as a chic adaptation of the Ford Foundation.

As for whoever would usurp a waqf and particularly the unambiguously "regular" characteristic of a waqf such as written and registered in 1320 by ash-Shaikh Abu Madyan, let his endowment speak for itself:

It is unlawful for any governor, official or tyrant to abolish this waqf or part of it, or change it . . . or endeavor to abolish it or part of it . . . He who does so or helps towards it . . . disobeys God and rebels against Him . . . and deserves His curse. Amen.

NOTES

1. Muk'dassi, the tenth century historian whose chronicle of Jerusalem is one of the earliest available manuscripts of its kind, wrote that "the territory of the Holy City is counted as all the country that lies within a radius of 40 miles from Jerusalem and includes many villages . . . This then is the land Allah—may He be exalted! —has called blessed. *(Quran* 21.71.)" Extensively quoted in Guy Le Strange, *Palestine Under the Moselms.* Beirut: Khayats Reprint, 1965, p. 86.

2. Al-Yaqut, *Mugam al-Buldan,* Vol 5, Beirut: Dar Sadir, 1984, p. 166.

3. See discussion of *fuda'il* by Walid Khalidi, introduction to Le Strange. Also A.L. Tibawi, Jerusalem. Beirut: I.P.S., 1969, and complete translation of two examples of *fuda'il* literature by Charles D. Matthews, *The Book of Arousing Souls,* New Haven: Yale University Press, 1949.

4. A.N. Pollak, "The Origin of the Country's Arabs," in *Molad.* 1967, pp. 297-303.

5. Le Strange, *op.cit.* p. 90.

6. Bernard Lewis, "An Apocalyptic Vision of Islamic History, "BSOAS XIII(1949-51) for translation of these texts.

7. Pollak, *op.cit.*

8. R.A. Nicholson, trans., *Tarjuman al-Ashwaq.* London: Theosophical Society Reprint, 1972, pp. 122-123.

9. Among his disciples are counted such spiritual luminaries as Abdul Qadr al Jilani, Muhyi-Din Ibn 'Arabi and Abu Hassan al Shazali.

10. My discussion of *waqf,* and in particular my quotation of the waqf of Abu Madyan, has been taken from A.L. Tibawi, *The Islamic Pious Foundations in Jerusalem.* London: Islamic Cultural Center, 1978, and his earlier work, *Jerusalem: Its Place in Islam and Arab History.* Beirut: I.P.S., 1969.

Chapter 10

Zion and the Two Jerusalems

Yitzhak Khayutman

THE URBAN DUALITY REPRESENTED BY JERUSALEM

The very name Jerusalem evokes in many people images not only of a city in this world but also of the world to come. My first thesis is that the name Yerushalayim-Jerusalem is very meaningful to our discussion, and is a predictor and an important key to world peace. It is indeed quite common to interpret the name Jerusalem as "The City of Peace," noting the similarity between the Semitic words for peace —Salaam and Shalom. Linguists may deny the past philological basis for this popular etymology and historians can easily show that few cities have known so much war and ongoing tension. Thus, there is an added tension because of the gulf between the "earthly" state of Jerusalem and its promised role as coded in her name.

In the prophecies and in the hundreds of mentions of Jerusalem in the Hebrew Bible she is called "Yeru, or Yoru, (there are no vowels in the original Hebrew Biblical text) Shalem." This name can be readily interpreted as literally meaning "(they) will teach Wholeness/Peace." This is the predictor I mentioned because the future tense is used. The Bible also gives clues of who the "they" are. It is surprising how few people have yet realized that the more direct connotation of the word Yerushalem is "Yerusha" which means "inheritance." So those who would teach wholeness and peace should inherit her. The story of Abraham's welcome to the city of Shalem ("Whole") (*Genesis* 14:18–19) and the Divine promise (*Genesis* 15:4–21) imply that Jerusalem is Abraham's inheritance to his children. But this also caused Jerusalem to become the scene for their family feuds.

It is just as surprising that while the original Biblical spelling is "Yerushalem," practically every Hebrew reader spells this name as

"Yerushalayim" which is in the dual form of Hebrew words, used for entities that come in pairs. So even the Israelis who vehemently swear in "the one Jerusalem" are meanwhile uttering the implication that there are two cities of Jerusalem. This is indeed paradoxical because the idea of wholeness and peace seem to be unitary, not dualistic. Wholeness is also associated with holiness, and Jerusalem's common predicate is "the Holy City" and in Arabic she is called "Al-Quds" —the sacred.

It is, however, clear that duality or multiplicity exist in this city. Between 1947 and 1967 Jerusalem was clearly divided by an international border with walls and barbed wire. The unification of Jerusalem in 1967 removed the visible borders, but there remains a marked division between the Arab and the Jewish cities which is often referred to as the division between Eastern and Western Jerusalem. Another physical distinction of two Jerusalems is between the walled Old City and the New City, both Arab and Jewish, built during the last 100 years.

We shall return to examine the spatial and ethnic division in some detail, but let us first realize that there is yet another dimension to the separation of the two cities of Jerusalem. There is a long tradition and many legends (Jewish, Christian, Moslem and others) that claim that, apart from the visible and material city "the Earthly Jerusalem," there is also a "Heavenly Jerusalem," a spiritual, (i.e., non-material) city which only the saintly few can perceive.

When we reflect on the idea of the two cities, physical and meta-physical, we may agree that perhaps all great cities have the two aspects, material and mental. The first aspect is the concrete assembly of material facilities and the resources committed to its construction, maintenance and operation. The second is the vast assembly of mental constructions which people hold concerning the city. We may thus speak of many cities as being dual cities—the one visible and physical and the other invisible and meta-physical or mythical. In terms of both the old Jewish Kabbalah and of a modern philosopher of science (Popper, 1980), these two cities belong to two distinct "worlds" of experience. These can be quite independent, yet they interpenetrate, and each influences the growth of the other. A known cybernetic model of urbanization (Forrester, 1969) makes much of the lag and possible disjunction between the image of the metropolis for migrants and the actual conditions they may encounter there.

The major demographic and cultural transformation of mankind in this century—the urbanization of mankind and the growth of world cities—is largely caused by this dual function of cities. The migrants from the villages to the slums of the burgeoning major cities of the developing countries may not improve their lot (e.g., Abu-Lughod, 1982 and her study of migrants to Cairo), though they get closer to being incorporated into the emerging global communications economy. The growing world cities provide major reference points and linkage nodes to the emerging "Planetary Brain" (Russel, 1983), and they are as yet the only such nodes in the developing countries.

It is noteworthy that an earlier account of planetary unification (de Chardin, 1955) already distinguished between two emerging layers of the planet, the urban "technosphere" and the cultural "noosphere," like the distinction between the human body and mind. This may mean that mankind may become unified not only by technology but also by a common mythos.

THE MYTHICAL JERUSALEM AS A DETERMINANT OF THE ACTUAL CITY

Jerusalem is possibly the epitome of this duality of the real and the mythical city. There is little doubt that de Chardin, a deeply Christian thinker, was influenced by Saint Augustine's theory of the establishment of the New Jerusalem, the City of God on Earth, and of the vision in the Book of Revelation at the end of the Christian Bible of the appearance of the Heavenly or the New Jerusalem. The part played by Jerusalem in contemporary global urbanization, together with her traditional symbolic role, and the disproportionate scale of the Arab-Israeli conflict in world politics all make Jerusalem not just a Middle Eastern city but an important world city and a major focus of the emerging Planetary Brain. My second thesis is that many of the current happenings in the concrete worldly Jerusalem can be understood only in light of the influence of the corresponding mythical city.

Jerusalem is so enmeshed in its myth that it is not even clear which came first, the real or the mythical city. Jewish legends claim that the Heavenly Jerusalem was created first as a model for subsequent earthly realizations. Common sense would, however, declare that since the Jews first had their glorious capital in Jerusalem and then were exiled from her, they must have developed the visions of restoration and the legends of the Heavenly Jerusalem only later. Whatever the case, the myth certainly preceded the modern Jerusalem. The massive investments made during these last decades in the growth of Jerusalem are understandable only in light of the immense Jewish emotional investment in the metaphysical Jerusalem over two millenia which culminated in a modern socio-political movement called "Zionism." Admittedly, this name, Zionism, means different and conflicting things for different people, but it literally means just

"Jerusalemism." The motto of the movement's founder was: "If you will it, then the myth becomes real."

We can follow the success of Zionism, and thereby of the most recent influence of the mythical Jerusalem on her earthly double, via the demographic trends in Jerusalem. If we start with the 1838 estimates by Robinson, we can find that the current "Judaization of Jerusalem" started about 140 years ago due to Jewish mystical revivals that preceeded political Zionism, but it was the latter that gave the force to "the return to Zion." The first reliable census for Jerusalem was made in 1875 and found about 20,500 residents, of whom 10,500 were Jews; in 1880 there were 24,000 people in Jerusalem, 13,920 of whom were Jews. At the beginning of the twentieth century, when Zionism was already a recognizable force, the city's population was estimated at 45,600 (15,200 Ashkenazi Jews, 13,000 Sephardi Jews, 8,700 Christians and 8,600 Moslems). The census of 1922 counted 62,578 people (33,971 Jews, 14,699 Christians and 13,413 Moslems) and before the 1948 war the population of the whole city was estimated at 165,000 (100,000 Jews, 40,000 Moslems and 25,000 Christians). The 1948 war brought a decline of population on both sides of the divided city (70,000 on the Israeli side and 40,000 on the Jordanian side). The Israeli rule brought an increase in the Western city population which reached 185,000 by 1967 whereas the Jordanian city reached a population of just over 60,000 people (including about 25,000 within the Old City walls). One of the significant changes after the reunification in 1967 was the restitution of the Jewish quarter of the Old City from which the Jews were expelled after its Jordanian occupation in 1948.

As noted earlier, one of the apparent dualities of Jerusalem is between the old walled city, which has many structures hundreds and even thousands of years old, and the contemporary city, which was built over the last 100 years. I use "contemporary" rather than the common term "the New City" to avoid confusing it with "the New Jerusalem" of the Book of Revelation. The latter is, in fact, similar to the common term of "the Eternal City" as referring to the Heavenly Jerusalem, the opposite of "the Temporal City."

Due to the recent trends noted above, both the Old City and the contemporary city are both Jewish and Arab. This united Jerusalem is made, in fact, of a mosaic of many diverse social and ethnic groups, and this diversity is one of the city's most notable features. Here is another dimension to understand. The orthodox Jews of Mea-She'arim versus the secular Israelis, or the different Eastern versus Western Christian sects, do not seem to belong to the same historic era, yet they exist side by side in Jerusalem. A visitor to Jerusalem may feel he is traveling through history as if he used some "time machine." "Contemporary" means existing in the "same" (externally measured) time. It does not mean synchronicity. Being in Jerusalem one may start doubting the facile Western assumption of "modern man" as the most up-to-date or future-oriented person. Certainly the orthodox, be they Jewish or Moslem, regard their own lifestyle as nearer to that of "the World to Come" of the future. Thus, we may regard some of the many divisions in contemporary Jerusalem as temporal divisions or as different degrees of infusion of the Heavenly Jerusalem into the image of the earthly city.

Jerusalem figures prominently in the three so-called "Abrahamic Religions" as the site for world formation, spiritual orientation, sacrifice, Resurrection, the Last Judgment and the symbol for final Redemption for all mankind (Werblowsky, 1973, 1983; the paper was handed in the conference to fill all the essential material).

In Judaism, Jerusalem is the Mount Moriah, the site of the Akeda (or "binding" for sacrifice) of Abraham's son Isaac. Legend says that Isaac did in fact die at that time and his soul departed there and then came back again. Other legends place the cornerstone for the formation of the world at Mount Moriah, as well as the gathering place for the dust from all over the earth to form Adam's body. More concretely, this was the place of Israel's past glory, the capital of David and the site of the First and Second Temples. Their destruction fixed Jerusalem as the hope and symbol for the restitution and the resurrection of the exiled people.

Christian myth takes Isaac's binding as a "type" (Frye, 1983), recapitulated and magnified by Jesus's Crucifixion and later Resurrection in Jerusalem. The Christian Bible acknowledges all of the Old Testament prophecies for Jerusalem's future role and ends with the vision of the New Jerusalem coming down from Heaven at the time of the Messiah's return.

In Islam, Mohammad first made a spiritual Hijrah from his hometown Mecca to Jerusalem where he ascended to heaven and where the downpouring of the Kor'an was initiated. Mohammad's physical and political Hijrah from Mecca to Medina and his return to Mecca in triumph came subsequently. The significance of Jerusalem/Al-Quds to Islam is discussed at length by Dr. Schleiffer in Chapter 9.

JERUSALEMISM AND UNIVERSAL ZIONISM

The mythological Jerusalem/Zion has spawned many eschatological images and revivalist movements throughout the world, not only for the Jews, who were scattered all around the world but remained united in their focusing on Jerusalem as the Paradise Lost and the Paradise to be regained, but also for Christians, Moslems and other groups worldwide.

There is a conjecture that the roots of Islam in the Arabian Peninsula are linked to Jewish attempts to rally the Arabs there to help liberate Jerusalem from the Christians. Certainly we may recall the Crusades, spurred by Christian outrage at Jerusalem's occupation by the Moslems as a sinister precedent of "Zionism." During their seige of Jerusalem (which united Moslem defenders) the crusaders had collective visions of the heavenly city. The crusaders' conquest helped bring a flowering of a "Zionist" literature in Islam—the Fadha'il al-Quds—tracts singing the praises of Jerusalem.

We find "Zionist" literature not only in the Hebrew prophets and in Islam but also in Western literature. Bunyan's (1678) "Pilgrim's Progress" to the Heavenly Jerusalem was the most popular text of English literature of its time, and later we find Milton and Blake constructing whole cosmologies and inspired epics in which Jerusalem plays a central role, so that Blake's praise of Milton's enterprise started with a vow to "build Jerusalem in England's green and pleasant land." This verse was later picked as the anthem of the British Labor Movement, reflecting its millenian and world-restituting ideals.

The same sentiment for human reconstruction as symbolized by Zion, Jerusalem and its Temple can be discovered in the secret order of the Freemasons in Europe and by groups of nonconformist Christians who left Europe for "The New World" and founded there hundreds of model communities, many bearing the name of Zion. We may perhaps even discern such secret "Zionist" motivations in the American Revolution itself, noting that almost all of the signers of the Declaration of Independence were Freemasons and that the Grand Seal of the United States seen on the one dollar bill carries the six-pointed star made of 13 regular (pentagonal) stars which is a primary symbol for the Heavenly Jerusalem.

The same symbolism of Zion can also be found in the developing countries. That same "Zionist Star" appeared as the symbol of many Bantu revivalist churches and sects (Werblowsky, 1973) which used Zion as their name, and the two million member-strong United African Church holds its mass meetings in so-called "Mount Zion."

Such movements may seem far removed from the modern Jewish political, and largely secular, Zionism which culminated in the re-establishment of the present-day Israel. Many leftist Europeans are anti-Zionist as are many Christians. For most Arabs "Zionism" is one of the dirtiest words imaginable. Yet paradoxically, such intense Arab and leftist anti-Zionism may itself be an inverted Zionism which centers on Jerusalem as an important focal point causing possible division and war, but it also contains possible seeds for higher order and unification centered on Jerusalem.

THE HEAVENLY JERUSALEM AS REDEMPTIVE ARCHETYPE

If Zionism is, as I claim, not an exclusive Jewish nationalist movement but a universal phenomenon, it must have some universal and primary meaning for the individual and for society. Zionism can be seen as the orientation towards "Jerusalem" and a drive to gather all the exiled and dispersed people into a safe home in the Middle East, the M.E. (where "M.E." can also allude to the psychological "Me").

Thus, Zionism may mean the psychic integration of an individual, the restitution from alienation through the return of the psyche to her home within. For the social group, Zionism also means the restitution from exile, dispersion, and powerlessness into a state of sovereignity, re-integration, and feeling of self-worth. I know that this is a touchy issue but I feel impelled to stress the point that in the Arab world, in the M.E., the Palestinians are, in fact, staunch Zionists and what they claim they want is precisely Zionism, both literally and metaphorically.

I have allowed myself to diverge very far from the common and conventional meaning of Zionism and Jerusalem, but there are many indications that there is a predestination about Jerusalem and an implicit plan which is beyond common understanding. This is the kind of belief that is the core of the Moslem trust (literally "Islam") in the inscrutable divine plan. In the development of the modern Jewish Zionism we had the doctrine of Rabbi Kook, the first Chief Rabbi of Palestine, that there is an implicit Messianic work in modern Zionism brought about unconsciously and even opposite to its declared secular ideologies. These days there is a growing new support for Jewish Zionism from many Christian sects in the U.S. who see Jewish Zionism as a compatible and needed stage in their own eschatological vision. Above all, there is a strong irrational feeling by Jews, Moslems and Christians that Jerusalem is a key to the mystery of the World to Come.

In order to come to closer terms with this sense we may have to go beyond words to those primary or archetypal forms that have been associated with Jerusalem by seers and sages as codes for their intuition. We may mention here the twelve- and the thirteen-fold forms as symbols of the Heavenly Jerusalem as well as the symbols of the star-and-crescent, the Star of David and the cross.

The form of the 12 divisions of the circle and the central thirteenth point may have derived from the 12 lunar changes during the solar year to the theories of heavenly influences held sacred in the ancient world. We find this form in the Bible in the 12 tribes of Israel as well as of Ishmael and of Essau's children. It stands to reason that this tradition was instrumental to the maintenance of the Temple and of the court of King Solomon where each tribe was to share in its maintenance for one month of each year. Even so, its occult aspect was primary and it appeared in the scheme of the camping of the tribes of Israel around Mount Sinai during their communal Revelation of the Torah and around the Mishkan (the Tabernacle) during their wanderings in the desert. This was to be the schematic model for the settlement of the whole land of Israel with natural allowance made for its very diverse geography. The arrangement of the whole Land of Israel into 12 tribal regions was kept in various Biblical accounts even when the identity of the tribes changed somewhat. In the prophetic visions, the whole land forms a mandala-type pattern with three tribes to each of the cardinal directions. In the visions of Ezekiel this twelve–fold form will return to prevail at the end of days. The visions of Ezekiel undoubtedly influenced the visions of the Book of Revelation which also mentions the restoration of the then already missing 12 Tribes of Israel and the appearance of the New Jerusalem coming down from heaven in the form of a giant cube (e.g., like the Ka'aba?) with 12 gates, each for one of the tribes to enter that perfect city. Other clear influences on the Revelation of John and even more on the Gospel of John are the Platonic-Pythagorean teachings from Alexandria such as those of the philosopher Philo the Jew who developed the concepts of the Logos and of The City of God. The Pythagoreans who revered the Platonic Solids considered the four known ones as symbols for the four "earthly elements" while they held as their great secret the fifth, the dodecahedron, as the symbol for the heavenly element. We may get closer to the secret by realizing that the dodecahedron has 12 equal faces, each a perfect pentagon (also a symbol for the human form). Each of these pentagons can be taken as the base for constructing another dodecahedron, resulting in a bunch of 13 equal and connecting dodecahedrons, thus multiplying that "heavenly element" and its influences.

The number 13 has strong occult connotations. While it is feared in the West, it is revered by the Jews, and I counted about 10 sacred uses of it in Judaism, from the 13 attributes of Divine Mercy to the Kabbalistic view of "the Assembly of Israel" (Knesset Yisrael) as "the thirteen petaled rose." Yet this is not an exclusive Jewish symbol, and graphic realizations of such a rose appear as the twelve-pointed star in the Rosary windows of Gothic cathedrals and in the Moslem Dome of the Rock situated in the sacred center of Jerusalem. It is the archetypal representation for the Heavenly Jerusalem.

Most of the above regarded the Heavenly Jerusalem as the ideal or "Platonic" form preceding its earthly realization. Christian and Moslem views of Heavenly Jerusalem see the Redemption as a "top to bottom" process of divine emanation or Grace. Jewish sources include also a "bottom up" description of the redemption where earthly actions precipitate the divine ones.

In Christianity it is the Cross, the junction of the vertical and the horizontal, that stands for the Redemption. The bleeding heart at the center forms the channel for Divine Grace to earth. This form can be seen in Jerusalem not only on the tops of its many churches but in the very plan of the Old City as it evolved over the centuries with its four quarters (Armenian, Christian, Moslem and Jewish) and the cruciform of the main streets dividing them. We have already surveyed the disjunctions in the modern world (and modern man) between East and West on the horizontal plane and between the material and the spiritual in the "vertical" plane. These are so clearly illustrated by Jerusalem that this city seems as perfect a stage as ever for the Messiah to come and bridge those gaps through whatever sacrifice this takes.

It is not correct, however, to see the present form of the Old City of Jerusalem as a simple Cross or Mandala. There is a fifth element there, the Temple Mount or the Haram ash-Sherif situated on approximately a fifth of its land area. Being almost empty, in contrast to the densely built Old City, and with the octagonal star of the Dome of the Rock in its center, the aerial view of the Old City is somewhat reminiscent of the Moslem symbol of the Crescent and the Star in its hollow. I am not sure of the full symbolism of the crescent, but I find it is evocative of the whole M.E. in the form of the historic "Fertile Crescent" inspired by a seemingly eccentric yet essential star.

The psychological importance of the Mandala and other symbols as mentioned here was explained in our time by C.G. Jung (1972) who elaborated the "theory of the archetype." Clearly the pattern of the Heavenly Jerusalem discussed here and elsewhere (Mitchell, 1973, 1983 and 1985) is a prime archetype of the Redemption and of psychological integration. To aid discussion and introduction of this archetype in the M.E., a shorter name may help, and I chose here the acronym "HEJERA" (for the *H*eavenly *Je*rusalem *A*rchetype) as a name that evokes the Islamic term "Hijra." Much like it, the HEJERA is a call for leaving the old partisan associations and the in-group orientation and to rise to the full dimensions of the divine calling.

THE HEJERA MODEL FOR
M.E. CONFLICT RESOLUTION

It is now time to apply the HEJERA model and to demonstrate its utility for helping bring peace to the Middle East. This will be done on the two levels introduced initially. I shall show in this section the political and cultural ramifications of the model by suggesting hitherto unrecognized and radical solutions. The next section will show how this model can be applied to the urban design and management problems of the earthly Jerusalem so that this city can become the key to and demonstration of the peace and wholeness her name implies.

The Future Ingathering of the Tribes

The twelve–fold pattern of the HEJERA represents primarily the 12 tribes of Israel who were given possession of the Holy Land by divine covenant. It is held alike by Jews and Christians that at some future time, immediately preceding the time of lasting peace, all 12 tribes will assemble again at Jerusalem (e.g., *Ezekiel,* 37). The modern Jews claim to be made up of two tribes, Judah and Benjamin, together with an admixture of Levites. The other tribes are said to be scattered among the nations of the world. The recognition of the missing tribes to make up the complete 12 is thus of practical importance. There have been hundreds of attempts made over the centuries to find the missing tribes with candidates ranging all the way from South America to Japan with as yet inconclusive results. On the other hand, there are contemporary groups that regard themselves as Israelites. It would appear that the practical general principle to follow is to allow the Israelites to declare themselves. Israel's recognition of them as legitimate Israelites could thus be offered to those who claim legitimacy and are impelled by Jerusalemism/Zionism toward the Holy City. There are various groups found worldwide who may choose to declare themselves Israelites. The case of the greatest interest here is the one close at hand—the case of the Palestinians in and around Israel.

Undoubtedly, this will be initially hard to swallow for both most Palestinians and Israelis, but let us examine some of the ramifications and allay some of the immediate suspicions which this idea is likely to raise. First, this solution does not entail the conversion of all Palestinians to Judaism, if for no other reason than the fact that Judah is but one part of the whole which is Israel. Secondly, this need not entail the massive influx of Arabs into Israel and the transformation of its demographic structure. As noted, the great majority of Palestinians live within the territorial boundaries of the British Palestine, now included in or controlled by Jordan and Israel. The HEJERA model implies, as is explained below, the centrality of Jerusalem within a multi-canton federation of Arab, Jewish and mixed regions. In this case the new Arab Israelites would live mainly where they already reside, albeit with enhanced civic rights, whereas new Arab migrants to Zion may settle initially and primarily in the Arab cantons discussed below. The important point is that those Arabs who come to identify themselves as Zionists would also recognize the Jews as such and recognize their legitimacy to stay in this land. This would remove, I believe, the biggest and most profound stumbling block and cause for instability in any feasible solution.

Centrality of Jerusalem in the Future Land

The centrality of Jerusalem in Zionist consciousness is bound to usher in the centrality of Jerusalem in the land—an influence of the Heavenly Jerusalem over the Earthly counterpart. As in Jungian psychology, there is a search for the self, for a new center beyond the Ego. This new center is first seen as external or eccentric, but once it is sufficiently recognized it starts to reorganize and reconstruct the territory (in the case of psychology, the psyche) until it becomes the real center. This is the case with Jerusalem. This tendency towards a center was expressed in Moslem Spain by the poet Ibn-Gabirol who gave this expression to his Zionism: "My heart is in the Orient and I am at the extremities of the West." In the past (1948–1967) Jerusalem had been divided and completely eccentric (both geographically and demographically) to Israel. But this could not remain a stable situation. Israel did not initiate the 1967 war and the re-unification of Jerusalem, but when King Hussain gave Israel the Casus Belli, the unification and annexation of East Jerusalem were, in fact, inevitable. Israel has been holding the "West Bank" for many years as a negotiation card, but meanwhile the influence of Jerusalem, i.e., of Zionism, has developed, and during the years of the Likud government formed to a policy of Jewish settlement in the West Bank and especially around Jerusalem. In the pattern which is thus developing, Jerusalem became the geographic center of the country. It is still eccentric demographically, however, so long as only Israeli citizens are counted and the rest are disregarded (as they presently are).

This Israeli settlement policy has gone so far that according to authoritative evaluation (e.g., of Miron Benveniste) a return of the "West Bank" to Jordan (or to a Palestinian State) is no longer possible. I am afraid that this evaluation is correct and the fear I express is of the consequences that this annexation will entail for Israel unless a new vision of Zionism is adopted. The vision of the Heavenly

Jerusalem explained here and expressed through the HEJERA model allows, I believe, a partnership with the Arabs in a Zionist vision and a justification to federation government.

To the extent that the HEJERA model inspires the creation of a federation-type arrangement for the whole West Bank of the Jordan (or the "Eretz Yisrael haShlema), it also allows an advantageous and fair unity to the whole land of Palestine/Israel on both sides of the Jordan. In this arrangement of the "Greater Palestine," Jerusalem would be eccentrically occidental geographically (unless the desert areas are disregarded) but demographically central.

The Future Federation of the Holy Land

It is instructive that the prophet Ezekiel, who introduced the image of the Heavenly Jerusalem and the detailed measures of the reconstructed Temple, also saw the restored land as divided into 12 regions for the 12 ingathered tribes. This is the ideal arrangement of the country for the time of lasting peace.

The modern interpretation of this vision is a federation of fairly autonomous regions in the land of Israel/Palestine. The example of the union of the Swiss Cantons is an appealing one, and federations are quite common worldwide, especially in lands of great ethnic and geographic diversity.

There are many good ecological, civic and cultural reasons to advocate a federation of over half a dozen regions even for "the smaller Israel" and to demand that the autonomy rule promised in Camp David for the residents of the regions of Hebron, Nablus and Gaza be granted first to the Jews of the Tel Aviv region, for example. But the chief practical reason for federation is, of course, ethnic-political. It is the fairest and safest way to give civic rights to the Arabs of the "West Bank." An independent Palestinian state is not feasible since it would create a strong polarization against Israel—a situation which could not remain stable. Even a three-nation federation including Jordan would be much better than any of the schemes currently discussed. Yet a more plural federation of some 6-20 regions would be still less polarized and thus inherently more stable. (Had Lebanon adopted such an arrangement, it might have saved that country from its current civil war.)

At present, nationalistic feelings run so high among both Israelis and Palestinians that such enlightened and practical solutions appear inconceivable. Even when the present Israeli premier, Peres, published one such plan in the past it drew no response, just as his mentor, Ben Gurion, did not manage to win his party to a cantonization plan back in the 1930s. Yet, since the Biblical vision of the New

Jerusalem, which is at the root of Zionism, does, in effect, contain or endorse such a plan, there is hope for the adoption of this scheme as this becomes recognized.

THE HEJERA MODEL FOR THE DESIGN OF THE EARTHLY JERUSALEM

The primary place to bring down to earth the influence of the Heavenly Jerusalem is, of course, the actual Jerusalem. Only in this way can Jerusalem become the unified whole that her name implies. Contemporary Jerusalem has a great diversity—and also much tension and contradictions. The HEJERA model may help to alleviate these tensions and help make Jerusalem the place for transformation, for the study of wholeness and transcendence, and for its demonstration. Let me illustrate a few possibilities.

Self-Government for Jerusalem's Neighborhoods

The canton-type organization of the whole country, fair and good as it may sound, may presently be too utopian. There are no political forces at present, Jewish or Arab, which are ready to champion such an idea. But there is a more evident need and a better likelihood for this reflection of the Heavenly Jerusalem to be applied on a local neighborhood scale in Jerusalem. To an extent this is already the case in practice—not only the Arab sectors but also the orthodox Jewish neighborhoods are largely autonomous and prefer to have only minimal contact with the central municipality. A largely unrecognized development in this direction is the many unplanned new Arab settlements around Jerusalem by ex-villagers attracted by the employment in the building boom the (thus possibly vain) "Judaization of Jerusalem" policy brought. The present trends of this policy, building massive self-contained neighborhoods like Gilo, Talpiot East and Ramot on the city's outskirts, with the resulting transformation of Jerusalem from a compact city into a metropolitan region, also suggest a pattern of local governments.

This is the pattern advocated by modern urban planning in many cases of metropoli. Moreover, there is a mounting political need for it. This need has its political opposition, and former deputy mayor Miron Benveniste lost his job for advocating more local rule for Arab Jerusalem, yet the case is politically feasible. Arabs are not likely to simply forget about Jerusalem and let Israel get away with whatever arrangements it imposes. In any future peace talks, Jerusalem will doubtless be a major issue and stumbling block. Outside mediators, including the U.S., are likely to suggest schemes which demand some changes regarding Jerusalem. Israel is bound to resist any suggestion to re-divide Jerusalem and to establish East Jerusalem as a separate city and capital of a separate Arab state or region. Obviously, Israel will persist in resisting the old United Nations plan for the internationalization of the Jerusalem region. The most feasible scenario of political accommodation will be to agree on some form of local governments for the distinct neighborhoods of Jerusalem.

The same political logic which advocates at least six rather than two or three regions for the country is no less valid for urban local rule. A single Arab "neighborhood" would constitute, in fact, a separate city. Three or four such neighborhood councils are thus more likely, and this then sets the impetus and scale for corresponding Jewish (and mixed) neighborhoods. This is lucky, perhaps even providential, since political considerations may support the pattern which is appropriate from the viewpoint of human and civic considerations. With some 8–15 candidates, it would be interesting to consider 12 councils as symbolically realizing the pattern of the Heavenly Jerusalem.

The influence of local rule can, and is likely to, serve as a model. Though the cantonization plan does not now seem readily feasible, this idea, if applied in Jerusalem, would bring the rest of Israel to follow its lead. Jerusalem is the head, and if many Israelis get used to the idea of local Arab councils in Jerusalem, they will come to regard mixed and Arab cantons in the entire country as natural.

Extra-temporal Status for the Old City of Jerusalem

There is one district of Jerusalem which is unique for the whole world and that is the walled Old City. In any future local rule plans for Jerusalem, the Old City will surely be regarded as distinct. This fact poses a unique opportunity for the realization of the Heavenly Jerusalem pattern.

The Old City can be regarded as the quiet center for the 12 busy sectors around it. Such a centrality of the walled and pedestrian-ruled inner city, which in turn contains the walled and open space of the Haram, which in turn contains the Dome of the Rock, is a clear recapitulation of the centrality of Jerusalem as expressed in the Talmud.

There is a political case for granting a special status to the Old City. Just because Israel is likely to resist the idea of the internationalization of the Jerusalem region (a plan which was resisted even more by the Palestinians in 1947), a special status for the Old City could be used as a political fallback position to defuse many further demands. The recent restoration of the Jewish Quarter and of real Jewish presence within the walls will enable Israel to leave the Old City safely to its own rule.

The above is merely a speculation or a political scenario. The relevant issue from the point of view of the HEJERA is the role of such a special city. The primary function for the Old City is that it shall become the center for religious and inter-faith studies—an ecumenical laboratory. Perhaps by having less commercial activity and class tourism, more room could be made for those pilgrims who want to come for spiritual pursuits. There is much demand for this and more institutes of Moslem, Christian and Jewish learning that could be induced to have their quarters in Old Jerusalem. The extra-territorial or extra-temporal status which could be granted to the Old City might be akin to the academic freedom enjoyed in a good university, though on a larger and more pluralistic scale. There should be a place where Moslems and Jews can pursue not only traditional, but also radical, innovative and even seemingly heretical interpretations of their religion—where adepts of the three Abraham- ic religions can meet each other and learn about the respective faiths first hand. It appears now (Yates, 1979) that the European Renais- sance was due not just to the Greek texts conveyed via Arab scholarship but also to the encounter of free-minded Christian mystics and scholars with Jewish Kabbalists who were expelled from Spain. My guess is that such common studies in Jerusalem will help to bring a renaissance for the whole Middle East.

REFERENCES

Abu-Lughod, Janet and Hay, Richard Jr. (eds.), "Third World Urbani- zation." Methuen Inc., 1982.

Augustine, Saint, "The City of God." Many editions.

Bunyan, John, "The Pilgrim's Progress." 1678.

Calvino, Italo, "Invisible Cities." (English version), 1972. Picador Books, (Hebrew version), Sifriyat Po'alim.

Cattan, Henry, "Repercussions of Israel's Occupation of Jerusalem." 1985, in this volume.

de Chardin, Teilhard, "The Phenomenon of Man." Fontana, 1955.

Cook, Michael A. and Crone, Patricia, *Hagarism: The Making of the Islamic World.* Cambridge University Press, 1977.

Forrester, Jay, "Urban Dynamics." MIT, 1969.

Frye, Northrop, *The Great Code: The Bible and Literature.* London: Ark Paperbacks, 1983.

Jung, Carl Gustav, *Mandala Symbolism*. Bolingen Series, Vol. 20, Princeton University Press, 1972.

Micell, John, *The City of Revelation*. Ballantine, 1973.

Micell, John, *The New View Over Atlantis*. Ballantine Paperbacks, 1983. Thames and Hudson, older version, 1972.

Michel, John, *Dimensions of Paradise*. Thames and Hudson, 1985.

Popper, Karl and Eccles, John, *The Self and Its Brain*. London: Routledge and Kegan Paul, 1983.

Rosenzweig, Franz, *The Star of Redemption*. Boston Beacon Press, 1972. (English edition of the 1919 German text)

Russel, Peter, *The Planetary Brain*. London: Ark Books, 1984.

Schleiffer, Abdullah, "Islamic Jerusalem as Archetype of a Harmonious Urban Environment." 1985, in this volume.

Werblowsky, Zvi, R., "The Meaning of Jerusalem to Jews, Christians and Moslems." Jaarbericht Ex Orient Lux 23, 1973. Reprinted 1983 by Israel Universities Study Group for Middle East Affairs, Jerusalem.

Yates, Frances, *The Occult Philosophy in the Elizabethan Age*. London: Ark Books, 1983.

DISCUSSION

Nasser

I want to begin by making some comments. I am a Palestinian, I was born in Jerusalem. I started out to be a Palestinian, then they started calling me someone who does not have a country. They called me a refugee. After that I was stateless. Then I was called a Syrian, a Lebanese, a Jordanian, what have you. Then they started calling me a terrorist. Today, I learned from Professor Khayutman that I am originally Jewish.

I am reminded of a story of Eskimos. Eskimos believe that the white man is originally Eskimo, so they have this story to tell you. They say one day a little Eskimo girl lost her way . . . and that's how the white man came into existence. I must admit that there is quite a bit of distortion in history and in realities. Basically you see, we the Palestinians have lived in Palestine for generations. We had deeds for the property and homes. The case is that people were brought from outside to take the place of the Palestinians, who were thrown out. Everything is a smoke screen to hide this fact. Before there was an Israel, there was Palestine. Palestine had its cities, its orange groves, its schools, its roads, its culture. So, Palestinians existed.

In 1969 Golda Meir, in an interview in London, said who are the Palestinians, they don't exist. Distortions. I am sure that the Jews were persecuted throughout history and I must add that primarily the Christian west persecuted them. The Muslims never persecuted Jews. And then you see, those people who were persecuted who knew what pain meant, who knew what suffering meant . . . they turned around to do the very same thing that was done to them. And under the name of democracy and under the name of shades of Zionists and Zionism, and under the shade of security, etc. They try somehow to hide the fact that people with rights have been thrown out and they are using might to keep them out. Jerusalem is my home town. I go often to Jerusalem. I look at it. It's sad, it has been mutilated. An invader came, another invader came, and when I walk in the streets of Jerusalem I look at the walls and see "Kilroy was here." And those people, those new invaders are writing "Kilroy was here." We want peace, we really want peace. And then shouldn't you want peace? Peace does not come through distortions. Peace does not come through confiscating land, mutilating people. Peace comes when you finally make a decision that you can exist, you can exist in this part of the world, as part of this region. Not as invaders, not as teachers, not as superior people, but as people part of the Middle East. I don't want to see in the future, there will be more blood shed, God forgives. Whatever happens God forgives us all for that, for anyone who did anything in terms of shedding blood. We don't want shedding blood anymore. We want peace, we want justice. You can live in this part of the world if you are just. There is a very ancient proverb. Perhaps it is also in Hebrew, I don't know, but I know it's in Arabic. It says "He who lives on an island must not make an enemy of the sea."

Ben-Dak

The truth is that this is the kind of session I usually like to avoid, not because the problem does not exist. I am very much aware that there are some of us who have had the experience of going through this, and go through it and have to relive some of the sorrow and pain and everything which has to do at least with Palestine. But the issue of a city such as Jerusalem where Jews and Arabs live together, have been living together, to me is no different from many of the other cities where we have the same phenomena. It's not only Jerusalem where Jews and Arabs are living together. Today we have it in Haifa, my hometown, we have it in Jerusalem, we have it in Tel Aviv, and Yafa which of course has been an Arab city, we have it in Akkah where Jews and Arabs live together and we have it in Beer Sheeba.

To me each one of those places represents some dilemma that can at once be looked at as a situation that is unique to that city. It also is something which reflects very much the basic problematics of the overall situation. I think it's very important to bear in mind that planning, inasmuch as it is happening now, has two basic problems. One is to deal with the past, and the past has been very awful. I'm not going to go through that, and I think it's almost idiotic to try to recount what Jews did to Arabs and what Arabs did to Jews. My basic philosophy of life is instead of looking at the disease and analyzing it in detail, the same amount of energy should always be focused on the solution. Sometimes by understanding something about the disease and focusing most of your efforts on the solution, you'll get a better situation altogether. With regard to cities I think that's even more true. I think that one thing however has to be clearly stated and it is in response to some extent to what I heard in Abdullah Schleifer's statement. I don't think Jews would ever consider living under Islam again and the fact that the western civilization has been so awful to Jews does not necessarily mean the implication that living under Islam was such a great heaven for Jews. The very basic thing is cultural violence which, if you live under some culture other than your own, you live a loyal life, it's something which is very, very important and has to be taken into consideration. It is one of the reasons why Israel is there altogether.

So one thing is very clear. I don't think the notions for instance for joint work should be taken more seriously than the notions of doing justice to Jewish law, Jewish customs, or anything else in Jerusalem. And a very careful analysis of the principle would mean the following. That Jews of today are planning the needs of a modern development of our cities. These cities' basic area of development is very small.

There's no way to do everything without injustice of some sort. At the same time I think that most important is really the general welfare of the situation, general welfare of the total population. That should be the only criteria. And I think that you should expect some sort of injustice of the sort that you mentioned. I would say that has to be minimized, but I don't expect any absolute in this game just like I never expected absolutes in the game in any other place where two conflicting religions have had something to do with each other. I would think that the criterion of compatibility is extremely important, but in Israel I think the question of space is getting to be serious, especially with regard to Jerusalem. I think the political dimension for the future is to make sure that Jerusalem is so important to Muslims, Jews, and Christians. This is one reason why there should be physical space left in the city, so that out of that space something very important can be developed for the future generations of the Middle

East. In a sense that if one time comes in the future it will not be too taxing to the city to do something in a common activity. In other words, I'm trying to say maybe one can talk about the future government for the region, or about the place where a Palestinian entity in Israel would have some sort of common advisory council or even a parliament. Maybe we will talk about the place where there will be a special university devoted to the interfaith discussions or clarifications. Right now, naturally, if I talk that way I sound very ridiculous to my colleagues. And quite often we have these difficult discussions. I'd rather do that. I very much like the idea of symbols that can be common, regardless of how silly they are now, or are going to be later. Maybe they are not the best ones but you've got to work at that level because if you really assume that hatred has to be part of the future, then eventually it's going to be the only part left. With reference to the space question, if you look at the master plans that have been developed in Israel now, so little of that is developed with the notion of what's going to happen in terms of combining forces. At least with regard to Jordan and Israel it seems to me that we have no luxury about it. Specifically, Jerusalem is by hook or by crook going to be related to the future relationship of Palestine and Israel, and in a larger sense, Jordan, Palestine and Israel. I'm not talking about the political solution. I'm talking about the importance and significance of the fact that this is where Judaism and Islam meet. The problems therefore have to be researched: that one is to plan to leave some space in the master design. Then there are the Christians. One cannot underestimate the hatred which Christians feel toward each other with regard to Jerusalem. Sometimes the one thing that will get Jewish and Muslim people together is the fact that they are a bit more rational about each other than the Christians are about each one of the small Christian groups. There are today approximately forty-eight different Christian groups that claim jurisdiction over Jerusalem and there are many places where the hatred has to do with specific spots.

It's no secret that Jerusalem's Mayor Collick wanted one time in the past to get a very strong representation of all the Christian communities to participate in the communication between Jews and Muslims and to create an overall interfaith council to deal with Jerusalem. In fact there was even the idea of giving such a council some political power so that the city council would be able to consider its decisions. But this has not come about not because of Muslim problems, not because of the Jews, but because the Christians couldn't really sit with each other. There were a lot of questions as to who should be represented, how many votes should each Christian group get, and so forth.

Nasser   Dr. Ben-Dak said we should not talk about what we are doing to each other. But Palestinians cannot simply ignore the daily hardships: the destruction of their homes by foreigners, the confiscation of their properties and lands. All these are factors of agony and destabilization in that area. We can't just forget them.

Munro   I just want to ask the question, in view of what has been said by both Dr. Joseph Ben-Dak and Dr. Khayutman I would assume that both are opposed to the idea of making Jerusalem the administrative capital of Israel. Would that be a fair assumption? The reason why I ask this question is fairly obvious. If one is thinking in terms of harmony, one is thinking of different societies living together, it would seem certainly a retrogressive step to make Jerusalem the capitol of a Zionist Jewish state. One seems to be loading the dice in the wrong direction. Am I right in assuming that neither of you are sympathetic to the idea of Jerusalem as the administrative capitol of Israel?

Khayutman I do propose to have Jerusalem as the capital for the Zionist state simply because Zionism and Jerusalem are the same thing. As far as the state of Israel goes, I've said that I for one, as an Israeli subject, do agree to look forward for other reformulations of my own country into other political arrangements. I proposed that Jerusalem be the capital of a federation of all this diversity. I am talking of Jerusalem historically, symbolically, metaphysically, which is a center of the multiplicity of the 12 tribes, the 12 signs of the zodiac, the multitude of human attributes. I see Jerusalem bleeding for uniting those things and I'm looking for a messiah or messiahs who will come and take this role of uniting it because this is a stage, and its center or capital is Jerusalem. So I see much further beyond Israel. I believe in the future God has for further and finer notions of what will be than we can conceive now. I have the deepest sympathy with Abdullah Schleifer's paper, and his search in Islam. I think that if we locked him and me and this gentleman from Palestine Jordan, together long enough, we would eventually brew up the solutions. Now we may not do it in this conference but I think that God in his wisdom has already done it. In setting up this stage, this pressure cooker of Jerusalem and the Middle East to brew us altogether with the pain, with the sense of history, with the whole range of human emotions, with rational and irrational thinking, we are stuck there and our only way is to go up, to transcend these problems and for me this is what Jerusalem and Heavenly Jerusalem represent.

Jerusalem is the stage: Mohammad did rise through Jerusalem. For the Jews they rise to Jerusalem and we speak about the Heavenly Jerusalem. I think God has set it as a point of contention as the stone of contention, but also as a point of going up from confrontation. If any place in the world was well designed for this purpose, this is it. Now about the Palestinian gentleman who spoke about all his pain. I think we simply have to sit and talk for hours. You know anything that I will say in one or two minutes is not fair, it would not acknowledge enough the pain and agony. But what I want to say right now, and this is nothing new, is that I did acknowledge your love of Jerusalem right away and I see in this love something, some force that hopefully can transcend the bitterness, the hatred, of the past. As Professor Ben-Dak said we can go through endless accounting of who did a bigger injustice here and there but we have to find ways of going beyond them.

Abu Khadra

It is not true that it's idiotic that we have to talk about what the Arabs did to the Jews and what the Jews are doing to the Arabs. If we don't face the realities, we will never be able to find any solution. We have to face that there are problems, and there are hostilities. I'd like to point out that in the Bible, Abraham was ordered to go from Mesopotamia to the land of Canaan and there were people living there before the Jews. And they were called the Canaanites. It's not true that the origins of all the people who were living in Palestine are Jewish. It's a multitude of nations that just came into the country at different periods of history and they constituted the population of Palestine in 1948 and before. You said that when the Arabs realize what the Jews went through in Diaspora, maybe some of the problems could be resolved. I'd like to ask you to look at it the other way around. Knowing what you have gone through during the Diaspora I hope you understand what the Palestinians are going through now. I am a second generation Palestinian, my father was born in Yaffa. I only had the very lucky chance to get a glimpse of my grandfather's home. Hopefully it's not demolished, I don't know, but probably it is, and that raises another question. What is happening to the Arab homes, the old Arab homes in the Arab cities that are now being confiscated? Are they all being demolished or are they being preserved? When I went "home," I was not allowed to get into my grandfather's house. It was completely closed and there was no way to get in and it was in a very bad shape. I'd like to ask you, "Can I, you said any Arab in Jerusalem can apply for citizenship and get it, can I as a second generation Palestinian apply for Israeli citizenship and get it and be allowed to go and live there, and in my grandfather's home?"

Mellanby

I was very interested in what Dr. Ben-Dak said that the 48 Christian denominations in Jerusalem all hated each other. I'm sure this is perfectly true and it is a very interesting phenomenon. I'm not sure it's important. I think that Jerusalem is an important religious city for different denominations. How important it is to the western countries of Christian tradition I do not know. That is to say I think that most of us, even those of us who still remain members of a Christian church are not very concerned about it. I have been to Jerusalem and it is to me rather like visiting Disneyland. If I am a Catholic I find where the resurrection took place in one tomb. If I am a Protestant I find another one. It is important as a focal point or a center, but the actual sites, the actual shrines that we see are of no great importance. And this is not true of all people of Christian tradition but I am sure it is true of 95%. I also wonder if it is religiously important to the Hebrew people. That is to say there are many extremely religious Jews but I have known many who are atheists. How important is the religious significance to them? And so I think that perhaps we are overdoing in some cases the complication, certainly the complication from a Christian point of view. It is important to a small minority, but I don't think that it need upset the whole question of how Jerusalem is going to be organized. I think let us keep the shrines, let us allow people to see them, but only as a minor question, not as the major question for the way the city is run.

Nasser

You say look it's God's will to have us sit here and seek solutions. It's brewing, like brewing hot. I couldn't help but perhaps see the bayonet and the bulldozer along with us. You're talking but you are talking at the same time when people, Arabs in Jerusalem lose their property, their land, their future. I must tell you that every time I come to visit Jerusalem, I am stripped naked, literally stripped naked on the bridge, searched, questioned, and questioned by faces that are alien to me as a man who grew up in Palestine with Jews. I went to school with Jews, we lived together in Palestine. And now you come here and you really tell me that it is a marvellous opportunity indeed and perhaps God willed that you and I and the rest of us would sit and find a way, forge a way out. How can we do that when your bayonets, bulldozers are now at work?

Galantay

I think you established the importance of the heavenly Jerusalem as an important place for the Jewish people. I also think nobody denies the right of the Jews to have access to the Israeli wall and to the holy places. It is another question however, that you can use these rights to claim Jerusalem to be the capital of Israel, because the fact that Jerusalem has been declared the capital of Israel has very important policy implications.

There are conflicting claims, for example as to the population distribution. We have one paper by Henri Cattan here which gives documented figures. I have in front of me an article by Teddy Collick which gives different figures. The latter claims that the Arab population in fact has increased. The former paper says that it has decreased. One thing is very clear to me. There are policy implications of having made Jerusalem the capital of Israel and these policy implications involve the population property relationship, land use, and urban structure.

There is no question that the policy implies a change of the existing population composition. Collick very clearly says, "This is a policy of the Jewish state to make the capital of Israel predominantly Jewish." And there is no question that there have been property changes; people's property has been taken away without compensation. Land use is being changed, urban structure is changed, without actually having involved the resident population in any form of consultation. The population has been changed by increased migration to Jerusalem by Jewish people and the expulsion of the Arab people. The modification of the demographic structure of a city of an area occupied in war and in the absence of a peace treaty is contrary to international law, contrary to the Charter of the United Nations, contrary to the United Nations resolutions. It has been condemned at the United Nations Conference on Human Settlement in Vancouver, where this specific question was raised. It is not exclusively a problem of Jerusalem because there are many other cases where occupied land, in the absence of formal peace treaties, result in population changes. For example, the United States does not recognize the occupation by the Soviet Union of the Baltic states and is opposed to the idea that the population of Riga for example, is becoming increasingly Russian by forced migration. Similarly, I do not approve of Rumanian actions which change the population of Hungarian cities like in Transylvania, by forced population transfers. So Israel had better think about this. If it wants to live in peace, I think some consideration has to be made to international opinion about this. It should also try to get some kind of agreement with the population that lives in this city. It also must figure out how to compensate these people for property taken and to give Palestinians access to their houses and the property of their ancestors. It is one thing for the Jewish people to have the right of access to Jerusalem, but it is another thing to make it a political capital of a new state and by policy, change its population, property relationships, land use and urban structure.

Ibrahim

Islam is an inclusive faith that does not negate previous religions. In our upbringing we learn that Judaism and Christianity and their prophets are our prophets. It poses no intellectual problem. Pluralism for me, as a Muslim, is not a problem, intellectually, or even existentially. And I think this is probably at the heart of some of the discussion. It is not so clear that this core of pluralism in Jewish thinking is well developed and that's probably where we should work. Israel had a chance, an advantage to rule supreme over this area for the last 20 years. I suppose if there was this core of pluralism entrenched in Jewish consciousness, it would have probably done different things than what have evolved in the last 15 or 16 years. All historical, international and even Israeli documents talk about the confiscation of land, under different pretexts; the demographic designs to alter the nature, not only of Jerusalem, but of the entire West Bank. As intellectuals and scholars, we have to contribute to a new vision not only for the Arabs and the Israelis, but for the whole Middle East. A vision that recognizes that pluralism is a way of the future and if we can preach that, then we have done something for our people, for ourselves and for our children.

With all my respect to spiritualism, I don't like to propagate or to perpetuate this new concept of God as a real estate agent, or God as an urban developer. Because under the pretext of God I'm allowed to do this and that. And we are told Zionism and Jerusalem are one and the same. Sure, spiritually they are one and the same. But that ought not be transformed into a geopolitical land confiscation practice under the pretext of God. I think, metaphors aside, we have to face reality. While this very emotional but very welcomed exchange between Palestinians and Israelis is well, let us recognize what's happening. Of course there is an equity in exchange, the anguished like Cattan, Nasser, and Abu Khadra, are very emotional. The victorious, like Ben-Dak and Khayutman are very kind and cool. I would suppose if they were in an exchange with Nazi Germans they would be different. They would be very emotional, just like Cattan, Nasser and Abu Khadra: I think this is something we have to recognize.

Ben-Dak

I find myself very often discussing and debating very emotionally these same issues in Israel because my position has been, among other things, to delay the decision on a formal statement about Jerusalem. But I have to say to you very clearly that we are here for one reason, we believe that one has to reconcile and one has to give a

great deal and one has to come forth and explain. The reality of
Jerusalem is important to Jews, I would dare say more than it is to
Muslims because Muslims have Mecca and Medina. Jews have only
Jerusalem and there is one of the very few things that has been very
clear in the mind of Jews all the time.

Another aspect is that for all those years that Jerusalem was
occupied by Jordan and the Jordanians were doing unbelievable
things to all those Jewish holy places, nobody cared about the fact
that the Jews were not allowed to come to Jerusalem. All those cries,
tears and whatever are coming now from the Palestinians and the
disenfranchisement in Jerusalem have not been there then because
Jews were not able to do anything about it. But Jews all the time were
talking about Jerusalem as the central place. We have several celebrations every year, that have been going on for about a millenium, that
Jerusalem is the key aspect of everything we do.

The point is that I can give you such an emotional statement. Well
of course I'm not going to do this. Maybe some other time. I think
what would really be the best use of our time is not to recount crimes,
to keep repeating them. To think about new designs. I really don't
want to see Palestinians that have left Palestine come back to
Palestine. I don't think it's going to be useful. I don't think it's right.
I'm not talking about every individual case. When you talk about the
individual pain it's really great, but you have to look at the collective
possibilities too. We have some possibilities for the future by realizing
very fully that in our generation the pain is going to be very bad and
very tough but we have got to think about the future generations.
One issue I would like to point to is not about Muslims and Jews
having pain, but the point that Professor Mellanby was bringing.
Indeed Christians have so much less to gain or lose with regard to
Jerusalem because most Christian groups are not that concerned. By
being willing to work out a position, they can really help the Jews and
Muslims and facilitate the situation to come forth. That has not been
happening.

Right now you should see how much energy and money is spent by
Christian groups concerning Jerusalem. For example, at the moment
they are building a campus near Jerusalem, a whole university is
going to be built in Jerusalem. Another example, one of the two
committees of the Catholic Church, is now devising a whole new plan
for what they're going to do in some area of Jerusalem. They are
secretly negotiating and buying land near Jerusalem to establish some
sort of ecumenical system. There's a great deal of energy put in,
there's no unity among Christians, and this does not help the Jews
and Muslims come forth together.

Schleifer   First of all I disagree with Professor Ben-Dak. Of the remarks he has made in the past half hour that most struck my consciousness as real, although it may be emotionally disturbing yet impressive, is his acknowledgement that he really doesn't want the Palestinians back. Now we have a starting point for some dialogue.

One of the things that always impressed me about Moshe Dayan as the possible man who could have seized a certain moment in history, aside from his credibility as a military man and a hawk, was the fact that he once wrote "If I were a Palestinian I'd be a member of FATAH for truly I recognize, according to the Palestinian, that we came to steal their land." Now to have that ability to perceive on that level was profound and it was a great tragedy he did not play perhaps the role that De Gaulle played in another similar environment. When you talk about entering the planning procedures of Israeli cities, it gives me the opposite feeling. It gives me a sinking sense that I've been invited by some French Algerian authority to discuss the planning of Constantine or Algiers, 1952—to come as a Muslim to discuss how the French will administer Muslim cities in which the Muslim populations were systematically expelled. I don't want to get into rebutting all sorts of individual points because this has been going on for years. My great grandfather was a Jewish merchant of Oddessa and he kept a Turkish passport for one reason, and for one reason only. Because he knew that whenever the pogromis showed up on the outskirts of Oddessa, he stayed because he could make a good living. He could skoot across into Islamic Turkey where there was tolerance. A tolerance, incidentally, which nineteenth century Jewish Orientalists did not deny. Quite the opposite, they extolled it, if only to make their Christian neighbors in Europe feel guilty. The point is they extolled pluralistic and tolerant Islam and the nineteenth century Jewish Orientals continuously talked about it. Salo Baron, for example, says there is simply no comparison between the pluralistic Islamic civilization and the European civilization from which the Jews suffered. And I quote here Shlomo Abneri in his utterly secular philosophy of Zionism. So again, we have to consider political aspiration. What Jerusalem are we talking about? Again, going back to the stories of my grandfather, the religious Jews emigrated to America because to emigrate to Jerusalem for worldly reasons, for real estate, was considered such a profanity and sacrilege that the overwhelming majority of Jews who did emigrate from the late nineteenth century were atheists.

And so we can see why my great grandfather who was religious used his Turkish passport to go to Jerusalem, because he had utter right as a Turkish citizen to go there. As did the millions of other

Jewish citizens of the Turkish empire who did not do that. My last comment, grievances. There are two aspects to a grievance - one is negative and one is positive. Now the negative aspect I would agree with Professor Ben Dak, is the grievance with which we sort of rub the salt into our wound and it gets us nowhere, and we should transcend it. But another type of grievance which is utterly vital and totally proper is a process called reconciliation. The Arabic concept of reconciliation that goes on all the time is a mediation. The grieved party has a grievance and he airs it, if only to enable he who has aggrieved him to take some sort of reconciliatory action, which usually involves sacrifice, either a sheep, a lamb, some money, whatever. Now in that context the discussion of grievances is utterly to the point and it is the only possible hope of reconciliation. For if you don't acknowledge these grievances which are due to the stolen properties, the hundreds of mosques that have disappeared from one end of Palestine to the other, etc., there cannot be any reconciliation. You talk about the Jordanians keeping the Jews from the wailing wall. Jordan went and signed a covenant of respect of the holy places contingent on the return of half a million refugees not to one wall, but to a thousand village walls. You have to recognize the grievance. You have to kill a sheep or pay money or whatever. Life is a cosmic soup and in that sense, the only hope is the airing of grievance and your ability some day, collectively, to come to terms with it. The grievances should be negotiated, because they are all negotiable. And I think this is our hope.

Khayutman

Israelis and Jews do not respect the hypocrisy in the condemnations of UN resolutions. There are many atrocities going on around the world of which the United Nations and other people are totally blind, simply because there is some power behind the injustice.

There is so much hypocrisy about the condemnation of Israel, that it's difficult for Israelis to see the genuine and just pain. We are in a sense traumatized in Israel about this (that we have done injustice) and it's a difficult problem. My grandfather came from Oddessa. He was in a movement which sought Arab/Israeli/Jewish reconciliation back in the twenties and the thirties. This movement included those Jews who founded the Hebrew University. There was an historical chance not to start this horrible wave of bloodshed. The reason they didn't have the impact in the Jewish community was not that the Jews couldn't care less about those Orientals, that's part of the story; but another part of it is because they couldn't find any counterpart among the Arabs. They'd been frustrated again and again, because of the Palestinian intransigence in not recognizing any legitimacy of anything Israeli or Jewish anywhere in Palestine. And there is a fantastic duplicity among Arabs and Palestinians in Israel. I'm not speaking in the physical context but the emotional one, I believe that something is missing here for the future of Islam and of Judaism which can only come through this reconciliation. I think that Islam has fantastic attributes but one of its followers' big weaknesses is that hardly any Muslim knows the Bible.

Saqqaf   I have two points to make at the end of our exchange. I want us to be very clear on something. I don't think the Muslims and the Arabs will ever, ever abandon Jerusalem, irrespective of balance of power, and that is the absolute minimum line that they draw. And it's up to us and up to the peoples of this area to work out an acceptable solution because Israeli sovereignty over Jerusalem is totally unacceptable as it exists now. And I know the Israelis do not accept returning Jerusalem to total Arab rule. We have to discuss and study the possibilities between these two positions that may exist for this very important city. The second point has to do with Professor Ben-Dak's comment. He said it is not right for Palestinians who left thirty years ago to return to their homes. At the same time, it is right for Jews who presumably left three thousand years ago to return. That logic is baffling.

Part V

Problems of
Over-Urbanization:
The Case of Cairo

INTRODUCTION

Cairo is the largest metropolis in the Middle East; in fact, it is one of the largest cities in the world. From its founding as a military camp 14 centuries ago, Cairo has grown rapidly. Today, over 10 million persons live in Cairo. The city cannot support so many—thus, there is an eternal shortage of houses, telephone lines, water supply, electric lines; there is a continuous congestion of traffic and people. Cairo has become a symbol of over-urbanization resulting from policies of over-centralization.

We have three papers on Cairo. Dr. Saad Eddin Ibrahim gives a summary of the historical evolution of the city's layout. Then his analysis tackles the important issue of class struggle within a growing city (in the economic sense as well as religious competition among the different religions and sects). Class relations are used as indications of the degree of political, social, and economic powers of each class group, especially the middle class.

Dr. Hoda M. Sobhi looks at the role of Cairo and its relationship vis-a-vis the rest of Egypt. According to the analysis, Cairo claims a preponderant portion of total resources available to Egypt. The home of only 20% of the Egyptians, Cairo claims 45% of the total food consumption, 60% of all communication systems, and a larger share of total investments. Yet it is not enough, and Cairo needs more. The primary reason is that Cairo's inhabitants have a higher per capita consumption and receive a higher per capita investment.

Finally, Dr. Abdel K. El-Ahwal discusses possible solutions to the over-urbanization problem of Cairo. He stresses the need for a rural-oriented development strategy that leads to decentralization. This can be done, he argues, through the integrated village development program which he discusses in his paper.

Chapter 11

A Sociological Profile

Saad Eddin Ibrahim

The history and sociology of Cairo are those of Egypt and, to some extent, those of the entire Arab region. Its size, splendor, power, and functions have been a reflection of this fact for the past 11 centuries. It is of little surprise, therefore, that the Egyptians themselves have used the same name for their country and their capital city, Misr, interchangeably, and the Arabs have admiringly dubbed this complex entity as "the Mother of the World" (Misr Umma Dunia).

This equation does not merely relate to a concrete physical entity, but describes a state of mind and spirit. To the Egyptians and their fellow Arabs, Cairo is at once a seat of political power, of artistic creativity and cultural pacesetting, of religious shrines and religious learning, of scholarships and higher education, of industry as well as entertainment. For Egyptians and fellow Arabs, Cairo, therefore, represents singularly what so many cities may pluralistically represent to their respective nations. In terms of regional influence, Cairo is the equivalent of the likes of Paris, the Vatican, Oxford, Hollywood, and Detroit combined.

As a giant national, regional, and international center with all the above functions and feats, Cairo is also gripped by giant problems. As much as the city is enriched and stimulated by the inputs of these concentric zones around it, it also carries their burdens. No one has analyzed the unfolding of this dialectic better than Janet Abu-Lughod in her masterpiece *Cairo: 1001 Year of the City Victorious* (Princeton: Princeton University Press, 1971). She skillfully recounted the story of Cairo, woven into its broader canvas—nationally, regionally, and internationally. In the following few pages I propose to expound a number of socio-political forces which have been at work in shaping this unique city in more recent times.

Present-day Cairo has evolved historically through a series of grand political designs. The four physical formations which constituted pre-modern Cairo were all envisioned and initially carried out by great military-political commanders or empire-builders. Al-Fustat was built by Amre Ibn al-Aas in 641 (21 H.); the Abbasid dynasty built Al-Askar northeast of it in 751 (133 H.); Ahmed Ibn Tulun added a third settlement adjacent to the second called Al-Qataai in 870 (256 H.); and the Fatimid Jawhar al-Sikkli built Al-Qahira northeast of the three settlements in 969 (358 H.). These four formations all started as military settlements for commanders and soldiers with a mosque and often a palace at the center of each. They were spaced by the 100 years Khaldunian Cycle of the rise and fall of Muslim dynasties. The four settlements were finally joined and fenced by yet another great military-political commander, Salahaddeen, before he set out on his campaigns against the European crusaders in 1187. Since that time, pre-modern Cairo assumed its physical unity and functioned as a single city. Much of the developments—physical and socio-cultural —which were to take place in the following three centuries under the Mumluks occurred within the confines of this single entity measuring about two square miles. So long as Cairo remained a seat of Egyptian power it thrived and prospered. As Cairo (Egypt) lost its political-military eminence with the Ottoman conquest (1517), the city began a decline in all spheres.

Not until the beginning of the nineteenth century was Egypt, and hence Cairo, able to start the struggle for autonomy from the Ottoman Empire. In this quest Cairo was the seat of two of that century's most ambitious empire builders. The first, Napolean, headquartered himself in the city briefly (1798), and tried to unlock its intricate physique and deep cultural secrets. To him, Cairo and hence Egypt, was a challenge and a gateway to the rest of the Orient. To Cairo and hence Egypt, Napolean was an equal challenge for he was a symbol of another world almost forgotten since the last showdown with the crusaders six centuries earlier. Many waters had run under that other world's bridges, but water stood still and stagnant under Egypt's and hence Cairo's bridge. Napolean stirred the latter, proba-bly too violently for the taste of Cairo. The hitherto slumbering city revolted against the French, and finally forced them out, ending the longest three years in Egypt's modern history. The traditional city may have been too weak to resist Napolean's initial onslaught, but it proved strong enough to foil his dreams.

Meanwhile, Cairo and Egypt were never to return to their earlier state of slumber, i.e., a backwater of the Ottomon Empire. For soon was to appear another rising star, Mohammed Ali (1805). More shrewd and more resilient, he attempted to modernize Egypt by circumventing its traditional structures. He created modern institutions parallel to the traditional ones, and allowed a pipeline to connect both. With these arrangements, he provided a strong material and manpower base which in a matter of two decades enabled Egypt to emerge as a giant regional power. Not only did Egypt secure a de facto independence, but also posed a deadly threat to the Ottoman Empire itself. This story is too well-known to recount here. But in the process of his quest for modernization and empire building, Mohammed Ali laid the seed for the dual development of Egypt and Cairo. For as he built parallel institutions to circumvent traditional ones, Mohammed Ali also began the process of expanding the modern Cairo—alongside the traditional Islamic city, to the northwest. Although most of Mohammed Ali's dreams were foiled by the European powers, the seeds and directions he laid for the future expansions of Cairo have proven more lasting.

Since Mohammed Ali's rule (1805–1849), there have been four big modernization attempts: under Khedive Ismael (1863–1879), during Egypt's Liberal Age (1922–1952), under Nasser (1952–1970), and under Sadat (1970–1981). Each of these big attempts left a lasting impact on Egypt and Cairo. Between Ismael's demise and the Liberal Age (i.e., 1881–1922) Egypt was under complete British occupation. Even then Egypt and Cairo did not cease developing. But it was a development mostly initiated by an alien power, deigned to serve its interests, and was carried out mostly by foreigners.

Ismael's vision of modernization was to turn Egypt into a piece of Europe and to make Cairo a European city. Turning his back on the traditional Islamic city, he moved the seat of power from the Citadel to Abdeen Palace. He seized the opportunity of opening the Suez Canal to hurriedly build new districts in the European style, complete with parks, broad streets, an opera house, street lights and additional palaces to accommodate his European guests. Many of these developments were to the west of the Islamic city—from Azbakiyya to the eastern banks of the Nile between Boulaq and Kasr al-Aini and across into the Gazira Island. Ismael's vision ended in a nightmare for Egypt. His designs and extravaganza saddled Egypt with heavy debts to European governments and banks. It led to growing intervention in Egyptian affairs; his deposing; a popular rebellion led by Egyptian officers against his successor (Khedive Tawfiq) in 1880–1881; and ultimately British occupation of the country (1881). Ismael had opened the doors of Egyptian society and economy to thousands of foreigners. With the British occupation, hundreds of thousands flocked through in search of fame and fortune. Most of them settled in Cairo and Alexandria. They settled in the new quarters created by

Ismael and constructed their own. They started and operated Western
–like institutions, and appropriated disproportionate shares of
Egypt's wealth—thanks to the capitulations, the legal shelter provided by the Mixed courts, and the protection of foreign powers. The
construction of Garden City and Zamalek occurred in the late
nineteenth and early twentieth centuries. Heliopolis and Maadi were
envisioned and started during this period too. The old city was very
much left alone. While its population was steadily growing, its area
remained fixed and its infrastructure completely neglected. As a
result, population density skyrocketed and its living conditions
severely worsened. The ambitious and achievers among its population moved out to the newer quarters, sharing the new fortune with
the foreigners. The old city, while still containing nearly half of
Cairo's population in the second decade of this century, was steadily
being marginalized socially and economically. The decline of its
guilds and crafts, its Ulama and merchants, had started with Mohammed Ali a century earlier. But with British rule, the pace of decline
was accelerated. While foreigners were the immediate beneficiaries of
this process, there was a new native social formation of technocrats
and bureaucrats. The genesis of this new middle class (NMC) was
laid in Mohammed Ali's time—the hundreds of students who had
been sent to Europe for training and higher education. But its birth
and maturity took nearly one century.

The new middle class knocked on the doors of power many times
since Urabi's Revolt in 1879. It was opposed by the combined alliance
of the royal aristocracy and foreign powers. The NMC tried again in
1919. This time it managed to mobilize the entire population in a
two-month uprising, reminiscent of the Cairo revolts against Napolean's armies. This time the NMC partly succeeded. The door to
power was half-opened—enough for the upper half of the NMC.
Between 1920 and 1950, Cairo lived a quasi-liberal age. A parliament
with two houses was created to fulfill the quest for political power. An
Egyptian banking industry was established to mobilize economic
power, and a modern university was created in response to the
educational needs. Likewise, cinemas and theaters flourished, and a
literary movement thrived. The upper echelon of the NMC was in its
heyday in the inter-war period and enjoyed all those benefits. It was
quickly turning into a bourgeoisie. Its successful banking encouraged
an industrialization venture. The Bank Misr group implemented
many projects ranging from large-scale industries such as textile
factories to motion pictures. In the process it was creating yet another
new working class. The latter, like the NMC, was long due since its
seeds were sown by Mohammed Ali, but was stunted or aborted time

and again by local despotism and foreign domination.

Cairo was the center of all these socio-economic developments. Members of the upper echelon of the NMC moved in big numbers to the newer and better quarters of Cairo—now as partners to and not intruders on the foreign residents. A tacit alliance was soon to develop between the newly bourgeoisied members of this class and foreign interests. The latter, long sensing the winds of change, were only happy to meet their Egyptian counterparts more than midway. The 1936 Anglo-Egyptian Treaty symbolized this new partnership. This treaty left out the lower echelons of the NMC, the growing modern working class, and traditional Cairoeans in the old city, all of whom grew restless during the late 1930s and throughout the 1940s. New parties and mass politico-religious movements appealed to them—notably the Moslem Brotherhood and Young Egypt Socialist Party (Misr al-Fatah). Their misgivings vis-a-vis the Egyptian upper class were no less than those against the British and the royal family. World War II added to their sense of relative deprivation and alienation. The burning of the modern business district of Cairo (developed respectively under Ismael, the British, and during Egypt's Liberal Age) in January 1952 was a dramatic display of their anger.

The 1952 revolution was to take place six months later. Led by Nasser, this revolution ushered in yet another big modernization attempt in Egypt's modern history. It was an attempt undertaken by the "left-outs" of the previous three decades—the lower strata of the NMC. They soon allied themselves with the new working class and the peasantry in the countryside. Much of the structural changes effected by the July Revolution were naturally for the benefit of this new alliance. One of the earliest acts of the revolution was to tear down the Kasr al-Nil Barracks—a symbol of both Royal and British Cairo. The whole upper class (big bourgeoisie and landlords) was removed from political power, and its economic power dramatically reduced. Urban rent controls were soon to follow (in 1958 and 1960) hitting owners of real estate and benefiting the tenants, i.e., the lower middle class and workers. This measure, while having an immediate equitable redistributive effect, was to have an adverse effect on the supply of urban housing in the long run.

Massive public housing projects were carried out in poor districts of Cairo (e.g., Zainhom, Ain al-Sira, Embaba, Helwan, and Shubra al-Khima). New areas were zoned and subdivided for the housing of technocrats who provided the backbone for the revolution's development drive. It is not accidental that Nasr City was designed not only for their residential housing but was also the preferred site for the State's planning organs—the ministry, the National Institute of

Planning, and the Central Agency for Public Mobilization and Statistics. Likewise, the Mohandiseen City (Engineers City) was designed to accommodate the housing needs of this vital group in any industrialization effort.

Cairo grew in size of population and area during the Nasser years (1952—1970). Big industries were started in the southern suburb of Helwan and the Northern area of Shubra al-Khima. New bridges were constructed across the river. New institutions of education and culture mushroomed throughout the city. The planning and urban forms created in those years may have left a lot to be desired from an aesthetic point of view, but for the forces which backed the revolution and grew in size and power through its programs, such developments were far superior than what they have had before.

Nasser's revolutionary drive had also turned Cairo into an Arab capital in the political sense of the word. His pan-Arabism induced thousands of Arab students, artists, journalists, and activists to make Cairo a favorite destination. The city's international flavor was further enhanced by Nasser's role in the Non-Aligned Movement and his support for national liberation movements in Africa and Asia.

Nasser's dreams may have overloaded both Cairo's and Egypt's capacity. These dreams came to a tragic halt in 1967. His military defeat at the hands of Israel boded ill for Cairo as well. For several years following 1967, with most of the country's resources earmarked for the war efforts, Cairo's infrastructure was not properly maintained, let alone expanded to keep up with continuing population growth. The rent control measures did not encourage the private sector to step in and help ease the growing housing shortage either.

When Sadat came to power (1970), he inherited the heavy burdens of the country and its capital city. By 1974, Sadat had evolved his own vision to deal with those burdens. His open-door policy ushered in another big attempt not only to deal with the problems but also to take off in all respects. His vision was reminiscent of Khedive Ismael. Sadat wanted to develop Egypt along a Western-style, with Western economic aid, and with Western technology and Western experts. If Paris and Rome were favorite models for Ismael, Los Angeles and Houston were favorite models for Sadat. He let loose private developers and speculators. When the cost of land skyrocketed, he proudly declared that his policies "had made Egyptian land very valuable." New luxury high-rise buildings mushroomed all over the city, replacing private villas, through massive slum clearance (e.g., Boulaq). Many first-class hotels were also started, and new highways and overpasses were constructed including the impressive Sixth of October Bridge across the Nile over Gazira Island.

This rapid and frantic urban development in Cairo was aided by the inflow of billions of dollars from Egyptians working in oil-rich Arab countries. A new wave of foreign influx (this time mostly Americans) added further stimulation and intensified the demand for luxury housing.

Sadat's vision was supported by an alliance of different forces which were to benefit from it. This new alliance was made up of the old bourgeoisie and landlords (who were never physically liquidated by Nasser); the nouveau rich who made their fortunes in Arab countries or from shady activities; and leaders of public sector corporations who had already reached the ceiling of promotion while still in their forties or fifties. It was a very potent alliance politically and economically, but small numerically. Left out of this bonanza were the vast lower middle class, junior bureaucrats and urban working class. As they saw their share in power and wealth steadily eroded and that of others leaping, these groups became more critical of the system.

An early sign of their frustration are the food riots in Cairo and other cities in January 1977. Reminiscent of the Black Saturday events 25 years earlier, the rioters in Cairo burned and sacked many of the material symbols of Sadat's city—night clubs, expensive cars, and police stations. The army was called in (as in 1952) to put down this uprising. In the aftermath some 100 people were killed in Cairo, and several times as many wounded.

Significantly most of those killed and wounded were from Bab al-Shiriyya, Boulaq, Shoubra, and Imbaba—the most densely populated districts of Cairo.

This early warning did not alter Sadat's vision. After a brief pause, his previous policies continued. In the following four years, dissent and anger were channeled through militant religious groups— Moslems and Copts alike. Religious confrontations and interreligious strife grew rampant. The most serious of these took place in Zawia al-Hamra, one of the poorest and most crowded districts of Cairo, during the summer of 1981. A few months later, convergence of several events culminated in a massive crackdown on the opposition and all religious dissidents. On October 7, 1981, President Sadat, and probably his dazzling visions, were assassinated by one of these extremist religious groups.

Cairo's development in Egypt's modern age must be seen against this socio-political sketch. The demographic forces of the entire country have been at work since the mid-nineteenth century. Now we turn to these less dramatic but equally important and more lasting forces.

TABLE 11.1
URBAN AND RURAL
POPULATIONS: 1907–1976

YEARS	TOTAL	URBAN	(%)	RURAL	(%)
1907	11,183	2,125	(19)	9,058	(81)
1917	12,670	2,641	(21)	10,030	(79)
1927	14,083	3,716	(26)	10,367	(74)
1937	15,811	4,382	(28)	11,429	(72)
1947	18,806	6,202	(33)	12,604	(67)
1960	25,771	9,651	(37)	16,120	(63)
1966	29,724	12,037	(40)	17,687	(60)
1976	36,556	16,092	(44)	20,554	(56)

Sources: Computed from official census figures.
Note: Numbers are in thousands.

Egypt's population has grown ten-fold in the last 150 years. Cairo's has grown thirty-fold during the same period. The story of this dramatic growth of the country and its capital is not unique in Third World annals. The difference is one of scale.

TABLE 11.2
THE DEMOGRAPHIC EVOLUTION
OF CAIRO AND EGYPT

Year	CAIRO*		EGYPT	
	Population	Average annual growth rate (%)	Population	Average annual growth rate (%)
1800	200,000	—	3,000,000	—
1900	600,000	1.4	10,000,000	1.5
1920	875,000	1.6	13,000,000	1.3
1930	1,150,000	3.0	15,000,000	1.1
1940	1,525,000	2.1	19,000,000	1.2
1950	2,350,000	4.8	21,000,000	1.8
1960	3,747,000	4.1	26,000,000	2.4
1970**	5,700,000	4.1	33,000,000	2.5
1980**	8,778,000	3.0	42,000,000	2.5

*Notes on sources: figures for the 1900–1950 period are based on adjusted census figures taken regularly every 10 years from 1897 to 1947 pro-rated to even decades. The 1960 figure is an actual census figure.
**Estimates issued by the Governor of Cairo, published in *Al-Misawar,* July 13, 1984, pp. 22–25, for greater Cairo which includes Cairo proper, the adjacent urban areas of Giza and Qaliobiya (Shubra al-Khima) governorates.

The country went through its "demographic transition" in the early decades of the nineteenth century. Death rates began their slow but steady decline; birth rates remained at their previous high levels. The inevitable result, with no migration out of Egypt, has been a steady population increase. At less than five million inhabitants, Egypt's population doubled in the course of the nineteenth century. By 1900 it had hit the 10 million mark. Since then the doubling time has become shorter and shorter. The second doubling, from 10 to 20 million, took 50 years between 1900 to 1950. The third doubling, took merely 28 years, i.e. from 20 to 40 million between 1950 and 1978. The growth trends are continuing with only a slight and erratic decline in rates of natural increase. For the last 30 years that rate ranged between 2.4% and 2.8% annually.

Egypt's urban areas grew steadily. Sluggish at the beginning, this growth has accelerated in this century. Not only have urban areas matched the countryside in natural increase, but they also began to incorporate some of the latter in the form of a rural-to-urban migration. Urban population grew from 19% of Egypt's total in 1907 to 33% in 1947 to 44% in 1976 (see table 11.1). At present it is estimated that half of Egypt's population reside in cities.

Rural-to-urban migration has been one of Egypt's many silent revolutions in this century, although its impact on the daily life of Egyptian cities is not so silent. The crowding, the confusion, and the noise of people and things are abundant and rampant. There are many reasons for the century-long trend of rural-to-urban migration: pressure on limited cultivable land, neglect of the countryside, lack of employment opportunities, the attraction of cities—where power and wealth and services are concentrated.

Cairo is our immediate concern at the moment. Like Egypt, it has witnessed a steady natural population increase. And like other Egyptian cities, it has absorbed an increasing share of the rural-to-urban migration. The city proper grew from an estimated 200,000 in 1800 to 600,000 in 1900, to 2.4 million in 1950 to 5.7 in 1970 to 8.8 million in 1980 (see Table 11.2). This is a fifteen-fold increase in this century alone, compared to only a two-fold increase in rural population, and a four-fold increase in urban population. As table 11.3 shows, Cairo was adding as many persons by natural population increase as it was from migration. The dominance of Cairo over Egypt's demographic and urban landscapes needs no elaboration. Currently, the city accounts for nearly 25% of the country's total population and about 50% of the country's urban population.

Cairo's land mass expanded steadily beyond its original Islamic core—the so-called traditional or medieval city today. Until the early

TABLE 11.3
NET MIGRATION TO CAIRO: 1907–1980

Period	No. of migrants for entire period	Average annual rate of migration to Cairo (%)
1907–1917	158,000	2.0
1917–1927	297,000	2.8
1927–1937	359,000	2.6
1937–1947	606,000	2.8
1947–1960	953,000	2.2
1960–1970	702,000	2.1
1970–1980	1,100,000*	1.9

Sources: Figures for 1907–1960 are from M.S. Abdul-Karim, "Emigration to Cairo," A *Report Submitted to the Greater Cairo Planning Commission,* 1968. The figure for 1960–1970 is from Gamal Askar, "The Population Explosion in Cairo," Al-Ahram al-Iktisadi (Dec. 1, 1972) and cited in John Waterbury, Egypt: *Burdens of the Past, Options for the Future,* Indiana Univ. Press, Bloomington, 1978, p. 127.
*The figure for 1970–1980 is our own estimate for the Greater Cairo area.

decades of the nineteenth century this built-up area was no more than two square miles. By the end of the century it tripled to six square miles. Semi-empty quarters adjacent to the Islamic core filled up: Azbakiyya and Boulaq. The genesis of new quarters to the north, northeast, and west were soon to witness an embryonic growth by the second half of the nineteenth century: Shubra, Abbassiya, Ismailiya, Mounira, Kasr el-Aini, Tawfiqiyya, and Helmiya. The names of most of these new quarters bear those of Egypt's successive rulers during the nineteenth century. The areas west of the Islamic City to the Nile had already been filled up, and bridges were constructed to connect Cairo proper to Giza on the other side. By the turn of the century both Garden City (an area between Kasr al-Aini and the eastern bank of the Nile) and Zamalek (an island in the Nile across from Boulaq) were to become the choice spots for residence of the upper class, foreign and native. By 1920, the land mass of Cairo proper had expanded around the Islamic core in three directions (west, north, and south) to an area of approximately 12 square miles. This rapid expansion (nearly six times the original medieval city) was aided by the introduction of tramways starting in 1896.

The first half of the twentieth century witnessed the physical consolidation of quarters built up a few decades earlier as well as the development of two new suburbs—Heliopolis and Ma'adi, to the east and south of nineteenth-century Cairo. These were designed in a European fashion at least in terms of physical layout. They were to be residential areas for the rising foreign and native bourgeoisie who could not be accommodated in Garden City and Zamalek. The gallant attempt of Baron Emphian, builder of Heliopolis, to give one of them an Islamic-Arab character may have succeeded as far as the outer appearances goes. The socio-economic contents and functions of Heliopolis (like that of Ma'adi) belonged to a different age hardly Arab or Islamic. It was the age of incorporating Egypt's economy and the upper stratum of society in the world capitalist system.

All in all, it may be said that between 1850 and 1950 the bulk of the present metropolis had developed. Pre-nineteenth century Cairo was no more than 10% of this urban mass. It was to shrink further in relative size during the three decades following the Egyptian Revolution of July 1952, as we will show later.

The three decades following 1950 witnessed the tripling of Cairo's population and more than doubling of its built-up urban mass. The area of Cairo proper grew from less than 40 to 88 square miles. Major new districts have been created since 1950—notably Nasr City to the east of the Old Islamic core in the triangle between Abbassiya and Heliopolis, Moqattam City to the southeast, and New Maadi to the south (east of Old Maadi). The housing strip stretching south along the Nile from Misr al-Qadima and Helwan has steadily claimed previously agricultural land. Helwan itself was quickly transformed from a leisurely suburb to an industrial district for most of Egypt's heavy industries.

Across the Nile from Cairo proper, the city of Giza extended westward all the way to the Pyramids (about nine miles) and northward all the way to Imbaba, incorporating several villages and transforming them physically and socio-economically in the process. For all sociological purposes this was an extension of Cairo, thus adding to its 132 miles another 60 miles. Along with the site of Cairo University, the National Zoo, the Orman Garden, and many villas along the western bank of the Nile, Giza has become the major recipient of Cairo's population spillover. New districts were planned and developed: Mohandiseen City, Professors City and Journalists City. Designed as single dwelling areas in the 1950s, these districts soon turned into high–rise building areas in the 1970s.

To the north of Cairo proper, the stretch between Shubra and rural Qaliobiyya was quickly filled up with both residential and industrial functions. Known as Shubra al-Khalma, this area (like Giza across the river) has become socio-economically an integral part of Cairo. It added some 18 miles to the 132 miles of Cairo proper.

Thus, all in all, the socio-physical entity called Greater Cairo is roughly 140 square miles, and is the home of more than 10 million of

TABLE 11.4
GREATER CAIRO: COMPONENTS OF GROWTH 1960–1976

URBAN UNIT Av. (%)	1960 POPULATION (000)	1966 POPULATION (000)	ANNUAL AV. GROWTH 1960–66 (%)	1976 POPULATION (000)	ANNUAL GROWTH 1966–76
Cairo Proper	3,353	4,220	3.9	5,084	1.9
Giza City	419	571	5.3	1,233	8.0
Shubra al-Khayma	101	173	9.4	394	8.6
Total	3,873	4,964	4.8	6,711	3.5

Source: Computed from official census data.

Egypt's population. In the early 1980s, Cairo proper accounted for roughly 63 percent of the total urban mass and about 70 percent of its population. Cairo proper has one of the world's highest densities— 12,800 per square mile. It has about 450,000 buildings and 2.5 million residential units.

Over the last century and a half, the old Islamic core of the city has shrunk in relative size and population. In Table 11.6, the data for Cairo proper is broken down by four major divisions: eastern, western, northern, and southern. The old Medieval city is entirely located in the eastern division. As the table shows, the city has grown all around it, reducing its relative size steadily. Up until 1907, the eastern division still accounted for half of Cairo's total population. By 1937 its share fell to no more than one third, and by 1976 its share fell to 19%. Measured against Greater Cairo, the population of the Islamic core would account for less than 10% today.

TABLE 11.5
GREATER CAIRO: CHANGING RELATIVE
WEIGHT OF COMPONENTS 1960–1976

Urban Unit	PERCENTAGE OF GREATER CAIRO'S POPULATION		
	1960	1966	1976
Cairo Proper	86.57	85.01	75.76
Giza City	10.82	11.50	18.37
Shubra al-Khayma	2.61	3.49	5.87
Total	100.00	100.00	100.00

Source: Computed from Table 11.4, above.

TABLE 11.6
CAIRO PROPER: DIFFERENT GROWTH
RATES OF ITS MAJOR DIVISIONS 1971–1976

YEAR	CAIRO	EASTERN (%)	WESTERN (%)	NORTHERN (%)	SOUTHERN (%)
1882	400,000	213,000 (54)	130,000 (32)	34,000 (9)	23,000 (6)
1897	590,000	320,000 (54)	160,000 (27)	76,000 (13)	34,000 (6)
1907	680,000	348,000 (50)	184,000 (27)	112,000 (16)	36,000 (6)
1917	800,000	376,000 (47)	216,000 (27)	170,000 (21)	40,000 (5)
1937	1,312,000	457,000 (35)	350,000 (33)	450,000 (34)	55,000 (5)
1947	2,091,000	670,000 (32)	512,000 (24)	800,000 (38)	109,000 (6)
1960	3,353,000	770,000 (23)	775,000 (23)	1,600,000 (48)	208,000 (6)
1966	4,220,000	840,000 (20)	928,000 (22)	2,110,000 (50)	338,000 (8)
1976	5,084,000	966,000 (19)	1,027,000 (20)	2,645,000 (52)	458,000 (9)

Sources: Computed from official census figures, following J. Abu-Lughod's classification of districts and extending it to cover 1966 and 1967. See Janet Abu-Lughod, *Cairo: 1001 Years of the City Victorious,* Princeton Univ. Press, Princeton, 1971, pp. 172–180.

TABLE 11.7
SELECTED INDICATORS OF CONCENTRATION
IN GREATER CAIRO IN 1976

INDICATOR	PERCENTAGE OF EGYPT'S TOTAL
Population	20.0
Manufacturing establishment	55.7
Industrial workers	48.5
Industrial production	51.5
Public investment	37.5
Public investment in water-delivery	48.5
Food consumption (1983)*	42.5
Telephone lines (1983)*	60.0

Sources: Computed or cited from official sources by John Waterbury, "Patterns of Urban Growth and Income Distribution" in G. Abdel Khalek and R. Tignor (editor), *Political Economy of Income Distribution in Egypt,* Holms and Meier, N.Y., 1982, pp. 319–324 and 328.
*Statement by Governor of Cairo, *al-Misawar,* July 13, 1984. p. 23.

The population of the Islamic core is only half of what appears in Table 11.6 under "Eastern." For, in reality, the eastern division includes a freak residential area known as the cemeteries of Cairo, referred to in urban literature as "the City of the Dead." Separated from Islamic Cairo to the southeast by Salah Salem Road and stretching along that road for several miles, the City of the Dead has been absorbing the spillover population of the Islamic core as well as the homeless from other parts of Cairo—including recent rural migrants. [Cairo's traditional burial places usually include a grave, one or two adjacent rooms, and an open yard (howsh), all surrounded by a fence. It is so designed as to enable relatives of the deceased to come for extended visits. Most of these structures are spacious, airy, and sunny, and could accommodate the living as well as the dead. For centuries the City of the Dead had a small population of burial-related functionaries, e.g., watchmen, undertakers, stonecutters, and Quran reciters. At times, wanted criminals and fugitives found shelter in the City of the Dead. In the last four decades, however, it began to attract other categories of population who could not find cheap housing elsewhere. In 1937 some 10,000 people were already residing in the City of the Dead. Thirty years later that population had grown ten-fold, i.e., to about 100,000. At present it is estimated to be close to 250,000.[1]

Cairo authorities reluctantly accepted the de facto situation and extended some municipal services—including water, electricity, schools, bus lines, and even a police station. Meanwhile, the residents of the cemeteries have engaged in normal activities found in similar quarters of Cairo. Groceries, bakeries and other service shops opened, and even some traditional industries (e.g., glass blowing) are located there.

By international standards, the City of the Dead would be considered a slum area. But by Cairo standards it offers better living conditions than many other slum areas of the city. The population density (about 12,000 persons per square mile) is not as high as it is in the Islamic core across the Salah Salem Road where it is about 36,000 per square mile. The general density average for Cairo as a whole is 12,800 per square mile. Some districts like Bab al-Shiaryya suffer from a density of 60,000 per square mile. Although the Islamic core of Cairo is densely populated, it is richly endowed with traditional culture and material symbols. It is the site of Al-Azhar Mosque and University, the Citadel, Cairo's most famous mosques, Khans, Mameluke tombs, traditional arts and crafts, bazars, and traditional coffee shops and restaurants. However, several new functions have been introduced in that district, notably warehouses and wholesale trade. These, along with a growing population density, pose the greatest physical and cultural threat to the Islamic core and its historical treasures. It is being squeezed from within and from without. Surrounded by other newer and faster growing districts, the demand is mounting for highways cutting across the Islamic core. The underground water level for its own population use and that of neighboring districts is rising and poses an added threat to its fabulous monuments.

In more than sheer metaphor, the Islamic core of Cairo has become an enclave of a remnant urban traditional culture, surrounded by a teaming megalopolis. Its fate is not entirely in the hands of its residents or even those who profess a keen obligation of guarding it. Nor is it clear in whose hands lie the fate of this Islamic enclave. Yet the enclave continues to muddle its way through the ups and downs of modern Egyptian history. Its "traditional culture" gallantly negotiates its survival with other modern and quasi-modern cultures of the megalopolis. One saving grace in this dialectic is that the megalopolis itself represents a bigger enclave in an otherwise semi-traditional society. Thus, the Islamic enclave within greater Cairo draws some of its strength from the larger society outside Cairo.

The larger society has continuously injected Cairo with waves of newcomers. While some of them are "select migrants" and hence "modern" or "modern-oriented," the majority of newcomers are "non-select migrants" and hence bearers of a traditional culture. This education has kept the terms of cultural exchange somewhat balanced within Cairo. Even some of the select migrants to Cairo in recent years, mostly university students or university graduates, have increasingly shown an aversion to modern metropolitan culture, if it means as it often does, "western culture." The growing Sufi orders and militant Islamic groups are embodiments of this trend. Thus, the Islamic enclave in Cairo is not entirely helpless or powerless in negotiating its survival with other sub-cultures. It has its own reservoir as well as voluntary secret cultural agents diffused throughout the city. In the 1970s an estimated 300 new nightclubs were opened in Greater Cairo—double the number for the previous 20 years. This was more than matched by the building of some 400 new mosques, mostly by private initiative—also double the number for the previous 20 years.

To say that Cairo has overwhelming problems is extremely stating the obvious. Its first problem is one of size. Greater Cairo now contains about one-fourth of Egypt's population. This in itself poses major problems of administration and manageability. None of Egypt's successive regimes in the last 100 years has been able to check its growth. Unwittingly, all of these regimes stimulated the city growth by concentrating power, economic activities, and services. Table 11.7 shows a few indicators of such concentration. A vicious cycle is at work; greater concentration of production and service functions in Cairo is at the expense of other cities and rural areas. The ambitious and needy population of the latter come to Cairo, often at rates *faster* than the city can accommodate. The government spends a disproportionate share to keep Cairo's population (old and new) from revolting. But it never spends enough.

A few examples may suffice. With only one quarter of Egypt's population, Cairo appropriates about half of Egypt's public spending on limited income housing. Yet at present it suffers from a housing shortage, short of 250,000 units.

Cairo consumes about 45 percent of Egypt's food. Yet, occasional food shortages and long lines in front of food cooperatives are familiar scenes in several of Cairo's districts.

The city consumes about half of Egypt's purified water, yet water shortages are frequent, especially in the summer months, and dwellers of higher floors eternally complain. Cairo's daily water consumption is 105 million cubic feet. But the capacity of its sewage and drainage network is only 70 million cubic feet. The excess (35 million) gushes out and creates sizable, hazardous ponds in most of Cairo's poor districts (and sometimes even in well-to-do districts). This phenomenon was directly responsible for the collapse of many buildings, especially those with shaky foundations.

As population grew, demand for land has mounted for housing and public buildings, and Cairo's green areas have steadily shrunk. Slightly more than one square yard per capita of green two decades ago, the share now is less than seven square inches, compared to 19 square yards per capita in Europe.

Cairo has equity problems. In the late 1970s about 40 percent of its population lived under the "poverty line."[2] Relations between education, occupation, and income are no longer congruous. Many of the poor are "new poors"—often with high school or university degrees. Many of the rich are "nouveau rich," often engaged in trade, smuggling, illegal currency exchange, land speculation, or other parasitic and dubious activities. Some of the nouveau rich are skilled, self-employed manual workers (e.g., plumbers, mechanics, electricians, masons, etc.). Nearly all the poor of Cairo (old and new) live in sub–standard housing. The Governor of Cairo (al-Misawar, July 13, 1984) stated that 35 percent of Cairo's 2.3 million housing units are too old and dilapidated to conform to safety health regulations. He further stated that about 25 percent of all new housing units are built illegally (wild-cat) and randomly without proper monitoring for safety and health standards.

Another side of the equity problem of Cairo is the emergence in the 1970s of parallel service institutions with vast differences in quality. Thus, along public schools and hospitals, for example, private ones have been established: the latter cater to the top five percent of Cairo's population; the former cater to the other 95 percent (the poor and middle classes). Similarly, much of the public expenditure on the city's transportation system has disproportionately gone to owners of private automobiles. In the 10 years of 1972–1982, the number of private vehicles more than tripled; public and semi-public vehicles also increased but at a slower pace. The new highways, overpasses and ringroads obviously cater mainly to commuters who own private cars.

The growing inequity in Cairo is part of that of Egypt. The top five percent of the country's population has raised its share of national income from 15 to 24 percent during the 1970s, while the share of the lowest 20 percent dropped from 17 to 13 percent. But it is in Cairo that this inequity is most glaring. About 200,000 of Egypt's estimated 250,000 millionaires are residents of Cairo. Another aspect of the glaring inequity is the vast salary differential among employees of the government, public sector, and modern private sector. Three persons with equal qualifications employed in those sectors could receive a monthly salary of E.100, 200, and 1000, respectively. The inequity has created instability in the job market, with a frantic race for modern private employment, whose demand is no more than 10 percent of Egypt's annual total.

All in all, Cairo's overcrowdedness, deteriorating physical infrastructure and public services are compounded for the majority of its population by glaring inequities of power and wealth. As there is a struggle for Cairo's soul, there is an even more intense struggle for the limited resources and privileges. Cairo's elite (top 5 percent) in

TABLE 11.8
GREATER CAIRO: MOTOR VEHICLES 1972–1982

Year	Private autos	Public and semi-public vehicles*
1972	80,559	17,736
1974	87,388	20,710
1975	94,564	31,481
1977	133,599	33,571
1982**	250,000**	45,000

Source: For the years 1972–1977, Ventral agency for Public Mobilization and Statistics (CAPMS), October 1978, cited in John Waterbury, "Patterns of Urban Growth and Income Distribution" in G. Abdel-Khalek and R. Tignor (editors), *The Political Economy of Income Distribution in Egypt,* Holms and Meier, New York, 1982, p. 333.
*The figures include taxi's and private buses which transport tourists and employees of public and private companies.
**Estimates by the Governor of Cairo, *al-Misawar,* July 13, 1984, p. 23.

recent years has been oblivious to the fate and conditions of the majority of the rest of the city's poorer quarters. The physical development of Cairo in the 1950s and 1960s was shaped by the lower middle class and the technocrats. It may have been austere and lacking in aesthetics, but not lacking in equity. In the 1970s Cairo's development was more vulgar and repleat with social inequities. The fight over Cairo's soul and body is far from being settled in the 1980s. The poor are crowded in older quarters, cemeteries, and are engaged in wild-cat housing and squatter settlements. The nouveau rich continue to be oblivious to the rest of the city so long as their immediate districts and homes are in good shape, and as long as they spend a good part of the year abroad. It is the middle classes, especially the lower rungs, which feel the squeeze, and the youngsters are steaming with frustration and anger. Much of Cairo's future, and hence of Egypt's, may very well lie in their hands.

NOTES

1. Some scholarly accounts put figures at 900,000. See, for example, M.F. al-Kurdy, "Cairo's Cemeteries: Population" in *Annual Book of Sociology,* no. 6 (Arabic), 1984 pp. 17–132. The figure is cited on p. 19.

2. For details see, Saad Eddin Ibrahim "Social Mobility and Income Distribution in Egypt" in G. Abdel Khalek and Ri. Tignor (editors), *The Political Economy and Income Distribution in Egypt,* New York: Holms and Meier, 1982, pp. 375–434.

Chapter 12

The Big Urban Bias

Hoda M. Sobhi

The pace of urban growth in the developing countries poses great challenges for national, regional and city policy–makers. To show how big these challenges are in the field of socio-economic development in such countries we should note that:[1]

- It is expected that 95% of the increase in world population up to the end of this century would take place in developing countries. 50% of this increase is expected to be urban population.
- The increase in the number of big cities has been quite tremendous in the last decade. The number of cities with more than four million inhabitants has increased from 28 to 41. In the developing countries this figure almost doubled; it increased from 15 to 27 big cities.

In cities of developing countries the problems faced by urban authorities are serious, yet the resources to deal with them are quite scarce. In addition, fundamental improvements in the institutional framework are considered an important prerequisite for more efficient and equitable urban growth. This is true since spatial development and the growth of any particular urban area are interrelated aspects of the same process of transformation experienced in all developing countries.

A diagnosis of the problems of urban policy in developing countries can be summarized as consisting of two interrelated phenomena. First, urban labor supply tends to expand more rapidly than urban labor demand; this limits the growth of urban wages and incomes, especially for unskilled workers. Second, the demand for urban services expands more rapidly than their supply; this leads to rising prices for urban land and housing, overcrowded housing, and shortages of essential services, all of which affect the urban poor especially. Since these imbalances are largely the result of inefficient management of labor demand and service supply by governments, the efficiency and equity of urban development can be increased by improving the policies that create the imbalance.[2]

The rising concern with the need for decentralization, the problems of rural-to-urban balance, regional inequalities, the growing squatter settlements and slums, and the rising backlog in urban services —these and other factors forced planners to realize that the spatial distribution of socio-economic activities cannot be treated independently from issues of national economic, social and political development. Development involves much more than just the expansion of output.

Economic development does not only mean maximum growth of output, but also optimal quality of growth. This implies a more balanced regional as well as sectoral growth. Confining development to the sector-branch pattern and neglecting the spatial dimension of the economy necessarily leads to the wrong economic decisions, negative and harmful effects on the natural environment, great disparities in the standards of living of the population, and losses in GNP because the regional growth potentials are neglected.[3]

For several essential reasons the need for a national urbanization strategy is much stronger among developing countries than it ever was in the developed countries. In practically all developing countries the role of the state is dominant. The government has an inevitable influence through its policies, the location of infrastructure investment, and the public enterprises it controls. In many developing countries national spatial development is marked by a higher degree of economic dualism and inequality among regions and urban areas. The rapid rate of growth of the population has led to the concentration of large groups of low-income households in a few large cities. This, in turn, complicated the task of development. Effective settlement strategies may alleviate this problem.[4]

THE URBAN BIAS OF
NATIONAL ECONOMIC POLICIES

A good understanding of the spatial effects of national economic policies is essential to developing countries. These policies have a definite effect on where people live and where they work. In countries that have begun to tackle their spatial problems seriously, the effect of the incentives on business location decisions is very strong.[5]

One major reason for the failure of national urbanization policies in developing countries is the exclusive concentration on problems of urban decentralization while ignoring the fact that national economic policies provide strong implicit incentives to locate in the dominant urban centers. Therefore, many of the objectives selected by policy–makers address the symptoms and not the causes of resource misallocation and severe regional disparities. The social and political objectives behind many announced spatial strategies are in clear conflict with the forces set in motion by national economic policy. Therefore, urban policies must make sure that national economic and social policies do not accentuate the concentration of population and economic activities in large urban centers.

The proper formulation of a national urbanization policy strategy requires the systematic discussion of three major aspects of population distribution and national settlement:[6]

1) The implicit spatial effects and biases of national policies

2) The appropriate policies to deal with problems of large cities such as congestion and pollution

3) The problems of regional inequality and the direct explicit policy instruments for the redistribution of economic activities

REGIONAL INEQUALITIES, PRIMACY AND CONGESTION

The great economic and social difference between regions sharply distinguishes the problems of a large number of developing countries from those of advanced economies. In the most advanced economies, the ratio between the poorest and the richest regions is in the order of two to one; in many middle-income countries this ratio can go up to ten to one. This contrast between the richer, more advanced regions and the poorer regions had led to differentiating the core region of a country from its periphery and to the notion of polarized development.[7]

In the developing countries there is a basic contradiction between the desire to reduce disparities among regions and the need to improve the overall efficiency of the national economy. In order to enhance future development in all the regions, growth in modern urban regions must be intensified, since they are the ones with high growth potential and high saving rates. They also generate investment surplus in the future which could be allocated to the less-developed and poorer regions. This is more or less the "trickle-down" theory in economic development. Of course, in the short run this is in direct contradiction with the goal of equity.[8] Therefore, there is little doubt that these pronounced spatial inequalities are associated with the biases of the above national economic policies. Inter–regional inequality is greater during the transition stage or intermediate level than at the low or high levels of development. The concentration of industrial development in growth centers is the result of attempts to derive the full benefits of external economies. This leads to a dual structured economy: a center of rapid intense growth and a periphery whose economy is either stagnant or declining. Later on, as the process of concentration of economic activities accentuates, the influx from the periphery to the center leads to congestion and over-urbanization.[9]

Here it is very important to distinguish between the concentration of a large percentage of total urban population in the largest city (primacy), and the existence of a large urban center in a country. These two conditions are not synonymous. Also, congestion is not synonymous with concentration of economic activities in space but refers only to situations where, at the margin, increases in concentration add more to total diseconomies than to total economies.

What matters here is economic efficiency and city size. Economic efficiency of a city is the net result of the benefits of urban agglomeration and the losses created by congestion and environmental deterioration. At the lower end of the size range, economies of scale increase rapidly as a city expands, but beyond a certain size the additional gains diminish rapidly.[10]

URBANIZATION TRENDS IN EGYPT

Egypt is highly urbanized for a country with its economic structure and per capita income. This phenomenon is not of recent origin, but has characterized the country from the beginning of the century. The over-urbanization is real and has increased with time.[11]

Many observers have noted that Egypt's over-urbanization is out-distancing its economic development in general and its industrialization in particular. Compared to Western societies which launched industrialization in the nineteenth century, Egypt is said to have twice as many urban dwellers as these societies had during their economic take–off.[12]

However, an opposite point of view exists. Gamal Hamdan, a distinguished Egyptian writer, does not think that Egypt is over-urbanized. He argues that modern civilization has reached a stage which is quite different from the post-industrial revolution stage. Urbanization is no longer a function of the degree of industrial growth; therefore, it is possible, and even natural, to have big cities without big industries. Or, at least it has become possible for the growth of big cities to precede industrial development as long as industrialization comes later and corrects the imbalance. In short, he considers the high rate of urbanization without industrialization a new pattern in modern societies and a natural outcome of modern advanced technology.[13]

Of course, there is no doubt that urbanization, provided it takes place within the right limits and necessary prerequisites, is a healthy and natural phenomenon. On the contrary, it is a sign of progress on the national level since it conforms with the long-term global trends. However, inasmuch as a great portion of our scarce capital is diverted away from industrial development in order to relieve the strains on urban infrastructure and services, there exists a problem of over-urbanization in Egypt.

Table 12.1 shows the dramatic rise in the share of urban population. The real jump to urban life came during World War II when the percentage of urban population suddenly jumped to 30%. For a whole decade after that the urbanization process continued rapidly, then it began to slow down. This trend is expected to continue, and by the year 2000, Egypt's urban population is expected to be 50%. This will give Egypt the same urbanization rate as the rest of the world by the beginning of the twenty-first century.

TABLE 12.1
URBANIZATION IN EGYPT
RURAL-URBAN (%)

Date	Rural	Urban
1907	81.0	19.0
1917	77.4	22.7
1927	77.1	22.9
1947	70.4	29.6
1960	62.6	37.4
1966	59.5	40.5
1976	56.1	43.9
2000	50.0	50.0

Source: G. Hamdan, p. 315.[13]

However, the situation is complicated since Egypt's pattern of urbanization has been dominated by the growth of the country's primary city, Cairo. The largest city in the Middle East and Africa, Cairo ranked the sixth largest among the capitals of the world in 1980.

Moreover, as Issawi notes, Egyptian regimes have been strongly urban biased for centuries, long before important substitution industrialization strategies were known. This urban bias has always been and continues to mean a bias to the capital, Cairo.[14]

THE RAPID GROWTH OF CAIRO

Cairo became a city of one million inhabitants for the first time in 1927. This was only the beginning. In the following two decades Cairo doubled its population, and by 1927, it represented 10% of the total population. By 1960, the Cairene population reached 3.4 million which was more than 13% of the total population. The growth continues unabated.

The Egyptian population grew 5.7 times in one century (1882–1976), while Cairo's population grew 12.7 times. This means that Cairo's population grew at double the national rate.

One very important fact is, the Cairo Governorate (85 square miles) no longer represents the true image of Cairo today. Greater Cairo, or the Cairo Metropolitan Region in the broad sense, is the true size of Cairo. The Greater Cairo area is 1160 square miles—that is 13.5 times as big as the area of the Cairo Governorate.

The Greater Cairo population was about six million in 1966, in 1969 the population increased to seven million. By 1976 the number rose to eight million. The 1983 estimates show that Greater Cairo's population was 9.3 million or 20.2% of the total population.[15]

Table 12.3 shows Greater Cairo's population in 1976.

TABLE 12.2
THE POPULATION GROWTH OF CAIRO PROPER

Year	Total NUMBER	Population RATE OF GROWTH	Cairo NUMBER	Population RATE OF GROWTH	Cairo TOTAL (%)
1882	6,712	—	0,398	—	5.7
1897	9,715	2.5	0,598	2.6	6.1
1907	11,287	1.5	0,678	1.4	6.0
1917	12,751	1.2	0,790	1.5	6.2
1927	14,218	1.1	1,064	3.0	8.2
1937	15,933	1.2	1,312	2.1	8.2
1947	19,022	1.9	2,090	4.7	10.9
1960	26,085	2.7	3,353	3.6	12.9
1966	30,076	2.8	4,220	4.1	14.0
1976	38,228	2.3	5,074	1.8	13.9

Source: G. Hamdan, *op. cit.,* pp. 288, 290.[13]

TABLE 12.3
GREATER CAIRO 1976

City of Cairo	5.084
CIty of Giza	1.246
City of Shobra el-khema	.394
Giza Markaz	.094
Imbaba Markaz	.407
Badrashain Markaz	.198
Kanater el-khayria Markaz	.141
Khanka Markaz	.151
Shebrin el-kanater Markaz	.065
Klayub Markaz	.185
Part of Saf Markaz	.032
Total	8.000 (million)

Source: CAPMAS, 1976 Census

In the year 2000, the Greater Cairo population may reach over 20 million. The total population is expected to be 66 million, 39 million of which is expected to be urban population. Therefore Greater Cairo is expected to represent about one-third of the total Egyptian population, and at least half of the total urban population.[16] The rapid population growth of Cairo has made its share in the country's population much bigger than the population percentage of the capital in other countries. Greater Cairo represents more than 20% of Egypt's population, whereas most countries' shares of capital population are about one-tenth of their total population. In this sense, Cairo today seems to be double its proportionate size.

THE MECHANISM OF GROWTH

So far, the important factor in the pattern of urban growth has been internal migration. There has always been great socio-economic spatial differences within Egypt, which created attractive pulling areas and disadvantageous out-pushing areas. Therefore, internal migration took place between a negative pole, i.e., the poor rural out-pushing overpopulated and underdeveloped areas, and a positive pole, i.e., the rich developed urban-pulling areas.[17] This means that internal migration in Egypt has always been urban-bound, and moreover, it has been mainly capital-bound too.

So long as the economic balance between population and agricultural productivity was acceptable, Egyptians had little inclination for internal or external migration. But once the traditional demographic equilibrium was undermined, this proposition no longer held. The steady population growth meant, among other things, mounting pressure on agricultural land, the result of which was the flight from rural to urban areas.[18]

The densely settled and impoverished countryside in Egypt is pushing people into the cities because they have no other alternative. Much of the migration to the cities seems to be a refugee migration from the countryside where increased population densities, diminished size of holdings, and falling income's have gradually squeezed out families in great numbers.[19]

The 1976 population census shows:[20]

1) The four urban governorates received 1,347,698 net migrants. This figure equals 17.4% of the total population of these governorates.

2) The Cairo Governorate alone received 998,560 net migrants. This figure represents 74.1% of the total net migration to the urban governorates.

3) Lower Egypt received a total of 461,677 new migrants from upper Egypt and the frontier governorates.

These conclusions represent the long-term trend of the redistribution of the Egyptian population. One can even find symptoms of this trend in earlier centuries. It is therefore a permanent and steadily growing trend.[21]

The problem of internal migration in Egypt lies in the fact that a great many unemployable people came to the urban areas, especially Cairo.

The influx of newcomers from rural to urban areas adds very little to the productive capacity of Egyptian cities. Most of these newcomers are what sociologists call "non-select migrants," i.e., migrants with little or no education, little or no savings, and little or no skills. Yet their presence in large cities taxes the already overloaded infrastructure and services. Yet, they are not incorporated into the modern sectors of the economy thus retarding their adoption of the typically "urban way of life." And because they have descended on the cities in large numbers, the newcomers tend to cluster on the edges of the cities. Their proximity to one another tends to reinforce rather than diminish their "rural way of life." This has given rise to a phenomenon now dubbed as the "ruralization" of Egyptian cities. The areas in which new rural migrants and the old urban poor concentrate have rapidly turned into slums—physically, socially and psychologically.[22]

The ruralization process is a function of the size of the rural influx. This means that its peak is reached in the capital Cairo, although

Cairo is at the top of the Egyptian urban life and urban hierarchy. This contradiction explains many of Cairo's features and problems.

ELEMENTS OF THE BIAS

One of the most important characteristics of Egypt has always been the very high degree of geographical centralism. Cairo seemed always to be the destination of the whole country. All roads lead to Cairo; it is the center of the valley as well as the center of the desert. This is true although, distance-wise, Cairo is not exactly at the center of the country, however, it is precisely at the center of the densely inhabited part.

The pattern of population distribution and densities make Cairo a natural demographic peak. In fact, one-third of the total population lives within a 45-mile radius of Cairo (according to 1976 census data).[23]

The administrative factor has always been a very important factor leading to more centralization. This is because Egypt is a hydraulic society and therefore the central government has always played a very important role in the economic life and prosperity of the whole country. Moreover, there has always been a strong relationship between the bureaucracy and the urban bourgeoisie, and based on this relationship it is said that the main Egyptian cities are cities of bureaucrats.[24] The administrative apparatus was always located mainly in Cairo, leaving the whole countryside totally deprived from the minimum level of its services.

Unfortunately, Egypt has always been divided into a big city, the capital, and a big village, the countryside. This has been the great contradiction and the peak of dualism in Egypt's history. There was always the glorious capital as contrasted with the poor countryside. This means Egypt was never a pyramid-shaped hierarchy of cities. In this sense, Cairo has conquered all other Egyptian cities, and this is the reason Egypt has a very imbalanced and skewed hierarchy of cities.

Feudalism, before the 1952 revolution, divided the country not only socially and functionally, but also geographically and spatially. Absentee ownership created two geographical classes: rich absentee landlords living in the capital, and poor landless peasants living in the countryside. Even after the end of feudalism, the same center-periphery relationship still existed in a much stronger form because of the growing bureaucracy, commercial bourgeoisie and later the industrial capitalists. Finally came the "infitah" (open-door) economic policy to give Cairo its highest stage of growth and to make it look like a giant on the Egyptian landscape.

THE BIAS OF NATIONAL ECONOMIC POLICIES

In the final analysis, Cairo is the heart of the Egyptian economy. Egyptian industry and agriculture—in addition to the government bureaucracy and all the services and amenities—seem to cluster around Cairo. The heart of Egyptian agriculture seems to be in the three surrounding governorates: Menoufia (dairy, meat and poultry production), Kalyobia (fruit production) and Giza (vegetable production). All the three specialize in providing the needs of Cairo. Similarly the peak of Egypt's industry lies with Greater Cairo too. About half of Egypt's industries are located in Shobra El-khaima north of Cairo, and Helwan in the south.

In general, we can easily say that all development efforts in Egypt have accentuated regional differences, increased the degree of primacy of Cairo, and increased the lack of social infrastructure in the rural governorates. This has been effected through a strongly biased regional allocation of investments:[26]

1) The first 1958–60 industrial program allocated 38% of its total investments to Cairo.

2) The first five-year plan (1960–65) allocated 20% of its total investments to Cairo. Cairo's share of industrial investments was 25%, 16% of electricity, 36% of investments in housing, and 37% of investments in services. Of course, if we add Giza and Kalyubia these shares would rise even further.

3) Figures of the transitional plan (1974–75) show the same trend, and so does the 1978–1982 five-year plan. Greater Cairo got 24% of the total investment.

The infitah economic policy is the peak of the big Cairo bias. In the absence of clear regional incentives, foreign investments in Egypt tend to strengthen the agglomeration tendencies prevailing in the spatial structure of the economy. Most foreign companies and businesses show their interest in locating in Cairo and its suburbs. This, of course, is due to the availability of government services, infrastructure, skilled labor, easy outlets to the rest of the world, accessibility to international communications and the huge market size.[27]

The geographic distribution of the inland projects that started production by the end of 1981 shows that:[28]

1) The governorate of Cairo received 196 projects, thus representing 61.4% of the total capital investments.

2) Second in order was Giza with 74 projects representing 11% of the total capital investments.

3) Third in order came Kalyobia with a share of 38 projects representing 5% of the total capital investments.

All this means that out of the approximate total of 436 inland projects, seventy-one percent are located in Greater Cairo. What aggravated the bias was the non-interventionist policy of the government. Things have been left to the mechanism of city growth, the mechanism which necessarily leads to more concentration of people and economic activities and therefore to bigger size all the time. Moreover, there was a severe lack of high-level political commitment to better distribution of economic activities throughout the country, and to stopping the octopus-like growth of the capital. Since Cairo was never meant to be of such a huge size, the vital importance of an effective settlement strategy and a sound national urbanization policy cannot be over-stressed.

THE STAGE OF DISECONOMIES: THE CONSEQUENCES OF THE BIAS

Cairo today is a city of great and acute contradictions. Cairo is the city of the rich and most fortunate. Over 200,000 millionaires live in Cairo. Only 5% of the Cairene population has all the power and wealth, while the rest suffers from Cairo's diseconomies of agglomeration.[29]

Cairo therefore has the severest class differentials in the country. It is estimated that 50% of Cairo's income goes to only 5% of its inhabitants. Therefore, Cairo's poor are the victims of its rich.[30]

Cairo today has become a real national issue because the congestion represents a frightening and vicious problem. All the positive externalities and the economics of scale Cairo had provided for a long time have now been exceeded by negative externalities and diseconomies of scale.

The rapid and sustained growth of urban population and the low level of resources available for housing and municipal services have all contributed to poor conditions in the cities, particularly in Cairo. Urban housing in particular seems to have steadily deteriorated since the early 1960s.[31]

On the one hand, there are the high modern and luxurious buildings in Zamalek, Maadi, Mohandesin and Heliopolis, and on the other hand, the tomb cities are getting more and more crowded every day. The population of the "Dead City" was estimated at 900,000 inhabitants in 1984, and the illegal low-standard houses represent 80% of the annual increase in housing units in Cairo, in spite of the fact that Cairo's share of public expenditure in subsidy to low-income housing is more than 50%. Cairo has an estimated shortage of 200,000 housing units today. Housing conditions in Cairo, probably the best served in Egypt, are very poor.

In 1970 only 44% of the buildings in Greater Cairo were connected to public or private systems of sewerage. Over 50% of the buildings did not have tap water supply. More than one-third of the buildings did not have electric connections.[33]

TABLE 12.4
ROOM DENSITIES FOR THE CITY OF CAIRO 1947–1972

Year	City Population	No. of Housing Units	Number of Rooms	Persons per Room
1947	2,090,064	448,333	1,039,742	2.0
1960	3,348,779	687,858	1,439,158	2.3
1966	4,232,663	779,789	1,559,578	2.7
1972	5,200,000 (Est.)	860,039 (Est.)	1,720,078 (Est.)	3.1

Source: Mahmoud A. Fadil: *Political Economy of Nasserism,* Cambridge Univ. Press, Cambridge, U.K. 1980, p. 128.

In 1984, room densities in Cairo reached a very high level. Some housing units, in districts like Babas-Sh'arriya, have 10 persons per room. The average of the old and poor districts of Cairo today is seven persons per room. In such residential units, it is quite usual for generations to live together in a single housing unit.[34]

Babas-Sh'arriya, the first destination for many bewildered new peasant migrants, now has a density of about 60,000 per square mile, three times the average of the slums of Calcutta or Djakarta.[35]

Looking at the problem from a different angle, we find that 400,000 of Cairo's dwellings are structurally unsound, and about 40% of Cairo's dwellings are on the verge of total collapse. The crisis is more aggravated by illegal urban squatters. We may distinguish between two basic types of clandestine squatters in Cairo: one form is roof-dwellers who build huts, shacks and the like on roofs of buildings in old districts of Cairo, which house about half a million Cairenes; the other is people living in the "dead city."[36]

The transport problem is even worse than the housing problem. Transportation reaches a standstill in the center of the city during rush hours, and the lines of cars are getting longer and longer. Today the cruelest problem facing anyone living in Cairo is the daily trip to work and the trip back home. This goes for those who drive their own cars, and in a much more dramatic way, for those who use public transportation. This is because there has never been any real coordination between working locations, especially industry, and dwelling locations. Therefore, a high percentage of the Cairene population works where others live, and lives where others work. The zoning system simply does not work. Moreover, there are more people than the vehicles could support, and there are more vehicles than the capacity of roads can handle.[37] This means that increasing the numbers of vehicles does not solve the problem; on the contrary, it complicates the problem.

An answer to Cairo's public transport system has been sought for about 30 years. The possibility of an underground system was first explored in 1954, and the cost was estimated at slightly below 770,000 U.S. dollars per mile (1985 rate of exchange). As the transportation crisis worsened, cost estimates have grown proportionately. In 1968 the cost of 12 miles running along the north-south axis of the city was estimated to be over five million U.S. dollars per mile (1985 rate of exchange). The five miles of track proposed to join the southern railway system with the northern metro, thus bypassing the highly congested central area, would cost approximately 12 million U.S. dollars per mile (1985 rate of exchange). In any case, the underground train system is presently being executed.

Of course, an underground system is the most expensive solution to the problem, and at the same time it may not be the perfect one. It is expected to relieve about 30% to 40% of the problem. There is also the fear that, in the future, this huge project would cause more growth and more concentration in the capital.[38]

Finally, the pollution problem of Cairo, i.e., noise, air, odors and sewerage, comes on top of all the other problems. The rate of pollution in Cairo has far exceeded the international safety levels. The physical density of the population, the huge numbers of vehicles, the absence of parks and green areas, the industrial siege around Cairo, and the sands and dusts of the surrounding hills and desert all add up to the problem. Therefore, the capital has developed a very unhealthy environment.

CONCLUSION

Cairo is a typical case of strong urban bias due to national economic policies. It is also a good example of many of the problems facing cities in the developing countries where resources to deal with such problems are quite scarce. Allocation of investments among governorates in Egypt illustrates the bias in favor of Cairo quite clearly. The results of the infitah policies show how the laissez-faire approach can only strengthen the trends of concentration of different economic activities, especially high income-generating activities in the primate region. The price the Egyptian economy has to pay today for this bias, which has long historical roots, is unfortunately a heavy burden. The social consequences of the resulting problems from this bias are quite serious.

NOTES

1. *Al-Ahram*, November 11, 1984.

2. Johannes F. Linn, *Cities in The Developing World*. New York: Oxford University Press, 1983, p. XIV.

3. Hoda M. Sobhi, "Problems of Regional Planning in Egypt" (in Arabic). A paper presented in a seminar in the National Planning Institute, Cairo, 1978.

4. Bertrand Renand, *National Urbanization Policy in Developing Countries*. New York: Oxford University Press, 1981, pp. 5–6.

5. *Ibid.*, p. 101.

6. *Ibid.*, p. 98.

7. *Ibid.*, p. 117.

8. Hoda M. Sobhi, "Regional Disparities and The Problem of Regional Allocation of Investments" (in Arabic). A paper presented to the 4th Egyptian Economists Conference, 1979.

9. Frank Stillwell, *Regional Economic Policy*. London: MacMillan Press, 1972, pp. 9–15.

10. Renand, *op. cit.*, pp. 107–108.

11. Kingsley Davis and Hilda Golden, "Urbanization and the Development of Pre-industrial Areas," in *Economic and Cultural Change*. 3, no. 1, 1954, pp. 6–24.

12. Saad Eddin Ibrahim, "Over-urbanization and Under-urbanism: The Case of the Arab World," in *International Journal of Middle East Studies*. Vol. 1, 1975, pp. 1–23.

13. Gamal Hamdan, *The Identity of Egypt, Part 4* (in Arabic), Alam El-Kotob, Cairo, 1984, pp. 320–321.

14. Alan Richards, "Ten Years of Infitah: Class, Rend (sic) and Policy Stasis in Egypt," in *The Journal of Development Studies.* 1983, p. 324.

15. Hamdan, *op. cit.,* p. 292.

16. *Ibid.,* p. 299.

17. CAPMAS, "Internal Migration in ARE." Ref. No. 215–01, Cairo, 1971, Sobhi, *op. cit.,* 1979.

18. Ibrahim, *op. cit.,* p. 10.

19. Davis and Golden, *op. cit.,* p. 50.

20. Abd-Elfatah Nassef, "Population Distribution in ARE." JNP Series of Working Paper, no. 21, 1982, pp. 9–11.

21. Hamdan, *op. cit.,* p. 302.

22. Ibrahim, *op. cit.,* p. 11.

23. Hamdan, *op. cit.,* p. 262.

24. *Ibid.,* pp. 271–273.

25. Sobhi, *op. cit.,* p. 13.

26. Hoda M. Sobhi, "The Impact of Multinational Enterprises on Regional Disequilibria." A paper presented at the 7th International Congress of Statistics, Computer, Social and Demographic Research, Cairo, 1982, p. 127.

27. CAPMAS, "Status of the Open Door Economy in ARE up to Dec. 31, 1984." Cairo, 1982, pp. 44–45.

28. *Al–Ahali.* no. 165, May 12, 1984.

29. Hamdan, *op. cit.,* p. 340.

30. Khalid Ikram, *Economic Management in a Period of Transition.* U.S.: Johns Hopkins University Press, 1980, p. 147.

31. *Al-Ahali, op. cit.*

32. Ikram, *op. cit.,* p. 148.

33. *Al-Mussaware,* no. 3138, Nov. 30, 1984.

34. Mahmoud A. Fadil: *Political Economy of Nasserism,* Cambridge University Press, Cambridge, UK, 1980, p. 128.

35. *Ibid.,* p. 129.

36. Ikram, *op. cit.,* p. 161.

37. Hamdan, *op. cit.,* p. 358.

Chapter 13

Integrated Village Development and the Housing Problem of Urban Egypt

Abdel K. El-Ahwal

_____**INTRODUCTION**

This paper is centered around the urban housing crisis in Egypt, especially in Cairo. Over–urbanization in Egypt in general, and in Cairo in particular, has reached alarming levels. The mounting housing pressures present a very challenging puzzle. A new section was recently added to today's Cairo near the famous Salah Eddin Castle. It is called the City of the Dead since it is built on a previous cemetery. Close to one million people are presently living among the dead. This is an example of the serious urban problems facing Cairo.

By examining the urban problems, this paper shows that Cairo's mushrooming over–urbanization has been misguided, misdirected, and misplanned. An integrated, carefully studied, comprehensive village development program is suggested as an integral part of an overall national development strategy. Cairo has been selected as a focal point of analysis for a variety of reasons such as:

1) It is a primate city and the largest and most densely populated in the Arab World and Africa.

2) It is burdened by many historical and socio-cultural legacies.

3) It dominates and shapes events in Egypt.

4) It has been exposed to many research projects and development plans, but its suffering is still growing.

However, Cairo is not an isolated island. On the one hand, it is at the heart of Egypt's urban metropolis, and on the other, it has deep impact on development and therefore is not limited to its physical boundaries, but contributes to the development of the whole country. Village development is given high attention in this paper because rural Egypt could play a major role in alleviating the pressing problems of urban centers and towns, especially Cairo. In addition, the rural sector has been and continues to be the main source of food and other supplies for the whole population. It also serves as a manpower pool for urban labor demand, a pool for capital formation, and an important market for urban products.

URBAN EGYPT AND ITS POPULATION STRUCTURE

Towards the end of 1984, Egypt's population approached the 48 million mark. About 55% of these live in a few urban centers, and the balance are distributed over more than 4,000 villages. It is not only the size of the population that affects Egypt's development, but more importantly it is the demographic characteristics of this population. The annual population growth rate has jumped from 1.14% in 1927 to 2.66% in 1982.[1] The population pressure is felt also through population density, especially in the cities. The population of Egypt lives on only 4% of the total land area of Egypt, and about one-third of the population lives in two cities—namely Cairo and Alexandria. Table 13.1 gives a breakdown of the urban population of the country.

TABLE 13.1
THE DISTRIBUTION OF EGYPT'S URBAN POPULATION IN 1976

ITEM	NUMBER OF CITIES	POPULATION	PERCENT OF TOTAL URBAN POPULATION
Big cities (100,000 or more)	20	11,967,868	(91%)
Small cities (50,000 to 100,000)	8	1,216,946	(9%)
Cairo & Alexandria	2	7,391,721	(62%)
Total	28	13,184,814	(100%)

Notes: Urban center is defined as the administrative capital of the province.
Source: Census Reports as quoted in Badco Company.

The urban population has steadily increased due to the normal growth, but more importantly due to the influx of rural inhabitants as Table 13.2 indicates.

TABLE 13.2
RURAL/URBAN POPULATION IN EGYPT

Item	Rural population	Urban population	Total
1960	16,120,980	9,863,703	25,984,101
1966	17,691,356	12,032,743	30,075,758
	(58%)	(40%)	(100%)
1976	20,589,801	16,036,403	36,626,204
	(56%)	(44%)	(100%)

Source: The Preliminary Findings of Internal Migration, CAPMS, Cairo, 1979.

The above data reveals that the urban population growth rate from 1960 to 1976 is about 64%. In the same period Cairo's natural population growth rate has been 70% or little more than the national rate. The annual urban growth rate in urban Egypt is nearly twice that of Egypt as a whole as Table 13.3 shows.

TABLE 13.3
ANNUAL GROWTH RATES
OF POPULATION IN EGYPT

Item	Rate of urban population growth	Rate of overall population growth
1897	1.1%	1.6%
1907	2.4%	1.3%
1917	4.0%	1.1%
1927	1.4%	1.2%
1937	4.4%	1.9%
1947	4.3%	2.7%
1960	4.1%	2.7%
1966–1976	3.5%	2.3%

Source: M. Sobhy Abdul Hakeem, *The Population Problem In Egypt.*[2]

THE RURAL URBAN DIALOGUE IN EGYPT

In his "The Origin and Growth of Urbanization in the World" Kingsley Davis emphasizes that the urban phenomena exercise their pervasive influence not only within the urban milieu but in the rural hinterland as well.[3] And for Robert Redfield, both the folk community and the urban center are mutually interdependent. In the Arab World especially, the urban centers are viewed as dynamic units of mutual exchanges and interactions with the rural areas. The roots of urban problems and crises, for Elkordy, lie mainly in the underdeveloped village communities.[4] The glitters of city lights and the perception of better opportunities and a more comfortable life attract villagers to cities. "Urban populations," as John Gulick asserts, "have always been replenished by migrants from villages." The political and commercial interests of city dwellers have also created major attractions. It is believed that villagers stand to lose by moving to the city.[5] The village migrant moves from a subsistence economy in which kinship ties and family relationships dominate life in a wholistic ecological, economic and socio-cultural complex. When the villager migrates to the city, he becomes totally estranged. One reason why Egyptian villages are badly underdeveloped is because they lose their educated, aggressive, and active young persons to the cities.[6] Another reason is the open-door economic policy of the 1970s during which no attempts were made to distribute the investment projects evenly. As a result, major investments were directed towards the traditional urban centers such as Cairo and Alexandria. The ongoing Second Development Plan in Egypt (1982–1987) does emphasize the development of the Egyptian village. However, the emphasis is not strong enough. It is my belief that Egypt's development will be imbalanced if the plan does not consider villages as an integral and dominant aspect of the cultural-production relationships. About half of the Egyptian people[7] still live in villages and about 68% of Egypt's exports are agricultural products. If Egypt is to progress rapidly and in a reasonable way, the urban bias in socio-economic policies and infrastructural investments has to be checked and thoroughly restructured.

Estimates indicate that from 40,000 to 60,000 feddans of fertile arable land are lost each year to urban encroachment[8] due to housing expansions, and ". . . land reclamation, though vigorously pursued by the government, has not yet kept pace with this encroachment." The recent rural statistics for the period between 1970 and 1978 indicate that an average of just 6,000 feddans per year have been reclaimed.[9] In light of the foregoing facts, certain conclusions can be reached as follows:

1) An absence of internal migration policies in Egypt

2) Imbalanced investment distribution in terms of the village-urban division

3) Urban biased development plans

4) Urban encroachments on the arable land

5) Limited success of the reclamation effort

If the situation continues in this direction, several things will happen:

a) Village manpower will be depleted.

b) The degree of self-sufficiency of the villages will decrease.

c) The village-urban imbalance of development will continue.

d) Housing in particular and urban services in general will continue to eat away arable land.

e) The quality of life in both villages and cities will deteriorate.

In a recent study on internal migration in Egypt, it was found that Cairo alone received 22.7% of the total rural exodus. The annual growth rate of urban-to-rural migration was 14.7% whereas the rural-to-urban migration increased by 84.8%.[10]

CAIRO'S HOUSING PROBLEMS

Some 35 centuries ago, Egypt's capital was Thebes which had a quarter of a million people.[11] In the fourteenth century, Egypt's capital was Cairo, which had a population of about one half million thus making it the most populous city in the Mediterranean basin. There were no housing problems since the documents refer to vacant houses in the city.[12] Cairo hit the first million mark in 1927 and exceeded its fifth million in 1976. Years ago, Cairo received a net inflow of 100,000 migrants each year. At the present, Cairo receives six immigrants every 10 minutes. Cairo consumes 45% of Egypt's food, and almost half of the country's clean water. It has 60% of Egypt's telephone lines. She is the city of striking contrast: the very rich who enjoy the splendor of life, and the homeless who live among the dead.

Over one-fourth of Egypt's manpower resides in Cairo.[13] Top managers in Cairo represent 63% of the capital's manpower structure.

By the year 2000, Cairo's population will be anywhere between 16 and 20 million people. One of the solutions proposed to deal with Cairo's over-urbanization is the concept of decentralization that was developed by the French to control the over-dominance of Paris.[14] This concept was adopted for Cairo and implemented in a fragmentary way. In 1979, an Egyptian committee was formed to chart out a national housing policy. But this committee was made up of technical engineers who knew how to build houses but knew very little about the socio-economic dimensions of urbanization. It should be noted that urbanization is not simply quantitative land use, finance housing materials, models, and technology.[15] Thus, the approach failed. Another concept for dealing with the over–urbanization of Cairo is the development of medium-sized cities. The third largest city in Egypt after Cairo and Alexandria is Tanta which has a population of only 600,000 people. Thus, the rural influx can be diverted to these smaller cities. It is obvious that no single strategy can provide the key to unlock the housing problems of Cairo. Even though the successive governments of Egypt in the last 50 years have been trying to reform Egypt's villages, still the villages suffer from subsistence living. The politicians are asking to turn the villages of Egypt into cities, and it cannot be done. Scholars, on the other hand, suggest improving the lot of the villages and stopping their "manpower drain." This latter direction may serve our purpose. Facilities and more services should be introduced in the villages, and projects that are established out of Cairo must be given incentives. Villages need to be developed within their own environment, in relation to one another, and in relation to the urban centers. Government employment should be directed to regions outside Cairo. An overall internal migration policy should be considered within the context of current and future population trends in Egypt.

Fifty years ago, one would have been surprised if an Egyptian villager gave any slight thought to leaving his village. Today, the bells are ringing loudly. In Egypt, as well as in the rest of the Arab World, officials are anxiously searching for an answer—an answer that is feasible, efficient and equitable. It is only through a well-thought-out strategy coupled with sincere and continuous efforts that the Arab city, especially Cairo, will be rescued. An integrated village development plan is an indispensable part of such a strategy.

NOTES

1. The Central Agency for Public Mobilization and Statistics (CAPMS), *Statistical Year Book of ARE 1952–1980*. Cairo, 1983, pp. 11–38.

2. M. Sobhy Abdel Hakeem, "The Population Problem in Egypt." A paper presented to the International Symposium on the Use of Family Planning Methods in Egypt, Cairo, 1981.

3. CAPMS, *Ibid.*, p. 24.

4. CAPMS, *Statistical Year Book of 1960*. Cairo, 1961.

5. CAPMS, *op. cit.,* 1983, pp. 11–38.

6. *Ibid.*

7. Kingsley Davis, "The Origin and Growth of Urbanization in the World." *The American Journal of Sociology,* Vol. 2, *March, 1955, p. 429.*

8. Mahmoud El-Kordy, *Regional Planning and Urban Development in Egypt,* Ector, INP, Mems no. 82, 1980, p. 2.

9. John Gulick, "Village and City Cultural Continuities in Twentieth Century Middle Eastern Cultures" in Ira Lapidus (ed.), *Middle Eastern Cities.* London: University of California Press, 1969, p. 122.

10. N. Kamel Marcus, *Rural Housing.* Training Course, INP, 1977, p. 2.

11. Fathy Abdul Fatah, *The Egyptian Village.* Daral Thakofa El-Geduda, Cairo, p. 40.

12. M. N. Abdul Raouf, *Agricultural Economic Development in Egypt.* Memo no. 314, INP., Cairo, 1975, p. 21.

13. Badco Company and Associates, *The Alternative Strategy of Urban Settlements in Egypt.* Cairo, 1981, p. 2.

14. *Ibid.*

15. CAPMS, *The Preliminary Findings of Internal Migration.* Cairo, 1979, p. 13.

REFERENCES

ALAHALY (The Citizens). An Egyptian weekly newspaper, May 12, 1984.

ALAHRAM (The Pyramids). An Egyptian daily newspaper, Dec. 14, 1984.

Davis, Kingsley, *The American Journal of Sociology.* Vol. 2, 1955.

El-kordy, Mahmous, "Regional Planning and Urban Development in Egypt." Ector, INP, Cairo Memo no. 82, 1980.

Hakeem, M. Sobhy Abdul, "The Population in Egypt: The Use of Family Planning Methods for Egypt." Symposium, 1981.

Lapidus, Ira (ed.), *Middle Eastern Cities.* London: University of California Press, 1969.

Morcos, Nabeel K., Rural Housing, Training Course, INP 1977.

Raouf, Mahmoud M. Abdul, "Agricultural Economic Developments in Egypt." Memo no. 314, INP, Cairo, 1975.

Saleeb, Raouf F., "Toward An Alternative Method to Confront the Housing Problem in Egypt." INP Seminar, 1982.

DISCUSSION

Ragette Egypt had urban development plans based on the creation of satellite towns to curb the influx to the large cities. Whatever happened to those towns?

Ibrahim I think the new satellite chain towns idea in Egypt was a good idea to start with. However, in their implementation, they have not fulfilled the promise. For example, you have the Tenth Ramadan City, one of the oldest towns which is on the way between Cairo and Ismaelia. It became in a few years a place where land speculators have taken most of the land, either bought plots or built up housing units without residing in them. Some factories have located there, but most of those who work in such factories commute back to Cairo every day. So after six o'clock in the evening, it is a ghost town.

Galantay I wonder whether the recent boom of investment in Cairo is not the direct result of the destruction of Beirut and the subsequent redirection of Gulf capital to Cairo. I am asking if Cairo's (Egypt's) economy is becoming increasingly dependent on the Gulf states—partly because of this capital investment and partly because of the remittances of the Egyptian migrant workers. So that if anything goes wrong in the Gulf states, Egypt could suffer.

I want to raise a question regarding the policy of creating New Towns. I think the policy failed because the New Towns are too close to Cairo and bring forth the importance and dominance of the capital. If they had been created further away perhaps they would have had a more positive impact and an independent role. Another urban policy was based on building up the canal cities which were destroyed or damaged in the war. This policy could have drawn some of the population influx away from Cairo if sufficient investments were made. A statement has been made that Greater Cairo has now reached a disproportionate size and is therefore clearly parasitical. This can only be judged by comparing the contribution of the capital city to the gross national product with the resources allocated to it. For example, Mexico City is frequently criticized for its enormous size, but while the consumption of the Mexican capital is absolutely disproportionate—to that of the rest of the country—so is its contribution to the national economy. I would like to check this same issue regarding Cairo.

The instruments that lead to the discrepancies that Dr. Khuri raised are all contained in Dr. Sobhi's paper. An urban bias by planners, by developers, by decision-makers, that concentrated much of the industry, much of the services, much of the power, in the capital. We can go into details but I think that's a story that's typical of most Third World countries.

Ibrahim

The point which Dr. Al-Ahwal mentioned, that you could not really have a successful urban strategy in Egypt, or in any country for that matter, without a well thought out rural strategy, has to be stressed. To my knowledge, Cairo did not benefit much from the Beirut crisis. Most of the entrepreneurs who fled Beirut went to Amman, Bahrain, and to some extent Cyprus, Paris, and London. They did not come to Cairo because Cairo's capitalist infrastructure as a free enterprise city was not yet well developed. After all, Cairo is coming out of a centrally planned economy. However, Cairo did benefit from the boom in the oil countries. It is part of the open-door policy, and the remittances that came were ploughed into mainly consumption and real estate speculation.

Alexandria, of course, has also grown at a rapid rate, but it has not taken the spillover or much of the increment of the net migrants to urban areas yet. The canal cities have been reconstructed, and Ismaeli, for example, is a rapidly growing town. It was far enough from Cairo and it has a competing pull-center. There is a potential of transferring population to Sinai, across from Ismaelia and Port Said, and that is again being talked about a lot, but little has been done about it. The contribution of Cairo to the GNP is probably high, but most of it is in the services, especially in the form of salaries and wages.

I would like to go back to Dr. Al-Ahwal on rural organization and village policy. It seems to me that it is impossible to tackle the problem of the great metropolis—Cairo, Istanbul, or any other big city—unless there is at least some attempt to stabilize the rural population. The one thing that can be influenced perhaps a little rapidly would be indeed to cut off the migration to the big capital cities. To achieve this rural development seems to be absolutely essential.

Galantay

It's not enough, however, to create rural employment, but one would have to make sure that those employed in rural areas have an income that is comparable to a person who does the same work in the city. It is not only a matter of job creation, but ensuring a more or less equitable income level for the urban and rural residents. That's the only way you can cut rural-to-urban migration.

Without a comprehensive rural development, upgrading of medium-sized towns and the creation of New Towns are not enough to solve the problems of the large metropolis. That means that rather than improving the situation, we will witness the continued degradation of the urban environment, at least for the next 20 or 30 years.

Zaim

There is a tendency for people to flow from the rural areas to the urban centers. Is there a regional planning system in Egypt which tries to establish some middle-sized cities, and tries to deviate this flow of migration into these areas instead of concentrating only on the two metropolitan areas, Cairo and Alexandria?

Al-Ahwal

There is in operation a regional planning decree that was issued in 1979. Even though six years have passed since that system was adopted, it has not really made a significant impact because of some organizational and administrative problems. Egypt is still working on finding the appropriate solutions to these problems which rise from over-centralization. That is why a rural-oriented development will divert the population flow to the new village towns. The new five-year development plan (1987–1992) especially stresses this aspect of socio-economic growth.

Part VI

Reconstructing Beirut

INTRODUCTION

Of the several cities discussed in this book, perhaps Beirut has the most recent urban history. As recently as the beginning of the nineteenth century, Beirut had less than 10,000 inhabitants. Thus, Beirut's urbanization is a phenomenon of the last two centuries. Many parts of Beirut, especially the busy downtown, have been destroyed by the long civil war. The city is an embodiment of the country's growing contradictions. It is an Arab country, yet intricately linked to Europe, especially its former colonizer, France. It has a secular system, yet it works on the basis of religious compartments. It is a highly urbanized society, yet it is fanatically tribalized. It is a "democracy," yet it has a pervasive feudal structure. It is an affluent society, yet it has some of the Middle East's poorest people. These and other contradictions are partly responsible for the destruction of Beirut.

Beirut was also Lebanon's primate city. In fact, the city housed nearly half of the country's total population. This primacy has helped make the city appear as an alien entity to the Lebanese. This explains, in part, the ease with which each party bombards the city, and the ease with which many of its affluent residents as well as the poor elements left the city to find other residences. The following three papers discuss the urban evolution of Beirut and the forces that shaped the city. They also discuss the efforts and plans to rebuild it along new foundations.

Chapter 14

An Historical Perspective of the City

John Munro

In order to place the reconstruction of Beirut in context, it is important to know something of the historical forces which have shaped its character, no less than the actual evolution of the city itself. One must remember that Lebanon is a pluralistic society, and while Beirut, its capital, is supposed to serve all Lebanese equally, there is some question whether this, in fact, has been the case. More specifically, some understanding of the two main tendencies which today dominate the Lebanese perception of themselves and their state is, I believe, essential for anyone charged with the responsibility of rebuilding the capital.

What one might call the "official" perception of Lebanon was enunciated by the present President, H.E. Amin Gemayel, on November 5, 1984, in an address to the Lebanese Army. In his speech he recalled his country's recent travail and announced:

> *The problem is not one of reform, because all of us aspire to have a democratic system, assuring social justice and equality among the people; the problem is rather attributable to foreign meddling in the domestic affairs of Lebanon.*[1]

Such a theory is held by a substantial proportion of the populace, and hardly a day passes without some passing reference in the press to sinister designs on the part of one foreign power or another, which may lead to civil dissent. On the other hand, perhaps equally numerous are those who suggest that even without foreign interference, Lebanon would have collapsed under the weight of its own internal contradictions.

The former defend Lebanon's autonomy and suggest that the country's confessional, demographic structure is at the very heart of its exceptional recent history, at least until 1974, a period during which inter-sectarian rivalries found a productive outlet in a wide range of cultural, entrepreneurial and political activities. Western-leaning Christians and Eastern-leaning Moslems in dynamic inter-action were responsible, so the argument runs, for the creation of an enlightened, open, prosperous society which served as an inspiration for other, less fortunate political entities which had been unable to resolve their internal, sectarian difficulties. Naturally, those who hold this view also continue to express faith in the so-called "National Pact," which guarantees Lebanon's various sectarian groupings their appropriate representation in the political power structure, suggesting that future political reform should involve only minor adjustments to the system already in place.

On the other hand, there are those who dismiss Lebanon as a political anomaly, and suggest that the reason why the state has held together for so long is more a matter of luck than sound judgment on the part of those who set the country's political course after independence. They demonstrate the numerous internal contradictions that exist in Lebanon, which have resulted in serious differences of ideology, economic well–being and opportunity. They call for the abolition of the National Pact and the removal of traditional, mainly sectarian leaders from the political scene, suggesting that if Lebanon is to survive, it will only be through a drastic overhaul of the present system or through the intervention of a foreign power capable of guaranteeing order, perhaps both.

Any student of Lebanese history will find ample evidence to support either view, and one's conclusions are as likely to be as indicative of one's own temperament as the truth. The optimists will tend to support the former argument, pessimists the latter. In any event, this is not the place to debate the merits of either case. Rather, we should simply be aware that for centuries the potential for inter-sectarian conflict in Lebanon has existed, that at times it has erupted in particularly violent form. During the past 150 years, especially, there have been innumerable attempts to contain it. Conflict, it would seem, has been the most prominent characteristic of the Lebanese experience, not harmony. The period of relative calm that existed between 1958, the date of Lebanon's first civil war after independence, and 1974, which witnessed the most recent manifestation of civil discord, should not beguile us into thinking that this is the norm. If this is so, then it might be more profitable to consider those factors which have been responsible for securing peace rather than those which prompted war.

Before proceeding further, however, it is well to remind ourselves that it is only comparatively recently that Beirut has emerged as a major, metropolitan center, its population characterized by a variety of different sectarian groupings. In the eighteenth century, Lebanon, though part of the Ottoman Empire, was but lightly ruled by the Sublime Porte in Constantinople.[2] It comprised a multiplicity of quasi-tribal groupings, each of which was largely self-sufficient. The mountainous terrain made travel across country rather difficult and this, together with the Lebanese reputation for being suspicious of strangers, meant that there was little inter-action among the various communities. Within each community a system of feudal loyalties ensured internal harmony. In 1820, however, the date of the so-called "Ammiyyah Uprising" in which the Druse peasantry rose up against the Maronite Christian clergy in particular and Christians in general, there were indications that the old order was under pressure, as the legitimacy of such institutions as hereditary, feudal authority, taxation, land tenancy and confessionalism came under attack.

Then, in 1831, Lebanon was occupied by the Egyptians under Mohammed Ali, who endeavored to impose his rule over the area as a whole, exacting heavy taxes and conscripting soldiers for his army. This led to further disturbances, notably in 1840, when both the Druse and the Maronites rebelled against their foreign oppressors. Eventually, the Egyptians were expelled from Lebanon and Constantinople re-asserted its authority once more, imposing a system of direct, centralized rule over its troublesome *villayet*. In short, by the 1850s, Lebanon was no longer a place where individual, tribal groupings exercised control over their own affairs more or less exclusively. Their authority had been largely superseded by a central government.

During this period, Beirut remained little more than a fishing port. However, during the latter part of the nineteenth century, it began to grow both in size and importance. There are various reasons for this. One reason was that in 1840, the *villayet* of Sidon was enlarged and Beirut made its capital. In 1864, a *villayet* of Syria was formed out of the *villayets* of Sidon and Damascus and sub-divided into five *sanjaks*, one of them being Beirut. Then, in 1888, a *villayet* of Beirut was formed from the *villayet* of Syria, and the city of Beirut became the administrative capital of the *villayet* bearing its name. In short, one of the reasons for Beirut's increase in importance was administrative.

Another reason was its security. During the 1830s especially, it was protected by the powerful Shihab leader, Bashir II, which meant that traders were encouraged to settle there and set up businesses. After Bashir's death in 1840, Mohammed Ali made Beirut his provincial capital, which led the French and the British to set up consulates there, followed by other European countries and the United States. Gradually, Beirut began to grow in commercial importance, its development receiving an especially firm boost as commerce between Europe and the East began to grow in the wake of the industrial revolution. Beirut, along with other eastern Mediterranean ports, began to handle an increased volume of trade, and in the 1850s and 1860s, when a carriage road between Beirut and Damascus had been constructed, followed some time afterwards by a narrow-gauge railway, its importance was confirmed.[3]

While economic opportunities in Beirut were clearly growing, in the mountains they were declining. Lebanon's most important cottage industry was silk-growing and processing, and before the construction of the Suez Canal, which opened up Far Eastern trade, Lebanon had been immune to competition from the silk growers of China, Japan and elsewhere. Gradually, cheaper silk from the Far East began to undermine Lebanon's export trade, causing considerable economic hardship. This prompted an exodus from the mountains to Beirut, and soon the city's population began to swell.

Therefore, during the closing decades of the nineteenth century, Lebanon was transformed from a mainly agricultural economy into one in which trade was beginning to assume increasing importance. Perhaps more importantly, the country had assumed a form of dual personality. There was the Mountain, where the old ways still endured; and there was Beirut, which, thanks to the presence of an increasing number of Westerners there, began to seem almost European in character.[4] In the Mountain, the sectarian, quasi-tribal groupings retained their independent status; in Beirut, there was some communal mixing, as more and more Christians were drawn to the mainly Moslem city. On the whole, both Moslems and Christians appear to have got on with each other quite well. Apart from the historical records, which support such a conclusion, we may also assume from the homogeneity of Lebanese architecture that Christians and Moslems appear to have enjoyed a similar lifestyle; the Beirut *suqs,* for example, were remarkably uniform in character, and even when the quarters were defined in terms of religious or ethnic identity, it is almost impossible to tell the difference between them.

Generally speaking, in spite of the large Christian influx into Beirut, this was not in itself a motive for discord. Indeed, it could be argued that Christians and Moslems complemented one another, at least economically. Christian trade was, for the most part, with the West; Moslem trade was either internal or with the Arab lands close by. Each depended on the other for its general prosperity.

Nevertheless, recognition of mutual, economic advantage may have kept upper-class Moslems and Christians from enmity. There were, however, other factors which provoked inter-communal resentment, especially among those living lower down the social scale, notably the way that Christians in Beirut appeared to be advancing more rapidly than the Moslems. Partly, this had to do with the fact that trade with the West was more lucrative than trade with the East. More importantly, legislation had been introduced by the Ottomans under European pressure which effectively raised the status of the Christian community as a whole. Previously, Christians, along with other *dhimmis,* or protected people, had been second-class citizens, paying special taxes and not being eligible for military service. Between 1839 and 1876, however, the *Tanzimat* was issued by the Sublime Porte under pressure from the European powers which provided a legal basis for all Ottoman subjects, regardless of their religion, being treated equally before the law.

Inevitably, Moslem frustrations spilled out onto the streets. In 1860, the civil war in the mountains sent shock waves through Beirut itself. In 1882, many Beirut Christians fled the city because of a number of incidents arising from a too enthusiastic observance of Moslem festivities, and by the 1920s, many—perhaps most— Christians in Beirut, at least, tended to see themselves drawn up against their Moslem fellow citizens in a state of open rivalry.[5] Thus, Edward Attiyah, in his autobiography, *An Arab Tells His Story,* begins one of his chapters with the words: "Christians versus Moslems: this was my first notion of human relationships. Moslems and Christians in antagonism to one another—two natural and inevitable groups, as natural and inevitable as the world itself."[6]

In spite of such sentiments, what kept Beirut society together was that while Christians and Moslems might clash on the streets, their leaders, drawn together by wealth and social position, remained on relatively good terms with one another. Therefore, whenever inter-sectarian conflicts did break out, the leaders of both sides took pains to contain the dispute, imposing order over the unruly elements of their respective communities by the weight of their feudal authority or social and economic prestige.

In a sense, one observed a somewhat similar situation in Lausanne in the spring of 1984 when the leaders of all Lebanon's warring factions convened under Syrian pressure to hammer out their political differences. There, together with their wives and friends, they wined and dined one another in apparent *bonhommie,* even though their followers were killing one another on the streets back home. However, one should not press the parallel too closely. Whereas, in the nineteenth century, Lebanese leaders were able to exert powerful control over their supporters, today this is not necessarily the case. In the past, feudal authority and economic and social prestige commanded obedience; today, egalitarian forces have whittled away at the leaders' pre-eminence, so much so that community leaders often appear to be bending to the will of their constituencies rather than shaping it.

Ironically, it is probably increasing democracy rather than its absence that is largely responsible for unrest in Lebanon today. After more than a century, the economic, social, cultural and, of course, religious distinctions between Christians and Moslems largely persist. What has changed is that Lebanon's leaders are, in many cases, unable or unwilling to control the masses when they take to the streets with their often justifiable grievances.

If the Lebanese are now no longer able to rely on the patterns of traditional authority to guarantee peace and stability, it would seem that a new system is needed to replace the old. And this would seem to imply a strong central government. Yet, as events of the past 10 years have shown—and as events continue to show—so deeply rooted are sectarian identities and affiliations, a strong central government in Lebanon has failed to emerge. Nor is one likely to emerge in the immediate future. True, the majority of Lebanese would, in theory, like to see a strong, centralized authority controlling their affairs, but in practice individual communities have only grudgingly yielded their traditional prerogatives. This is especially true of the Christian community which, conscious of its minority status and anxious to preserve its cultural identity in the face of what it perceives as a possible inundation by hostile Moslem forces, continues to press for decentralization.

Thus, the Christians seek to retain Lebanon's pluralistic educational system which allows all schools considerable latitude with respect to their curricula and administration. The Moslem majority, on the other hand, would like to see the system changed in such a way that the government would exercise its authority to ensure that all schools followed more or less the same program and to guarantee certain minimum standards of education. Behind these proposals lies the determination of the Christian community to maintain the generally superior status of their schools, and an equally determined move on the part of the Moslems to ensure that their schools are placed on an equal footing with those of the Christians.

In other words, if a strong central government that would claim the allegiance of the population as a whole were to be installed, it would only come about when the barriers of suspicion and mistrust have been removed. And after 10 years of civil war, those barriers are as strong as ever. The Lebanese army may have bulldozed the ramparts thrown up by the rival militias, and there is little doubt that considerable progress has been made with respect to providing increased security for all. Even so, the psychological barriers still remain. If these too are to be eroded, some encouragement will have to be given to communal inter-action.

This is something that is unlikely to be achieved by legislation alone. Opportunities will have to be provided for members of Lebanon's different communities to mix more freely. In this context, the reconstruction of Beirut is of paramount importance. Recent fighting in Lebanon has effectively divided the capital into two: the Christian east and the mainly Moslem west, the two communities separated by what has come to be known as the Green Line. Along that line, material damage is more apparent than anywhere else in Beirut, and today there is a half-mile-wide belt of ruined buildings and open spaces from which the rubble of destruction has been removed, stretching from the sea into the southern suburbs. It is this area in particular which has become the focus of attention of those who would seek to create a suitable environment for inter-communal mixing.

Thus, several schemes have been suggested that would attract Lebanese from all communities to a rebuilt downtown area where they could mix freely and hopefully regain some sense of mutual trust and respect. Essentially, what is envisaged is the reconstruction of the old *suqs* which traditionally catered for both Christians and Moslems; the restoration and possible re-location of central government offices; the construction of major facilities for entertainment; the provision of open spaces for rest and recreation. Whether such a visionary scheme will actually be implemented is, of course, by no means sure. Lebanon is a country whose very *raison d'être* often seems to be commercial exploitation; it is also a country firmly dedicated to *laissez-faire* economics. Under these circumstances, it is likely that there will be considerable opposition to any plan such as I have described.

Moreover, the kind of reconstruction plan that would provide an opportunity for intercommunal mixing begs the question whether or not Christians and Moslems—not to speak of other groupings within those two major communities—genuinely wish to submerge their identities in favor of some nebulous ideal of statehood.

Professor Fuad Khuri, in an earlier paper included in the present volume, has described what he calls the "endogamous" tendency of Arab culture which reinforces community affiliations at the expense of nationhood. If he is correct in his assumptions, then the whole idea of reconstructing the downtown area of Beirut is open to question, at least under the terms of a government-controlled plan. Perhaps, instead of investing large amounts of public money in such a project, one would be better advised to develop the city's various mini-centers which form the foci of different communities' activities. Under these terms, one could leave the reconstruction of downtown to individual *entrepreneurs,* who would rebuild this area in accordance with their individual and presumably economically inspired perceptions.

To put it another way, even supposing one were able to solve the legal and material problems associated with the reconstruction of downtown Beirut so as to provide an appropriate environment for communal intercourse, is this the kind of arrangement which most Lebanese genuinely desire?

NOTES

1. *The Daily Star.* November 6, 1984, p. 4.
2. For this section of my paper, I have relied heavily on Samir Khalaf, *Persistence and Change in Nineteenth-Century Lebanon. passim.*
3. See Leila Tarazi Fawaz, *Merchants and Migrants in Nineteenth-Century Beirut.* pp. 69–70.
4. *Ibid.,* p. 108.
5. *Ibid.,* p. 115.
6. Edward Attiyah, *An Arab Tells His Story.* p. 10.

REFERENCES

Antonius, George, *The Arab Awakening.* London: Hamilton, 1938.

Burckhardt, John L., *Travels in Syria and the Holy Land.* London: J. Murray, 1822.

Churchill, Charles, *Mount Lebanon: A Ten Years' Residence from 1842–1852.* London: Saunders and Otley, 1853.

Fawaz, Leila Tarazi, *Merchants and Migrants in Nineteenth-Century Beirut.* Cambridge, Mass: Harvard University Press, 1983.

Harik, Iliya F., *Politics and Change in a Traditional Society, Lebanon, 1711–1845*. Princeton, NJ: Princeton University Press, 1968.

Hitti, Philip, *Lebanon in History*. London: Macmillan and Co., 1957.

Hourani, Albert, *Syria and Lebanon*. London: Oxford University Press, 1962.

Jessup, Henry H., *Fifty-Three Years in Syria*. New York: Fleming, Revell Co., 1910.

Kerr, Malcolm, *Lebanon in the Last Years of Fuedalism. 1840–1868* Beirut: Catholic Press, 1956.

Khalaf, Samir, *Persistence and Change in Nineteenth-Century Lebanon*. Beirut: A.U.B., 1979.

Salibi, Kamal, *The Modern History of Lebanon*. London: Weidenfeld and Nicolson, 1965.

Smilianskaya, I.M., "The Disintegration of Feudal Relations in Syria and Lebanon in the Middle of the 19th Century, 1800–1914," in *The Economic History of the Middle East, 1800–1914,* Charles Isawi ed., Chicago: University of Chicago Press, 1966.

Chapter 15

Reconstruction: Theory and Practice

Friedrich Ragette

After 10 years of intermittent civil war, Beirut holds a special position in the context of Middle Eastern cities. In fact, it has become the subject of serious scientific study concerning the secret of its survival as a functioning community in the absence of public order and security.[1]

It is obvious that in its present state Beirut is the very opposite of a "harmonious environment for modern man," although up to the tragic events which led to the civil war in Lebanon, this city was the envy of the region by seemingly offering the very conditions we are discussing today.

These were based upon full freedom of movement and speech; no restrictions on banking or trading; a free press; an adequate supply of housing at reasonable rents; a very low inflation rate and a booming economy, which was rapidly using up the reserves of open space and attracting large numbers of non-Lebanese residents.

This is not the place to discuss the complex political events which brought this to an end, but in hindsight we may realize that much of glittering pre-1975 Beirut was not golden at all, and one could submit that even without civil war, Beirut as well as Lebanon would have developed serious problems of overpopulation, over-exploitation and ensuing environmental disaster.[2]

Recent years have brought significant changes in our concepts of both "harmonious environment" and the characteristics of "modern man." We are actually in an exciting period of transition where man the exploiter is supposed to be changing into man the conserver. Beirut is an excellent example of super-exploitation which in its early stages was hailed as progress. However, as more and more people were suffering for the profit of a few, a growing opposition made itself heard, challenging the traditional *laissez-faire* mentality.

This coincided with new attitudes by "modern" man in general towards his environment, and I wish to propose that the political, economic and social changes which will have to be introduced to solve the Lebanese dilemma will have to be in tune with them. Below I shall try to list some of these attitudes as I see them.

- Decentralization: Instead of central governmental action the decision-making process should start at the local level, with neighborhood administrators being easily accessible. Only such decentralization will assure the best condition for most of the people.

- Regional Identity: Instead of melting into an international mass society, man should enhance his ethnic characteristics. Architecture should stress the elements of the region to which it belongs and respond to environmental factors such as climate, local materials, traditional practices and styles. Under these circumstances people are more likely to identify with their surroundings and feel at home.[3]

- Local Action and Participation: Instead of applying synthetic solutions on a large scale, problems should be solved at the local level by small steps in an *ad hoc* fashion. Teams of specialists should keep in close touch with the recipient, invite his participation in the planning process and allow for his self-expression in the ultimate product.

- Resource Efficiency: Instead of assuming a position as master over his resources, man should recognize his dependence on nature and live in harmony with it. He should use energy, water and land sparingly and assume his responsibility for future generations by maintaining the ecological balance.

- Pragmatism: Instead of pretending that we have the means of creating the perfect environment for man, we should recognize this as an illusion and aspire to obtain the most suitable solution for each problem without preconceived ideas.

These attitudes are sustained by the recognition of man as an individual or as a member of a well-defined group. The traditional Middle Eastern city satisfied most of the above conditions in a very natural manner.[4] The individual house, which usually had clearly defined quarters for guests, men and women was designed for comfort and energy efficiency by proper orientation and consideration of lighting, air circulation and privacy. In more severe climates, specific summer and winter quarters or even distinct day-and-night accommodations were arranged around courtyards. In the mild climate of Beirut, with its abundance of water, the construction of detached houses surrounded by gardens was preferred.

Clusters of houses usually belonged to one clan which itself was part of a neighborhood that could easily be sealed off and defended. Usually it was part of the quarter of a particular ethnic or religious group which had its place of work and communal facilities within walking distance. Thus, frictions between different communities as well as commuting needs were reduced, while the common suq, major places of worship and the *serail* provided contact with other segments of the society.

The hectic and largely uncontrolled growth of Beirut, together with the impact of the automobile, destroyed much of the traditional city pattern. City planning was reduced to attempts at coping with the worst traffic problems, while the zoning laws—even if enforced —allowed the exploitation of land, irrespective of existing scale or pattern and led to exorbitant densities.[5]

For a while, this was seen as the price for entering the family of developed nations and of forging a dynamic and progressive society. However, the pre-illusion that ethnic and religious barriers had been overcome proved false. Today, the mosaic character of the Lebanese society has become visible through armed demarcation lines and accentuated segregation, in spite of the fact that once clearly defined neighborhoods were broken up by demolition and redevelopment well before the recent fighting.

The inherent weakness of the public authorities in strife-ridden Lebanon entailed a continuous erosion of the quality of life in the city—chaotic traffic conditions with very inefficient public transport facilities; poor public schools; lack of parks and children's play areas; proliferation of pollution through uncontrolled garbage disposal; unabated noise levels and unrestricted parking. The war has added three problems—deficient water and electricity supplies and a great measure of physical insecurity.[6]

However, it is noteworthy that the very factors which have sustained sectarian conflicts in Lebanon, such as local community allegiances at the expense of national unity, or private enterprise detrimental to the common good, or self-reliance in the absence of public action, are also the elements which allowed a city like Beirut to survive during the past few years.

The future of Beirut will depend largely on the manner of its reconstruction, which poses three major problems.

1) *The conceptual problem:* How should we plan? What should we build? This should be based upon a comprehensive assessment of the given situation and a consensus regarding what the future city should be like. After the first phase of destruction during 1975–76, a group of French and Lebanese experts prepared the 1977 Master Plan for the Center of Beirut.[7] The plan was officially adopted by the government but actual work did not start before autumn 1982. By that time the over-all situation had changed significantly, necessitating a re-evaluation of the 1977 plan. Oger-Liban, the organization entrusted with the reconstruction of downtown Beirut, organized in June 1983 a competition for further design proposals.[8] Later events again blocked the reconstruction work.

2) *The legal problem:* Despite all political troubles, the central government must adhere to due process; to expropriate real estate is very time-consuming and costly in Lebanon. The 1977 plan was adopted under the impact of the initial experience of the civil war and largely used the formula of real estate trusts where all landlords would participate equally in the optimization of their holdings through replanning. Since it is very difficult to arrive at a legalized plan, the authorities want to avoid any further changes. This explains the lack of publicity and the quiet development of detailed designs. However, broader participation in the planning process was one of the main demands of the members of a symposium dealing with the reconstruction of Beirut.[9]

3) *The financial problem:* For decades the economic boom of Lebanon defied explanation by international experts. This puzzle was accentuated when years of civil disturbance and destruction hardly affected the value of the Lebanese currency (except over the last few months), kept land values soaring, and resulted in only limited shortages in the supply of goods. The primary reasons for this are the free economy of Lebanon; the regular inflow of money from the countless Lebanese working abroad; and, it seems, the fact that for many the fighting was good business, bringing in cash from many sources.

As recently as 1983 the opinion was voiced that Lebanon could finance the reconstruction herself and need not go begging for funds.[10] Only recently has the Lebanese economy finally showed signs of serious problems, as demonstrated by the decline of the Lebanese pound.

Probably under the impact of heavy economic pressure only will Lebanon's various factions effectively compromise and open the way for a new deal towards a lasting peace. Hopefully, this will lead to an enlightened reconstruction which shall turn Beirut into a truly

Middle Eastern city with a harmonious environment for modern man. To accomplish this, reconstruction must encompass the city and its suburbs and be part of a regional strategy for development. The architectural challenge, however, lies in the city center.

While 10 years of armed struggle have led to segregation along lines of religion, kinship and ethnicity, the new downtown will have to resocialize the Lebanese and provide the framework for a new togetherness and civility.[11] Furthermore, it should demonstrate the existence of a new Lebanon by providing appropriate civic and national facilities.

The brief reconstruction effort undertaken by Oger-Liban has already exhibited a new sensitivity to environmental, historical and contextual values (see Figure 15.2). By meticulous restoration of whole successions of buildings of near-forgotten downtown streets and the preservation of large suq areas as pedestrian zones, a positive step has been made. But while keeping memories of the past as a link with the future, we have to introduce those elements which were previously missing. In the case of Beirut the greatest deficiency was the lack of a convincing expression of its function as a national capital. Maybe this was the correct image of Lebanon, as a very young nation composed of many communities, each striving to preserve its particular interests. Thus, monuments in the town center either represented the bygone power of past rulers or local opposition to them. All the built-up achievements of the new state were scattered in the metropolitan area, probably according to the availability of building sites.

It is significant that the town center emerged as the dividing line between the major Lebanese factions which neither could conquer and which was destroyed in the process. In a way, this proved that it belongs to the whole country, and it should emerge as the nucleus of a new Lebanon. The task, therefore, is not just reconstruction but edification of the new Lebanon.

Sketch proposals to this effect were made by students of architectural schools (Figure 15.3) and by visionary professionals (Figure 15.4). Some stress the creation of interlinking squares free from vehicular traffic, while others reach out with grand avenues to express major axes and relate new coastal developments with existing landmarks.

However, the reconstruction effort must go beyond the creation of monuments; it must lead to a more viable city as a whole. To achieve this, essential changes in Lebanese priorities are necessary. Above all, the excessive commercialization of Lebanese society, where everything is subject to the profit motif, must be curbed. This calls for fundamental changes in public administration, a demand which has been made for decades and is imperative to spark the necessary reforms. Taxation needs to be effectively administered and must be extended to include land holdings. (Certain enterprises simply should not be profitable.) Construction of desperately needed housing for middle-income and low-income families must be encouraged and the rent laws further revised.[12] A modern public transport system must be developed, which is the only solution to the formidable traffic problem. Without such reforms developments will continue in the wrong direction and further conflicts will be inevitable.

The real tragedy of Beirut and of Lebanon as a whole is the tremendous discrepancy between its potential for becoming a model for the interaction of a free and pluralistic society, living in a natural setting of extraordinary beauty and enjoying a geographic location with superior possibilities for trade and cultural exchange, and the present reality. I am convinced that a better future must and can be built from within.

NOTES

1. David Hill, Research Proposal: *Survival Mechanism of a Modern City in Civil War,* (unpubl.). College of Design and Planning, Denver, CO, 1984.

2. Livre Blanc: *Beirut 1985–2000.* Direction Generale de l'Urbanisme, 1973.

3. Christopher Alexander, *A Pattern Language.* Oxford University Press, 1977.

4. Fazlur R. Khan, "The Islamic Environment: Can the Future Learn From the Past?" *The Agha Khan Award for Architecture,* Proceedings of Seminar One, Aiglemont, 1980, pp. 32–38.

5. Gregoire Serof, "Visions of Tomorrow," *Beirut of Tomorrow.* American University of Beirut publishers, 1984, p. 94.

6. Samir Hage, "Planning for Quality of Life." pp. 102–108.

7. *Plan Directeur d'Amenagement du Centre de Beyrouth 1977.*

8. Concours International d'Architecture: "Beyrouth, Reconstruction du Centre Ville," in *Oger-Liban.* June, 1983.

9. Friedrich Ragette, minutes of discussion, *Beirut of Tomorrow.* p. 131.

10. Raymond Mallat, "Finance Plan." pp. 25–26.

11. Samir Khalaf, "Sociological Reflections." p. 22.

12. Eric Peterson, "Housing and Reconstruction." pp. 37–48.

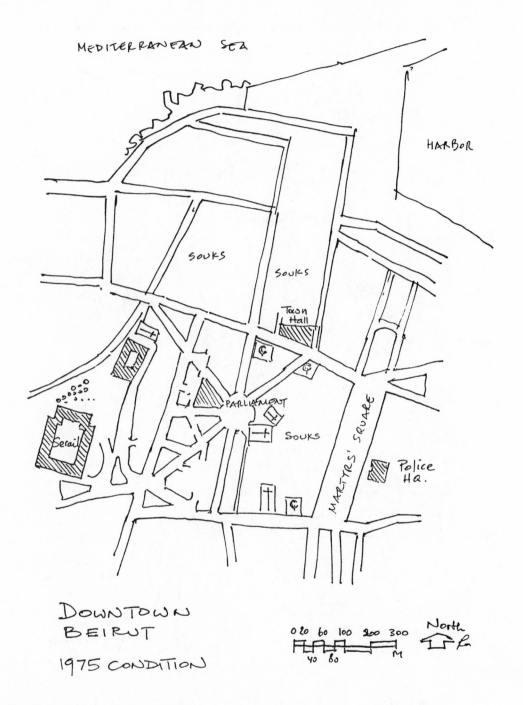

Fig. 15.1: *Downtown Beirut—1975.*

Fig. 15.2: *Principal organization of the town center according to Oger Uban.*

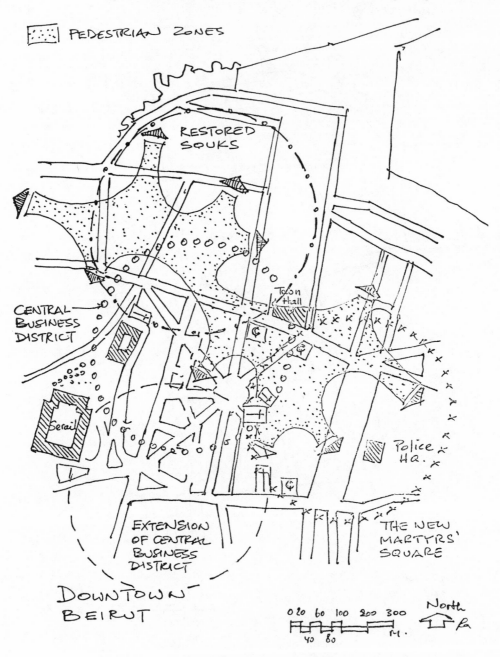

PRINCIPAL ORGANIZATION OF THE TOWN
CENTER ACCORDING TO OGER URAN

Fig. 15.3: *Downtown Beirut—Emphasis of squares.*

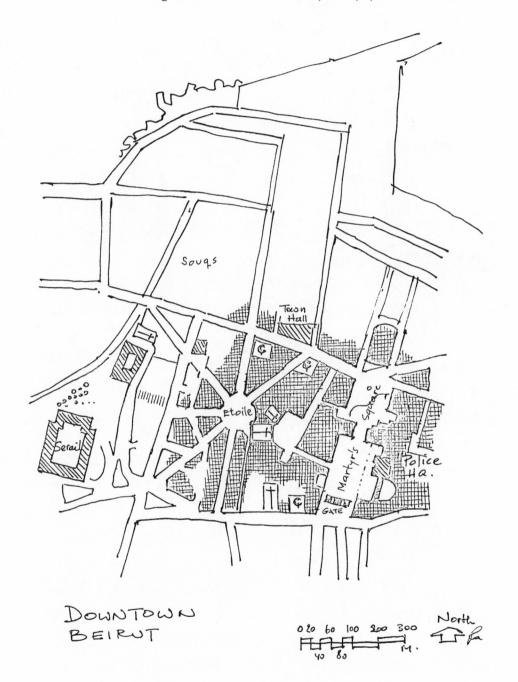

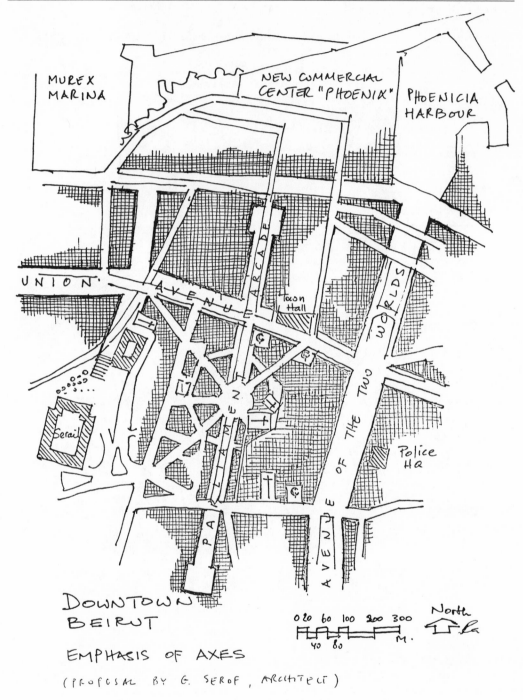

Fig. 15.4: *Downtown Beirut—Emphasis of axes.*

Chapter 16

A Pictorial Essay of the Reconstruction Process

Hana Abu Khadra

A city almost as old as man himself, Beirut has been the home of many different cultures, all of which have left traces and influenced the city's development. Until 1853, Beirut was a completely fortified seaport of about one quarter of a square mile, surrounded by gardens. From 1840 to 1876, expansion to the east and to the west resulted in the demolition of the remaining city walls, and since that time Beirut has developed and expanded in all directions, despite the surrounding steep slópes. By 1970, Beirut had become, to a certain extent, the cultural, business and commercial center of the Middle East.

Today, inhabited by more than a million persons, the city has been severely damaged by intermittent fighting. Beirut has always been a city of contrasts, conflicts and contradictions, but even today it refuses to die.

As the city grew, Beirut assumed certain social and ethnic groupings that had an impact on the distribution of the population as well as the activities they engaged in. Even so, until 1975, Beirut's central business district was the financial, commercial and cultural center for all Lebanon. After that date, things changed, and as a result, other parts of the city assumed increasing importance, each of them, in one way or another, acting either as a supplement or substitute for downtown. Thus, *suqs* in Raoucheh and Sanayeh appeared as a replacement for the main downtown suq, and other areas, such as Mazra'a, Mar Elias, Moawad, Sassin, Zalqa and El Zouq, all developed in importance as they catered to displaced merchants and businessmen.

At the same time, many residential districts were destroyed and their inhabitants displaced, which created exceptionally high density areas in other parts of the city, often exceeding legal limits. On the other hand, the industrial areas retained their locations on the outskirts of the city, even though many factories were either damaged or destroyed. Both the international airport and the seaport functioned intermittently, depending on the state of security, sometimes operating at almost full capacity and at others being closed for extended periods of time.

Today, in Beirut, a sense of disorganization prevails as a result of the ineffectiveness of the central government and the diminished role of the judicial system. Solutions to all forms of urban problems tend to be improvised, which on occasion only leads to the creation of more complex problems.

Over the years, Beirut has developed from a pedestrian city to one with a maze of vehicular streets. From time to time, several plans have been suggested to improve the circulation of traffic in and around the city—as, for example, those by Efli, Eccochard and Dauger—but none of them have been effectively implemented. Looking to the future, it has been suggested that a major north-south highway with interchanges and exits connecting it to the different parts of Beirut should be constructed. Internal highways designed for through traffic were to be constructed, each having a minimum of cross intersections with smaller streets, the idea being that this would reduce traffic problems and congestion. Unfortunately, Beirut's streets were not designed to support the traffic load that exists today, and it is only with careful planning that serious traffic problems may be overcome.

As the city grew, the architectural style of the buildings changed considerably, exhibiting a wide variety of influences and resulting in a continuous struggle between the forces of tradition and modernism. In an effort to produce a subtle marriage of styles, forms and techniques, individual architects have not always been successful. Consequently, architectural innovation has obscured or blurred the face of the traditional city. With the growing influence of the so-called "international style," Beirut has become a mosaic of unrelated shapes and forms. As the city continues to grow, new buildings keep climbing higher and higher. Arches and bay windows are replaced by glass curtain walls, porches by modern shops and the traditional pitched red-brick roofs by huge chillers and mechanical systems. Even so, in the midst of this chaos, the traditional city still struggles to assert its presence, a scattering of old buildings reflecting a past style that refuses to die.

The nucleus from which the present city of Beirut has grown is part of today's devastated central business district. In this area, one may still see the remains of some historic buildings and the sites of those which have all but disappeared may still be traced. Many streets still carry their old names, faint reminders of their historical past. As the city grew, the old town became a center for most of Beirut's activities, as well as its suburbs and the country as a whole. In the mid to late 1960s, however, this area was not able to accommodate all the needs of the fast-growing population. Consequently, other centers of activity in Beirut and the outer suburbs became more and more important. This trend was accentuated as a result of the fighting which broke out in 1975, and by 1978 the downtown area had become completely deserted.

In other words, the destruction of what one might call "Old Beirut" had been going on for several decades before the civil war delivered its *coup de grace*. In the late 1920s, for example, under the rule of the French mandate, the governor ordered merchants living in the center of the city to vacate their shops within 48 hours in preparation for their demolition. A French planning team then began to implement a scheme for re-designing the old town, creating a Place d'Etoile, with large, wide streets emanating from it, the most important of which became known as Ma'arad Street, running down to Allenby Street. Nobody opposed the plan, and soon new streets were constructed over the ruins of the old. Around 1930, European-style buildings were created in the area around Ma'arad all the way to the west of the Place d'Etoile. Prior to this date, the area consisted of groupings of several small suqs, each specializing in the sale of a particular kind of merchandise. Thus, there was the egg suq, the shoe suq, the clothes suq, the jewellers' suq, and many others. A few of these remained after the demolition-construction boom of the 1930s, and they continued to engage in business until the events of 1975-76, namely the Suq Tawil-Ayyas and Suq Sursock-Nouriyeh. Meanwhile, demolition and construction continued, and in 1959 the so-called "Small Serail" was razed to allow for the enlargement of the Place des Martyrs, an area also known as al-Bourg, taking its name from an old Phoenician watch tower that had once been there.

During the 1960s and 1970s, the forces of modernization continued to change the face and character of the downtown area. By 1975, what was left of old Beirut and the surrounding area was veiled by a forest of shop signs and neon lights. After the worst of the fighting there had died down, most of the genuinely old buildings were revealed to have suffered irreparable damage.

In 1977, several planning teams, some of them French, surveyed the area, and after being commissioned by the Lebanese government, several of them produced a "Plan Directeur," which was supposed to serve as a guide for future rehabilitation and reconstruction. As it turned out, actual attempts at reconstruction did not take place until early 1983, in the wake of the Israeli invasion.

During this latter period, several issues were raised, all of which have considerable bearing on the actual process of reconstruction.

1) Some of the oldest and most interesting buildings (namely the suqs Sursock and Nouriyeh) had been demolished; others, though damaged, were still capable of being rehabilitated. However, in some cases, individual owners had quickly intervened to restore their premises, which meant that a concerted plan for reconstruction had become more difficult.

2) After a preliminary survey, some areas which had suffered minimal destruction were classified for facade restoration. Work was begun in these areas, namely Ma'arad, Allenby and Foch, but many buildings were, in fact, empty shells, and renovation of their interiors was left for a later date. Also, much of the restoration of the facades was not executed with the proper degree of expertise.

3) As work began in the downtown area, problems of ownership began to emerge, as well as problems relating to rentability and tenure. As the buildings were old, some of the claims to ownership were exceedingly complex, requiring detailed and often time-consuming investigation. Thus, determining who is responsible for bearing the cost of renovation and repair has become a major problem, one that is not likely to be resolved in the near future.

4) At one point, four blocks of buildings were designated as prototypes for reconstruction. They were evaluated and carefully surveyed, and eventually restoration work was carried out with satisfactory results. However, in executing the work, the following problems emerged:

a) The high cost of reconstruction meant that when the renovated premises were available for use, only those able to pay high rents would be in a position to make use of them. This would obviously be a determining factor in what the buildings would be used for and the class of clientele which would patronize them.

b) As for the restoration work itself, it became clear that those artisans capable of executing it were difficult to find and expensive to employ.

c) Updating the structures so as to accommodate heating and air-conditioning units required special skills and careful study. Many of the buildings did not lend themselves to such modification.

d) Disputes over ownership, tenancy and liability for the expense of reconstruction were often so intense that it appeared that reconstruction would be delayed while such problems were being resolved.

Finally, it is clear that the reconstruction of downtown Beirut is a large-scale project, requiring careful planning and study before work can actually start. It would also seem reasonable to suppose that, as the area was used by a large proportion of the city's population, large numbers of people should be consulted and invited to share in the planning decisions. However, this can only be done in the context of an educational program designed to enlighten citizens about the problems related to reconstruction, both practical and aesthetic. It is also important to realize that the whole downtown community has been uprooted and displaced. Therefore, even if the downtown area is restored to something like its original appearance, it will be especially difficult to recapture the character of the area, with its small shops, winding alleys and bustling commercial activity. Perhaps, what Beirutis like to think of as downtown has been lost forever. Nevertheless, this should not mean that we are ready to abandon all attempts to recapture something of its spirit. One should make every effort to save what we can of "Old Beirut" so that it may serve as both a symbol and inspiration for generations to come of a city that refused to die.

DISCUSSION

Before 1975 Beirut achieved something like a metropolitan role, and it was one of the major financial places in the eastern Mediterranean. It also became kind of a little Paris for the Gulf oil states. As a result of civil war and anarchy, all this is lost.

Galantay

To focus on construction as a public policy is only to undermine an enormous amount of effort of construction and reconstruction. What you have listened to is only the public effort and, of course, because of the collapse of the state there is a lot to be desired along that line. But this does not mean at all that construction and reconstruction in Lebanon and in Beirut has not been taking place on a private level. An enormous amount of construction and reconstruction has been

Khuri

taking place through private efforts.

And to isolate the center of the town and communicate it to the outside world as the reconstruction of Lebanon and of Beirut is to undermine an enormous and admirable effort.

Ibrahim

Certain aspects of this case strike me. First, here is a prime example of the withering away of the state without a revolution, but through a civil war. The society continues, it reproduces itself over and again despite the ravages of war and the tormentation of destruction and so on. That's admirable because, at least in these bleak times, it does rekindle my hope since it is an example of human determination to survive. Second, many Middle Easterners know that, despite all the destruction of the war, Beirut remains one of the viable and efficient cities in the Middle East. That's why I'm a constant visitor to Beirut. I can still have my books published in Beirut. So much can get done in Beirut which cannot get done in Cairo or many other cities. This is again a point that testifies not only to the determination of man to survive, but also to the fact that the Lebanese have managed to weave a viable entity called Beirut. Third, the Lebanese are slowly recognizing that history cannot be reconstructed, and that the new Beirut will have to emerge along different lines—lines that utopian liberals and secularists may not like, but with which they have to live. Because an enclave developing in the midst of an otherwise semi-traditional or traditional society has its follies, has its blind allies. It could lead to what it led to in Lebanon.

Maybe, Beirut and Lebanon have to be cantonized. I think this, coming from an Arab nationalist, may seem ironic. But if this is a reality, why not accommodate it without forfeiting the future. The green line, that half-mile-wide strip dividing east from west Beirut, could become a hub of new possibilities. Rebuild the quarters along communal lines, allow their own inner dynamism to take place, but then have this green line turn into parks and into marketplaces.

Munro

What made Beirut such a sparkling success also brought its downfall, and that is to say the incredible capability of the individual citizen. I don't think any other country in the world could have endured 10 years as we have endured in Lebanon and still survive, and still offer a reasonable standard of living. The personal, individual initiative in Lebanon is very sharply defined indeed. It has rather interesting implications for the reconstruction process. We've heard about the plans for the reconstruction of Beirut. Now my somewhat anarchic theory is that this plan was only a facade. You cannot attract funds into a country without having a plan. What you want to do is to give a morale boost and let the private sector carry on as best it can behind the facade of a planning structure.

So this reconstruction plan was a deliberate effort to stimulate the local, regional and international initiatives to reconstruct Beirut and Lebanon. My feeling is that this reconstruction plan was never really intended to be taken seriously. It was an indication that Lebanon was about to get on its feet once again; it was an indication that yes, it was safe to reinvest in Lebanon again; it was an indication to governments to bring money in so that the reconstruction process would start, but actually what was felt all along was the individual would refurbish his office front to the best of his ability, do what he could to get on his feet and start anew.

So, I think, in speaking about reconstruction plans, particularly in Lebanon and I suspect elsewhere, one shouldn't take everything at face value. I think perhaps we should see more strategems for development rather than blueprints for development.

Ragette

A Lebanese slogan states: "A young country six thousand years old." So along these lines, I'm very sure Lebanon will regain itself, and if there's any indication to this, it is in its very survival under such adverse conditions till now. Because the key to the metropolitan character of the town is not the physical structure, it's the people, and the people are there. The question is how long will it take before the hostilities end and reconstruction starts. Unfortunately it is taking much longer than we ever dared to believe. Also I must stress that the private reconstruction was really impressive and the risk-taking ability of the Lebanese is tremendous.

Abu Khadra

I believe that the downtown area is the most problematic part of the Beirut reconstruction. Historically, it played an important role, and it can still play a similar role in the future. It is the only identity of the old town—the only example of what the old town of Beirut used to look like in terms of architectural identity. Therefore, adopting it as a public project is very important. It's one of the largest stretches of land that has witnessed great destruction and its private reconstruction is going to be very difficult.

A. The city of Beirut

Until 1835, Beirut was a completely fortified seaport town of about one–quarter mile square and was surrounded by gardens. From 1840 to 1876 expansion, into the east and west, demolished the last walls and from there it has been developing and expanding in all directions, despite the steep slopes, into "modern" Beirut. By 1970 Beirut had become the cultural, business, and commercial center of the Middle East.

Today, inhabited by more than a million people, the city has been severely affected by the forces of destruction.

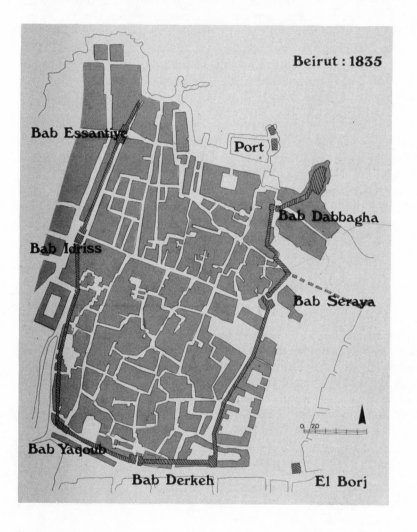

Fig.1: *Beirut in 1835.*

Fig. 2: *Beirut in the mid–1800s.*

Fig. 3: *Beirut in the 1930s.*

Fig. 4: *Beirut in the early 1970s.*

Fig. 5: *Beirut in 1983.*

B. The transportation network

Beirut has grown from a pedestrian city to one with a maze of vehicular streets. The future plan for the vehicular circulation network around greater Beirut calls for a major north–south highway with interchanges and exits connecting it to the different parts of greater Beirut. Other highways should go through the city without encountering the smaller streets, thus reducing the traffic jams.

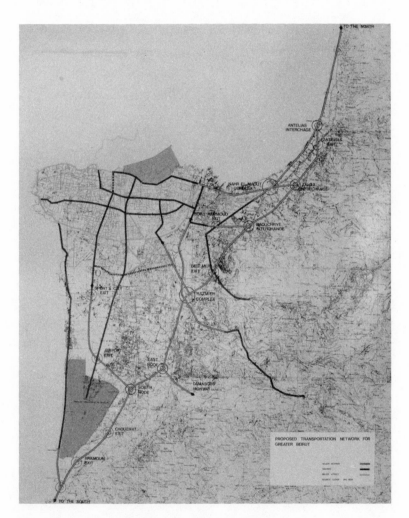

Fig. 1: *Proposed transportation network for greater Beirut.*

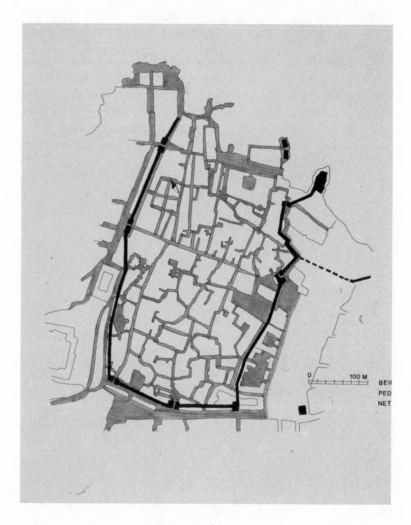

Fig. 2: *Pedestrian street network: Beirut, 1835.*

C. The displacement of activities

Until 1975, Beirut's central business district was the financial, commercial, and cultural center for all of Lebanon. In Beirut other important commercial districts had been in existence and were rapidly growing as well. However, the war changed the organization of activities. As the central business district was totally destroyed, other areas assumed larger importance.

Residential districts were destroyed, their inhabitants displaced. The industrial areas maintained their locations on the outskirts of the city. The airport and the seaport have been functioning according to the security of the situation.

A sense of disorganization prevails in the city as solutions to problems are being improvised, frequently resulting in more complex situations.

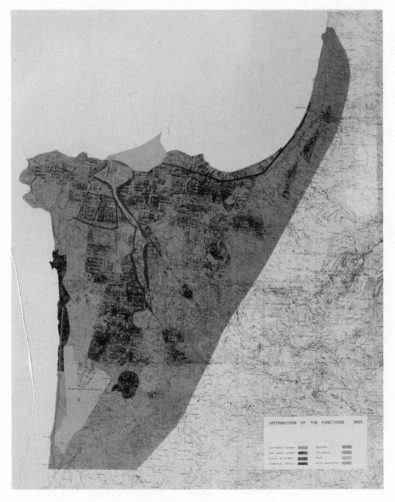

Fig. 1: *Distribution of functions, 1984.*

D. The evolution of the architectural style

The architecture of the city displays a continuous struggle between the forces of tradition and modernization. With the growing influence of the international style, the city has become a mosaic of unrelated shapes and forms. Today, as the new city is growing, the traditional style still struggles to assert its presence.

Fig. 1: *Evolution of the architectural style.*

Fig. 2: *Evolution of the architectural style.*

Fig. 3: *1985.*

E. The city center

The nucleus of Beirut has grown from the city center which, when that area became a center of combat, resulted in tremendous damage to the existing buildings. In 1977, the government commissioned several consulting offices to prepare the "Plan Directeur" for the reconstruction and redevelopment of the downtown area.

Fig. 1: *Souk Ayass, 1973.*

Fig. 2: *Souk Ayass, 1983.*

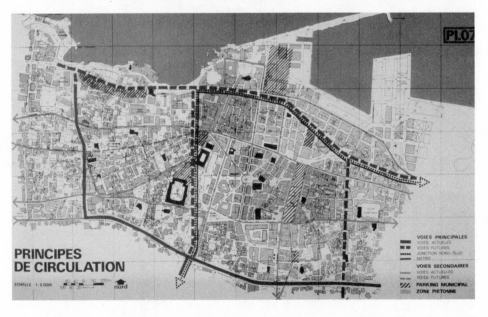

Fig. 3: *The "Plan Directeur."*

Fig. 4: *Rue Allenby, 1983.*

Fig. 5: *Maarad after restoration, 1983.*

Fig. 6: *Central business district of Beirut, 1973.*

Fig. 7: *Souk Nounieh, 1973.*

Today, the area lies in total devastation as consulting offices try to evaluate the changing situation day by day. Several attempts at reconstruction have already taken place. The real work, however, can only be planned and executed when real peace prevails in the area.

Fig. 8: *Souk Ayass, 1980.*

Fig. 9: *The central business district, 1983.*

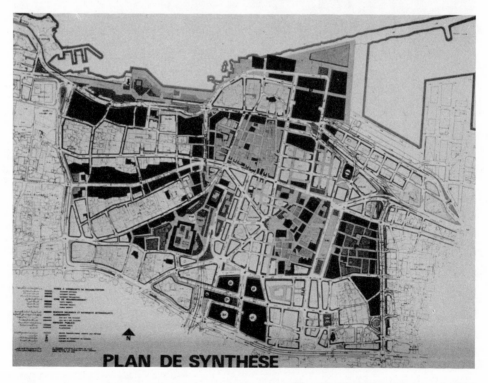

Fig. 10: *The "Plan Directeur," 1977.*

Fig. 11: *Maarad Street after restoration, 1983.*

Photos in this section appear by courtesy of the following people: Dr. Joseph Phares; Colonel David Ourfalian, of the Ministry of Defense; Mrs. Samia Nassar and the APSAD; Professor Jay Randle, chairman of the School of Architecture of the American University of Beirut; and to the students of the School of Architecture, class of '86 and '87, American University of Beirut.

Part VII

Issues in Turkish
Urbanization

INTRODUCTION

Turkey has achieved a certain degree of balance in the distribution of its urban centers. Although the Turkish Republic inherited from the Ottoman Empire a country which was dominated by the Istanbul metropolis while the remainder of the country was heavily rural, the urbanization trend was gradually and steadily transformed. Istanbul, at the northwestern corner of the country, continues to be the most heavily populated urban center of the country. Yet, a large urban center has evolved in the central plains, around the capital city, Ankara. A third major urban center developed around Izmir and the Aegean Sea; a fourth urban center grew along the southern Mediterranean coast close to the Syrian border, and its major city is Adana; and many smaller urban centers have grown in the eastern and central parts of the country as well as along the coast of the Black Sea. This distribution of urban centers, based on a conscious plan, has given the country a balanced spatial growth as the three maps that follow indicate.

Yet, unlike many cities in the Middle East, Turkish cities suffer from serious squatter and slum settlements known as gecekondu. The influx of rural peasants, especially from the poorer eastern part, has given Turkish cities a major problem. Coupled with problems relating to a high population growth, the over-crowding of poorer segments of the Turkish cities is posing an increasing difficulty.

Three Turkish scholars shed light on the urbanization trend. Professor Zaim gives an informative overall description; Professor Alkin details the environmental issues (pollution) associated with urban industrialization, and Professor Cam discusses the impact of urbanization on political activity.

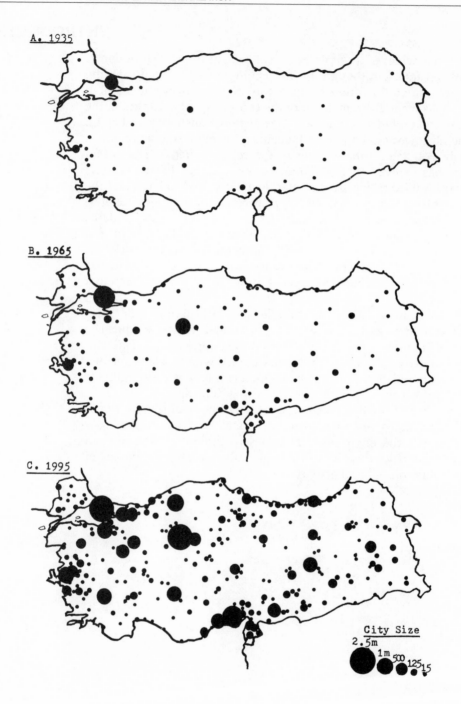

Figure 17.1 *Rate and Distribution of Urbanization in Turkey.*

Chapter 17

Urbanization Trends in Turkey

Sabahaddin Zaim

THE PROBLEM OF URBANIZATION

Urbanization is one of the most important socio-economic problems of both the developed and developing countries. The population of the world increased by 2.6 percent per year between 1920 and 1960, and 3.6 percent between 1950 and 1960, and 1.7 percent between 1975 and 1980. In developed countries the figure was 2.7 percent between 1950 and 1960, and in Europe the figure was 0.4 percent between 1975 and 1980. The figures are much higher in the developing countries, reaching, in many cases, double the average of developed countries. As a consequence, developing countries have a higher rate of urbanization.

The urban population of the world was about one billion in 1960, and has nearly doubled by 1985. Urban populations in the developing countries increased by 120 percent between 1940 and 1960, while in the developed countries the percentage of increase was only 50 percent. The population of cities with over 500,000 inhabitants has increased four times in developing countries, and just two-fold in developed ones. The number of cities with over one million inhabitants increased from 11 in 1900 to 75 in 1950 and reached 162 in 1970. In spite of the rapid urbanization movement in developing countries, however, the percentage of urban population (23 percent) is less than the developed countries (61 percent). This is shown in Table 17.1.

Urbanization, in a narrow sense, is a population movement which leads to the increase in quantities both in the population and the numbers of urban centers. Urban population increases due to the positive difference between birth and death rates of population on one hand, and due to the migration from rural areas to the urban centers on the other.

TABLE 17.1
WORLD URBANIZATION 1920–1980 (IN MILLIONS)

	1920	1940	1960	1980
1. World population	1.860	2.295	2.291	4.430
a) Developed countries	673	821	976	1.630
b) Developing countries	1.197	1.474	2.015	2.800
2. World urban population	360	570	990	1.800
a) Developed countries	260	385	580	860
b) Developing countries	100	185	410	940
3. Big cities (over .5 m)	107	180	352	680
a) Developed countries	93	135	221	350
b) Developing countries	14	35	131	330

Source: United Nations Statistics.

The share of migration is much more than the natural increase of population. The bulk of the world population was living in rural areas up to recent times. The over–concentration of urban population is a phenomenon of the twentieth century. In one century the world population has changed from primarily rural to primarily urban. Such a rapid change has created a lot of repercussions on the socio–economic and politico–cultural structure of societies. Therefore urbanization is not just a demographic phenomenon, it is the result of development. Economic development, especially industrialization, has stimulated the movement of people to cities and has transformed agricultural societies into urban conglomerates.

THE URBAN CONCEPT

a) Population Criteria: According to this criterion, population centers of over a certain population (in Turkey it is 10,000) are considered as urban centers. The United Nations uses the 25,000 benchmark.

b) Administrative Criteria: In official business of the State Institute of Statistics in Turkey, the province and district capitals are considered to be urban centers.

c) Economic Criteria: Population centers are considered urban where a major part of the economic activities is non–agricultural. There are some other sociological criteria as well. The biggest cities are specified as metropolitan centers or world cities. These metropolitan centers cover larger areas.

URBANIZATION IN TURKEY

If we take the population criterion (over 10,000 inhabitants to comprise an urban center in Turkey), the percentage of Turkish urban population increased from 16 percent to 45 percent between 1927 and 1980. Under this criterion, 20.3 million people out of a total population of 44.7 million were living in urban areas in 1980. This is shown in Table 17.2.

TABLE 17.2
PERCENTAGE OF TURKISH URBAN POPULATION
(FOR LOCALITIES WITH 10,000 OR MORE
INHABITANTS)

Census year	Percentage	Census year	Percentage
1927	16.4	1955	22.1
1935	16.6	1960	25.1
1940	18.0	1970	34.8
1945	18.3	1975	37.4
1950	18.5	1980	50.2

Source: Prime Ministry, State Institute of Statistics, Census Reports.

If we classify the urban population according to the size of the cities, more than half is located in big cities with over 100,000 inhabitants. This is shown in Table 17.3.

TABLE 17.3
DISTRIBUTION OF URBAN
POPULATION ACCORDING TO
SIZE OF CITIES

Cities	Percentage of total urban population		
	1970	*1975*	*1980*
100,000 and over	54.1	56.2	55.7
50,000–100,000	10.1	13.6	55.7
25,000–50,000	17.3	14.5	14.5
10,000–25,000	17.4	15.7	15.2
	100.0	100.0	100.0

As seen in Table 17.3 the concentration is stronger in the larger cities. Roughly 70 percent of the urban population live in cities which have over 50,000 inhabitants. But the percentage of middle-sized cities (with 25,000 to 100,000 residents) has increased from 28.3 to 29.1 percent.

If we calculate the urban population according to the administrative criterion, up to 1975 the ratio of urbanization is comparatively higher. These figures are shown below. In this case, the percentage of the population in urban centers is 43.9 percent, representing 19.6 million out of a total of 44.7 million inhabitants.

TABLE 17.4
PERCENTAGE OF URBAN POPULATION
IN ADMINISTRATIVE CAPITALS

YEARS	PERCENTAGE	YEARS	PERCENTAGE
1927	14.2	1955	28.8
1935	23.5	1960	31.9
1940	24.4	1965	34.4
1945	24.9	1970	38.5
1950	25.0	1975	41.8
		1980	43.9

Source: *Census Reports.*

If we take the municipality criterion for urban centers, then the percentage of urbanization becomes much higher. In that case, 60 percent of the total population lived in urban centers in 1984. This is shown in Table 17.5.

TABLE 17.5
PERCENTAGE OF URBAN POPULATION
IN MUNICIPAL CENTERS

		ESTIMATED		
	1978	1983	1984	1989
Number of municipalities	1710	1676	1702	1774
Population of municipalities (millions)	23.9	28.1	29.1	34.3
Percentage of total population	55.7	58.8	59.6	63.2

Source: State Planning Organization.

So let us compare the three criteria mentioned above for 1980, and see what percentage of Turkey's population is urban and how many people live in urban centers.

TABLE 17.6
URBAN POPULATION IN TURKEY IN 1980

	URBAN POPULATION *(in millions)*	PERCENTAGE OF WHOLE POPULATION
Cities of 10,000 or more	22.458	50.2
Provincial/district centers	19.645	43.9
Cities with municipalities	28.100	59.6
Total population	44.737	100.0

Source: Prime Ministry, State Institute of Statistics.

Rapid urbanization demanded that the government pay attention to controlling the over-concentration of population in the three main metropolitan centers: Istanbul, Ankara and Izmir. Regional planning has been used as a device to establish some small or middle-sized cities around these metropolitan centers, and to blockade the rural migration movement in these areas.

This target has been achieved to some extent, especially after 1975. Between 1975 and 1980; the percentage of population in the three main urban centers against the total population was stabilized. This is shown below.

TABLE 17.7
SHARE OF TOTAL POPULATION OF MAIN METROPOLITAN AREAS

YEAR	TOTAL POPULATION (MILLIONS)	POP. OF ISTANBUL, ANKARA & IZMIR (MILLIONS)	PERCENT OF TOTAL
1945	18.970	1.386	7.4
1950	20.947	1.617	7.7
1955	24.065	2.185	9.1
1960	27.755	2.709	9.8
1965	31.391	3.350	10.7
1970	35.605	4.237	11.9
1975	40.348	5.361	13.3
1980	44.737	5.983	13.4

Source: Prime Ministry, State Institute of Statistics.

Due to regional planning around Istanbul, Ankara and Izmir, some small cities have been newly established and they have absorbed the newly arriving migrant population. For example, in the area surrounding Istanbul, there were only 36,168 inhabitants in 1945. This figure jumped to 1,604,852 by 1980. This means that surrounding the city's 2.8 million inhabitants are an additional 1.6 million in smaller satellite cities.

Metropolitan Istanbul today begins at Tekirdag in European Thrace to the west and extends to Izmit and Adapazari in the east. The same pattern is found in Ankara and Izmir. In Izmir, the central city of 800,000 people is surrounded by a circle of small cities with a total of 500,000 additional inhabitants. This represents a shifting of population from the central parts of metropolitan areas to their outskirts. In the suburbs of the metropolitan centers, newly-arrived migrant poor people encircle the city with slum dwellings called *gecekondu,* meaning "built in the night." In the large metropolitan areas then, population expands more rapidly on the periphery than at the center. This is demonstrated below.

TABLE 17.8
INCREASE IN CITY POPULATION

PERCENTAGE INCREASE OF POPULATION		
	Total province	Central city	Suburbs
Istanbul	3.9	1.9	7.5
Izmir	3.3	3.1	3.5

The average increase of urban population in Turkey was 3.04 percent between 1975 and 1980, while in Istanbul, in the main city center, the rate of increase was only 1.9 percent. Therefore the rate of increase for all of Istanbul province (3.9 percent) was above average for Turkey. The rate of increase in Izmir was 3.1 percent, in Ankara 2.3 percent, and in Adana 3.5 percent.

The highest percentage of population increase has occurred mainly in the Eastern Province centers, where growth ranges from 5 to 7.5 percent.

TABLE 17.9

Eastern	Hakkâri	7.5 percent
Provinces	Van	6.1 percent
	Diyarbakr	5.7 percent
Central	Kaysbri	5.0 percent
Anatolian	Niğde	5.0 percent
Provinces		

But if we consider the quantitative increase, the biggest cities are, of course, ahead of the others. For example, the population increased from 1975 to 1980 in Istanbul, Ankara, and Izmir by 45,000, 35,000 and 24,000 respectively, while Hakkari and Diyarbakir increased by only 18,000 and 3,000 per year during the same period.

REGIONAL PLANNING

Due to the industrialization and urbanization movement in developing countries, the concept of regional planning has been a popular subject in recent days. First, we have to define the terminology. A region is a part of a country which has some specific characteristics and is larger than a city. The main characteristics of a region are related to its economic, social and geographic structures. Regions are described either according to their physical characteristics (agricultural regions, climatic regions, etc.) or to the administrative and geographic structures of a country (e.g., the big city regions such as the Marmara region around Istanbul) which aim to solve the problems of a big city; the state regions that aim to balance interregional differences in federal systems; the special-problem areas that aim to decrease unemployment and increase income level (such as Eastern Anatolia region); and the homogenous economic regions that aim both to provide documents to the State-Plan and to make easier its application. Regional planning also has different meanings, as the word "region" does, and can be categorized in four groups: resource regions, the big city areas, functional areas and economic development regions.

THE MAIN REGIONAL PLANS

Marmara Region

The Regional Planning Office of the Ministry of Construction and Settlement started the Marmara Project in 1960. The main reason was to find solutions for economic and social problems of Istanbul, and to try to ease the burden of urbanization on this major city by stimulating the creation and improvement of development centers. This region is divided into three sub-regions: a) Thrace (including Edirne, Kirklareli, Tekirdag) which represents the average level of development in Turkey; b) Southwestern Marmara which is a less-developed area (Çanakkale, Balikesir); c) Eastern Marmara (Istanbul, Kecaeli, Sakarya, Bursa, Bilecik) which is the most developed part of Turkey.

As the first preliminary project, Eastern Marmara was chosen. The conclusion of the project research has been published. The following are subjects that were studied in this project:

1) The characteristics, functions and importance of the region; estimation of the future functions, principle activities and targets for the development of this region

2) The economic activities and industrial sectors; their current structure and development potentials

3) Demographic and physical structure of the region

4) The current level of and the need in future for the infrastructural investments

5) Financial, administrative and legal aspects of the project and plan

6) Urbanization problems, and the possibilities for the new development-centers around Istanbul

7) Alternatives for resettlement, the localities and amount of investment and the timing of the project

This project was re-studied in 1967 according to the conclusion of the 1965 industrial census and practical evolution. A new Urban Planning Committee was established and this committee prepared the general Urban-Plan of Istanbul.

The region of Thrace was studied in 1965 in collaboration with an expert group provided by the OECD. The study was finished at the end of 1968 and published in English and French. After the accomplishment of the study of southwestern Marmara in 1968 the whole Marmara project was published in 1971 by the Ministry of Construction.

Aegean Region

The first study started with the Muğla pilot project. Muğla Experience: Köyceğiz-Dalaman Development projects. Due to the earthquakes of Muğla in 1957, Fethiye was destroyed. For the reconstruction of the area, first Fethiye, then Muğla was chosen as a pilot project region. The OECD and UNESCO helped in this project. But the conclusions were not so successful. The approach to this project was rather similar to community development, except that the development stages were planned. Later the project was made to cover the whole Aegean region. In 1966 a local bureau was established in Izmir.

There are six provinces in this region: Izmir, Aydin, Denizli, Manisa, Muğla and Uşak. Before the general project started, a touristic study was made for the area between Bafa Lake and Cesme and for the "Denizli-Pamukkale Touristic Settlement System" which was published in 1966 after some preliminary small projects were published as "Izmir Metropolitan Area Studies" in 1967, and "Izmir Urban Area" in 1968. The final "Aegean Region, Regional Development, Urbanization and Settlement System" came out in 1970.

Antalya Region

Antalya, Burdur and Isparta provinces are in this region. Here the studies were also started as a pilot project in 1959, called the "Mediterranean Development Project." The project had three main targets: a) to make the basic studies necessary for the development of the region; b) to have a preliminary study for Turkey and other Mediterranean countries; c) to educate the Turkish research staff.

This was a joint study made by NPO and FAO. Later, RPO also joined the study team by taking over the physical aspect of the project. In 1971, the final study was over and published by RPO under the title of the "Antalya Regions, Regional Development, Urbanization and Settlement System."

Western Black Sea Region

This region covered Zonguldak, Bolu and Kastamonu provinces. Zonguldak is the center, and the first study was started there in 1969 by RPO. The project had two targets: first, to find solutions for the problems of the ailing steel and coal industries; second, to educate the research staff. These studies were completed and the conclusion was published by RPO in 1971 under the title of the "Western Black Sea Region, Regional Development, Urbanization and Settlement System."

Eastern Black Sea Region

This region covers 10 provinces and is divided into two sub-regions. The first is the Samsun sub-region which contains Samsun, Amasya, Giresun, Ordu and Sinop. The second is the Trabzon sub-region which covers Trabzon, Artvin, Rize and Gümüşhane. The first research was carried out in Trabzon and the conclusion was published as "The Inventory of Trabzon Province" in 1967. In this project, the natural resources, demographic and economic potential of the region were studied.

Cukurova Region

This region has Adana which is the fourth biggest city in Turkey. The Cukurova project was started in 1962 by RPO; NPO joined the project in 1963. At first, the economic structure of the region was studied. Later, land use studies were made and the economic sectors were taken into the project. Both central and local institutions collaborated in these studies and technical aid was provided by AID and the OECD. The first preliminary draft was published in 1966 and the final report came out in 1970 under the title of "Çukurova Region; Regional Development, Urbanization and Settlement System." In the final report special attention was given to the resettlement problems of the population. This analysis was done to enable inter-regional comparisons. Another aspect of the project was to make some proposals for the population transition from Çukurova to the Eastern Anatolian region to achieve the balanced interregional development target of the National Plan. On the other side, studies were made in detail about the Içel seashore and Iskenderun-Dörtyol-Payas areas.

Middle Anatolian Region

This region covers 13 provinces and is divided into five sub–regions. Ankara, Eskisehir, Kayseri, Kenya and Sivas are the centers of these sub-regions. The Ankara sub–region includes Çankiri, Çorum, Kirşe-hir and Yozgat provinces; the Eskişehir sub–region includes Afyon and Kütahya provinces; the Kayseri sub–region includes Nevşehir and Niğde provinces; Kenya and Sivas are independent subdivisions as they are big enough provinces.

Regional planning studies of Middle Anatolia were finished in 1970 and the related report was published by PRO, under the title of "Middle Anatolian Region, Regional Planning, Urbanization and Settlement System." The characteristics of the region, the potential capacities for development and the problems of the areas were studied in this plan and a new settlement project was analyzed.

The analyses which were made in this plan allow for inter–regional comparisons. Following an introductory survey, the study gives an in-depth study of the sub–regions. The sub–region studies cover Ankara sub–region agricultural analysis, recreation planning of Ankara city, program studies of Ankara province, general urban planning of Ankara city, touristic planning of Nevşehir, which was done with the collaboration of the Ministry of Tourism, planning possibilities of Çankiri province, socio-economic structure of Kenya, and development potentialities of Sivas province.

Eastern Anatolian Region

This region contains 30.3 percent of the population and 20 percent of the area of Turkey, which includes 19 provinces. It is divided into five sub–regions, the centers of which are Elâziğ, Diyarbakir, Erzurum, Gaziantep and Van.

The studies in this region started in 1965 and covered the area of the Keban Dam. The conclusion of the studies was published in 1968 by RPO, under the title of "Elazĭğ-Keban Physical Settlement Plan."

Later, the study of the whole region was completed and published in 1970, under the title of "Eastern Anatolia Region, Regional Development, Urbanization and Settlement System." Miscellaneous projects included NPO's other studies to integrate the regional plans into the national plan.

According to the studies made by NPO, a model was prepared for the urbanization and urban development centers. They are classified in five groups according to the 94 socio-economic criteria: all are development centers—metropolitan, regional, provincial, district and rural.

According to the conclusion of these studies, these centers are fixed as shown below.

1) Current metropolitan centers—Ankara, Istanbul, Izmir

2) Metropolitan centers for future development—Bursa, Adana, Elâzĭğ, Samsun

3) Regional development centers—Eskişehir, Gaziantep, Kayseri, Sivas, Erzurum, Diyarbakir, Antalya, Trabzon, Van, Kenya, Malatya

This short explanation clearly shows the vital importance of regional planning for Turkey in light of the rapid industrialization and development aimed at creating job opportunities for the increasing population and improving the standard of living of the population. As resources are so limited, investment selections and decisions related to the localities, timing and sectors of economic activity are necessary to maximize returns and minimize waste.

THE REASONS OF URBANIZATION

Urbanization is stimulated by the three factors of pushing, pulling and connecting. The first factor is pushing the rural population to urban areas. Connecting factors are related to the improvement of transportation facilities, which carry the people from villages to towns and cities. Pulling factors are the socio-economic advantages of the urban life which attract the rural population.

In Turkey, all of these three factors are playing their roles in the rural migration movement into urban areas.

Pushing factor: In spite of the gradual decrease in the percentage of the rural population, about half of the population is still living in rural areas. The percentage of rural population decreased from 76 percent in 1927 to 56 percent in 1980.

In 1984, 60 percent of the labor force was in the agricultural sector, but their share in the total national income was only 19.3 percent.

It means that, roughly, every 3 percent of the labor force which is in the agricultural sector received only one percent of the income in 1983. In current prices, per capita income in agricultural sectors was 90 U.S. dollars, while total per capita income (including agriculture) was 494 U.S. dollars. It means that agricultural income is less than one-fifth of the average income. Therefore, both the employment opportunities, e.g., demand, are not enough in the agricultural sector to absorb the increasing labor supply on one side, and the income level for the people who are employed already in agriculture is comparatively low. The size of land per family is so small that in many cases it is not enough to provide sufficient income for a moderate standard of living. These are the main pushing factors.

TABLE 17.10
SHARE OF AGRICULTURAL SECTOR
IN NATIONAL INCOME

YEARS	SHARE OF INCOME (%)	SHARE OF LABOR FORCE (%)
1960	55	75
1965	36	75
1970	30	68
1984	19	60

Connecting Factors: These are transportation and communication facilities, which improved rapidly and facilitated the migration movement from rural to urban areas. The share of these sectors in national income increased from four percent in 1938 to 8.5 percent in 1984. The number of trucks and buses increased by 187 percent and 274 percent respectively between 1953-65. Table 17.11 shows this tendency. The highways system has also improved rapidly.

Pulling Factors: Industrialization has the pulling function for urbanization, because industrial concentration in urban centers created demand for labor and absorbed the excess labor supply in rural areas. The experience of Republican Turkey is no different.

The first push was given by the legislation of the Industrial Promotion Law. After 1930, the etatist movement and state industrial investment was the second push to stimulate industry through state capitals which spread throughout Anatolia. After 1950, during the administration of the newly established Democratic Party, came the third push for industrialization through free enterprise movements

TABLE 17.11
TRANSPORTATION VEHICLES
(IN THOUSANDS)

Vehicle	1958	1960	1970	1980	1982
Motorcycle	7	9	61	134	178
Automobile	34	46	138	711	782
Truck	40	57	71	170	186
Bus	8	11	16	31	34
Pick-Up Truck	—	—	52	157	171
Minibus	—	—	21	66	71

Source: Prime Ministry State Institute of Statistics.

and private investments which were concentrated in big cities. During this period (1950-60) industrialization rapidly improved and was concentrated in metropolitan centers like Istanbul, Ankara, Izmir, Adana and Bursa. Labor migration and urbanization increased.

In 1927, there were only 65,000 employers, including small-scale industry, employing 257,000 people. Ninety-one percent of these places were small-scale industries employing less than 10 people.

In 1950, the number of employers increased to 99,000, and employees reached 354,000. Small-scale industries were still predominant. In 1964 there were 161,000 plants and 680,000 employees; 19 percent of the plants were big-scale industries. In 1980 there were 177,000 small employers employing 455,000 people and 9,700 big-scale industries with 850,000 employees. A total of 1.3 million people were employed by 186,000 employers. The share of large industries was five percent in employers and 64 percent in employment.

This is shown in Table 17.12.

TABLE 17.12
GROWTH OF TURKISH INDUSTRIES
AND EMPLOYMENT

Years	Employer (thousands)	Employment (thousands)	Share of big industries: employer (%)	employment (%)
1927	65	257	1	9
1950	110	354	2.2	12
1964	161	680	3	19
1980	186	1264	5	64

Source: Prime Ministry State Institute of Statistics.

In summary, we can say that, up to 1980 small-scale industries were predominant. After 1980 the concentration of industry in the hands of big holdings have gradually changed the structure of industry.

The number of people employed increased from 1.3 million in 1970 to 2.5 million in 1982. The share of industry in national income increased from 11 percent in 1927 to 32 percent in 1984. The share of industry in the labor force increased from six percent in 1927 to 16 percent in 1980. If we take the average value-added as one, the ratio of agricultural value-added decreased from 0.54 in 1962 to 0.33 in 1984; while the ratio of industrial value-added increased in the same period from 2.06 to 2.31.

BIG URBAN CENTERS AND THE STRUCTURE OF THE LABOR FORCE

Industrialization created demand for labor and pulled the rural population into urban centers. But during 1950-70 the pushing factor was greater than the pulling functions of industry. Therefore in this period, in the big industrial urban centers, urbanization was ahead of industrialization. We conclude therefore, that the labor force employed in the service sector is higher than industrial employment in the cities.

According to the results of the research of the State Institute of Statistics, migrant rural workers suffer from disguised unemployment in the cities.

Their value-added is much less than the normal industrial worker's. That is, the percentage of migrant rural workers who mostly dwell in the *(gecekondu)* slum areas is 44 percent in Izmir and 12 percent in all of Ankara. But this percentage reached 22 percent, 54 percent or even 70 percent in some poor districts of Ankara. These people usually take up such professions as peddlers, hawkers, shoe-shiners, doorkeepers, janitors, porters, street-sweepers, and so on.

SOCIAL AND ECONOMIC EROSION

The industrialization process brings with it pulling and pushing factors. Everywhere, there is some difference between the forces of these two factors. It is neither possible nor desirable to reverse these functions. The important point is that these movements should not be left unorganized, thereby leading to some socio-economic difficulties.

Rural migrants come to the city with aspirations (dreaming of some wonderful life in the new city), but in many cases they are disappointed, and young energetic peasants are transformed into lazy and wasted people in the urban streets. In addition, when the cities are overcrowded with these rural migrants, all urban functions become limited and break down, especially in transportation facilities, housing, traffic, parking, school and hospital facilities, water and electric services, and so on. The final result is the prevalence of slums.

The pulling factor of industrial life attracts some wealthy people of village areas as well. In this way, the accumulated capital of rural areas is channeled into urban centers; however, it is used to increase consumption rather than to increase investment capacity.

The problem is to find an optimal site for the cities. After a certain size, the cost of service increases, and it becomes difficult to satisfy the necessary minimum needs of the urban people. But the optimal size cannot be decided only according to the cost of services. Urban centers have some positive functions as well. They create income and increase productivity. The problem is to keep the balance between the positive and negative attributes of the city to reach an optimal size.

In Turkey, there are many shortages in providing enough services to the inhabitants of big metropolitan centers like Istanbul, Ankara and Izmir. But since 1970, due to planning, and the concentration of industry in the hands of big holdings, over-crowding in metropolitan centers like Istanbul, Ankara and Izmir has been controlled.

In the big cities like Istanbul, Ankara and Izmir, the structure of the labor force has changed, and the rate of industrial employment increased. This is shown below:

Table 17.13
PERCENTAGE DISTRIBUTION OF
EMPLOYED HOUSEHOLD MEMBERS

Sectors	Istanbul	Izmir	Adana	Bursa
Agriculture	0.2	1	4	1
Industry	39.2	40	41	47
Trade	30.0	32	33	25
Service	29.5	26	20	26
	100.0	100.0	100.0	100.0

Source: State Institute of Statistics.

Only in the middle-sized cities located in industrialized Eastern or Central Anatolia is the service sector dominant. See Table 17.14.

TABLE 17.14
PERCENTAGE DISTRIBUTION OF
EMPLOYED HOUSEHOLD MEMBERS

Sectors	Erzurum	Trabzon	Kayseri
Agriculture	2.6	—	3
Industry	20.6	24	35
Trade	36.9	34	27
Service	39.9	33	35
	100.0	100.0	100.0

URBANIZATION POLICY

After 1962, the governments pursued different urbanization policies for each five-year period. In the first five-year plan (1963-67), the strategy was to achieve an optimal size for urbanization, balanced regional development and reorganization of local administration, stressing industrialization, dealing with housing problems and finding solutions for slum (gecekondu) areas in big cities.

In the second five-year plan (1968-72), the urbanization policy changed slightly. Instead of an optimal-size concept, urbanization was stimulated, as an economic indicator of economic development. Governments promoted the enlargement of big cities and Istanbul, Ankara, Izmir and Adana were considered as regional centers.

In the third five-year plan (1973-77), the strategy was again to stabilize the enlargement of big cities, as such big centers were stimulating luxurious conspicuous consumption and curtailing the saving and investment possibilities of the country.

The fourth five-year plan period (1978-83) stressed the regional planning and regional balanced development.

In the fifth five-year period (1984-89), the strategy for urbanization becomes clearer. The aim is to provide balanced regional development. Therefore, the government will stimulate the increase of the number of medium-sized cities (with 50,000 to 500,000 population), and will do its best to spread the economic activities into such cities instead of concentrating them in big metropolitan centers. The target is to reach a 4.6 percent increase of urbanization during the plan period. According to the estimate of the fifth plan, the urban population (living in the cities with 20,000 or more population) in 1989 will reach the level of 28 million inhabitants, which means 52 percent of the total population. Table 17.15 shows this evolution.

TABLE 17.15
URBAN AND RURAL POPULATION BY
CENSUS YEARS (IN THOUSANDS)

Years	Total pop.	Urban pop.	%	Rural pop.	%
1927	13,648	3,300	24.2	10,342	75.8
1935	16,158	3,803	23.5	12,355	76.5
1940	17,821	4,346	24.4	13,475	75.6
1950	20,947	5,244	25.0	15,703	75.0
1960	27,755	8,860	31.9	18,895	68.1
1970	36,605	13,691	38.5	21,914	61.5
1980	44,737	19,645	43.9	25,092	56.1
1982	46,312	20,673	44.6	25,657	55.4
1983	47,788	21,600	45.2	26,188	54.8
1984	48,812	22,600	46.3	26,212	53.7

Source: NPO, census reports.

URBANIZATION AND THE LABOR FORCE

The following conclusions have been reached on the co-relations between urbanization and the structure of the labor force during the development process in Turkey.

1) As the urbanization process increases, the labor force-participation-ratio decreases. The main reason is that the female labor force-participation ratio is rapidly decreasing in urban life. Beyond this main point there are some other points which lead to the same direction, such as the education years, the decrease of the working age due to pension, the increase of the number of students, prisoners and invalids, as well as the improvement of productivity.

2) The male labor force participation rate is increasing together with urbanization, which is parallel to the increase of potential male-labor force ratio. This is shown in Table 17.16.

3) a) According to the age classification of the labor force, the ratio is higher in the villages for all categories, while in urban centers, the ratio is lower for the age groups of 15-19 and over 45. If we compare only the male population of 20-45 years, there is not much difference of participation rates between urban and rural areas. In urban centers, both the quantity and ratio of economically non-active female populations is high for all age groups.

   b) According to sectoral distribution of the labor force, the ratio of agriculture decreases while the ratio of industry and service

TABLE 17.16
LABOR FORCE-PARTICIPATION
RATES IN 1982 (%)

CITIES	MALE	FEMALE	TOTAL
Istanbul	68	14	41
Izmir	64	13	39
Adana	74	13	43
Bursa	72	10	41
Eskisehir	68	9	38
Kayseri	67	7	37
Erzurum	73	7	38
Trabzon	77	11	45
Zonguldak	67	14	40
Total cities of Turkey	69	11	40

Source: Prime Ministry, State Institute of Statistics

sectors increase in line with the growth of urban centers.

c) Due to urbanization, the ratio of female labor force in the service sector increases.

d) By the urbanization process, the percentage of the wage earners increases, while the ratio of unpaid family workers decreases.

e) Due to the urbanization process the percentage of the labor force engaged in agricultural occupations decreases, while the ratio of the labor force engaged in technical and professional occupations increases.

4) In the less-developed areas the level of urbanization is ahead of the level of economic development. These areas are over-urbanized. In such areas, cities are overloaded with an excess of labor force, which cannot be absorbed in the economic activities. Therefore, urbanization should not be accepted as an *aim,* but just as a *means.* It should be organized and kept under control to avoid waste, and social imbalance, and to stimulate full-employment.

5) The pushing factors of villages are stronger than the pulling factors of cities. The excess labor force has migrated to other countries as visiting workers. Today, roughly one million Turkish workers —and together with their families, 2.4 million Turkish citizens (this includes the workers)—are working abroad.

6) In 1982 the structure of the Turkish labor force was as follows:

a) In urban populations (over 12 years of age) 40% are economically active. Out of this urban labor force, 86 percent is male and 14 percent female.

b) In the male urban population, 69 percent are economically active; 15 percent are students, and 7 percent are retired.

c) In the female urban population (over 12 years of age), the percent of economically active population, or the labor force participation ratio, is only 11 percent, while 74 percent of the female population are housewives, and 10 percent are students, and a total of 89 percent are out of the labor force. Therefore, the non-market production of housewives, such as knitting, housekeeping and so on, are not counted in the calculations of national income.

7) The process of urbanization increases the quantitative content of social insurances, and the income-tax payers, and the level of income taxes.

8) If it is necessary, family-control systems should be practiced in the rural areas. There is no need to follow it to the urban centers because urbanization itself is the best family-control device.

9) Urbanization has some positive influences upon the better contribution of labor into production, through more output, higher productivity and higher skill. Therefore, it may be advisable to improve a big city in such less-developed areas to function as a regional metropolitan center. This is the strategy which has been adapted and put into practice in the fourth and fifth five-year plans.

In conclusion, we can say that urbanization in Turkey quantitatively has a positive influence by increasing the male labor force, and a negative influence by decreasing the female labor force. Quality-wise, the influence of urbanization is definitely positive. The important point is to avoid over-concentration in a few cities and to spread the urban population into middle-sized cities. Over-concentration in a few cities creates disguised unemployment.

In some parts of Turkey there is some over-urbanization. In terms of demography of Turkey, the country still has a large potential capacity for urbanization. The important point is to keep regional balances in development and this has been accepted and already put in practice in the fifth five-year plan.

REFERENCES

Atalik, Gunduz, *Criterions for Urbanization for Economic Development.* Istanbul, 1967, Ph.D. thesis, Istanbul Technical University.

Gokcen, Ahmet, *Rural Migration 1965-1982.* Ankara, State Planning Organization, no. 1107, 1971.

Ministry of Construction, *Housing Statistics.* Ankara, no. 2, 1974.

Regional Planning Conference, *Istanbul.* Istanbul, 1967.

Stewig, Reinhard, *Structure of Istanbul.* Istanbul Chamber of Commerce, Istanbul, 1965.

Stewig, Reinhard, *Istanbul.* Istanbul Chamber of Commerce, Istanbul, 1965.

Technical University of Istanbul, *The Last 25 Years of Urbanization.* Istanbul: Istanbul Technical University Press, 1984.

Tuna, Orhan, *Housing Policy in Istanbul.* Istanbul: Istanbul University Press, no. 2300, 1977.

Tuncer, Baran, *The Future Population and Economy of Turkey.* Istanbul: Turkish Development Foundation Press, 1977.

Turkish Society for Housing and Planning, *Development in Regional Planning.* Ankara, 1964.

Yucgel, Unal, *Administrative Problems of Urbanization.* Istanbul: Istanbul Technical University Press, 1982.

Union of Chambers: Industry of Turkey, *Republican Statistics.* Ankara, 1983.

Yavuz, Fehmi, *Urbanization.* Ankara: Ankara University Press, 1956.

Yavuz, Fehmi, et al., *Urbanization.* 1973.

Yazgan, Turan, *Urbanization and Socio-economic Structure of Turkey.* Istanbul: Istanbul University Press, 1968.

Zaim, Sabahaddin, *City and Regional Planning and Industrial Zones in Istanbul.* Istanbul Univ. Publication no. 1781, Istanbul, 1971.

Zaim, Sabahaddin, *Population Problem of Turkey.* Istanbul: Bogazici Press, 1973.

Zaim, Sabahaddin, *Regional Planning in Turkey.* Istanbul: Istanbul University Press, 1971.

Chapter *18*

Environmental Problems of Urbanization

Erdogan Alkin

Turkey, like every other ambitious developing country, did not care much about the environmental problems that industrialization and urbanization could create. It seemed a luxury to use the already scarce financial resources for the measures which could limit the hazards that a rapid urbanization would bring to the environment. But we must remember that rich countries had failed to take the environmental problems seriously until the beginning of the 1960s.

This paper will initially explain the bottlenecks of a rapid development strategy, and thus the causes of the negligence of environmental problems. This explanation must not be taken as an *apology;* it merely states the facts. Secondly, the environmental problems of urbanization and the newly emerging environmental policies will be briefly summarized.

THE BOTTLENECKS OF DEVELOPMENT

After World War II, especially during the 1950-54 period, Turkey had contradictory ideas on economic development. Foreign experts had prepared many reports on economic prospects for Turkey which were even more confusing. Turkey tried to establish new industries and to modernize the agricultural sector at the same time. If foreign exchange reserves had not been exhausted in a short time and if the favorable climatic conditions had continued, those efforts could have changed the economic destiny of the country. But in a developing country it is not wise to depend on so many "ifs" and to make historical speculations. The rest of the story, as for every developing country, consists of chronic balance of payments' difficulties, high rates of inflation, insistence on maintaining an overvalued currency, etc. Coupled with this is of course the International Monetary Fund's insistence on the rapid implementation of stabilization measures. The new economic stabilization policies caused stagnation which lasted until the beginning of the planning period.

After 1963 the Turkish economy experienced a stable and balanced development throughout the First Five-Year Development Plan (1963-67). However, towards the end of the Second Five-Year Plan period (1968-72) inflationary policies, mainly as a result of deficit financing in the public sector, were observed. In the face of a trend rapidly leading to crisis, the government then in power decided to take a series of measures in 1970. The third devaluation in the republic's history was made and the Finance Law, consisting of measures supporting the financial resources of the public sector, was put into effect.

These measures gave quite positive results during the first few years. For example, the devaluation of the Turkish lira encouraged exports and workers' remittances and led, in 1973, to the first surplus in the current accounts in the last 30 years. But after 1973, increasing import prices following the energy crisis, and inflationary domestic policies which were pursued mainly because of domestic political instabilities, led to an overvaluation of the Turkish lira, and thus to stagnation in exports and to a rapid increase in imports. These indicators, however, were neglected by the economic authorities.

The government which assumed power in 1979 and the following governments were determined to pursue a programme of structural adjustments. The outlook for the full period of the Fifth Plan (1985-89) is more promising. These improvements should restore Turkey's credit-worthiness considerably.

However, even if Turkey's credit–worthiness is fully restored, will it be possible to ensure a continuous flow of foreign credits on a large scale to support the future development efforts? To find a definite answer to this question the present conditions of the world economy must be considered in a realistic way. Turkey, as every developing country, faces a dilemma. Implementation of a simple stabilization program may restore the internal and external economic equilibria but cannot solve the employment and income distribution problem. Without solving those problems, it is almost impossible to restore social and political stability. In order to solve those problems a rapid development program supported by a continuous flow of sufficient foreign aid must be implemented. But under the present conditions of the world economy there is no way to secure sufficient foreign credits. And so the country is trapped in a vicious cycle.

Therefore, it must be well understood why Turkey cannot spare enough capital to fight the environmental problems caused by her own industrialization efforts. This is the second dilemma which Turkey, again as every developing country, faces. The industrialization process accelerated at the expense of the traditional sectors, such as agriculture. Table 18.1 indicates that the share of industry in gross national product rose from 10.7% in 1950, to 15.3% in 1960, to 25.3% in 1980, to 26.4% in 1983.

TABLE 18.1
GNP SHARES OF THE MAIN ECONOMIC SECTORS (%)

Years	Agriculture	Industry	Manufacturing	Services
1950	45.5	10.7	8.9	43.8
1955	42.7	12.2	10.2	45.1
1960	40.9	15.3	12.6	43.8
1963	39.3	16.0	13.9	44.7
1967	32.7	19.3	16.43	48.0
1973	27.5	20.1	17.4	52.4
1978	25.3	23.0	19.5	51.7
1980	22.6	25.3	21.4	52.1
1981	23.1	26.5	22.6	50.4
1982	22.1	25.6	21.6	52.3
1983	21.4	26.4	22.5	50.2

Source: SPO Statistics.

THE ENVIRONMENTAL PROBLEMS CAUSED BY URBANIZATION

A lot of causes are responsible for Turkey's environmental problems. These problems are becoming more and more serious with every passing day. The first attempt in the direction of solving these problems must be definition and the presentation of the problems as a whole.

Air, water and soil pollution are the three main environmental problems in Turkey. In this chapter the causes of these problems will be explained briefly.

a) *Air pollution:* There are two main reasons for air pollution in Turkey. One of them is industrialization and the other is urbanization which can also be explained to a large extent by industrialization.

The rapid urbanization which has been taking place since the

1950s is one of the main causes of air pollution besides industrialization. The pollution in crowded towns is mainly caused by rather
primitive heating systems, fuel burning techniques and poor fuel
quality.[1]

b) *Water pollution:* Besides the agricultural activities and wastes in
settled areas, urbanization is one of the main causes of water
pollution. There are very important regional water pollution
problems in Turkey. The most problematic regions and water
resources are the Bay of Izmit, Gemlik Bay, the Golden Horn (in
Istanbul), Sakarya River, Porsuk Stream, Nilufer Stream, Simav
Stream and Ankara Stream.[2]

Twenty-five percent of the total sewage, dirty water and industrial wastes of Istanbul are disposed of in the Golden Horn.
Physiological effects of certain heavy metal ions play an important
role in the pollution of the Horn.[3]

c) *Soil pollution:* Urbanization plays an important role in the pollution and the destruction of agricultural land. The use of agricultural land for construction sites is one of the most important
environmental problems in Turkey. The development of the towns
in the fertile plains of western, central and southern Anatolia
caused the loss of high quality agricultural lands in those areas.

d) *Other environmental problems:* There are other environmental
problems besides air, water and soil pollution in Turkey. Other
pollution problems concern flora and fauna, solid wastes, pesti-
cides, noise, and energy production. But to save time, these
problems will not be discussed here.

We have repeatedly stressed the impact of rapid urbanization on
the environmental problem, be it air, water or soil pollution. Over the
last few decades, Turkey witnessed a dramatic expansion in its urban
population. Today, the urban population makes up nearly half of the
total, as shown on the following page.

The growth or urban population is over three percent whereas the
total national increase in Turkish population is just over two percent.
Therefore, the growth in the number of city dwellers is partly due to
the internal migration or rural inhabitants to the city. To substantiate
this point, we can analyze the rate of urban growth in the different
regions of the country. (At the end of this paper, Table 18.6 gives
detailed population growth rates in the cities and villages of the
different provinces of the country.)

It is no surprise that the regions with the large urban centers
witness a higher influx of rural populations, in spite of the govern-

ment efforts to control those flows. Table 18.3 gives a distribution of urban growth rates by region.

AUTHORITIES AND ORGANIZATIONS CONCERNED WITH ENVIRONMENTAL PROBLEMS IN TURKEY

The Office of the Undersecretary for the Environment is the main public body concerned with environmental problems. This office,

TABLE 18.2
CHANGES IN URBAN AND RURAL POPULATIONS

YEARS	TOTAL (1000)	POPULATION IN URBAN CENTERS	%	YEARLY INCREASE RATE (%)	POPULATION IN RURAL AREAS	%	YEARLY INCREASE RATE (%)
1950	20,947	5,244	25.0	2.2	15,703	75.0	2.1
1955	20,065	6,927	28.8	5.6	17,138	71.2	1.7
1960	27,755	8,860	31.9	4.9	18,895	68.1	2.0
1965	31,391	10,806	34.4	4.0	20,585	65.5	1.7
1970	35,605	13,691	38.5	4.7	21,914	61.5	1.3
1975	40,348	16,869	41.8	4.1	23,479	58.2	1.4
1980	44,737	19,645	43.9	2.0	25,092	56.1	1.3

Source: 1980 census.

TABLE 18.3
POPULATIONS AND ANNUAL GROWTH RATES BY REGION

AREAS	TOTAL	PROVINCES & DISTRICTS, CITIES	SUB-DISTRICTS & VILLAGES	% RATE OF INCREASE TOTAL	CITIES	PERCENT PER ANNUM VILLAGES
TOTAL	44.7	19.6	25.1	2.06	3.04	1.34
Thrace	4.3	2.4	1.9	2.59	0.92	4.95
Black Sea Coast	6.2	1.7	4.5	1.47	2.82	0.97
Marmara & Aegean Coast	8.4	4.1	4.3	3.17	3.84	2.54
Mediterranean	3.9	1.9	2.0	3.11	3.93	2.36
Anatolia West	3.2	1.3	1.9	1.30	3.31	0.03
Central	11.0	5.2	5.8	1.51	2.94	0.31
Southeast	2.0	1.0	1.0	1.50	3.06	0.06
East	5.7	1.9	3.8	1.76	3.54	0.91

Source: 1980 census.
Note: Numbers are in millions in first three columns.

attached to the prime minister's office, was established in 1979. Besides this office, some ministries and the State Economic Enterprises are also concerned primarily with the pollution problems.

TUBITAK (Turkish Scientific Research Foundation) and the universities carry out research and analytic studies on environmental problems. There are also voluntary organizations such as the Environmental Problems Foundation of Turkey, Turkish War on Air Pollution Association, Association for the Protection of Nature in Turkey, the Environmental Engineering Sciences Association, and so on. During recent years these voluntary organizations have taken successful steps to warn and enlighten public opinion about the environmental problems.

The real legal support which these institutions and authorities deeply needed came very recently. The principle of environment protection is included in the new constitution. This represents a significant step for Turkey and places important responsibilities on the government and on every resident of the country. The most important one of these responsibilities is the provision of the "Environment Protection Law." This law was enacted through promulgation in the official gazette on August 11, 1983.

Environment Protection Law No. 2872 has introduced new and significant regulations in Turkey regarding the solution of environmental problems. In the third article this law introduces a major innovation. According to this article, those who pollute will be held responsible. The law also authorizes the highest official of the local administration to halt the activities of the plants which cause pollution. Another innovation introduced by the law is the creation of the

TABLE 18.4
ENVIRONMENTAL SHARE IN TOTAL
INVESTMENTS OF SOME ENTERPRISES

NAME OF ENTERPRISE	SUB-SECTOR	SHARE OF ENVIRONMENTAL INVESTMENT
SEKA	Paper and cellulose	1.5 percent
ETIBANK	Mining	16.8
DDY	Railway transportation	4.7
MKEK	Machinery, chemicals	5.3
SUMERBANK	Textiles	2.4
TKI	Coal mining	0.4

Source: State Planning Office.
Note: Data for 1983.

"Environmental Pollution Prevention Fund."

Although the institutional support for environmental control came only recently, and in spite of the meager resources allocated for these activities, serious efforts are made in this regard. The highest environmental investments are naturally in the "polluting" industries. Table 18.4 gives the environmental share in the investments of some of these industries.

In addition to environmental investments by the industrial sector, significant similar investments were made by the other sectors. Notable among these are the agriculture and service sectors. Table 18.5 gives the share of environmental investments in the allocations of those two sectors.

TABLE 18.5
SHARE OF ENVIRONMENTAL
INVESTMENTS IN TOTAL INVESTMENTS

Year	Agriculture sector (percent)	Service sector (percent)
1980	0.2	0.9
1981	7.0	0.9
1982	2.9	0.6
1983	5.8	1.0

Source: State Planning Office.

CONCLUDING REMARKS

At the end of this paper one very important question must be asked: how effective are the environmental protection measures in Turkey that have been taken to date?

The answer, unfortunately, is not a satisfying one. Like every developing country with limited financial resources, Turkey has not been able to take serious steps to prevent air, water and soil pollution which have been caused by rapid urbanization and industrialization. People of developing countries must realize that the future cost of pollution will be higher than the cost of the environmental investments they face today.

There are a lot of urgent problems which need immediate solutions in every developing country. However only small groups in these countries are aware of the fact that environmental problems are also urgent problems. For that reason international support is necessary for the solution of environmental problems in all developing countries.

TABLE 18.6
YEARLY POPULATION INCREASE RATES
BY PROVINCES DURING THE 1970s
(ALL FIGURES ARE PERCENTAGES)

Province	Total	Cities	Villages
Adana	36.11	47.21	23.21
Adiyaman	19.16	50.79	7.24
Afyon	9.73	23.80	3.73
Agri	23.72	40.14	17.58
Amasya	10.58	27.70	1.55
Ankara	33.52	42.26	6.95
Antalya	25.99	46.72	15.34
Artvin	1.38	15.85	− 1.97
Aydin	14.43	27.23	7.45
Balikesir	12.93	27.48	4.17
Bilecik	5.70	26.76	− 5.65
Bingol	25.09	43.91	19.80
Bitlis	32.97	44.74	26.82
Bolu	15.56	29.78	11.45
Burdur	11.09	32.00	0.94
Bursa	30.35	42.44	17.09
Canakkale	8.19	26.40	0.53
Cankiri	− 1.13	25.45	− 9.34
Corum	9.82	29.71	2.62
Denizli	16.58	37.66	7.18
Diyarbakir	29.18	45.06	16.43
Edirne	13.81	24.47	6.70
Elazig	15.66	21.03	11.88
Erzincan	2.11	19.71	− 5.79
Erzurum	15.75	37.08	5.67
Eskisehir	16.87	33.55	6.57
G. Antep	28.77	44.04	6.81
Giresun	6.10	33.52	− 2.19
Gumushane	− 2.53	13.15	− 5.81
Hakkari	41.84	75.22	31.18
Hatay	37.07	41.50	33.87
Isparta	15.44	32.54	3.25
Icel	35.64	54.45	19.63
Istanbul	45.15	27.80	80.94
Izmir	32.58	34.11	30.83
Kars	5.92	11.62	4.13
Kastamonu	0.97	19.40	− 3.70

PROVINCE	TOTAL	CITIES	VILLAGES
Kayseri	26.25	47.38	9.52
Kirklareli	9.73	24.98	0.01
Kirsebir	11.24	42.91	− 2.36
Kocaeli	43.74	52.47	34.64
Konya	19.90	38.94	7.58
Kutahya	12.21	38.54	1.59
Malatya	17.22	29.61	9.80
Manisa	15.63	28.10	7.45
K. Maras	33.30	53.34	22.70
Mardin	22.07	47.13	11.26
Mugla	17.24	35.13	12.48
Mus	25.54	45.96	20.02
Nevsehir	11.15	29.65	4.12
Nigde	22.61	49.29	11.13
Ordu	15.89	36.37	10.26
Rize	13.48	27.94	8.71
Sakarya	17.85	24.77	14.23
Samsun	20.51	38.15	12.42
Sirit	32.87	50.25	22.25
Sinop	3.91	21.39	− 0.22
Sivas	2.46	25.66	− 8.75
Tekirdag	17.46	35.44	4.16
Tokat	14.38	31.16	7.34
Trabzon	10.36	29.85	4.47
Tunceli	0.43	20.89	− 4.92
Urfa	11.34	31.78	− 3.77
Usak	17.51	39.19	4.38
Van	36.37	57.54	27.20
Yozgat	8.27	34.46	1.00
Zonguldak	24.96	34.80	20.50

Source: 1980 Census

NOTES

1. Environmental Problems Foundation of Turkey, *Environmental Profile of Turkey,* Ankara, 1981.

2. State Planning Organization, Commission Reports on Environmental Problems, 1981–83.

3. F. Baykut, *Pollution in the Golden Horn* (in Turkish). Istanbul, 1976.

Chapter 19

Urbanization and Political Behavior

Esat Çam

Urbanization is a critical process in both capitalist and socialist states. Ideologies and policies are influential in shaping events. Historically, urbanization is a result of the Western industrial revolution. However, in developing countries, urbanization seems to be a result of colonialism and imperialism, and it's identified by Westernization.

We define urbanization as the increase in both the number and the population of cities. Although the rate of population growth is 2–3 percent annually in general, the increase of population in cities is approximately 6–7 percent.

Urbanization is not only related to trends in population, but is also the result of economic and social changes in the structure of the society. Urbanization is a process of economic and industrial development, increase in number of cities, social organizations, division and specialization of labor, all of which shape human behavior and relations in cities. The early emergence of urban centers has produced a fundamental cleavage between the more modernized life of city people and the more traditional village-based people.

Population in Turkey tremendously increased after World War II. In these years, the expansion of usable land in villages required a larger labor force. Furthermore, the Marshall Plan accelerated the decline in the death rate through investments in health and nutrition.

If we take all Turkish cities with more than 10,000 inhabitants, their share of total population grew from 18.5 percent in 1950 to 45.4 percent in 1980. Table 19.1 indicates the evolution of this trend.

TABLE 19.1
PERCENT OF TOTAL
POPULATION IN
CITIES OF 10,000
PERSONS OR MORE

Years	Percent
1950	18.5
1960	25.2
1970	35.7
1980	45.4

Even though the Turkish population growth rate was 2.5 percent in the last 30 years, urban areas grew by 6.1 percent yearly. By contrast, rural area populations grew by 0.9 percent per year. The population distribution between cities and villages for the 1927–1980 period is given in Table 19.2.

From 1950 to 1980 the number of cities with a population of more than 10,000 was increased from just over 100 to 320 cities in 1980.

One of the main reasons for rural-to-urban migration results from concentration of farmlands. Table 19.4 gives the number of landless households in the various regions.

TABLE 19.2
POPULATION OF CITIES AND VILLAGES
BY CENSUS YEARS

Census year	Total	Cities		Rural areas	
		Population	%	Population	%
1927	13,648,270	3,305,879	24.2	10,342,391	75.8
1935	16,158,018	3,802,642	23.5	12,355,376	76.5
1940	17,820,950	4,346,249	24.4	13,474,701	75.6
1945	18,790,174	4,687,102	24.9	14,103,072	75.1
1950	20,947,188	5,244,337	25.0	15,702,851	75.0
1955	24,064,763	6,927,343	28.8	17,137,420	71.2
1960	27,754,820	8,859,731	31.9	18,895,089	68.1
1965	31,391,421	10,805,817	34.4	20,585,604	65.6
1970	35,605,176	13,691,101	38.5	21,914,075	61.5
1975	40,347,719	16,869,068	41.8	23,478,651	58.2
1980	44,736,957	19,645,007	43.9	25,091,950	56.1

**TABLE 19.3
NUMBER OF TURKISH
CITIES WITH MORE THAN
10,000 INHABITANTS**

YEARS	NO. OF CITIES
1950	102
1960	147
1970	239
1980	320

**TABLE 19.4
HOUSEHOLDS WITHOUT
USEABLE LAND, BY REGION**

REGION	PERCENT
Middle Anatolia	77.9
Black Sea Region	76.8
West Anatolia-Marmara	72.6
East Anatolia	90.5
Mediterranean	82.5

Thus, in addition to rapid population growth, economic deprivation accelerated migration from rural areas to urban areas. The rapid mechanization of agricultural activities reduced the demand for labor, thereby leading to unemployment. The unemployed simply drifted to cities. However, surveys indicate that villagers tend to migrate to the large cities rather than the middle-sized towns. Thus, the share of cities with 100,000 inhabitants or more in total urban population grew from 43.8 percent in 1950 to 65.2 percent in 1985. Table 19.5 gives the shares of various size in the total urban population.

At the same time, the number of cities with 100,000 inhabitants or more grew from two in 1927 to 41 in 1980. Table 19.6 shows the number of cities with populations of more than 100,000.

Of course, a few cities (Istanbul, Ankara, Izmir, Adana, and Bursa) claim a large percentage (roughly 40 percent) of the urban population itself. This, of course, gave Turkey a few primate cities.

Parallel to difference in population growth rate among cities is a difference in population density. High population density is associated with the more developed regions such as Marmara, West/South/Middle Anatolia, whereas the backward regions such as East Anatolia and the Black Sea have very few low densities.

TABLE 19.5
DISTRIBUTION OF CITY POPULATION
ACCORDING TO SIZE

	YEARS				
CITY SIZE	1950	1960	1970	1980	1985
10,000–20,000	22.9	15.8	14.3	10.8	10.1
20,001–50,000	23.2	21.9	20.3	15.2	12.7
50,001–100,000	10.1	17	11.1	10.7	12
Over 100,000	43.8	45.3	54.1	63.3	65.2
Total	100.0%	100.0%	100.0%	100.0%	100.0%

A detailed study of Istanbul as a special case in Turkish urbanization is helpful. The population of Istanbul is expected to be 10 million by 1995. It plays an important role in the economic development of the country. For example, its share in the GNP is around 21 percent yearly, and one-third of all industrial activity is concentrated in Istanbul. However, almost 50 percent of its population lives in "gecekondu" (slums). In other words, Istanbul faces a steady rise in its population because of the continuous inflow of people who are unskilled, unemployed, abysmally poor and marginal to the city's economy and social organization.

Even in comparison to the other large cities (including the capital Ankara) we find most of the inhabitants work in the modern (industry and services) sector as Table 19.7 indicates.

TABLE 19.6
CITIES WITH MORE THAN
100,000 INHABITANTS

CENSUS YEAR	100.000—NUMBER OF GREAT CITIES
1927	2
1935	3
1940	3
1945	4
1950	5
1955	6
1965	14
1970	20
1975	38
1980	41

TABLE 19.7
DISTRIBUTION OF LABOR FORCE IN
LARGE CITIES BETWEEN INDUSTRY
AND THE SERVICE SECTOR IN 1980

CITIES	INDUSTRY	SERVICES
Istanbul	38.9%	50.2%
Ankara	20.1	69.6
Izmir	34.7	53.6
Adana	31.7	45.9
Bursa	40.4	41.4
Eskisehir	30.9	53.3
Over 100.000	32.6	56.8
Other Cities	8.8	15.8
Turkey	11.5	20.9

EFFECTS OF URBANIZATION ON POLITICAL BEHAVIOR

Modernization theory assumes that there is a positive relationship between socio-economic development and political participation. According to Karl Deutsch, parallel to social modernization will be political integration of people, spread of political information, and political consciousness. Deutsch names this process as "social mobilization." However, political participation cannot be explained only in terms of voting behavior. On the other hand, Daniel Lerner accepts urbanization as the first stage of modernization because urbanization stimulates literacy rate, education level, usage of mass media, and economic and political participation.

In general, we can say that political participation in urban areas is greater than in rural areas, because of more highly developed organization. The experience of Turkey is not different. In all election

TABLE 19.8
VOTING RATES IN RURAL
AND URBAN AREAS

ELECTION YEARS	RURAL	URBAN	AVERAGE
1961	76.4%	83.2%	81.0%
1965	66.2	73.3	71.3
1969	56.3	68.1	64.3
1973	63.2	69.6	66.8

years, the percentage of urban dwellers who exercised their voting right is always higher than their rural counterparts. This is true despite the efforts of landlords who try to mobilize their rural sharecroppers. Table 19.8 gives this comparison.

A growing voting power in the cities is controlled by the "gecekondu" population. By 1980 there were 1.15 million gecekondu dwellers in Turkish cities, by 1983 there were 1.28 million, and by 1985 they are estimated at 1.5 million. The powerplay becomes interesting once we recognize that more than 50 percent of these people are concentrated in the five major cities (Istanbul, Ankara, Izmir, Adana, and Bursa). This situation allows for a target-oriented direct political campaign.

Moreover, the second generation "gecekondu" population has been even more politicized due to efforts by the Republican Peoples Party (RPP) which secured most of their votes. The party has a left-oriented philosophy which appeals to the urban poor. Table 19.9 compares the changes in voting patterns in the five large cities which can be attributed to the gecekondu votes.

TABLE 19.9
VOTES IN MAJOR CITIES

Province	1961		1973	
	RPP	JP	RPP	JP
Istanbul	33.8	28.5	48.9	28.8
Ankara	36.6	29.2	44.8	31.2
Izmir	35.5	40.9	44.6	39.7
Andana	37.7	19.0	49.2	56.0
Bursa	25.0	53.0	31.5	48.2

The Republican Peoples Party (RPP) is a left wing party; the Justice Party (JP) is right wing.

The growth of urban centers with the rise of the gecekondu votes would have eventually led to a left-controlled government. However, the trend was stopped in 1982. According to the constitution of November 7, 1982 (article 68), the existence of extreme left and right wing parties is forbidden. Still, the main characteristic of the distribution of votes between the two main political parties will remain a predominant feature in Turkish political life.

The causes of this deep polarization were many. However, in 1983 the newly emerged Motherland Party (MP), which is oriented politically toward the right, gained some ground. We can say, nonetheless, that for the next national elections, Turkey will probably return to its traditional trend of left-right polarization. Urbanization may, in part, be responsible for this phenomenon. The disenchanted have been shoved either to the left, or they have returned to traditional values which are part of the right-wing party's philosophy. Yet, the interaction warrants further analysis.

DISCUSSION

Mellanby

The points made here about environmental damage are very important; they are also subjects which give rise, in some cases, to a good deal of misunderstanding. One of the important things here is that we must always make sure we identify what is causing the damage, and we must also therefore try to cure the things that are actually doing the damage.

Galantay

One major contribution to air pollution, not only in Istanbul but in all Turkish cities, is, among other things, the lack of public transportation. A city the size of Ankara should have either a metro system, a subway system, or an electrified rapid suburban train system. The picturesque collective taxicabs which exist in great numbers contribute to congestion, and much of the pollution comes from very badly maintained private cars, taxicabs, and trucks.

Ben-Dak

I want to address the question of garbage disposal in the whole area. What do you do with the stuff? One thing that struck me while visiting Brazil is that the government decided to apply the law strictly regarding pollutant industries, even in the face of much-needed industrial growth. The question applied to your case of the public law 2872 is: have there been any plants that were closed down because they were polluters? Your answer to this question is a good indicator as to how serious the government is about pollution control.

Mechkat

Is there any private voluntary initiative at the local level to control pollution in the Turkish cities? International support can also be solicited. I wonder how much this issue has been brought to the attention of the local and international communities.

Phares

Some people regard pollution control as a luxury in developing countries. I address especially Professor Alkin and insist that talking about environmental protection and pollution control is not a luxury. How can we have harmony in a polluted environment? I would also add another dimension of this deterioration of the environment. It is the social dimension of pollution. It is all around the world and especially the Middle Eastern cities. Slum areas are growing more rapidly than the cities they surround. So between 20 percent and 40 percent of the people in cities are slum dwellers.

Saqqaf

If we go back to the pattern of urbanization that has evolved in Turkey over the last 50 years, we can see that it is multi-polar. There are at least five or six distinct regional urban centers. This helps distribute the population as evenly as possible throughout the country. It would be interesting if other Middle Eastern countries reduce the overwhelming role of their primate cities (usually capital cities) and pursue a multibased urban development policy such as in Turkey.

Part VIII

The Future Middle Eastern City

INTRODUCTION

More than anything else, the future Middle Eastern city will require two services—communication and municipal. So indicate the authors of the next two papers. The availability and adequacy of these two services will determine the dynamism and growth of our cities. Communication is critical for the development and efficiency of urban living, without which progress cannot be achieved. The inefficiency and inadequacy of the telephone service in Cairo, for example, has forced many companies and agencies to communicate by telex within the city itself. This issue is not only critical within a city, but also among cities in the Middle East and elsewhere. Professor Ben-Dak looks at this issue with an eye to the future. The analysis especially covers mass communication media (such as television) by using satellites. Municipal services are very lacking, especially in the poorer and crowded parts of the cities. Massive investments in public parks, children's playgrounds, and public promenade areas have been transformed into places where garbage is piled. The streets are covered with dust and various kinds of trash. Professor Mellanby looks into this issue. Drawing on his vast experience, he directs his analysis toward possibilities of pollution control through recycling.

Chapter 20

Communication in the Middle East City of the 1990s

Joseph Ben-Dak

URBANIZATION, COMMUNICATION, EMULATION

Communication has been part and parcel of the very process of urbanization. As Arab nationalism grew, especially in the cities of Cairo, Alexandria, Damascus and Beirut, it was the printed media that made clarity of the message possible and combined it with a tacit or open modernism among intellectuals. On the other hand, it was radio broadcasts that facilitated the growth of urbanization and Arabism among the masses.

In the early fifties, television entered the scene. Television, indeed, has become the moving communication instrument in such populations as the Jordanian Bedouins, where as early as 1978 even the nomadic tents had television antennas.[1] Cassette players and transistor radios are ubiquitous throughout the Middle East, but television is quickly becoming ubiquitous in virtually all the cities of the region, regardless of income bracket.

Typical of this trend is that in Egypt in the late 1950s, between 55% and 77% of rural Egyptians attended to radio and 20% read newspapers. In 1960 some studies suggested a moderate growth of newspaper reading.[2] This later "fact" is not borne out by a 1974 study where 97% of the Egyptian peasants are said to listen to radio, 76% watch television and 31% read newspapers.[3] On the basis of two recent studies it can be stated that in the 1980s (reviewing both urban and rural Egypt), between 89% and 96% listen to radio, between 64% and 95% watch television and about 43% read newspapers (Talaat 1980; Egypt 1981).[4]

When one compares such statistics with the illiteracy rate, the relationship between the urban process and communication is further suggestive. In 1976 in Jordan, the illiteracy rate was 29.3% (70% in 1952) and in Egypt in 1978, the illiteracy rate was 56.5%.[5] Small wonder why governments, aware of the high rate of illiteracy in the rural sector, stress and budget more electronic media, as change agents in agricultural development and health care impact planning.

Information is thus assured of better dissemination and reception. Radio and television are also the tools of political and cultural integration, bringing to the village and to the small or larger outlayers of settlements the value system nurtured in the city. In this sense, the development of electronic media in the Middle East advances a process of empathy and emulation.

The new capacity to transfer sights, physical and spiritual ecology (e.g., Al-Aqsa Mosque), color, focus, recognizable faces, traditional symbols and the fuller impacts of oratory skills and music has worked and contributed to two directions of emulation which co–exist, often happily, in the media of the Middle East. One direction is depicted by Mahmoud Esh-Sherif:[6]

> *Amongst the Arab Peoples, there is a strong feeling of belonging to one Nation bound together by a common language, and a common cultural heritage. The present political division of the Arab World is viewed by many as an abnormal transient phenomenon, and that one day, the Arab World must be united again. Regardless of the feasibility of the fulfillment of such a dream in the near future, its magnetism has a strong sway over the masses. The Arab Media have played, and are still playing, a major role in sharpening this consciousness, and in giving it various tangible forms. The Arab Leagues Pan-Arab Festivals, exchange of Radio and Television programmes, and the cooperation in the Arab Satellite Project which will be launched early next year are all signs of this deeply rooted yearning for Arab unity, which the media are fostering and boosting among Arab Masses.*

Successful, or relatively successful, emulation of this type can be identified in Jordan where the process of detribalism, especially sedentarization in earlier times and identification with the state in recent periods, have been pivotal impacts of electronic media. All Jordanians (East Bankers) are tribal in the sense that they relate their descent from one or another of the hundreds of Jordanian or nearby (Syrian, Iraqi or Arabian) tribes. Yet, for a steadily increasing number, tribal allegiance is either meaningless or peripheral to their lives and feelings.[7]

King Hussein is projected in the Jordanian media as a unifying source, everlasting and empowering in both state and international politics and especially in the Arab world. Amman, the city, is the primary locale to identify with and perceived as the significant political ecology of Jordan. This is projected and transmitted in every news edition, and virtually in all public interest or military programs on television. The result, indeed not only due to communication, is that prestige is primarily connected to being involved in the urban centers (and not tribal or familial ascription).

The process of urbanization in major cities such as Zarqa, Salt or Irbid exhibits sometimes less advanced emulation (typified, for instance, by spatial tribal residence patterns), but throughout Jordan communication has short-circuited the traditional urbanization. Being a *Fellahin,* or identifying with *Fellahin* manners of behavior, is the logical and historical next step to moving out of tribalism. It is rather a rare next step and is looked down upon by Jordanians. While the origin may be tribal, and is hailed as such, the next empirical, and ultimately satisfying, development is in living in Amman and immersion in the city, complete with its politics and symbols.

THE DEVELOPMENT OF A MODERN COMMUNICATION CHOICE

Emulation can be not only an effective agent in raising affective relationships or collective cohesion (under conducive environment) but a major force in personal career decision, choice of marital lifestyle and individual modernization.

Jureidini and McLaurain following K.S. Abu-Jaber have pointed out that whether it is perceived as a force for growth, development and constructive social change ("the revolution of rising expectations") or for restlessness, discontinuity and destructive violence ("the revolution of rising frustration"), emulation is definitely impacting the present generation of communication receivers. It also provides "a portrait of what the present generations (the plural is important, as generational differences must be considered) see and will act upon in the future."[8]

A good case to exemplify this type of emulation is the role Israeli electronic media play in Jordan and in southern Lebanon. The term "generations" is applicable here in the very sense used above. The Palestinian refugees of the wars of 1948 and 1967 especially, their children, and Arabs who have grown with no direct encounter with Palestinians have all been absorbing information from Israel, which, *de facto,* created urban needs and aspirations. What Kamal Abu-Jaber states regarding the impact of Palestinians in Jordanian society can also be suggested as an impact of the *Israeli media* on Jordanians:

> *The Palestinians brought with them to Jordan a healthy respect for modernity, knowledge and awareness of the twentieth century. Their frustration and anger (were) also accompanied by . . . hard work and the need to achieve. Politically mature, they began placing demands on the machinery of the state for services, job opportunities, facilities and other amenities of life.*[9]

The observant social scientist needs no unusual imagination to realize that the Palestinians have become the pathsetters, if not the personalization of the Israeli "value system." The latter was projected especially in the Arabic, but also in the widely watched Hebrew television. Palestinians tend to watch Israeli TV broadcasts and, here, while animosity and frustration linger on, continued emulation provides for growing similarity in personal choices and preferences among Palestinian Jordanians, East Bankers, Israeli Arabs and Israeli Jews.

Emulation with the role model of Israeli society is responded to by the power of neighborhood communication also in Israel. TV watchers in northern Israel, especially in the urban centers of Kiryat Shmona, Zefat, Tiberias, Nazareth and the shore cities of Haifa, Nahariya and Akko, spend a great deal of their viewing hours (normative: 6:00 p.m.–10:00 p.m.) with Arab-originated television. Jordan's French program (Channel 6) which normally includes news, a series and a "France Today" miniprogram, is popular among Israeli French speakers, especially of Moroccan and Tunisian origin, at 6:00 PM–7:15PM.

At that very same time, Israelis, Lebanese and some Syrians, especially of younger generations, watch Lebanon's Christian English language station which, at that time of the day, tends to broadcast Western series. During the same time slice, Israeli Arabs, Arabic-speaking Jews, Jordanians and Lebanese tend to watch Israeli-Arabic television which includes, among others, programs on "problems and solutions" and "between citizen and government" programs which highlight a rational, often instructive and democratic way and process of dealing with urban life in Israel.

Jordan gets more Israelis watching at 7:30 PM (news in Hebrew) through 8:00 PM and again at 10:00 PM–10:30 PM (news in English). Christians in Israel look for the "700 Club" on the Lebanese Christian station.

In summary, it appears that not-necessarily-planned cross-viewing has developed a market situation and that TV viewers choose what they like to see—and be affected by—from the modernity message of nearly the total TV programming of the Near East. Learning about each other in the context of the city is already taking place in both directions.

VERTICAL AND HORIZONTAL COMMUNICATIONS: THE CHALLENGE

Some of the best reasons for change in the communication systems permeating the Middle East lie in that urban masses, as well as urban elites, are not happy with the present patterns.

Governments, by and large, have not been able to use media to contribute significantly more to the aims of individual and societal development. There is a government realization, for instance, in Egypt that an effective communication system is an essential element in modernizing health delivery systems, in producing literate and trained workers for industry, and in bringing about effective participation in the making of a nation.[10]

But, even though efforts were directed in this direction, the results call for new measures. Television broadcasts on health, for about four hours weekly, and three hours on radio programs are insufficient, an Egyptian government report indicates. This is the very same point that prevented Syrian government communications from achieving their objective.

Communications in the urban setting of the Middle East, probably more than most mass media theoreticians have stipulated so far, must be born out by a reinforcement of their contents and social climate by both vertical and horizontal networks among the people listening to and receiving the medium.[11] Ithiel de Sola Pool offers the proposition that people tend to develop informal networks of communication and sensitive "decoding" techniques when government-controlled mass media become powerful.[12] By these "instruments" they second-guess what is actually happening and actively exchange views that differ with those sanctioned in the formal media.

The need to change is most obvious in Egyptian government and scholarly work. The first problem, that of vertical communication, is illustrated by Talaat:[13]

> . . . *Government plays a major role in development of pro-*
> *grams and policies. It has been considered sufficient just to*
> *tell . . . of these policies. Communication has been a one-way*
> *traffic in Egypt. Dependence has been on telling the people,*
> *rather than encouraging them to seek information or talk over*
> *decisions, or express their needs and wishes. Most research*
> *studies focus on vertical communication, from the national and*
> *state capitals.*

The new communication mode will have to be a communication in which the government takes into consideration what messages and requirements are developed by the recipients of communication. This is the first meaning of a desired two-way communication.

The second meaning is in the informal fostering of the medium. Again as Talaat examines it:[14]

> . . . *Change will not take place unless those who are expected to*
> *change know and accept the reasons, the methods and the*
> *rewards for changing. New skills will not be learned unless they*
> *are taught, and unless individuals are motivated to seek teach-*
> *ing. True national participation in economic and social develop-*
> *ment will never come unless communication flows up as well as*
> down the channel between the national leaders and the rural
> people. *It is through this two-way process of communication*
> *that the understanding and cooperation of people can be*
> *enlisted to achieve community and national goals. It is through*
> *communication that influences are brought to bear to change*
> *traditional way of living and working, during the "ascent" to*
> *modernity.*

The new communication mode will have to enlist actual involvement of people, especially group and face-to-face communication in order to analyze, clarify, review and spread the communication. Much of it depends on eliciting public support such as the volunteers in the process of Egyptian family planning. The foundation herein exists for such activities as:

1) Parents-children review of TV programs on violence, assessing its antecedents and deciphering its meaning for daily life

2) Aged viewers (senior citizens) discussion and representation groups

3) Political debates, clarification, etc. between government and people, between student groups, high schoolers, clubs, etc.

4) Government research or sponsored research into appropriate
social activities supporting and benefiting active communication

5) The function of learning from formal communication especially
when a computer aided facility is available and, hence, the facility
of repeating and development of gradual feedback is available to
individuals or groups of citizens.

COMMUNICATION-AIDED PARTICIPATION IN THE URBAN SCENE

When the essential components of urbanization in the Middle East
are brought up in the context of modern communication, it appears
now that one of Daniel Lerner's classical propositions regarding
modernity in the Middle East has gained a really new and important
meaning.[15] Lerner, already in 1964, suggested that actually living in a
city is not in itself necessary to the development of a "modern"
outlook and, hence, to a "modern" way of life. Lerner's model,
simplified, suggests that literacy and exposure to the mass media
stimulate empathetic imagination, which in turn stimulates the
mental mobility and openness to change. Rephrased by V.F. Costello,
it is Lerner's thesis that a general model of modernization, which
follows an autonomous historical logic, may be applied to the Middle
East.[16] Each stage in the process of modernization tends to generate
the next stage by some mechanism that operates independently of
"doctrinal" or "cultural" variations. Physical concentration is the first
stage which leads to impersonal communication and so to literacy.
Literacy creates the capacity to operate a media system which is the
second phase of modernization. Once a society has over 10 percent of
its population living in cities and has over 40 percent literate, then
new desires and satisfactions are both feasible and growing, and the
third phase of modernization—that of media participation—is under
way, to be followed by a fourth development, the phase of political
participation.

   Lerner's empirical studies in the 1950s could not have foreseen the
power with which the media system effects the modernity process of
the third and fourth stages in the Middle East of the late 1980s. Egypt
nowadays, for example, uses medium wave radio stations of 500
kilowatts (KW) at Batra, Abis and Giza. Saudi Arabia has no less than
58 television stations of moderate power, mostly of 5 KW and some of
stronger signal (Qurayat has 80 KW and Dammam has one station of
40 KW and another of 20 KW).[17] The media capacity to effect

TABLE 20.1
MIDEAST COMMUNICATION—SELECTED INDICES, 1984

Country	Population in approx. millions	Percent urban	Percent urbanized in recent decade	Key radio broadcasts and targets[19]	Color TV sets	TV color system[20]	Key locations, organizations and authority	Languages and broadcast hours
Egypt	46m	45	3	Arabic, Arab World, Sudan, Red Sea Coast, English, French, German†, Greek, Armenian,†	350,000 (4 mill. incl. black & white)	SECAM B	Cairo, "Egyptian Radio & TV Corporation," 50 stations	Arabic 0800-2130 Limited Br. on Fri., Sun.
Iraq	12m	64	10	Arabic, Kurdish, Turkuman, Assyrian (Persian, Urdu, Hebrew, English in the "Foreign Service")	535,000	SECAM B	"Baghdad Television," Government, limited commercial, 15 stations	1400–2100
Israel	4m	83	1	Hebrew, Arabic (English, French, Spanish, Portuguese, Russian, Persian, Yiddish)	600,000	PAL B & G	Jerusalem and Tel Aviv, "Israel Broadcasting Authority," (IBA) and "Instructional Television Centre," (Educ.), 20 stations	1530–2300 06–1530 Limited Broadcast on Fri., Sat.

Country								
Jordan	3m	44	1	Arabic, English	20,500 (201,000 including black & white)	PAL B & G	"Jordan Televison Corporation" (JTV) from Amman. 6 stations for each of 1st & 2nd program	
Lebanon	3m	63	1	Arabic, French, English, Ammenian (Radio Voice of Lebanon; Voice of Hope; Christian)	450,000	SECAM B	Beirut: "Tele-Liban" (Gov't.) 7 stations (3 in Beirut) & Middle East TV (Christian)	Arabic, French, English 1530–2200
Syria	10m	48	3	Arabic, Turkish, English, Hebrew, Spanish, French	40,000 (405,000 including black & white)	SECAM B	Damascus: "Syrian Arab Television Gov., Commercial 10 stations	1600 (Friday 1200–) –2200
Sudan	20m	15	4	Arabic, English	109,000	PAL B	Omdurman: "Sudan TV Service," Gov., Commercial	1630–2130
Yemen A. Republic	8m	14	8	Arabic	150,000 plus 400,000 black/white	SECAM B	YAR TV, Sana'a 3 radio stations in Sana'a, Taiz, Hodeida	1600–2300 English TV news at 1930

participation in the sense of physical mobility, that is, the basic character reformation that accompanies modernization, can be reached deep in the rural or non-urban sectors of the average Middle Eastern country. Empathy in the sense of identification with another person's situation can be reached already in the form of TV broadcasts that are sent one way, from government to the people. Table 20.1 summarizes some pertinent data.

Table 20.1 demonstrates that:

a) There are elites that use a high degree of communication facilities in each of the eight countries.

b) Governments control virtually all media productions, facilities, etc.

c) Local stations (relay and reinforcement) are already fairly prevalent in the 1980s.

d) There is a relationship between a high degree of urbanization (Israel, Iraq) and availability of color sets (and presumably other high technology communication products).

e) There are two defined groups of technical facilities in color broadcasting: SECAM B (Egypt, Iraq, Lebanon, Yemen, and Syria) and PAL B (Israel, Jordan, Sudan).

f) There is a certain interest in broadcasting with an appeal to local populations and to the neighboring states not only in Arabic but also in languages of local minorities (e.g., Hebrew, Armenian).

g) There is an interest in broadcasting to foreign elements in the region (English, French) or outside it (e.g., via shortwave radio to Europe).

These seven properties of media in the Middle East of the 1980s can be used to predict and illustrate seven emerging properties for the 1990s. It can be said that even in the present growth of urbanization and, given logical options, trends that are likely are:

1) Elites will push for *more of a variety of communication,* the most likely being interactive television and local area networks (LANs). These are Western, next logical extensions of well-to-do urban elite use of media. This is most likely to appear first among the "haves" in the large urban centers and may later be shared by the middle classes, whose status and percent in the total population will grow. Emphasis will be on both information sharing and "conver-

sation." The present growth of computer consumption is a natural precondition to this development. Location of such elite high-consumers can easily be identified, e.g., in Cairo's districts of Bab-Al-Hadid and silver coast.

2) Pressure to enter the media market will come from *private sectors* especially in the predicament of a growing democratization and evolving commercial benefit to entrepreneurs and investors. Again, this trend may effect particularly the urban centers and their immediate hinterlands. It is likely that both the need to governmentally control populations and Islamic rejection of too much Westernization will oppose the trend of uncontrolled communication markets. But the evidence partly documented above suggests that the urban, modernity-seeking element is already strong in most Middle Eastern cities and will grow in impact and needs even more in the coming decade.

3) *Local communities* may, more and more, consider the promise of interactive television, given the growth of the city, its problems and its government. The Middle East's unique local communities that are homogeneous and different from one another are the natural candidates to be wanting to hear and be heard both in government circles and throughout their own reference community in a manner best served by an interactive medium. Thus, Alexandria, Egypt's second urban center, for example, with its religious groupings (Copts, Jews, Foreign-Christian, etc.), each located in a cluster associated with a social status is a case in point. Kuwait City may also face the question of allowing the homogeneous clusters of Iraquis, Palestinians, Saudis, Indians, Pakistanis and Egyptians to participate in local politics via the interactive medium. Clearly, the spatial segregation of citizens and non-citizens is defined clearly as "original" Kuwaities and "others" by a 1948 law. However, if Kuwait is to overcome the bitterness felt by the foreigners, media is one way to reach an acceptable mode or representation.

4) With the process of modernization continuing, *prices going down on media technology,* and Arab elite pressure to bring communication progress into *their* homes, the relationship between city growth and preoccupation with interactive media is to positively grow.

5) *Cooperation between governments* in the field of communication is likely to grow too and, in itself, lead to further development and test of the electronic communication field. In similar sense to McLuhan's media-equal-message, it appears that, once inter–

governmental adjustment in color systems has set organizational coordination, *that,* in turn, sets in motion testing for new grounds. Opportunities will become feasible and, gradually, legitimate not because of conscious decision-making but, rather, because of natural extension of the need to do different and new "projects," partly just learning from experimentation in communication elsewhere in the globe.

The two forerunners of this type of inter–governmental cooperation are the "Arab States Broadcasting Union" (ASBU), 1969 and the "Islamic States Broadcasting Services Organization" (ISBO), 1975. The first organization has been instrumental in making Arab League bodies aware of the need to invest in radio and television regional development. The technical center is located in Khartoum, Sudan; training for ASBU is pursued in Damascus, Syria, and the audience research center is located at the Iraqi establishment for radio and TV, Baghdad, Iraq.[18] Thus, there is already a form of intercity cooperation between Khartoum, Damascus and Baghdad that has slowed a bit because of the polarization of the Iraqi-Syrian relationship, but that is in search of further growth. The ISBO which extends to 44 state members is aiming explicitly to use media to propagate Islamic teachings and to further cooperative relations. It has been involved during the 1980s in production of radio and TV programs teaching Arab language by audio-visual means and has conducted training of personnel for broadcasting corporations. The net effect of these developments on the process of urbanization may be too complex to assess here but several tentative suggestions can be made even now:

a) Islamic and modernity messages will *coexist* in media broadcast and, therefore, in the minds of men. To the contrary, this will be a natural outgrowth of national TV having side-by-side programs "birds of different feathers," but also in closing the gap between the religious preacher, (i.e. Quran interpretation) being the main or sole representation of religion on the Arab media, and a more western religious program type of relating everyday life to Islam.

b) Standardization and homogeneity will gradually surface in terms of inter-city comparison of program development, broadcasting style, choice or pool of programmes, and risk taking with new types of programming, including interactive television and experimentation with audience participation.

c) Influence from and intergovernmental relationship with Arab oil producing countries will become a pivotal asset *and* issue in Arab countries, especially as Arab world wide communications are feasible.

6) *The place of minorities, of ethnic groups and of language groups other than Arabic* is likely to receive attention in countries that today already engage in targeted communication to such groups. "Key radio broadcasts," are one such indication (see Table 20.1). To the extent governments allow representation, cultural growth and give-and-take with such groups, it would be mainly a question of funding and community organization to develop either inner-community communication or inter-community programs. The most likely setting for this trend to unfold is in the larger urban centers where such communities dwell, and, in fact, are likely to positively mobilize to advance such experimentation, for example, in fostering a more active participation in city-wide politics. It follows that in this latter case, it can be done as a by-product of city-wide wiring of neighborhood centers to city hall and enlisting the support of all neighborhoods to interact with politics, politicians and with other communities in the immediate or remote environment.

7) The possibility of *Arab-Israeli interactive communication* will appear as a feasible undertaking, gradually, especially if the aforementioned trends produce results of the sort that will make Middle Eastern communication more open, experimentally minded and a copy of the urban process as a wholesome series of phases in, and toward, *political participation.*

PARTICIPATION: THE TECHNICAL CHOICES

The previous discussion suggests that communications in the urban scene of the 1990s will have to contribute to several objectives such as: (a) national, state and especially city empathy with a possible role in political participation and services; (b) individual and group modernization including such prospects as learning-at-home for the aged; (c) vertical and horizontal communication, complete with supporting groups; (d) variety of communications uses and choices; (e) government reasonable control and intergovernment cooperation; (f) the involvement of new participants in all of the above including entrepreneurs, minorities, local micro-communities; and (g) the Arab-Israeli interface.

We can turn now to what is already happening in the Arab World.

Arabsat is a communication satellite serving a regional consortium in the Middle East.[19] This is a low-power, C-band satellite. The original American model for this type of satellite was built in the 1970s to carry telephone calls for RCA, Western Union and the other common carriers, i.e., a U.S. domestic "bird." Nowadays, the Arabsat and the similar Indonesian Palapa systems are used to feed television within a wide geographical range. Arabsat broadcasts in Arabic throughout the Middle East, and to and from Europe. While some of its first uses were in transferring economic and financial information, its program can be used to accommodate many of the objectives described above. It is difficult, in view of only a backdrop of information, to predict or suggest what such a satellite will do for urbanization in the Arab world.[20] Molniya programs indicate the experimentation program is of prime importance. Such experimentation can provide planning concepts and notions of practical connection between and among urban centers in the Arab world and extend educational programs to a variety of local communities and fairly remote ones, thus creating a basis for intensified emulation and modernization throughout the region. It can give a push for local organizations and groups and possibly new types of social entrepreneurs to provide both vertical and horizontal support to government-positive programs of social change, interfaith dialogues when the times come and possibly even non-governmental initiatives. Table 20.2 suggests a rough outline for possible experimentation and demonstration that can make Daniel Lerner's notions of political participation a real undertaking in the Middle East of the 1990s.[21]

On the technical side, one must surmise that the field of communication has every feasibility of developing efficient networks in the region. Data available on Middle Eastern macroprojects does indeed suggest that when such targets are considered priorities, the funds and organizational initiatives are there to make it a reality. Consider Table 20.3 for an illustration of urban and telecommunication projects as to document this potential.[22]

POLITICAL PARTICIPATION: ULTIMATE COMMUNICATIONS

Much of what is technically feasible today will only improve and get priced right for the needs of the Middle East in the 1990s. The contents, however, with regard to "who will participate," "for what" and "with what set of constraints and inducements" is less apparent. The urban scene in the Middle East is compounded of elements of unity and diversity. Its unity is generated from the common, indigenous origins of urbanism, stamped in the Arab world by the culture of Islam. The key questions superimposed on all other queries regarding communication is whether political participation will include a state-level (or regional-level) democratic process and whether this process will include a legitimate Israeli-Arab "conversation." Media's typical role in the past was to report violence, reasons for violence and to propagate more of the same.

The media has served in the past also as an element of Arab-Israeli interaction in either providing a scene or an "ecology" for a typical debate of inner-city Jews and Arabs on Israeli radio or TV—or as a stepping stone or "event" that actually brought upon the debate. Thus, the Israeli movie, "Behind Bars" where Jews and Arabs are depicted in jail got Arab youth of Jaffa and young Israeli Jews of Tel Aviv's district of "Kerem Hateymanim" (Yemenite Jews neighborhood) to engage in a series of discussions.[23] Even this minute contribution is rare in the role of Middle Eastern media.

It is only natural that when so much violence has surfaced in the urban scene, people tend to react to it, and rational people whose communities conflict would like to study the nature of a possible solution or bone of contention. Without much speculation, the growing frequency of several types of crime are true indications that the 1990s will involve more kidnapping, murders, school violence, youth-gang street fights, and property and sexual offenses, some of which will be of unsurpassed cruelty. The shocking murders of female soldier hitchhikers in Israel or the Lebanese massacres in Palestinian camps are cases in point. These incidents will happen in Israeli-Arab context but the media will be one reason (among a few) that *crime will be learned and used and repeated in all other contexts of the Middle Eastern city.*

The simple logic of learning from examples is possibly the best available. Inter–active television can bring pain, sense of a given justice, demands and background and contrast it all with an equally legitimate parallel and factual presentation of the opposing position (or people, group, neighborhood). One cannot stop and should not prevent televising terrorism or violence but allow the large range of factual material and debate to enter the consciousness of the viewers, be it children or politicians.[24] This might be a good direction to take in all TV but is an especially strong argument in favor of *adopting inter–active television.* The latter could provide an alternative to regular, official expression and will be one significant path to unleashing the coming steam of the urban ethos of the 1990s in the Middle East.

It is only hoped that notice and further elaboration on how to do it will indeed be demanded by ruling elites concerned about the future of our cities.

TABLE 20.2
PRIORITY AREAS AND PRIORITY CRITERIA FOR SATELLITE
EXPERIMENTATION AND DEMONSTRATION

1	3
Clusters of populations that can benefit if efforts will:	*Target populations* that can benefit if efforts will:
1. Respond to the special requirements of education in the *remote regions.*	1. *Properly use existing community institutions and mores.*
2. Respond to potential learners' groups that are *isolated physically from society.*	2. Utilize extensively, *culturally relevant materials and staff.*
3. Develop educational alternatives for *migrant and other socially disadvantaged populations.*	3. Foster positive ethnic identity and capitalize on *community homogeneity.*
	4. Build creatively on the special relationship between *parent and child.*
	5. Respond to educational needs of *total communities and gender and age groupings.*

PRIORITY
EXPERIMENT
OR
DEMONSTRATION

2

Exposure or distribution of cost/benefit servicing by matching:

1. *Large populations* with educational service.
2. *Large quantity materials* with users.
3. New, alternative and repeated educational uses with *existing resources.*
4. Capital expenditures and initial investments with *local contribution.*

4

Local communities in which education efforts will:

1. Fulfill educational needs that are currently *unfulfilled.*
2. Include making the target group *aware of such needs.*
3. Utilize extensively local *capabilities and abilities.*
4. Stimulate community *self-help* to education and educators.
5. Employ effective *"basic management technology."*
6. Build on a realistic assessment of *target groups' strength.*
7. Build on a *continuing program* of education improvement.

5

Experimenting/demonstration organizations that are:

1. *Viable,* (creative and efficient).
2. Capable of utilizing *resources* effectively.
3. Geared toward *long-term involvement.*

TABLE 20.3
MIDEAST MACROPROJECTS

Project Name	Location	Curr. invest-ment ($Bill.)	Curr. compl. date	Stage	Owners	Lead project managers
1. Saudi Arabia Gas Processing, Pipeline	Saudi Arabia	21.0	1985	Contract let	Aramco	Fluor
2. Telecommunications System—Phase I	Egypt	20.0	1983	RFP	Areto	Con. Telephone Co. Gen. Tel. & Elec.
3. Al Jubail Industrial City	Saudi Arabia	20.0	1997	Underway	Sabic	Bechtel
4. Trans-Turkey Highway	Turkey	14.0		Plan	Turkey Government	Spec.
5. Iraq Telephone System	Iraq	10.0		Plan	Iraq Government	
6. South of Riyadh New City	Saudi Arabia	10.0	1983	Plan	Saudi Arabia Government	
7. Yanbu Industrial Project	Saudi Arabia	10.0	2006	Contract let	Sabic	Parsons, Ralph M. Fluor
8. Ruweis Industrial Centre Infra-structure	Saudi Arabia	10.0	1992	Contract let	Abu Dhabi Natl. Oil	Fluor
9. King Khalid Military City	Saudi Arabia	7.0	1985	Contract let	Moda	U.S. Army Corps Eng. Morrison, Knudsen
10. Road Pavement	Saudi Arabia	7.0		Agreed	Saudi Arabia Government	Korea Highway Corp.

NOTES

1. Paul A. Jureidini and R.D. McLaurin, *Jordan: The Impact of Social Change on the Role of the Tribes.* Washington D.C.: Praeger, 1984.

2. Fathallah El-Khatib and Gordon Hirbayashi, "Communication and Political Awareness in the Villages of Egypt," *Public Opinion Quarterly.* Vol. 22(5), 1958 pp: 357-363; Lewwis Melika, *Leadership in an Arab Village.* Cairo: Sirs El-Layan, 1963 (Arabic).

3. Illiya Harik, *Political Mobilization of Peasants.* Bloomington, IN: Indiana University Press, 1974, p.140.

4. Shahinaz Talaat, *Mass Media and Social Development.* Cairo: Anglo-Egyptian Bookshop, 1980 (Arabic) and Radio and Television Union, *Evaluation of Radio and Television Programs During 1980.* Cairo: Department of Research and Statistics, 1981 (Arabic).

5. Kamal Abu-Jaber, *The Jordanians and the People of Jordan.* Amman: Royal Scientific Society Press, 1980, p.109; Ministry of Education, *International Day for Anti-Illiteracy.* Cairo: Department of Adult Education, 1978 (Arabic).

6. Mahmoud El-Sherif, "Freedom and Social Responsibility of Arab Media." Paper presented at the Seventh World Media Conference, Tokyo, Japan, November 1984. p. 5.

7. Jureidini and McLaurin, *ibid.,* p.40.

8. Jureidini and McLaurin, *ibid.,* p.36, 86.

9. Kamal Abu-Jaber, *ibid.,* p.12.

10. In this assertion we closely follow the arguments developed by Shahinaz Talaat, *The Social Responsibility of the Media Towards Development Issues in Egypt,* (preliminary report). Faculty of Mass Communication, Cairo University, 1984.

11. See for instance, Karl W. Deutsch, *Nationalism and Social Communication: An Inquiry into the Foundations of Nationality.* Cambridge: MIT Press, 1966. We follow here in the same rationale and logic developed for Jordan by Jureidini and McLaurin.

12. Quote in Jureidini & McLaurin, *ibid.,* p. 35, 85.

13. Talaat 1984, *ibid.,* p.11.

14. Talaat 1984, *ibid.,* p.12.

15. Daniel Lerner, *The Passing of Traditional Society: Modernising the Middle East.* New York: The Free Press, 1958, London, 1964.

16. V.F. Costello, *Urbanization in the Middle East.* Cambridge:

Cambridge University Press, 1977.

17. Data on TV sets, broadcasts, color, organizations, etc. are taken mainly from *World Radio TV Handbook,* 1984, pp.396-441.

18. *World Radio TV Handbook,* 1984, p.64.

19. Anthony T. Easton, *The Satellite TV Handbook.* Indianapolis, Indiana: Howard M. Sams, 1983, especially pp.42-43.

20. See for example, Koag Levins, *Arab Reach: The Secret War Against Israel.* Houston, 1983, p. 133, 230, where a connection between the Houston financial community and the Arabsat is drawn. Data of value regarding planned experimentation or steps beyond c-band type satellite were not found in the middle of 1984 (in the public domain).

21. See also, Joseph D. Ben-Dak, *Priority Areas and Priority Criteria: Guidelines for Selecting Projects.* Washington D.C.: U.S. National Institutes of Education Satellite Experimentation Program and Practical Concepts Incorporated, 1976.

22. Manabu Nakagawa, *Macro Creative Science-Harmony of the Natural and the Human.* Tokyo: Dep. of Economics, Hitotsubashi University, 1984. Reference is given in this working document to work done by Kathleen J. Murphy (1983).

23. Israeli papers, November, 1984.

24. Consider the position of P. Schlesinger, G. Murdock and P. Elliott, *Televising "Terrorism": Political Violence in Popular Culture.* London: Comedia Publishing Group, 1983.

Chapter 21

The Provision of Essential Services in the Future City

Kenneth Mellanby

INTRODUCTION

During the last 100 years in all parts of the world, cities have been established, and have grown, at an unprecedented rate. In Western Europe four-fifths of the population lives in cities and large towns. In Australia the vast majority of the inhabitants live in the state capitals. In the Middle East this process may be less advanced, but the rate of urban growth, although it started later than in Europe, is now much more rapid, and is expected to continue at an even greater pace. The pressing issue relates to rapid urban growth, and what type of city will result. Will it be possible to guarantee a reasonable quality of life to the inhabitants?

Rapid urbanization in the Middle East has only been made possible by the introduction of modern technology as part of the development process. It is this advance in technology which has provided essential services. Life for some (the poor) in all cities has not been pleasant, but it has been possible. The city dwellers have been provided with water, food and shelter sufficient to enable them to survive, though the mortality among different groups has differed considerably. The rich enjoy a better living standard than the poor. It is also apparent that, although technology has provided some necessary facilities, its effects have not always been beneficial. Misused, or not properly controlled, it has damaged and polluted the environment and seriously reduced the quality of life. This technology has also replaced the local architectural heritage of the Middle East. Yet technology has also contributed to the comfort of all citizens when properly used.

In the Western world, many cities are today losing population. This means that their problems are very different from those of the rapidly growing metropoli of the Middle East. In Britain urban pollution has recently been largely controlled so that the air is cleaner than it was 100 years ago, and central London enjoys as much sunshine as rural areas at the same latitude. The river Thames which was so polluted that it supported no fish 30 years ago is now breeding salmon, a species most easily damaged by adverse conditions. Western cities suffer from a lack of population in their centers rather than from trying to support too many people in these areas. The current movement is to outer suburban estates and even to the countryside. "Commuters" are replacing the farmworkers whose occupation has disappeared because of the mechanization of modern agriculture where a tiny working force produces, today at least twice as much food as was produced at any date in Britain's history up to 30 years ago. Pollution control in a rapidly growing city is a much more difficult problem.

In any expanding city, it is important that the services provided should be sustainable; that is, they should remain as effective, or become more effective, as the city grows. There is justifiable concern that, on a global scale, man is using up the world's resources in such a way that he is condemning future generations to deprivation and suffering. This could happen with Middle Eastern cities in particular. For example, those that rely on underground water supplies are likely to exhaust them when their need is greatest and when it may be impossible to obtain water from other sources. Frederich Ragette used the term "resource efficiency" when dealing with the reconstruction of Beirut, and the same principle must be generally applied. Planners must attempt to make the most efficient use of the resources which are available to them on a long-term basis.

Efficient long-term planning depends on accurate forecasting, something which has seldom been possible. The population forecasts for Middle Eastern cities are frightening, but will they be fulfilled? While there may be uncertainty about long-term numbers, there is little doubt that rapid growth will continue in the immediate future, and that more and better facilities will have to be provided. It will be wise to take current decisions in the expectation of further growth; if this is less rapid than expected, it will relieve the pressure on the authorities.

It is impossible for me to consider in any detail all the services needed by a growing city. I shall not deal at all with the important problem of air pollution, which has caused too much trouble in both the West and the East. The Japanese, where unbridled industrial development after the last war took place at the expense of the environment, have shown how, at great expense, this can be controlled. South Korea is trying to introduce effective controls before too much damage is done. It is obvious that it would be wise for any expanding city to follow the Korean example, notwithstanding the temptation to try to maximize wealth-producing activities as soon as possible.

Much has already been said about the type of building being erected today. Many of these are not entirely appropriate for their situations. It is true that when electricity is cheap and plentiful, it is possible to provide an acceptable working climate in any type of building, no matter how hot—or how cold—it is outside. But many of us have experienced the misery of living in the tropics in rooms designed for air-conditioning when there is a prolonged power failure. The traditional type of architecture which took advantage of the climate often provided the most comfortable living conditions.

Cities depend on transport to bring food in, and to move people about. Here the problem differs in the shrinking cities of the West and the growing cities in the Middle East and the Third World. In Britain we are coming to rely more and more on private cars. Though there are inefficiencies and traffic congestion is often a serious problem, recent studies show a decreasing role for public transport. With rapid urban growth this solution is unlikely to be effective, and the need for efficient public transport is likely to increase.

Yet, the most problematic aspect of a growing Middle Eastern city has to do with two basic services.

WATER SUPPLY

I propose to deal in more detail with water supplies and with the disposal of waste. Water is the substance most essential to all living organisms. Unless human beings get some two quarts a day of water to drink, they die. It is best if this water is clean, unpolluted and free from organisms causing disease, though many populations survive on very dirty drinking water. This produces a high infant mortality rate, but those who survive generally have sufficient immunity to avoid, or at least tolerate, further disease. Those only receiving the minimum survival ration of water with none for washing and other purposes clearly have a very low quality of life, and all city authorities attempt to provide more adequate water supplies.

Water is a scarce resource in the Middle East, and people have evolved an efficient system to use it in the past. The situation in Sana'a showed that, in the old city, wells supplied adequate water, which, carefully used and recycled, even allowed green gardens to flourish. Yet, Middle Eastern city dwellers have rapidly increased their consumption of subsidized water. Cairo, for example, uses 105 million cubic feet (over 3,000 million quarts) of water a day. This is a very substantial fraction of the purified water available in the whole of Egypt. It compares with the wasteful use in cities like New York and is greater than the minimum needs of the inhabitants by some 150 times. Much of this water probably goes to waste through defective pipes, which certainly overloads the sewage system causing widespread pollution. It may be that the water from the Nile allows Cairo to be so prodigal, but there are few cities elsewhere which would allow such water consumption on a long-term basis.

There are various ways in which water economy is possible. Where there is a water-borne sanitation system, there is no need to use potable water to flush the water closets. In situations near the sea, salt water may be used. It may be possible to provide a separate and limited supply of clean drinking water. Often a decision will have to be made as to whether water closets and a sewage system are practicable. In many situations, even in quite large cities, some type of earth closet is used, and there is an efficient collection of night soil, which, after composting, is recycled as a plant fertilizer. This system needs to be operated carefully, otherwise it may spread disease. But it can be efficient and may be worth considering on future developments. A sewage system, with its prodigal use of water, may not always protect the environment. In the nineteenth century, London introduced effective sewers but the untreated effluent was discharged into the Thames. This had the result of "killing" the river, totally eliminating fish, and, in the summer, causing such a stink that Parliament (on the bank at Westminster) was unable to sit even when the windows were covered with blankets soaked in vinegar in an attempt to reduce the nuisance.

Most Middle Eastern cities get their water supplies either from underground aquifers, or from the collection of rain or from the desalination of sea water. As already indicated, underground supplies, which are often "fossil water" accumulated many years ago when the area had a higher rainfall, may be limited in quantity and liable to be exhausted. Even in Britain where the rainfall greatly exceeds the consumption, some aquifers have already been seriously depleted. Thus, many large blocks of buildings in London found it cheaper to sink deep wells for their water supplies than to pay water companies to supply them. Already some have abandoned this policy, as they were having to go deeper and deeper to obtain sufficient water. In many islands when quite small amounts of underground fresh water have been pumped to the surface, salt water is sucked in from the sea and makes the supply undrinkable.

Rainfall in the Middle East does not replenish the exhausted aquifers, and this may be a bad omen for growing cities.

In some countries water is brought long distances from areas of high rainfall to supply the needs of the drier or more heavily polluted regions. Before a city becomes dependent on water from another district or even from another country, the authorities should make sure that the supply will not be arbitarily interrupted, particularly where there is no alternative supply.

A third possible source of fresh water is by the distillation of sea water. This can only make an important contribution when a source of free or very cheap energy is available. This is true of some oil producing countries where much natural gas of high calorific value may be blown off into the atmosphere. With fuel bought commercially, distillation is at present much too costly to produce much more than drinking water. It is often suggested that solar energy could be used, and so it could, but solar stills are not very productive. It would be possible, particularly in countries with plenty of sunshine, for drinking water for most houses to be produced by solar stills on their roofs, but that is about all. It may be in the future that solar power may be used more effectively, but this depends on the unforeseeable results of research. If there is plentiful cheap energy from fusion or another source, this could alter the whole situation, but planners would be unwise to rely on this if other sources are likely to be exhausted.

WASTE DISPOSAL

Man is an untidy animal, and refuse has always been a problem. When our ancestors lived in caves they threw their waste onto the floor where it built up and eventually left insufficient head room for the occupants. Anthropologists and other scientists have learned a great deal about the food and habits of early man from a study of these deposits.

When man started to live in towns, he still allowed his wastes to accumulate on the floor and in the street. Recent investigations in York (England) of Viking life in the ninth and tenth centuries show how unhygienic the city dwellers were. They also seem to have been surprisingly careless with their jewels and money. Archeologists have made fruitful studies of their deposits. In a similar way, investigative journalists today rummage around in the dustbins of the famous and notorious in order to write scurrilous articles in the gutter press about their extravagant eating and drinking habits.

Food wastes carelessly deposited obviously encouraged vermin, including rats and mice, which were also involved in spreading diseases like plague. In the Middle Ages the streets of London were at least partly cleaned by kites, birds which, in Britain, have now become a scarce, endangered species restricted to the Welsh mountains since their urban food supply has been reduced. I would not wish to advocate a policy, even on conservation grounds, which encouraged their return to our cities. But in many cities, for instance Ibadan in Nigeria, goats roam the streets living mainly on the refuse thrown out of the houses. They thus make a modest contribution to hygiene as well as providing milk and, eventually, meat for the population. Such recycling is seen in some parts of the Middle East, though it is generally discouraged by the authorities. Perhaps this is a mistake in a world of diminishing resources.

The refuse so far considered consists mainly of food residues, ashes, broken pottery, discarded and worn out clothing, furniture and similar materials. That produced today is often very different, particularly in the West and in the more affluent communities. In fact, it could be said that, in some cases, those with a high standard of living produce so much objectionable refuse that they seriously reduce their quality of life.

In the West we certainly have not solved the problem of waste at all satisfactorily. The streets of both New York and London are a disgrace, with overflowing plastic bags of objectionable material spilling over the sidewalks. Most of this is, eventually, collected and either buried or burned, but not before it has done much damage to the environment. The refuse consists partly of waste food, and it has been calculated that in New York alone this could provide more than is actually consumed by 10 million Third World peasants, and which in hot weather decays and stinks abominably. There is also plastic and paper wrappings most of which are unnecessary and which sometimes cost more and use more energy in their production than the goods which are wrapped, not to mention the vast quantity of paper which is discarded.

Efficient waste disposal is not necessarily dependent on the authorities having much money to finance the service. In the Seychelles, not one of the wealthiest countries, there is no house-to-house collection, but bins marked "Keep Seychelles clean" are located at strategic points so no one has far to go to get rid of his rubbish. The bins are emptied daily without fail, and the workmen usually take care to remove any material which has overflowed onto the surrounding ground. The refuse is then taken to a landfill site, where it is compressed, covered with soil and, in due course, produces useful reclaimed land.

In an ideal world there would be little waste material, as most of what is now thrown away would be recycled and reused. Unfortunately, in wealthy countries, recycled materials are generally more expensive than new. In Britain some waste paper is in fact recycled, but this is seldom a commercial proposition. Where it works, free labor from public spirited groups like boy scouts collect and sell the paper, and while this may raise useful sums of money for worthy causes, if the collectors were paid even a minimum wage for their time, the operation would be run at a loss. In some communities recycling can be organized, particularly where the wages paid are low. Much paper is recycled in Sri Lanka, where foreign currency to import wood pulp is scarce. In Hong Kong, large blocks of apartments have employees who sort out refuse into some five categories —food residues, paper, tins, plastic and the remainder, so that the amount left to be buried is comparatively small.

It clearly depends on the city authorities whether refuse is or is not a serious problem. Many materials plentiful today will become scarcer as resources are exhausted and the world population grows. It is to be hoped that cities in the Middle East will learn from the failures and the few successes in other countries. Clearly, it would be sensible to try to reduce the volume of refuse, to recycle what can be reused, and to get rid of the remainder as effectively as possible. Many Middle Eastern cities are fortunate in having potential landfill sites near at hand. Properly managed, these should produce no adverse environmental problems.

Perhaps one of the most objectionable features of life in many countries is the litter which disfigures the city streets and the countryside. This is a serious social problem whose solution depends on the will of the authorities. In Britain you can be fined for dropping litter in the street, but the law is seldom enforced. In Hong Kong, on the other hand, anyone offending is immediately arrested and heavily fined. The population accepts this and helps with enforcement, so the streets are clean. Will it be possible to obtain equal public involvement in Middle Eastern cities?

DISCUSSION

Mass communication is potentially among the more counter-productive elements of our society. Its impact on the "fellaheen" at the economic level is clear. There is also a political dimension to it. One of the things that struck me about Morocco which I visited 10 years after its independence and then returned some 20 years later, was that French television was able to achieve what colonialism could

Schleifer

not accomplish in 50 years. The French troops were able to occupy the streets of Morocco but they were never able to penetrate into the sanctity of the homes of Morocco, and now that has happened. And the society has gone through an extraordinary transformation. The Moroccan no longer has pride in his traditional dress and his manner, and the effect of television has been devastating.

Munro   It is always assumed that greater communication means reduction in tension. It's been my experience in the Middle East that the electronic revolution has brought about greater fragmentation rather than coherence. In Lebanon, there was a survey undertaken a couple of years ago about the viewing habits of Lebanese television watchers and the results were fairly predictable. The upper class, Westernized part of the population watched "Dallas," and the lower-income groups who were not particularly Westernized watched "Abu Milhem." The distinction is very important, in fact, I saw myself—one day on Lebanese television back to back—one show of "Abu Milhem" which is a very popular program with the lower class Lebanese, and "Eight is Enough." Now in the "Abu Milhem" program it was said that a girl had lost her virginity in a car accident, and this was regarded as a tremendous tragedy. The father was saying "My God, my God, anything but this, anything but this. I would rather you'd lost an eye, an arm, anything!" Immediately after that program, in "Eight is Enough," you have a father giving birth control advice to his unmarried teenage daughter. Now this surely is leading to tremendous polarization of the Lebanese society between the Westernized upper-middle classes and the still Arabized lower classes.

Saqqaf   I couldn't agree more with Professor Mellanby's analysis, just thinking of Yemen and Sana'a in particular. I think a study has been done as to the rate of "water depletion" in Sana'a and it has found that every year Sana'a's water table falls by 36 inches. And it's becoming a real problem for Sana'a. To some extent, the government has started steps to control new industries within Sana'a itself because the city cannot support the rising number of people. It's, I think, a very, very valuable statement to make at this stage and we should recognize that.

Ben-Dak The point I want to make has to do with an aspect which is called the demonstration effect. It's important to bear in mind what this actually means. In satellite communications and in general technological gadgets, the most important technological developments, as far as contribution to people, when we talk about demonstrations, is to measure people's reactions and interactions through samples. First of all, put it to use with a limited number of people and measure the effect. Then we proceed full scale from there.

Conclusion

Urbanization is not new to the Middle East. The world's first urban societies most probably emerged here some 6,000 years ago. Famous cities rose in different parts of the Middle East forming the focal points of successive civilizations. These range from the Mohenjo-Daro and Harrapa cities of the extreme east (today's Pakistan) passing through the fabled cities of central Asia such as Anachosia and Aria (Qandahar and Herat in today's Afghanistan, Bactria (Balkh), Maracanda (Samarkand); the royal cities of Susa and Gabae (Isfahan) in modern Iran; the luxurious Sumerian, Babylonian, and Assyrian cities of Assur (Ashur), Akkad, Babylon, Calah, Dur-Sarrakin, Eridu, Kish, Nippur, Nineveh, Ur, and Uruk (Biblical Erech) all in modern Iraq. Further west in the Levant, there rose the famous cities of Al-Quds (Jerusalem), Aleppo, Carchemish, Damascus, Gomorra, Megiddo, Palmyra, Petra, and Sodom. To the south and along the western, eastern and southern parts of the Arabian Peninsula rose the merchant cities of Mecca and Yathrib, and the Yemeni cities of Marib, Timna', Shabwa, Zhafar, and many other cities in Oman and Bahrain. Crossing the Red Sea and along the banks of the Nile River existed the magnificent royal cities of ancient Egypt, Memphis and Thebes, along with the many work colonies such as Kahun and Tell El-Amarna.

Most of these cities preceded the Greco-Roman cities and surpassed them in size and splendor. In terms of history, the first Middle Eastern cities date back to the fifth century B.C. whereas the first European cities came to exist only 2,000 to 3,000 years later. Even in size, Middle Eastern cities were much larger.

Babylon and Thebes each covered 2,500 acres in the middle of the first millennium B.C. Nineveh covered 1,850 acres, Uruk 1,100 acres, Calah 800 acres, and Dur-Sarrukin 600 acres. By comparison, the first European urban center, Athens, which, at the time of Themistocles was considered unusually large and populous, covered only 550 acres.[1]

The second phase of Middle Eastern urbanization came with the rise of Islam. Many cities were founded, and older cities were invigorated. The most famous of the newly founded cities are Basrah and Kufah (636-38 A.D.), Cairo (640), Qayrawan (668), Tunis (681),

Qum (701), Almeria (756), Fez (807), etc. Among the cities rejuvenat-
ed by Islam were Mecca and Medina, Sana'a and Taiz, Damascus,
Balkh, Bukhara, Herat, Grenada, Cordova, Al-Quds, Samarqand,
Seville, Tashqand, Istanbul, etc.[2] But, urban growth spurred so
strongly by Islam was later slowed down remarkably, and almost
stagnated. Case studies of urban conditions in various cities like
Cairo,[3] Damascus,[4] and Aleppo [5] indicate a marked deterioration,
although Andre Raymond convincingly argues to the contrary.[6]

Yet, it is the final phase of Middle Eastern urbanization that is most
dramatic. Over the last 100 years, the number of Middle Eastern
cities, and the sizes of these cities, rose at phenomenal rates. Today,
many of the countries of the Middle East are more urbanized than the
countries of south Europe and always more than the Third World.
Some 50% of their total populations live in cities today.

This rapid urbanization poses several critical issues which need
proper attention and direction on the basis of a clear vision. Paramount among these issues are:

a) *City character:* The rapid urbanization phenomenon has transformed the character of Middle Eastern cities. In most cases, this
transformation meant that traditional Islamic quarters have been
replaced by "modern" secular and development-oriented quarters. This has led to basic changes in the social, cultural, and
religious fabric of the society. If Middle Easterners have a preconceived model of their societies, then the urbanization pattern will
have to be adjusted so that it is compatible with that model.

b) *Reconstruction:* All the countries of the Middle East, without a
single exception, have been at war with their neighbors one or
more times since the beginning of this century. In addition, many
of them have gone through agonizing civil wars. The end result
has been massive destructions of urban settlements. So, reconstruction issues become very important in such a volatile part of
the world.

c) *Over-urbanization:* The pace of urbanization is faster than the
abilities of the society to equip the cities with the necessary
infrastructure and services. Although a major part of national
public investments go to urban centers, it is still not enough.
Thus, a constraining urban policy, and a more effective national
comprehensive development plan are badly needed. A reversal of
the urban trend is not likely, but measures to curb its phenomenal
growth could succeed if rural-oriented investments are encouraged.

d) *The medina:* Modern urbanization has broken out of the old physical entity—the medina—and has sprawled aimlessly to cover a much larger area. In fact, many Middle Eastern cities today have two or more urban pattern forms with different lifestyles and physical structures. Where the old medina persists and continues to be the home of a substantial number of people, official policies have tended to "protect, revive, and restore" it as part of the Islamic heritage. This is true in Aleppo, Baghdad, Cairo, Jerusalem, Damascus, Istanbul, Herat, Lahore, Mosul, Sana'a, Fez, Tunis, etc. However, where the old medina was small or subject to intensive transformation, the old traditional sector of the city is virtually lost, as in Algiers, Beirut, Jeddah, Kuwait, Manamah, Taiz, Tehran, etc. The issues of old medina –new city relations are colored by the strong aesthetic and religious attachment to the old faced by utilitarian considerations, especially regarding the high costs that will be incurred if total restoration of the old is envisaged.[7]

There is total agreement that urbanization will continue as a dominant and dynamic force in the population landscape of the Middle East. Essentially, this is not a negative evolution since cities provide the framework that challenges and releases the best of an individual's and society's abilities and potentialities. Yet, we must be willing to accept the issues concurrent with urbanization: the heterogeneity, the variety, the crowdedness, and the unpredictability inherent in the city.[8] This is the nature of the situation, and it requires our visionary efforts to plan, build, and rebuild our cities.

The need for a clear direction for managing our cities cannot be over-emphasized for future development. Decisions regarding the cities should be based on a long-range plan. Governments, groups, and individuals should free themselves from commitments emanating from past ad-hoc arrangements dictated by expediency. Managing our urban environment distinctly entails the responsibilities of the physical organization as well as what the Chicago School urban sociologists call the "human ecology."[9] This human ecology in Middle Eastern cities incorporates a rich Islamic heritage which has to be studied and revived. But we need not blindly emulate the past since that would neither be feasible nor in our interest. The preservation process must be selective and must be adapted to our modern needs. The challenge of preservation/revival of our urban Islamic heritage is, in colloquial terms, how not to throw out the baby with the bathwater. The experiences of Al-Quds/Jerusalem, Cairo, Damascus, and Fez are useful in this regard. At all times, however, urban planners in the Middle East should look to the future and its needs rather than what had existed in the past.

NOTES

1. Ira M. Lapidus, *Middle Eastern Cities.* Berkeley: Univ. of California Press, 1969, p. 5.

2. R. B. Sergeant, *The Islamic City.* Cambridge, U.K.: UNESCO, 1980, p. 15.

3. Marcel Clerget: *Le Caire,* Vol. 1, Cairo, 1934, p. 178.

4. Jean Sauvaget, "Esquisse d'une histoire de la ville de Damas", in *Revue des Etudes Islamique.* 1954.

5. Jean Sauvaget, *Alep: Essai sur la developpement d'une grande ville syrienne des origines au milieu du XIXe siecle,* Vol. 1. Paris, 1941, pp. 238-39.

6. Andre Raymond, *The Great Arab Cities in the 16th-18th Centuries.* New York: New York University Press, 1984, pp.5-9.

7. Carl Brown (ed.), *From Medina to Metropolis: Heritage and Change in the Near Eastern City.* Princeton, New Jersey: The Darwin Press, 1973, pp. 28-32.

8. Elizabeth Geen, Jeanne Lowe, and Kenneth Walker (eds.), *Man and the Modern City.* Pennsylvania: University of Pittsburgh Press, 1963, pp. 4-5.

9. Such as Robert Park, Ernest Burgess, Donald Bogue, and others.

Contributors

Hana Abu Khadra (Palestinian holding Lebanese nationality) is an Architect and Instructor at the Architecture Department, University of Beirut.

Erdogan Alkin (Turkish national) is Professor of Economics at the Faculty of Economics, University of Istanbul and Director of the Istanbul University Research Center.

Ahmad Attiq (Yemeni national) is an Engineer/Architect and Director-General of Planning, Ministry of Municipality and Housing, Sana'a.

Joseph Ben-Dak (Israeli national) is Professor of International Business with wide-ranging experience in the business community and academia, former President of the Israeli Peace Research Society, and currently chairman of the Board of the Tri-Alpha International Corporation.

Esat Çam (Turkish national) is Professor of Political Science at the Faculty of Economics, University of Istanbul.

Henry Cattan (Palestinian holding French nationality) is an international Jurist and Writer, former Professor at the Jerusalem Law School, and Member of the Palestine, Jordanian, Syrian and Lebanese bars. He represented the Arabs of Palestine at the General Assembly of the United Nations during 1947 and 1948 and is author of many books.

Thomas Cromwell (British national) is Secretary-General of the PWPA-Middle East, and Publisher of The Middle East Times.

Abdel El-Ahwal (Egyptian national) is Professor of Sociology at the Institute of National Planning (Socio-Cultural Planning Division), Cairo.

Ervin Galantay is an Architect and Professor and Chair, Department of Urbanism, Swiss Federal Institute of Technology. Professor Galantay is the author of many publications on urbanism.

Saad Eddin Ibrahim (Egyptian national) is Professor of Sociology, American University, Cairo, Secretary-General of the Arab Human Rights Organization, and Secretary-General of the Arab Thought Forum. Dr. Ibrahim has written widely on different aspects of social evolution in Egypt, the Middle East, and the Third World.

Yitzhak Khayutman (Israeli national) is Senior Researcher in the Desert Research Institute (on regional educational development), Ben Gurion University. He has done significant work in cybernetics and educational computer games.

Fuad Khuri (Lebanese national) is Professor of Social Anthropology, American University of Beirut. Professor Khuri has published several books on the socio-cultural transformations of Arab societies.

Cyrus Mechkat (Iranian national) is an Architect and Professor at the School of Architecture, University of Geneva, Switzerland. He has researched and written on various urban projects in Iran, North Africa, and Switzerland.

Kenneth Mellanby (British national) is Professor and Director Emeritus, Monks Wood Experimental Station, England.

John Munro (British national) is Professor of English, American University of Beirut. Professor Munro has spent the last 19 years in Lebanon, thus he has witnessed Beirut reach its peak and fall. He is also the Beirut Correspondent for The Middle East Times.

Sari Nasser (Palestinian holding Jordanian nationality) is Professor of Sociology, University of Jordan, Amman. He is also author of the book *The Arabs and the English,* as well as several other articles.

Ali Oshaish (Yemeni national) is an Engineer/Architect and Official at the Ministry of Municipalities and Housing, Sana'a, working especially on the preservation and revival of Old Sana'a.

Osman M. Osman (Egyptian national) is Associate Professor of Economics at the Institute of National Planning, Cairo and is presently teaching at Sana'a University. Dr. Osman is especially working on modeling and research applications in development plans.

Joseph Phares (Lebanese national) is Professor of Urban Sociology at Kaslik University. Professor Phares has written several books and articles on urbanization.

Fritz Piepenberg (West German national) is a Journalist and Author, and is The Middle East Times Correspondent in Yemen.

Friedrich Ragette (Austrian national) is Professor and Chair, Department of Architecture, American University of Beirut. He is the editor of the book *Beirut of Tomorrow—Planning for Reconstruction.*

Abdulaziz Saqqaf (Yemeni national) is Associate Professor and Chair, Department of Economics, University of Sana'a and Secretary-General of the Yemen Economic Society. He is also author of several books and articles.

Abdullah Schleifer (American national) is a Distinguished Visiting Lecturer in Mass Communication at the American University in Cairo. At different times, Mr. Schleiffer was Correspondent to NBC, Jeune Afrique, The New York Times, and others. He is the author of *The Fall of Jerusalem.*

Hoda M. Sobhi (Egyptian national) is an Expert in Economics at the Institute of National Planning (Department of Regional Planning), Cairo. Dr. Sobhi has also been lecturing at the National Institute of Public Administration in Sana'a.

Sabahaddin Zaim (Turkish national) is Professor and Chair of Labor Economics and Industrial Relations, Istanbul University. He is also Visiting Professor at Cornell University, Munich University, and King Abdulaziz University in Saudi Arabia.

Index

The index is of personal proper names and major themes. The numbers in parenthesis refer to footnotes. The numbers in **bold face type** refer to pages written by the subject. Tables are indicated, while other references to the subject may appear on the same page as a table.